McClain Printing Company

Parsons, West Virginia

www.mcclainprinting.com

River on the Rocks

Skip Johnson
with Rob Johnson

Edited by
Peter & Elizabeth Silitch

Book Design and Layout by
Neal Gentry, Wolfpen Digital
www.wolfpendigital.com

International Standard Book Number 0-87012-661-X
Library of Congress Control Number 2001118466
Printed in the United States of America
Copyright © 2001 by Skip Johnson
Herold, West Virginia
All Rights Reserved
2001

First Edition 2001

McClain Printing Company
Parsons, WV 26287
www.mcclainprinting.com

To Birch,
this eternal
river on the rocks

Table of Contents

Preface   ix
1   The Origins of Birch   1
2   Skyles and Boggs   13
3   Shay It Isn't So   33
4   Birch Village   51
5   Powell's Mountain   67
6   Cora Brown   85
7   Little Birch   101
8   Long Run   111
9   Herold and Wolfpen   125
10   The Rocks   141
11   Big Run Meets Lower Keener   161
12   If We Were Counting   185
13   The Blue Hole   205
14   Leatherwood Country   229
15   The Floods of Birch   249
16   The Big Timber Era   261
17   Creatures Large and Small   269
18   William Strange   297
19   The Doctor and The Preacher   311
20   The Indians   325
21   The Poem   341
22   A Much Studied River   351
Epilogue   360
The Tributaries of Birch River   362
Flora   365
Fauna   369
Populations, 1860 - 2000   372
Bibliography   375
Index   379

Illustrations

Falls Rock below Herold, Frontice
Big Eddy Rock, Title Page
Meadow Fork and Back Fork, 2
Former Dr. Dan Kessler house, 9
View, the Highest Elevation, 12
Site of the 1894 shootout, Boggs, 14
Henon Fleming; circa 1942, 14
Cal Fleming Tombstone, 18
The falls, largest on Birch, 27
Skyles bottom today, 31
Head of Skyles Creek, 32
The Eakin Lumber Company, 39
The Shay Engine used by Eakin, 44
Eakin's Barnhart log loader, 46
Skyles logging crew; Tom Reger, 50
Historic concrete bridge, 55
The Little Gulf Station in Birch, 56
Former Birch Village P. O., 61
The Bubbie Hole of Birch River, 64
Aerial view of Birch Village, 66

High point, Powell's Mountain, 68
Powell's Mt. elevation sign, 71
Shanty Branch sign, 75
Henry Young Monument, 81
Powell's Creek and Tug Fork, 84
Cora Brown, 1920's, 88
Cora Brown's house, early 1900's, 90
The restored house of today, 90
The Cora Brown bridge, 92
Frank Given Hole, rocks begin, 94
Henshelwood Eddy, 100
At the Jack Johnston Rock, 100
Smiley face on Little Birch hill, 103
The Ward Garee Low Gap, 113
Birch River Junction, Canfield, 116
Scenic Birch River Sign, 124
Bridge on Birch above Herold, 124
Louis Johnson, 126
The Herold horseman, cir. 1905, 127
Herold in 1941, 131
The old schoolhouse today, 140
Falls of Birch below Herold, 145
The scenic Abner hole of Birch, 150
Rocks near Feedtrough Run, 153
Cliffs like this one at Herold, 155
Bill Gillespie, 159
Jim Brown, 159
The rock at Jack Johnston's, 160
Warder S. Dean, 162
The Lower Keener Eddy, 163
The Perrine Ford, 165
Long Shoal below L'wer Keener, 166
The dynamited Reynolds Rock, 168
Pig Shoal plout, 170
The Devil's Backbone, 172
The celebrated Falls, Herold, 179
Fast Hollow rock, largest, 179
The Big Eddy rock, 1700 tons, 180
The sixteen foot falls, Boggs, 180
End of the rocks, Raven Eddy, 181
Small rocks, at Lower Keener, 181
Jumble of rocks, Lee Jack Plout, 182
Day lilies brighten Birch River, 182
Royal Fern rock above Herold, 183
Large rocks at Fast Hollow, 183
The scenic falls below Herold, 184
Swift water above Abner hole, 184
The snake that upset the canoe, 186
The Willis Long plout, 188
The Martha Butcher hole, 188
The Lee Jack plout, 191
The Abner, 194
Smallmouth bass, 198
The storied Blue Hole, 206

Mouth of Middle Run, 215
Lon Smith, 218
Former Twistville Post Office, 227
The Raven Eddy, 228
The Smith Eddy, 228
Birch near Leatherwood Run, 230
The Duffield Eddy, 239
The Lower Turn Hole, 242
Mouth of Birch, railroad trestle, 245
Swinging bridge at Glendon, 247
Lester Hayes Jr.'s muskie, 248
Doug Given's record deer, 248
Aerial View, Lower Turn Hole, 248
Birch River at normal stage, 250
Birch River at flood stage, 250
Fallen Hemlock below Herold, 258
Birch at flood stage, at Herold, 260
Flood stage, falls below Herold, 260
Warder P. Dean, 262
Splash dam remnants, Slabcamp Run, 265
Dogwood in Bloom on Birch, 272
Mountain laurel, 276
Rhododendron, 277
Morel, 284
Deer at Freda Woods's, Birch, 288
Watersnake, 295
W'm Strange sketch, Clinton Curtis, 296
Possible routes, W'm. Strange, 308
Willie Lewis, 313
Norman Goad, 319
Indian sketches, Ben Gibson, 326
Artifacts, Ray Reip collection, 333
Thomas Dixon, 342
Thomas Dixon tombstone, 346
Dam site, Lower Turn Hole, 356
Proposed Resevoir, 1971, 359
Sunset on Lower Birch, 361
Three county population, 372
Braxton County Population, 373
Nicholas County Population, 373
Webster County Population, 374

My Peace

Down the path
Past age old familiar trees
Looking for something,
At times I think I've lost me

It took a while for me to learn that nothing comes for free
And the price I've paid is high enough for me

Feeling the cool sand under my feet
I walk to the river's edge and drop to my knees
Tears streaming down my face (sorry, daddy, I know you said to never let them
see you cry)

I look towards heaven
And whisper, "Thank you God for creating this place"
I look to my right and see a little girl with her sister and grandmother
Standing in the river and laughing so freely
I look to my left and see a woman laughter is now a stranger to
And in front of her mother saying forbidden words (the snake made me)

Leaning forward I see my reflection in the river
And wonder what happened to the innocence
Cupping my hands I wash away the tears
And just that easily the water changed me
I feel a smile starting to break through
Here on this river's edge it doesn't matter if I was never quite as good
Sometimes afraid, alone and misunderstood

Here my ancestors' voices whisper through the trees
This river calms my mind, soothes my soul
And I can be that little girl again laughing so freely
This river fills the emptiness that seeps into my heart

Standing up I walk into the river 'til I reach the middle and I whirl around
Splashing water everywhere and laughing, for I have just found me
I am that little girl and I am that woman
Raising my hands to the sky I realize that here I am free to be both
Here I am not afraid, I am no longer alone, I am surrounded by family
And God is as far as I can see

Birch River. Thank you God for sharing this with me
My piece of heaven here on earth, my peace

-- Vicki Johnson Bossie

Preface

During the two years I worked on this book, I gained a new appreciation for the beauty of central West Virginia and for its people. I took the advice of history writer Stephen Ambrose, who said: "Never write about a battle until after you've visited the battlefield." With that in mind, I walked much of Birch River, knocked on many doors, and was barked at by most of the dogs in three counties. More than ninety nine percent of the people I met were friendly and eager to help, and I am grateful to them. In that sense, this book is a community product.

There were special moments, including early on when Bill Armentrout took me to the highest elevation on the Birch drainage, a 2,792 foot ridge near Cowen, and many months later when I sat with Dana and Dolsie Corley on their sun porch facing the mouth of Birch at Glendon, and watched the afternoon sun glistening on the river.

A poignant moment came when I walked onto a knoll overlooking the Devil's Backbone of lower Birch with Marjorie Young, who was born nearby. She told me about helping her late husband clear trees sixty years ago from the land on which we were standing.

Many people shared their stories with me. Most of them appear in the book, but a few do not. Bill Dunn told about a property deed in which one of the calls went to "a horse standing in the field," and Medford Teets, who was my "right arm" on lower Birch, told of a deed that specified "a turkey nest by the side of the road."

A gentleman who lived in the Birch community long ago rarely got to town. Some neighbors persuaded him to accompany them to Sutton, and when he saw all the electric lights, he exclaimed: "Boys, no wonder the price of lamp oil is so high."

- - -

Birch is a river that must be seen daily in all its moods to be appreciated. I thought of this one cold February day in 2001. The late afternoon shadows stretched halfway across the river, leaving the remainder bathed in sunlight, and the contrast was strikingly gorgeous.

Sometimes a river is best viewed through a child's eyes. Eddie Rowan, a longtime friend from Charleston, brought his grandchildren, William, now six, and Caroline, now four, to Herold several times during the drought summer of 1999. William was old enough at the time to be fascinated by everything: the rocks, the crawfish, the tiny bugs, the water spiders, everything that moved, ebbed, and flowed. "We live five minutes from the city," said his mother, Ann Rowan Evans, "and this [the river] is a delightful source of wonderment to him."

In the end, it all came down to the river, and fittingly it got in the last word. It had been very benign during most of the dry May of 2001, but at the moment I was completing this project, heavy thunderstorms erupted and overnight Birch became a raging torrent. Paul Roche, who lives at the Falls below Herold, had not seen it that high. He woke up the next morning, looked out toward the huge rock that fills his picture window, and had only one word to say: "Wow!"

- - -

The collective effort that went into the writing of "River on the Rocks" was extensive, and I acknowledge the help of everyone, and am most grateful for it. There is not a page in the book that doesn't contain the contribution of someone other than myself.

If we accept the saying that a picture is worth a thousand words, then my nephew, Rob Johnson, contributed seventy thousand words to the book through pictures, plus another thousand words in "Birch River, a Summer for the Ages" in the "If We Were Counting" chapter. This chapter was my personal favorite because I like to fish Birch, but I wouldn't have fished it as extensively as I did without Rob's enthusiasm and energy.

Rob and Eddy Grey were the architects (cartographers I believe is the correct word) of the Birch watershed map, which turned out to be a classy, miniature, folded version of the book. Their work speaks for itself, and I suspect it is unique for a book about a West Virginia river.

Peter and Elizabeth Silitch, the book's editors, spent many hours wading through twenty two chapters and assorted other of my writings, and their contributions to the finished product were impressive and welcome. Our editing sessions spilled over into literary discussions of varying stripes, and I am tempted to write another book to assure that they will continue. Peter Silitich and Neal Gentry helped with the indexing.

Bill Gillespie and Jim Brown took time out from their work to visit Birch, "weighing" the rocks, cataloging the flora and fauna, and advising me on the geological forces that shaped the rocks and the river corridor. One day Jim and I crawled through rhododendron to measure a large rock, and I marveled at life's roll of the dice that had brought the two of us to that moment in time.

Neal Gentry, my neighbor and owner of Wolfpen Digital, a digital media production business, was an enormous asset in book layout and design, not to mention dealing pleasantly and equably with my total, abysmal, and astounding lack of knowledge about such things.

Lyle Stokes, who lives in the Los Angeles area, reached across four time zones to construct the population graphs for the three counties through which Birch flows, and Ward Eakin, who lives in New York state, provided priceless history of the Eakin Lumber Company operation on Birch.

Numerous federal, state, county, and municipal agencies, and other entities, were invaluable in providing information: The West Virginia Department of Highways, especially its historian, Harold Simmons; the West Virginia Geological Survey; the U.S. Geological Survey; the Army Corps of Engineers (special thanks to Jim McCormick, resource manager at Sutton Lake, and David Karickhoff of the hydraulics and hydrology section at Huntington); the West Virginia Department of Agriculture; Mike Arcuri, supervisor of the water quality section of the West Virginia Division of Environmental Protection; the West Virginia Division of Culture and History, especially historian Greg Carroll and senior archaeologist Joanna Wilson;

Marshall University biology professor Tom Pauley, who was of considerable help; Artie Barkley, shop foreman at the Cass Scenic Railroad; the county clerk's offices in Nicholas, Clay, and Braxton Counties; Webster County circuit clerk Karen Morris and retired judge Boonie Sommerville; Webster County assessor Dana Lynch; Cowen recorder Sharon Hart; Roger Conrad of the Braxton County assessor's office; and the public libraries at Sutton, Gassaway, Summersville, Cowen, and Craigsville, all of which were extremely helpful.

The life blood of any extended writing project is in being asked, "How's the book coming?' and in that regard I owe a debt of gratitude to Kevin Teets, my friend on Keener's Ridge who never failed to ask that question; to Ferrell Friend, a former Charleston Gazette colleague who was supportive from the beginning; to George and Doris Beam of Keener's Ridge; to their son, Joe, who flew my brother, nephew, and me down Birch River to make a video several years ago that proved to be the impetus for this book; to the late Del Thayer, whose encouragement was an inspiration and whose untimely death in April of 2001 was a sad moment; and to Lowell and Nancy Knight; Reggie and Judy Carte; Rose DeMoss; and Herb and Ann White.

Many others helped in various ways: Glenn Longacre Jr., who is writing a book on Elk River and was willing to share information with me; Frank Johnston, a fellow Herold native whose research was of immeasurable help; Braxton County realtors Dave and Roy Huffman; Tom Vance, who lives on the road to the Lower Keener Eddy; Gerry Milnes, coordinator of folklore at the Augusta Heritage Center at Davis & Elkins College; Lec Bowman, my first contact at Cowen on the very first chapter; Ewell Ferguson and GTR, Inc. for use of their Xerox Document Center; Jim and Steve Nicholas of Nicholas Family Monument Sales; Doug Huff, West Virginia's preeminent sports historian; Bill Dixon, a longtime friend and the great grandson of Thomas Dixon of "Hills of Birch River" renown; Margaret Brenner of the Wheeling Area Historical Society; Irene Crites of the Mustard's Last Stand ice cream and sandwich shop on old U.S. 19; Ruth and Anna Lee Lewis; Jim Lewis; Mary Goad Calhoun; Junior and Annie Murphy and their sons, Mike and Mark; and Eleanor Carte Byrnes.

Brenda Hickman of Gassaway, who dispenses genealogical history at the Gassaway Public Library, was always willing to dig for information. Her family history on Henry Young, her great great grandfather, gave that saga a special touch. To me personally, it revealed that the man who sleeps in the lonely grave on Powell's Mountain was my great great uncle.

I discovered in the course of writing this book that everybody must have a website, or risk being left behind in the dust of antiquity. Therefore, thanks to my nephew, Rob Johnson, and to Cherie Downey, our website consultant, for designing www.scenicbirchriver.com, which has drawn "visitors" in numbers that have astounded me.

The website was given a considerable boost by Lola Given of Frametown, whose E-mail contacts greatly increased the number of online visits.

Finally, whenever I needed an attentive ear, I went to my neighbors, Denzil and Gerry Baughman, on Adams Ridge. Denzil grew up, as I did, with the object of the book's affections. He put it this way:

"In the beginning, God created Birch River."

One

The Origins of Birch

Two Forks Meet in the Woods

Back Fork and Meadow Fork tumble off a mountain near Cowen, Webster County, and join in the woods in a picturesque setting of hemlock and rhododendron on Evergreen Mining Company property.

Immediately below where they meet is a rock shute with a series of small drop-offs. Although the calendar said late March 2001 when I went there, the banks were lined with ice. The two streams continue on a few hundred yards as one, and link up near the entrance to Evergreen with a small branch coming down from the Cowen direction to the east. There, alongside West Virginia Route 82, with berms too narrow to pull off and pay homage, officially and modestly begins the river of this book.

Back Fork and Meadow Fork are considerably larger in drainage area, totaling almost four and one-half miles of mountain streams, and thus are the principal water sources for the beginning of Birch River. But the smaller branch is recognized locally as the head of Birch, and I became convinced after tramping around the area on several visits that, geographically speaking, this designation is correct.

Pinpointing the exact start of a river is difficult, because drainages tend to occur hither and yon, and they defy precise classification as to which one is the actual beginning before they finally meld into one obvious stream. An example is Elk River and its two forks, Big Spring and Old Field, both of about equal size. An argument could be made for either one of them being the fountainhead of Elk. But in the case of Birch, we may as

Where Meadow Fork and Back Fork meet. Photo by Joe McPherson

well start with Larry Riffle and Bill Woods.

Larry Riffle lives at the top of Birch Mountain where W.Va. 82 levels off and Big Ditch Lake comes into view. His side yard slopes down to a wooded ravine where two rivulets meet in a classic "Y" at a little flat sprinkled with delicate, light green lady ferns. It is a nice setting for the start of a river, however modest this start may be. If I were to pinpoint the very head of Birch, I would point slightly to the left of the mailbox by the road that says "Riffle Pottery," and stake my claim there.

Larry and his wife, Carolyn, built a new studio and gallery on a wooded knoll overlooking Big Ditch Lake. Larry is the potter; Carolyn weaves rugs and placemats. Both are native Webster Countians, he from Jerryville and she from Cowen.

Bill Woods lives almost at the top of Birch Mountain, which isn't really a mountain but a hill, and is the divide between the Birch and Gauley River drainages in the area. The head of Birch begins on the western side of the hill.

It is just beyond Bill Woods' property line, between him and Larry Riffle, where the two small hollows come together. The single rivulet, thus formed, runs through Bill's yard. At his property line are four stately white oak trees that, in their way, announce the origin of Birch. When he took me to the hallowed ground, our presence was announced by the joyous barking of his son Roy's coon dogs.

The rivulet goes through a culvert underneath the road leading to Larry Perrine's house, and there joins a small brook coming in from the north of about one-half mile in length. The brook is called the Chris Hollow for Chris Miller, who once lived there. The present owner of the property is Ralph Miller of Cowen (no relation to Chris).

From there, the waters from the two "Y" hollows, the rivulet, and the Chris Hollow trickle down off Birch Mountain, or Birch Hill, cross under the highway, and meet the merged Back Fork and Meadow Fork to humbly begin Birch River.

Bill Woods has lived on "the head of Birch waters," which is the way his property deed describes the location, since 1943, and he wouldn't have it any other way. "Nothing ever happens around here," he explained. "That's why I like it so well." Bill's great grandparents, William Woods and Jane McElwain Woods, settled on the head of Birch in the 1800s. She died in 1908; he died in 1914. William and Jane Woods were the grandparents of Anna Mae Woods Fletcher of Cowen, who was born on the head of Birch.

Bill Woods' neighbors are his brother, Frank Woods, who works for the Department of Highways; Larry Perrine, who works for CSX; and Charles McElwain, who worked for A.T. Massey and Evergreen Coal Companies, and as a surveyor for a firm that did contract work for Brooks Run Coal Company.

Anna Mae Woods Fletcher was born near the Tollgate Rocks, an ill-fated rock formation on the old county road that ran from the present Evergreen entrance to Welsh Glades near Cowen. She and her brothers and sisters played on the rocks. The origin of the name Tollgate Rocks, or Devil's Tollgate, as the formation is also called, is elusive. The best explanation seems to be that two of the rocks had a natural passage between them, thus resembling a tollgate.

But these rocks, and another rock above the road that was part of the formation, were mostly destroyed by work on the old county road at some point prior to the building of present W.Va. 82 in the late 1930s.

Although Cowen is commonly known as the place where Birch begins, the town is actually located on the Gauley and Elk River drainages, primarily on Gauley. The West Virginia Geological Survey pinpoints the drainage divide as approximately one-third of a mile north of the Cowen town limits. From there, the drainage is north into Laurel Creek, a tributary of Elk River, or south into Gauley.

Big Ditch Lake, the 55-acre fishing impoundment that was built by the Division of Natural Resources and the U.S. Soil Conservation Service in 1969, is also mistakenly believed to be the start of Birch, but geography and geology dictated long ago that it would drain entirely into Gauley, the famous whitewater stream. Only a few hundred yards separate Big Ditch from the start of Birch, and I've often wondered how much the physiography of Birch River would have changed had the Big Ditch drainage tilted Birch's way. Certainly Birch would have had a bigger water volume, and it too may have become a major whitewater attraction.

Big Ditch Lake owes its existence to Hans McCourt, who represented Webster County in the State Senate, and to Carroll Greene, who was executive secretary of the State Soil Conservation Committee. McCourt was in an especially advantageous position as chairman of the Senate Finance Committee, and later Senate president.

Big Ditch Lake is on a tributary of Big Ditch Creek, hence its name. The creek flows from Cowen south into Gauley River.

The Harry Howard and Clyde Smith farms were located at the present lakesite. Clyde Smith's wife, Lelia, who died on July 16, 2000, at age 102, had her family bring her to the lake perhaps once a year from her home at Upper Glade, and she would walk around the lake. She did this until her 99th year.

- - -

Cowen (population 500 to 600) is a railroad town. It was established by the West Virginia and Pittsburgh Railway Company in 1892 and incorporated in 1899. The first post office came about in 1893 when it was moved to Cowen from Welsh Glades, a community located about one mile away on the road to Camden on Gauley.

Cowen and the Baltimore and Ohio Railroad began a long association in 1900 when the West Virginia and Pittsburgh merged with the B & O. Later the B & O merged with the Chesapeake and Ohio to become Chessie System, and then Chessie System and Seaboard merged to become the present CSX.

Passenger trains ran through Cowen from 1900 until 1956. Four trains stopped at Cowen daily enroute between Richwood and Grafton. Two of the four runs were discontinued over time, and, on June 20, 1956, the final two were discontinued, thus ending an era. C.L. (Lanky) Henderson, an Upper Glade native who came to Cowen in 1926, recalls precisely the daily schedule when there were four trains:

9 a.m. (Clarksburg bound).
11 a.m. (Richwood bound).
2:30 p.m. (Clarksburg bound).
5:06 p.m. (Richwood bound).

Anna Mae Woods Fletcher remembers that it was a social occasion to turn out and meet the Sunday train. Her mother ran the Home Hotel, a two-story structure that was located across from the depot.

Harold Carpenter, who retired in 1992 as trainmaster at Cowen after thirty nine years on the railroad, rode the last passenger train out of Cowen to Richwood. There was no ceremony at the end, just an air of finality. Harold doesn't recall anything particularly special about the trip, except that the nostalgia of the moment attracted a lot of railroad buffs who crowded the passenger and baggage cars.

Even coal trains no longer run through Cowen. That era ended in 1994, and the track has been removed from Allingdale to Richwood. Allingdale is a community on W.Va. 20 between Camden on Gauley and Craigsville, about ten miles southwest of Cowen.

But coal trains still run from Grafton to the Cowen yard. They are loaded at the Brooks Run Coal Company near Erbacon and at the Evergreen Mining Company tipple just north of Cowen. Evergreen has been mining coal on the head of Birch since 1991, and is the only current mining operation and the only industry on the entire river. Small mines were sprinkled all along Birch early in the twentieth century, most of them of the house coal variety. The defining structure on upper Birch is the Evergreen conveyor belt that crosses W.Va. 82 just west of the start of the river. The enclosed, green-painted belt is of German design and is unique in that it curves. It carries coal from Evergreen's operations on the south side of Birch to its railroad loading tipple on Laurel Creek, a distance of slightly over two miles.

In the 1930s, Cherry River Boom and Lumber Company had a large band mill on the head of Birch just below where the Evergreen conveyor belt crosses.

- - -

The Cowen railroad depot was vacant when I visited there in June 2000, but new life had been breathed into the landmark structure through a $199,844 state transportation enhancement grant to the town to buy and remodel the depot as a museum. Two passenger cars, built in the 1800s, will be restored at the same location. One was the personal living car of John T. McGraw, a railroad tycoon at the turn of the twentieth century.

When Harold Carpenter went to work for the railroad in 1953, nine crews worked out of Cowen. Spur lines from the Cowen marshalling yard ran to coal mines on the Williams and Gauley Rivers. At one time, Cherry River Boom and Lumber Company operated a railroad from the junction of the Williams and Gauley Rivers to Jerryville, which is located on Gauley near where Webster, Pocahontas, and Randolph Counties come together.

One of the great railroad names in West Virginia history is the Strouds Creek & Muddlety, a twenty-one mile coal hauling line that went from the B & O track at Allingdale to just beyond Muddlety, a Nicholas County community near Summersville (see "Powell's Mountain").

The B & O leased the SC & M track and paid a royalty for coal hauled over it, as did CSX later. Strouds Creek & Muddlety was the successor to the Birch Valley Lumber Company railroad. Strouds Creek heads near Tioga and empties into Gauley River at Allingdale, and is named for Adam Stroud, an early settler.

Steve Davis, a Summersville lawyer who represented the Strouds Creek & Muddlety, points out that the railroad's slogan was "Linking Muddlety With the World." In a 1958 article in the Charleston Gazette's State Magazine Section, L.T. Anderson said the railroad "wanders rather aimlessly through the ramp fields of central West Virginia, its path much like that of a happy child, picking daisies." The SC & M is no longer in operation, and as of 2000 a change in ownership left the future of the track in question.

The last and only piece of rolling stock belonging to the railroad was a restored caboose that has been transported to the town of Wellsboro, Pennsylvania, and remains there for public display. Most of the stockholders of the parent company of Strouds Creek & Muddlety Railroad were from that vicinity.

The B & O Restaurant at Cowen is a story in itself. That was its official name from the time it was opened around 1945 until it closed in 1995, but railroad employees knew it affectionately as "The Beanery." The restaurant building, which was located adjacent to the tracks and near the shop, included forty sleeping rooms, and a lobby and television room. Layover railroad crews stayed there, and for a time so did state police and conservation officers. There are still layover crews on the coal runs from Grafton to Cowen, but they are transported by cab to a motel at Summersville.

Dorothy Handschumacher of Craigsville managed "The Beanery" from January 1971 to its March 1995 closing. She served the final meal to a crew of six railroad men.

A spectacular wreck occurred on the Cowen-Grafton run in 1982 on the bridge over Sutton Lake near Centralia where the track comes out of Elk Tunnel. As the coal train came out of the tunnel, the horrified crew saw that the bridge was on fire. The engineer made a decision (it turned out to be the right one) to charge full speed across the bridge rather than stop on it. The engine barely made it across the bridge before derailing. About sixteen coal cars derailed on the bridge, and four of them toppled into Sutton Lake, and are still there. The crew escaped unharmed. The cause of the fire was never determined.

- - -

Cowen itself had a fiery beginning. In 1911, an arson fire destroyed a considerable part of the downtown. A picture of the aftermath shows that only the Central Hotel escaped undamaged. Then in 1914, another fire came along. It started in the Lemley and Mills store building and destroyed four other buildings before it was stopped. Lemley and Mills was a two-story structure with dry goods upstairs and groceries downstairs.

There may be a thing about Cowen and fire. According to *Heritage of Webster County*, the Moccasin Rangers of Cowen, one of the militia units formed in West Virginia during the Civil War, joined with, or were joined by, Confederate cavalry in torching a house in Sutton in December 1861. The fire quickly spread in the little community of frame dwellings, and soon much of the town was in ashes.

Cowen was first called "The Glades" because of the existence of a large glade (an open space surrounded by woods) at the present townsite. A considerable portion of this glade remains today, and gives Cowen the appearance of small towns in Northern Ontario, which are typically surrounded by grassy, spaghnum bogs called muskeg. The elevation of Cowen is 2,244 feet, which places it in the top fifteen among West Virginia municipalities. Davis in Tucker County is the highest at 3,101 feet, and the highest incorporated town east of the Mississippi River.

In 1860, when Webster County was created and named for orator and statesman Daniel Webster, the name of "The Glades" settlement was changed to "Webster Glades." Botany lost out to commerce, however, when the town was incorporated in 1899 and the name was changed to Cowen in honor of John K. Cowen, director and one of the principal stockholders in the West Virginia and Pittsburgh Railroad.

John K. Cowen was a business partner of Johnson N. Camden, the Lewis County native who, according to Bill Byrne, grew up in Sutton, and was twice elected to the U.S. Senate (1881-87 and 1893-95) when he was living at Parkersburg. Camden had a town named after him too, but not without a struggle. When he built the West Virginia and Pittsburgh R.R., he also built a sawmill at Lane's Bottom near Cowen. When Lane's Bottom was incorporated in 1904, the name was changed, naturally, to Camden. But the U.S. Postal Service balked, pointing out there was already a Camden in Lewis County. Johnson N. Camden was successful in getting "on Gauley" tacked onto the name of his Camden, and so it still is today. But he was not successful in turning Camden on Gauley into the resort town that he had envisioned. Instead, Webster Springs seized that prize, at least for a time.

In addition to being a builder of railroads, Johnson N. Camden was also an oil magnate, an owner and operator of coal mines, and a fisherman. In his classic book, *Tale of the Elk*, Bill Byrne said that Camden was probably West Virginia's first millionaire.

Camden on Gauley was known as a rough and tumble town during its heyday in the early 1900s, but not when Henon Fleming was police chief. Henon Fleming was involved in the celebrated shootout at Boggs on Birch River in 1894 (see "Skyles and Boggs"), and later became police chief at Richwood and Camden on Gauley. Bill Byrne was a lawyer, and he successfully defended Fleming in his trial at Webster Springs that resulted from the Boggs affair. Byrne wrote many years later that Fleming "had the reputation of a splendid officer." One reason may have been that his reputation had preceded him as a result of the Boggs shootout. In short, people were afraid of him.

Lanky Henderson was a young constable in Webster County in 1926 after Henon Fleming's days as the Camden on Gauley policeman had ended, and once he had the unenviable task of delivering a warrant on Fleming involving a misdemeanor of some sort. Henderson approached with some trepidation the area where Fleming lived. He didn't know Fleming, and when he saw a man walking along the road, he stopped and asked directions. The man walked over, put his hand on Henderson's shoulder, and said mildly, "Sonny, I'm the man you're looking for."

Fleming explained that he could not accompany Henderson to the courthouse that evening, but that he would be there the first thing in the morning. He was, and he promptly settled whatever the warrant was about.

"He was a tall and slim man," Lanky Henderson said of Fleming, "a businessman in a way, and a good man. After that [the warrant arrest] I considered him one of the best friends I ever had."

- - -

Lanky Henderson, who was ninety five years of age and possessed of a remarkable memory when I interviewed him at his home in the spring of 2000, held a variety of jobs in addition to constable. He worked in a lumber camp, and for the Department of Highways, was Cowen postmaster, then mayor of Cowen, worked for the Alcohol Beverage and Control Commission in Charleston, later for the Webster County Board of Education, served as a justice of the peace, and often appraised timber.

An earlier Cowen icon was Doctor Dan Kessler, a native of Rupert, Greenbrier County, who came to Wainville on Laurel Creek in 1891 when the railroad was being built, and moved to Cowen in 1895. He lived there for twenty five years. His Victorian-style home with a porch on two sides on West Railroad Avenue is still a Cowen showplace.

Former Dr. Dan Kessler house

The present owner is Joyce Blattenberger, a Webster Springs native. She and her husband, Donald, bought the house in 1989. Donald Blattenberger, a Pennsylvania native, died in 1992 before he could complete his renovation plans for the house, but it is still a classic.

In 1906, Kessler built the Gauley Sanitarium, a three-story, well-equipped hospital, but closed it in 1913 when it became too much of a financial burden. It was turned into a rooming house for girls who were attending Cowen High School, and in the early 1930s the top story was removed and it became Cowen Grade School. The school gave way to consolidation in 1976. The final use of the building was as a furniture store. The building still stands on a knoll across from the entrance to the Erbacon Road.

Kessler practiced medicine throughout the Birch, Laurel Creek, Gauley, Elk, and Williams River country, and was also a businessman. In 1916 he opened the first commercial coal mine in Webster County on Laurel Creek, and he was interested in timber and became an agent for the West Virginia Pulp and Paper Company.

He was living in Weston at the time of his death in 1945 at the age of eighty two. His story is told in the book, *Doctor Dan* written by Thelma and Kent Kessler.

Another well-known Cowen resident of the Doctor Dan era was his brother-in-law, George A. Herold, who owned a general store, and in 1921 served a term in the West Virginia Legislature. He also established a store and post office at Herold on lower Birch River, hence the name of the community. George A. Herold's home still stands near the Cowen Post Office, but has been vacant for a long time. The Cowen store building no longer exists.

- - -

Cowen High School, authorized by the voters of Glade District in 1910, is gone, too. A picture of the first class in 1911 hangs on the wall at the municipal building. Its members were Mayme Harold, Georgia Crites, May McCoplin, John Smith, Goldie Exline, Clyde Talbert, Emma Gardner, Zenia Kelly, Rebecca Woods, Eva Holister, Ernest Miller, and

Chilton Bobbitt.

Charles T. Dodrill, author of *Heritage of a Pioneer*, was born at Beech Bottom (now Wainville) on Laurel Creek and attended one of the early terms at Cowen High. He was principal of Cowen Grade School, and later became a lawyer in Huntington.

From an athletic standpoint, Cowen High School is defined by basketball player Don Svet, the Camden on Gauley native who became one of West Virginia's all-time top scholastic scorers. He averaged 40.3 points per game in his senior year in 1955, and once scored fifty four points in a game against Meadow Bridge. His senior-year average was a state record at the time for a single season, and still ranks second in that category to Paul Popovich of Flemington, whose 41.8 points is the record. Svet's coach, Beecher Hinkle, is retired and lives at Craigsville. Svet is a U.S. magistrate judge at Albuquerque, New Mexico.

Bud Stutler, who coached at Cowen after the Svet years, had a player, Mickey Smith, who once scored fifty two points in a game. Smith is living in Bristol, Tennessee, and manages a used car lot. Stutler retired in 1976 and lives in Cowen. The following year was the last for Cowen High School. Consolidated Webster County High School opened at Upper Glade in 1978. Cowen High, which was located across the road from the Doctor Dan Kessler hospital, has been torn down, and the exploits of Svet, Smith and others in its basketball gymnasium are only echoes.

Harold Carpenter, the retired trainmaster, was a senior on the 1953 Cowen football team. Although he was two years ahead of Svet in school, he remembers Svet as a place-kicker for the gold and blue-clad Bulldog football teams, as well as a basketball star. In Carpenter's senior year, Cowen defeated Richwood in their annual Wagon Wheel clash. "I believe that was the last time we won the Wagon Wheel," he recalls. The Cowen High School football field was located at the present site of Glade Elementary School. Harold Carpenter is the great-great grandson of Solomon Carpenter, who was born under a rock on Laurel Creek (see "William Strange").

The first football game I ever saw was between Sutton and Cowen, and was played on the fairgrounds field below present-day Sutton Dam. I didn't know much about shoulder pads and other accoutrements of football players, and I thought those were the biggest people I would ever see in the world. The outcome of the game has long since faded from memory, assuming I ever knew in the first place.

Although Cowen was a railroad town, its major private employer now is Leslie Bros. Lumber Company. The company founders were William and Clyde Leslie Sr., who went into the logging business in 1950 and followed with a sawmill in 1968. The present owner of the company is Larry Leslie, son of Clyde Sr., who passed away in 1989. John Leslie, Larry's brother, owns a John Deere dealership near the lumber company. Leslie Bros. Lumber employed one hundred and twenty people, as of late summer 2000.

- - -

Birch River begins just west of Cowen at an elevation of 2,300 feet, but the highest point in the one hundred and forty-three square miles of drainage is 2,792 feet. This Peak of Birch occurs on an unnamed ridge three miles southwest of Cowen on the headwaters of Meadow Fork. I named it Ashton Place in honor of Ken Ashton of the West Virginia Geological Survey, who identified it to me as the Mount Everest of the Birch drainage.

The Birch watershed elevation drops 2,017 feet from Ashton Place to the mouth of the river at Glendon. En route, the river travels 36.6 miles through Webster, Nicholas, and Braxton Counties, and that journey is the subject of this book.

Bill Armentrout not only agreed that Ashton Place is the Peak of Birch, he also took me there. Bill, who is retired from Island Creek Coal Company, has quite a stake in the origins of Birch River. He owns at least half of Meadow Fork, which flows squarely through his three hundred acre farm on Meadow Fork Road southwest of Cowen. Further, his property comes close to Back Fork, the other half of the twin tributaries that contribute the most water to the start of Birch.

We unfolded a topo map of the Cowen quadrangle on the hood of my car and studied it, while at the same time eyeing the surrounding hills. For several months I had planned to visit Ashton Place, but I wasn't familiar enough with the area to trust my judgment on exactly which of the ridges it was, nor did I know which roads to take to get there, assuming there were roads.

"I have good news and bad news," Bill told me when I drove up to his home in the valley of the Meadow Fork. "I've found the 2,792-foot ridge, but it may not be 2,792 feet any longer." He explained: "The area was strip-mined a few years ago, and at least some of the ridgetop, if not all of it, was reduced in height."

That would have opened a whole new can of map reading to determine the highest point of the Birch watershed.

But we headed for Ashton Place, after a visit with Fred and Dolly Hickman just down the road from the Armentrouts. Fred is a native of Meadow Fork. He and his wife now live in Ohio, but spend a lot of time at his homeplace in the summer. The topo map was unfolded again, this time on Fred's vehicle. He deliberated, looked at the surrounding ridges, and nodded his approval of Ashton Place as the Peak of Birch.

Approaching Ashton Place, the former mining roads began running here, there, and yonder. It was like one of those puzzles, called "mazes," with an intricate network of passages, where the trick is to work your way from A to Z. But because of our earlier reconnaissance, we quickly recognized Ashton Place when it came into view, and I breathed a sigh of relief when we saw that the entire ridgeline had not been reduced in height. One part of Ashton Place was obviously still 2,792 feet.

We walked to the crest of the mined area. In the distance, looking northwest, we could see Evergreen Mining Company (not the company that mined on Ashton Place) and the Back Fork drainage. Looking east, we could see the Meadow Fork

The view from the highest elevation in the Birch drainage

drainage, the town of Cowen water tank, and, purplish in the summer haze, a far ridge that runs toward Point Mountain on West Virginia Route 20 between Cowen and Webster Springs.

"From my decidedly prejudiced standpoint," I said to Bill, "the best part of this splendid view is the one that looks toward Meadow Fork and Birch River."

He nodded.

"Do you agree?" I pressed, unwilling to accept a simple nod.

He nodded twice.

I accepted two nods, primarily because Bill held the keys to his truck, and it was getting along in the afternoon.

But it was pleasant on Ashton Place. The sun was shining, a red-tailed hawk circled in the air currents, and a cool breeze came off the high point and ruffled my thin shirt. From where we stood, everything was downhill for Birch River.

Two

Skyles and Boggs

The Twin Cities of Upper Birch

The settlement of Skyles, named for surveyor Jacob Skyles, lies at the mouth of Skyles Creek, which is on a corner of the Nicholas-Webster County line. Skyles Creek enters 24.1 miles above the mouth of Birch and 4.8 miles above Birch Village. The neighboring hamlet, Boggs, is located four miles farther upstream at the 28.1 mile mark.

Combined, these "Twin Cities" have a rich history of timbering, logging trains, hunting, and colorful characters.

And then there was the shootout.

The famous duel at the O.K. Corral in Tombstone, Arizona, on October 26, 1881, where the Earp brothers and Doc Holliday took on the Clantons and McLaurys in what evolved into the most celebrated gunfight in Old West history, had little on the January 14, 1894, shootout at the Boggs Store and Post Office, where the Fleming brothers took on Cap Hall and two associates.

In terms of number of participants and number of dead and wounded, the Boggs shootout rivaled its western counterpart.

There were a total of eight participants at the O.K. Corral, or more correctly behind the corral, and a total of five participants at the Boggs Store and Post Office. In both cases, the gunplay erupted at close range. In sixty seconds at Tombstone, three Clanton associates were dead, and two of Wyatt Earp's brothers were wounded. In the narrow confines of the Boggs Store and Post Office, two died and three were wounded in probably about the same time.

The bloody happenings at Boggs have as many different versions as the number of people telling them. But perhaps it is best to rely on the account of a lawyer who was one of the defenders of Henon Fleming in Webster County Circuit Court.

The lawyer was Bill Byrne, a cult figure among those interested

Site of the 1894 shootout at Boggs

Henon Fleming; circa 1942
Photo courtesy of Ruth King

in West Virginia history, and particularly Elk River history, because of his book, *Tale of the Elk*, which first appeared in installments in *West Virginia Wildlife* magazine and in the Braxton Democrat from 1927 to 1931, and was later published in book form.

Byrne and fellow lawyer A.J. Horan were appointed by the court to defend Henon Fleming, who had been indicted for murder as a result of the violent shootout, in which, according to Byrne, at least twenty two shots were fired.

The incident had its roots in Wise County, Virginia, where an entire family had been wiped out in what became known as "the Pound Gap murders."

Byrne wrote that the Halls, "justly or unjustly," sought to pin the Pound Gap murders on the Flemings. The two Fleming brothers sought safety on upper Birch at the home of a brother-in-law, who lived near Boggs. They were said to have become well liked in the community, and minded their own business, a prized commodity.

Some accounts say the two factions were feudists; Byrne calls them "two bitterly opposed clans." But Ruth King of Richwood, a grand-daughter of Henon Fleming, doesn't believe they were feudists, at least not in the classic sense, although there was probably "bad blood" between the two factions.

The Fleming brothers made a weekly visit on a certain day to the

Boggs Store and Post Office for supplies and their mail, and this punctuality proved to be fatal to one of them. A reward for the apprehension of the brothers had been offered by Wise County authorities, and Cap Hall, George Branham, and Dock Swindall discovered where the Flemings were staying, and made their way to Boggs. There they found out about the regular visits, and, according to local legend, hid in a cellar near the store and waited.

Byrne wrote that Hall, Branham, and Swindall followed the Flemings into the store, six-shooters in hand, yelling "Hands Up!" The Flemings had either ridden horseback or walked to the store, probably coming down Barnett Run and then upriver the short distance. From the shootout site, Barnett Run hollow is visible where it enters Birch. Calvin Fleming was standing at the counter to the left of the door, reading a letter that postmaster Billy Boggs had handed him, and Henon Fleming was reading over his shoulder. The shooting started. Calvin Fleming, who had a reputation for being quick on the draw and was therefore the initial target, was hit three times and killed instantly. Henon Fleming was the target of fifteen shots, according to Byrne's account, and himself got off four shots, with deadly effect.

Henon Fleming was hit in the mouth, tearing away all the teeth on the left side of his jaw, and the bullet lodged in his left shoulder. Branham was hit twice and died a few hours later. Swindall was hit twice, but survived. Henon Fleming's fourth shot had passed through Swindall's windpipe and grazed Hall's temple. Byrne wrote that Fleming was in the act of firing a fifth shot when a bullet from the pistol of one of his two remaining adversaries struck the cylinder of Fleming's revolver, locking it, and part of the bullet plowed up Fleming's arm, leaving a large welt to his elbow. Henon Fleming was going for a smaller pistol in his belt, but fainted from loss of blood before he could use it, and there the shootout ended.

Byrne said that as soon as Henon Fleming and Dock Swindall recovered sufficiently, they were removed from Billy Boggs' house, where they had been taken after the shooting. Henon Fleming was lodged in the Nicholas County jail at Summersville, where he further recuperated, and Swindall was taken to his home in Virginia. The likely route of Fleming's journey to Summersville opens another page of West Virginia history. The story is that he was handcuffed, placed in a wagon and brought first to Cowen. This version, which was printed in *Heritage of Webster County*, says that the wagon stopped in the vicinity of the George A. Herold store, and that Viola Herold, wife of the store owner, washed Fleming's wounds and generally treated him kindly. Years later, Fleming met Viola Herold by chance, remembered her, and thanked her for the kindness she had shown him. Lanky Henderson of Cowen, who knew both Henon Fleming and Viola Herold, said he personally heard her tell the story of when Fleming was brought to Cowen. Ruth King, a granddaughter of Henon Fleming, said she has also heard this version.

The likelihood, then, is that he was indeed brought from Boggs to Cowen by wagon, and then on to Summersville by the same transportation. There existed at that time an unimproved dirt road called the Summersville and Slaven Cabin Road (West Virginia Geological Survey) that started at Summersville and ran eastward through Craigsville, Allingdale, Camden on Gauley, Cowen, Webster Springs, Monterville, and Valley Head. Its eastern terminus was Slaven Cabin, a community on the eastern slope of Shavers Mountain, just west of the present town of Durbin. Henon Fleming was probably taken to Summersville on this road.

While he was recuperating from his wounds at Summersville jail, rumors arose that an attempt would be made by his family or friends in Virginia to break him out of jail, so authorities moved him in the dark of night to the Kanawha County jail in Charleston.

Meanwhile, a circuit court in Webster County had indicted him for the murder of Branham, and a similar clandestine journey was made from Charleston to Webster Springs for the trial, which began on November 9, 1894.

The trial lasted only two days, and the result is told in Law Orders Book Five at the circuit clerk's office at the Webster County Courthouse. The record of the full trial, including exhibits and statements of witnesses, was ruined years ago when a section of the courthouse roof blew away in a storm, and old records stored in an attic were destroyed. But the following entry in the Law Orders Book tells of the beginning of the trial:

> The State vs. Hennon Fleming, Indictment for Felony [court documents spelled his name Hennon, but his descendants say the correct spelling was Henon]:
>
> This day came the state by the prosecuting attorney [E.H. Morton], and the defendant was led to the bar of the court, in custody of the jailer, assisted by counsel, whereupon the defendant demurred to the indictment and says the same is not sufficient in law, which demurrer being considered by the court is overruled, whereupon the defendant pleaded not guilty, and thereupon a panel of twenty jurors were drawn from those in attendance at this term, and pronounced competent and free from exception by the court, from which panel the prosecuting attorney struck off two and the defendant struck off six, leaving the following named twelve as the jury for the trial of this case, namely Joseph H. Bennett, Phillip Schuemacher, Sampson

Hammons, Jacob Graff, G.L. Brady, E.J. Isenhart, Harman L. Brown, Wm. J. Chandler, S.S. Hines, W.C. Anderson, Lewis Garvin, and Jacob Hinkle, who were sworn according to law, and after hearing part of the evidence, were committed to the custody of D.H. Sizemore, deputy for P.J. McGuire, sheriff of Webster County, who was first duly sworn for the purpose, and the prisoner was remanded to jail, and this cause continued until tomorrow.

The entry was signed by W.G. Bennett, the circuit court judge.

The trial entry for the following day, November 10, 1894, says simply that the jury acquitted Henon Fleming:

> This day came again the state by the prosecuting attorney, and the prisoner was led to the bar in the custody of the jailor, and the jurors herein in custody of D.H. Sizemore, deputy sheriff of Webster County, to whose custody they were on yesterday committed, and the jurors after fully hearing the evidence and arguments of counsel and instruction by the court, were sent to their room to consider of their verdict, after which they returned in court and upon their oaths do say we, the jury, find the defendant not guilty. Therefore it is considered by the court that the defendant be discharged from said indictment.

The record for the same day shows that the twelve jurors in the Henon Fleming trial were each paid four dollars for their two days of jury duty.

A second felony indictment had been brought against Fleming as a result of the Boggs shootout, and it was promptly dismissed on April 30, 1895, with this entry in the Law Order Book: "The prosecuting attorney with the assent of the court, declines to prosecute further in this behalf, therefore it is ordered by the court that the defendant be discharged."

With the 1894 trial, and the dropping of the second indictment in 1895, the saga of the shootout officially came to an end in Webster County.

Henon Fleming was also later found not guilty in Virginia of the Pound Gap murders. He returned to West Virginia, as did two of his brothers, and they lived in Webster or Nicholas Counties the remainder of their lives. Ironically, Henon Fleming became police chief at Richwood, and later at Camden on Gauley. Ruth King and another granddaughter, Kathryn McCoy of Rainelle, have a picture of their grandfather, taken in 1908 when he was police chief at Richwood, posing with a daughter of Devil Anse Hatfield when she was visiting in Richwood. The grand-daughters believe he was police chief at Camden on Gauley around 1915. He had a reputation as an excellent officer, perhaps one reason being that his reputation had preceded him as a result of the Boggs shootout.

Henon Fleming's brothers who came to West Virginia were Orbin and Al Fleming. Madalene Hivick, who moved to Camden on Gauley in 1924, remembers that Al Fleming lived near her at that time. Glenn Longacre Jr., of Cherry Falls, recalls that Al Fleming bought and sold timber in his later years. Longacre met him in the 1950s at Dixie, Nicholas County, on timber business.

Henon, Orbin and Al Fleming are all buried at the Fleming Cemetery at Cottle. Henon Fleming died on November 18, 1943, at age seventy eight. He was twenty nine at the time of the Boggs shootout. His gravestone gives his name as Samuel Heenan, but his granddaughters say "Heenan" is an incorrect spelling. A great-grandson who lives in Cottle is named Henon (Mac) Fleming. Mac was part of Calvin Fleming's name.

Henon Fleming's wife, Catherine Vanover Fleming, died in 1926 and is also buried at the Cottle cemetery. A Colorado blue spruce and two yucca plants are growing at their graves. Catherine Vanover was a native of Kentucky. She and Henon Fleming were married in Kentucky on September 8, 1887. The marriage certificate lists him as a resident of Pound, Virginia.

The 1900 Webster County census shows that Henon and Catherine Fleming were back in West Virginia by that time. They had four children living, including three daughters and a son. At the time of the census, Henon Fleming was a night watchman for the railroad.

Calvin Fleming is buried at the Boggs Cemetery on a hillside above the mouth of Barnett Run, near where he was killed. The name on the tombstone identifies him as P.M.C. Fleming, the date of his birth as October 15, 1872, and the date of his death as January 14, 1894. Thus, he was not quite twenty two when he died in the shootout. Ruth King said her grandmother sold eggs and butter to obtain money for the monument that was placed at Calvin's grave. The story is told that Calvin Fleming was buried outside the Boggs Cemetery as it existed one hundred and seven years ago, perhaps because a stigma was attached to the way in which he died. But time has, in a sense, changed the location of his grave. Many more people have been buried there over the years, and his grave is now very much inside the cemetery.

Cal Fleming tombstone

Ruth King was nineteen when her grandfather Henon Fleming died. She spent a lot of time with him at Cottle, and remembers him well. "He was a tease," she said, "and he could cuss mules with the best of them. He didn't cuss around the house, but he could turn the air blue around his mules [mules seem to do this to people generally]."

Kathryn McCoy remembers her grandfather as "a good-hearted person. He was always joking. I thought a lot of him."

Henon Fleming was the community "dentist" at Cottle, an avocation shared with Peter the Great of Russia. Chester Kerns, who lives near where Henon Fleming lived (the house no longer exists), remembers having a tooth pulled by him. Afterwards, the "dentist" gave him salt water to rinse his mouth. Kerns recalled Henon Fleming as being "tall and slim." "Yes, he pulled teeth for people," Kathryn McCoy said. "One time he was going to pull one of my teeth, and I ran off. Being a little girl, I didn't want my tooth pulled."

At the time of the shooting, the Boggs Store and Post Office was located in a large Birch River bottom just above Barnett Run between Skyles and Boggs. According to *Heritage of Webster County*, the community of Boggs is named for David Boggs, father of Billy, who settled in the area following the Civil War. The shootout site is directly across the river from the present Walnut Grove United Methodist Church. The property owners are Bill and Sharon Riddle, who have a stable for the riding, training, and boarding of horses. Bill Riddle is also a logger.

Bill Riddle's great-grandfather, William Roberts, who died in 1960 at around one hundred years of age, told his great-grandson that he came to Boggs on the day after the shooting and that Henon Fleming was still there and bound so tightly that breathing was difficult. He persuaded whoever was guarding him to loosen the binding, which they did. The Flemings had worked for William Roberts on Board Fork of Beaver Creek near Tioga, where he had a sawmill and also farmed. Roberts was one of many people who were said to have come to the Boggs store the day following the shooting to learn more about it.

Billy Boggs, the storekeeper, is said to have wisely taken refuge behind the counter while the carnage unfolded. He died a few years after the shootout.

- - -

For whatever reason, maybe accessibility provided by the broad river bottoms, there were more early settlers on upper Birch than on its lower counterpart.

Another, perhaps more plausible, theory is that the excellent hunting and trapping on upper Birch lured the early settlers there in the first place, and they simply stayed and raised families. The most common origins of settlers on Birch seemed to have been Bath, Alleghany, Rockbridge, Botetourt, Augusta, and Rockingham Counties in Virginia, and Greenbrier, Pocahontas, and Pendleton Counties in present West Virginia.

One of the pioneers of upper Birch was Isaac Rose, a Revolutionary War veteran who is buried between Birch Village and Skyles midway along a gravel driveway across W.Va. 82 from Ronnie Collins' residence. Isaac Rose came into the area from Pennsylvania, as did his wife, Margaret Forsythe Rose. They had six children, one of whom, William Rose, served in the War of 1812 (See "The Blue Hole"). Isaac Rose's tombstone says simply: Isaac Rose. Revolutionary Soldier. 1753-1829. There is no tombstone at the site for his wife, who died in 1843 at age eighty six.

On June 24, 1979, a marker was placed at the Isaac Rose grave by a chapter of the Daughters of the American Revolution.

Madalene Hivick, who lives at Camden on Gauley, is a great-great granddaughter of Isaac Rose. Her grandfather, Fielding Rose, was a Confederate soldier in the Civil War.

Another Revolutionary War veteran and native of Ireland, Adam O'Brien, left his initials in a cave on Road Fork (or Left Fork) of Skyles Creek. According to Gerry Milnes' 1999 book, *Play of a Fiddle*, about traditional music, dance, and folklore in West Virginia, O'Brien moved around a lot in his pursuit of hunting, trapping and fighting Indians. Milnes wrote: "He was of Irish birth, lived to be more than one hundred years old, fought in the Revolutionary War battle of Point Pleasant, and left his initials on rocks and trees and in caves throughout the area. It is said that he sired a child at age ninety two!"

- - -

Bearhunter Billy Barnett may have given Barnett Run its name, and if not, he was short-changed. The story of Billy's fight with a bear, which occurred on the head of Poplar Creek or on the dividing ridge between Poplar and Barnett Run, is legendary. Various accounts exist, but William C. Dodrill, in his 1915 book, *Moccasin Tracks and Other Imprints*, says he got his version from Bearhunter Billy himself. Dodrill, also known as Rattlesnake Bill, was born in 1861 just above the mouth of Poplar, and lived until 1921. His book has contributed significantly to preserving the lore of upper Birch.

Rattlesnake Bill Dodrill was a legend in his own right. Bill Byrne of *Tale of the Elk* fame and Rattlesnake Bill were fishing companions, and

Byrne wrote this about him: "Rattlesnake Bill was a schoolteacher in the winter time, and a wild man in the summer time, and early in our acquaintance we discovered that we had much in common, that is, during the wild season. Many a day and night we have spent together in and along the banks of the raging Elk. He died a few years ago, and in him passed one of the most ardent anglers and all-round wildlifers it was ever my good fortune to meet."

In his account of Bearhunter Billy Barnett's encounter with the bear, Rattlesnake Bill Dodrill wrote that Billy shot a very large bear, and, after reloading, went up to the bear, which jumped on him. They rolled downhill, and eventually Billy killed the bear with his hunting knife. In the fight, Billy suffered a severe thigh wound, whether inflicted by the bear or by his own knife isn't clear, but probably by his own knife. With his hands a mass of wounds, he bound up the cut with strips of cloth torn from his shirt, and then tied a bloody cloth around the neck of his dog, and repeatedly whipped him until the dog ran home to sound the alarm, so to speak.

He was found around three o'clock the following morning, weak from loss of blood. Dodrill said the man who found him carried water in his boot, Billy having become almost delirious from thirst because of the loss of blood. He was carried home on a litter, and spent weeks recuperating. He was always somewhat lame afterwards, Dodrill wrote.

Carl Davis of Coon Creek, Braxton County, a great-grandson of Bearhunter Billy, told a postscript to the story: "Great-grandfather was in bed, and those gathered around were telling him what he should have done. 'Now, my friends and neighbors,' Billy replied, 'you would have done exactly as I done, and you might have made a worse job of it.'" (Carl Davis was killed on November 24, 2000, in a farm tractor accident on Coon Knob).

William C. Barnett was born in 1816, and died in 1896 at age eighty. He is believed to be buried in the Barnett Cemetery near Boggs. There are over twenty graves in the cemetery marked only by slabs of rock, and Bearhunter Billy's is probably one of them. He lived in a cabin in the woods nearby. Because county makeups were changing at the time, it is said that he lived in three different counties, but in the same house at the same place. Exactly where he lived is not known, but, if the story is true, the possibilities are Kanawha, Nicholas, Braxton, and, of course, Webster, which was formed in 1860 as the last county created before separation from the Mother State, Virginia. From 1860 on, he definitely lived in Webster County.

Kanawha was formed in 1788, and covered a wide area; Nicholas was formed in 1818 from parts of Kanawha, Greenbrier, and Randolph;

Braxton was formed in 1836 from parts of Lewis, Kanawha, and Nicholas; and Webster was formed in 1860 from parts of Nicholas, Braxton, and Randolph.

Rose Barnett Rowh, a great-granddaughter, lives across from the Barnett Cemetery with her husband, Benson Rowh. She recalls a bearskin that covered a trunk in the ancestral, one-hundred-year-old, now vacant home in front of where she lives. She believes this may have been the bearskin of Bearhunter Billy's celebrated confrontation.

In addition to being a bearhunter of great renown, Bearhunter Billy was also well known as a gunsmith. William C. Dodrill wrote that a Barnett-made rifle was highly prized, and that the name was "a guarantee of honest workmanship."

The time of his fight with the bear is unknown, but it occurred sometime after 1836, the year he married Charlotte Rose Barnett, who is mentioned in accounts of the episode. Billy and Charlotte had nine children. One of their sons, Levi J. Barnett, had eighteen children. Levi Barnett was a circuit rider (a preacher who traveled around within an assigned territory; because they traveled on horseback, they were often called "Saddle Bags Man.").

Early residents of upper Birch seemed to take their bear hunting seriously. In a November 15, 1983, interview with Gerry Milnes for the Augusta Collection, Booth Library, Davis & Elkins College, Fred Roberts told about his grandfather, Neal Roberts, shooting, but not killing, a bear on Poplar Creek. The bear and Fred's grandfather's dog took up the fight. "Grandfather knocked the bear loose from the dog with his fist," Fred Roberts related. "He was much of a man, Grandfather Roberts was."

Descendants of Bearhunter Billy still live in the Boggs-Skyles area. One enclave of Barnetts on W.Va. 82 put up a sign which says "Barnettsville. Population 6." There were also familes with the surname Christian living in the same area years ago. A protracted revival meeting was being held, and one day the preacher called a mid-afternoon break. He asked someone if he was a Christian (meaning a professed follower of Jesus), to which the reply came back: "No sir, I'm a Barnett."

- - -

Some say that the man who came to the wounded Bearhunter Billy's aid with water in his boot was named Baughman, which opens another chapter of Birch River lore.

Christopher Baughman, who may have been that man, migrated from Boutetourt (pronounced "Botetot") County, Virginia, and settled on Birch River in 1823, according to an article by Ronald Hardway in the

1984-85 *Webster Independent*, a publication of the Webster County Historical Society. According to Gerry Milnes' research, Christopher may have introduced the mountain dulcimer to central West Virginia.

Christopher Baughman was a miller and farmer by occupation, and he had a thirst for land. By virtue of his own purchases, plus a Virginia land grant of 1,800 acres in 1856, he eventually owned more than 2,000 acres. A son, John, later became an even larger landowner, with approximately 3,000 acres of valuable farming and timber property at the start of the Civil War.

Hardway wrote this about Christopher and Rachel Glasburn Baughman, whom Christopher married in 1813 while still in Boutetourt County: "They are the Baughman pioneers in central West Virginia and the progenitors of the Baughman family in Nicholas, Braxton and Webster Counties."

Christopher Baughman died in 1861 at age seventy three, and is buried on a tiny flat above present West Virginia 82, a stone's throw from the mouth of Skyles Creek, with his first wife, Rachel, who died in 1843 at age fifty two. Christopher remarried after Rachel's death, and his second wife may be buried there also, although the weathered tombstones are difficult to read, and two of them have toppled over. Christopher is known to have been living near the mouth of Skyles in 1849, and probably lived there the remainder of his life. Whether he lived in the same place throughout his thirty eight years on upper Birch is not known.

William C. Dodrill wrote in *Moccasin Tracks* about an imaginary trip he took up Birch River from the mouth of Skyles to Mill Creek beyond Webster Springs in 1849, and the only residents of upper Birch then were Christoper Baughman, his son John, Bearhunter Billy Barnett, and Henry Cutlip.

Samuel Baughman, youngest son of Christopher and Rachel, bought a tract of land on upper Keener's Ridge near the Nicholas-Braxton County line in 1849, beginning a Baughman presence in Braxton County that continues to this day. Samuel died in 1879 at age fifty two, and is buried at the family cemetery on Keener's Ridge near Morris.

Samuel's son, Henry Baughman, eventually lived on Birch River at Herold, and was the last grist-mill operator in that community, and maybe the last on Birch. His steam-powered mill was a Herold fixture until the late 1940s. He learned the trade working in his brother Cornelius' mill, which is believed to have been located on Birch River at the mouth of Coalbed Run. Henry's sons, Newman and Edwin, lived in the Herold area most of their lives. A daughter, Ora, moved to Upshur County. Another daughter, Oma, lived in Herold for a time, then moved to Charleston, but returned to the community and was living in Canfield at the time of her death.

This Baughman lineage had a shaky start before coming to Birch. The patriarch, Heinrich Baughman, a native of Germany, arrived in America in 1739 and lasted sixteen years. He was killed by Shawnees when they attacked his log blockhouse fort at the mouth of Muddy Creek on the Greenbrier River near Alderson in 1755. Nineteen other settlers died with him, but among the survivors were Heinrich's wife and three sons. One of the sons, Henry Junior, was the father of Christopher, the upper Birch settler.

- - -

Another early settler on upper Birch was George Mollohan. In a paper on Birch River written in 1982, Glenville State College history professor John Hymes Jr. said that "historians generally agree that around 1800 George Mollohan, an Englishman from Bath County, Virginia, moved to [the Skyles area]. Legend holds that Mollohan lost his life at an old age while attempting to pass through the wilderness from Birch River to the Sutton area to visit his son. Mollohan was apparently nearly blind at the time, and when his horse strayed off the path he was never able to find it again. His saddle blanket and gloves were found hanging on a tree in the area." Another account says his horse was found grazing nearby in bottom lands. But Mollohan's body was supposedly never found.

The book, *Heritage of Webster County*, says that a George Mollohan came to Birch from Greenbrier County around 1805 or 1806. Greenbrier was formed in 1778 from parts of Montgomery and Botetourt Counties, Virginia. According to this source, he settled on Birch near William (English Bill) Doddrill, who arrived there in 1799.

Elias (Lise) Sanson arrived in the Boggs area in the late 1800s and is called in the book, *Moccasin Tracks*, "one of the last great hunters in Webster County." Michael Dilley, who grew up in the Boggs-Skyles area and presently lives at Huttonsville, has done extensive research on the families of upper Birch. He found that Sanson was born in Pike County, Kentucky, in 1835, moved to McDowell County, West Virginia, and left there about 1888 bound for Birch River. "I don't understand why they all left McDowell," said Dilley. "The way I understand it, the government did a geology survey about 1887 or 1888, and found large deposits of coal. McDowell became a booming county in 1888. Why did they leave when all this was going on? Maybe the coal company bought them out."

Perhaps it was the lure of the happy hunting grounds of upper Birch. In *Tale of the Elk*, Bill Byrne speculates that the existence of good hunting and trapping was what brought so many early settlers to the upper section of Birch. He wrote: "The earliest settlers of that locality were hunters who went for the deer and bear and wild turkey which there abounded, built a camp here and there, and being so pleased with the prospect, these camps were succeeded by log cabins to which these hunters moved their families, cleared out a few acres for a garden, corn, 'tater and sorghum patch, and took up their permanent abode."

William (English Bill) Dodrill, who settled on Birch in the Boggs-Skyles area in 1799, is said to have come there after hearing of the exceptional abundance of wild game, fish, and fur-bearing animals on upper Birch. English Bill had been a friend and hunting companion of Daniel Boone at Point Pleasant and Charleston, and therefore had a keen appreciation of fertile hunting grounds.

The head of Poplar Creek between its main branch and Panther Lick Branch seemed to have been a magnet to hunters. This area abounded in acorns, beechnuts, native American chestnuts, and hickory nuts, which made it attractive also to bear, deer, and wild turkey. At over six miles in length, Poplar is the second largest of all Birch River tributaries. Only Little Birch River is larger at 19.84 miles. The long, deep hollows and high mountains of upper Birch are quite impressive. The elevation where Poplar begins, for example, is 2,325 feet.

Bill Byrne wrote about a hunting trip he took in the late 1800s up from Birch Village. He called it "Ford of Birch," there being no bridge then, and, by the way, no road upriver. His hunting party followed "a pack-saddle trail," but apparently the hunting was worth it, although he didn't elaborate.

- - -

Upper Birch is of course smaller than its lower counterpart, does not possess the huge boulders that mark the lower river, and is more accessible. Or at least it is now. West Virginia Route 82 runs along the entire seventeen miles of upper Birch from Birch Village to Cowen.

But it was once an adventure. The road originally went up the left side of the river at Birch Village, and came back into what is present W.Va. 82 above the Birch Elementary School. That would of course have necessitated fording the river. From there on, the adventure continued. In his history of Eakin Lumber Company, including its operations at Skyles, Ward Eakin wrote:

> By 1920, cars began to show up at Skyles and you could get to Cowen and downriver to Big Birch. You could walk about as fast as a car could go. If you met another car

someone had to back up to pass. There were no bridges and of course you drove through and along the river all the way.

He listed various cars owned by Skyles residents in the 1920s, when partly disassembled cars were shipped by train to Cowen and assembled there: Frank Gawthrop had a Stearns-Knight, Earl Delung had an Oldsmobile, Bert Brown had a Star, Bert Marshall had a Durant, Jake Neal had a Dodge, Eck Mollahan had a Durant, Frank Harris had a Star, Lee Windom had a Durant, Gene Dean had a Baby Overland (four-cylinder) with solid disc wheels, Bracky Dean had an Essex, Big John Dodrill had a Scripps-Booth (a big, fancy car), Howard Case had an Auburn, Russ Marshall had a Pontiac, Jack Mollahan had a Star, Simons (no first name listed) had a Jewett, and Thayer (no first name listed) had a Hupmobile. Tom Reger, the woods boss at Skyles for Eakin Lumber Company, drove a Model T Ford, and later a Durant.

"All roads were dirt," Eakin continued, "but a few had a rock base. Bridges were few and far between. You spent more time driving in and through creeks than you did on the road."

"You could expect to have at least one and maybe two flat tires on any trip. These first cars were all touring cars. That is: no windows, no heat, and no air conditioning except by Mother Nature. Along with the good clean air you had to literally eat dust and bugs. If it happened to rain, you were in bad trouble. Not only from the slick and rutted roads, but also from the rain blowing inside the car. Someone had to get out and 'put on the curtains.' These were snapped around the windows and had a cellophane window in each one. Note: Have you ever had a flat tire in rain and on a muddy road? Everyone in the car had to get out in the rain as the tools were always carried under the rear seat. If you had a spare tire you were lucky. If not, it was a couple of hours trying to jack up the car, get the inner tube out of the tire, get it patched, placed back in the casing, pumped up with a hand pump, and then back on the car."

Ah, the good old days.

There is a bewildering array of cars on the road today, but the more things change, the more they stay the same. A 1925 booklet, *Know Your Own State*, put out by Standard Oil Company of New Jersey, lists eighty nine different makes of cars! All of the above are listed except Scripps-Booth and Pontiac. Among the names that will resonate with car buffs today are Hudson, Nash, Packard, Pierce-Arrow, Studebaker, Stutz, and Willys Knight. The latter with Overland was forerunner of the company that produced the Willys Jeep of World War II fame.

In a September 2, 1985, interview with Gerry Milnes for the

Augusta Collection at D & E College, former Skyles resident Trace Ratcliff told about trading an overcoat for a Model T Ford, which was supposedly the first car of that make on Skyles.

- - -

Upper Birch has the largest falls on the river. They are located one-half mile below Barnett Run in Webster County, near Boggs, and are approximately sixteen feet in height, and fifty feet wide. Nothing else compares in size, although the falls of lower Birch below Herold are spectacular because of the large rocks that surround them.

The pool below the falls, which is surrounded by rocks and rhododendron, is a favorite of swimmers. Myrtle Roberts Riddle, who lives on Bragg Run at Boggs, was born near the falls, and she remembers being attracted to the pool at about age five. To discourage her from wandering down to the stream alone, her parents told her there was "a turtle as big

The falls near Boggs are the largest on Birch

as a washtub" that lived under a rock that serves as a diving board. "I believed this story for several years," she said, "but I began to have doubts because I never saw it, and soon the turtle story faded away."

There is also a smaller falls above the main one that is picturesque in its own right. It is called "the Scootin' Falls" because the river has carved a perfect chute in the rock where kids can "scoot down the chute."

The Boggs falls provided power for many years to a classic old grist mill that was built in 1883 by Bearhunter Billy Barnett, and to a later replacement mill. Such mills were sprinkled all along Birch River in the late 1800s and early 1900s. "Grist," an Old English word, is defined by Webster's New Collegiate Dictionary as "a batch of grain for grinding." In most cases, the grain was corn. Early on, people couldn't "run to the store" for a loaf of bread as they do now.

The original mill sat on the bank immediately below the falls; the replacement mill was on top of the falls, where a flume fed the water to turn the wheel. The flume for the original mill was chiseled out of rock at the top left of the falls, and is still visible.

The Boggs mill is more commonly associated with the McCoy family, which bought it from the Barnetts and operated it and a 1930s replacement for many years. The replacement mill was severely damaged by a flood in 1954, and has since ceased to exist.

The McCoys were Reverend W.L. McCoy, who died in 1919; his wife, Maggie, who died in 1938; and a son, Buck McCoy, who died in 1986. All are buried on a hillside behind the home of Gary Dilley, who keeps the area around the falls clean and provides a picnic table for visitors. Reverend McCoy was a stone mason, in addition to being a preacher and miller. The stone cellar at Gary Dilley's home was made of stones of McCoy's handiwork.

The mechanic who kept the mills running over the years of McCoy ownership was a son-in-law, Jack Evans, who also built the replacement mill.

Both of the mills at the falls were of the "overshot" variety, meaning they had vertical wheels that required falling water to turn. There was another mill downstream that was commonly referred to as "the little mill," and is believed to have also been built by Bearhunter Billy Barnett. It was a turbine mill, meaning it had a horizontal wheel fixed to the millstone shaft, and was run by the normal flow of the stream. In either instance, the wheels turned the stones, which ground the grain. The stones contributed a common phrase to the English language: Something or someone is described as "a millstone around your neck." Stones from old grist mills are occasionally seen around the state as lawn decorations.

It isn't clear whether the original mill at the falls or the little mill downstream came first. Wilkie Barnette of Drennen (he spells his name with an "e"), a descendant of Bearhunter Billy who has done considerable family research, believes the little mill came first.

The original mill at the falls is pictured in *West Virginia Yesterday and Today*, a 1930s history book written by Phil Conley and Boyd Stutler which was familiar to schoolchildren of that era. The mill's location isn't given; the caption simply says "An Old-Time Water Power Mill." The picture was taken by Shirley Morton.

One of the enduring stories about the era of the McCoys at the mill is that Maggie McCoy periodically heard the sound of a wagon, but the wagon never materialized. To this day, it is referred to as "the Ghost Wagon." Another ghost story of upper Birch is that Tom Bragg and Dick Roberts of Boggs were driving about one-half mile above Boggs and saw Tom's deceased mother, Ellen Greene Bragg, walking on the road. The vision was so real that they slowed down to avoid hitting her.

Ruby Boggs Roberts, who was born in 1912 and lived all her life in a landmark two-story white house at Boggs, loved upper Birch and the grist mill. In the 1960s, when she was president of the Webster County Development Commission, she attempted to have a mill rebuilt for the sake of posterity, but, according to a 1994 story in *Wonderful West Virginia* by Robert Bowers, the attempt failed either from lack of funds or lack of widespread interest. The magazine story was accompanied by a marvelous color picture of the falls taken by Ron Snow.

When W.Va 82 was authorized for paving, the Greenbrier County contractor had no place to house and feed his men. Ruby Roberts agreed to house and feed the entire crew of ten, and the work proceeded. W.Va. 82 was blacktopped in 1938. Ruby Roberts died in 1993 at age eighty one. Her husband, Glen Roberts, died in 1982 at age eighty two. One of their sons, Skip Roberts, and his wife, Mitzi, live at the mouth of Barnett Run near the homeplace and near the Boggs Cemetery, where Calvin Fleming is buried. Skip Roberts works for Evergreen Mining Company at the head of Birch near Cowen.

- - -

Bragg Run, which enters Birch at Boggs, is named for Jim Bragg, the first settler on the run. He came there around the time of the Civil War, and amassed a considerable amount of land. His son, Lewis Bragg, worked for Eakin Lumber Company at Skyles, and also helped build W.Va. 82 in the 1920s. Lewis Bragg's sons, Albert (Abb) and Clint Bragg, still live on Bragg Run. Abb Bragg worked in the woods, worked in coal mines at Tioga and Buckhannon, worked for the B & O Railroad at Cowen as a brakeman, and drove a school bus in Webster County. Clint Bragg worked for the State Department of Highways.

- - -

The aforementioned English Bill Dodrill was probably the earliest white settler on Birch River. His story is told in *Heritage of a Pioneer*, the 1967 book by Charles T. Dodrill, and in 1994's *Heritage of Webster County*.

English Bill was born either in eastern Virginia or eastern North Carolina around 1750. Family tradition holds that he became a soldier in the English army during the Revolutionary War and was part of Lord Cornwallis' army that surrendered to the revolutionists on October 19, 1781, at Yorktown, Virginia.

He was a tailor by occupation, and apparently a very good one, and plied his trade in the area of Winchester, Virginia, where he and other English soldiers were loosely held as prisoners of war. One day, on one of his rounds, he simply never returned, but even at that he stayed at the prisoner of camp longer than did many of his comrades.

He melted into the American scene, and met and married Rebecca Lewis Daugherty, daughter of plantation owner George Lewis of Cowpasture, Virginia, in 1782. Rebecca's first husband had been killed by Indians.

In 1784, William and Rebecca Dodrill and their children (they had two at that time and eventually eight), headed across the mountains as part of the great migration that pushed the frontier westward. They joined other settlers at Point Pleasant at the mouth of the Kanawha River. Charles T. Dodrill wrote that their two small children, a son, George, and a daughter, Mary, were carried in a basket strapped to their mother's horse during this arduous journey.

Then English Bill met Daniel Boone, the five-star figure of the American frontier, and *Heritage of a Pioneer* suggests that Boone and English Bill may have trapped for beaver on Birch River.

Boone, in his eternal wanderings, came to Point Pleasant soon after English Bill, and the two became friends, neighbors, and fellow adventurers in hunting, trapping, surveying, and trading in furs and ginseng.

Boone later moved up the Kanawha, settling four miles upstream from present day Charleston. English Bill and his family followed, and settled at Clendenin's Fort at the mouth of Elk River. Threats of Indian attacks were the primary reason for the move. Boone had warned of preparations by the Indians to resist any further encroachment on their lands.

When Boone became a delegate from Kanawha County to the Virginia General Assembly at Richmond, English Bill accompanied him and sold pelts and ginseng.

Charles T. Dodrill wrote of Boone and English Bill:

"His [Boone's] home while in the vicinity of Point Pleasant was on Crooked Creek. Just two years before, William E. (English Bill) Dodrill and his family had come to the mouth of the Great Kanawha River under the leadership of Andrew Lewis Jr., Thomas Lewis, and William Lewis.

"Boone and English Bill became friends. Together they enjoyed many hunting and trapping expeditions in the valley [Kanawha] until Boone left the valley for Missouri sometime between 1795 and 1799. They trapped for beaver on the waters of the Elk and its tributaries *including the waters of Birch River*" (author's italics).

Wanderlust eventually took hold of both men again. Boone continued his relentless trek westward, and died in Missouri in 1820 at age eighty six. English Bill and his family returned to the Virginia plantation and stayed there until about 1797, when they headed back across the mountains. This time they settled on Peters Creek near present-day Gilboa, Nicholas County, but in 1799 they left Peters Creek and moved to Birch River either at the mouth of Bragg Run at what is now Boggs, or closer to Skyles. Bragg Run was first known as Doddridge Run, which was an early spelling of Dodrill, and English Bill apparently owned land there, if he didn't live there. In any event, he built a cabin and spent the rest of his life on upper Birch. The eighth and last child of William and Rebecca Lewis, a daughter named Rebecca, was born probably at Boggs in about 1800.

One hundred years later, my mother was born at Boggs. My grandfather worked in a lumber camp at Boggs the winter of my mother's birth, and my grandmother accompanied him. The following spring, after my mother was born, they returned to Braxton County.

English Bill Dodrill is believed to have died on Bragg Run sometime after 1818. Where he is buried is unknown, but two possibilities are

Skyles bottom today, site of former lumber town

the Boggs Cemetery at the mouth of Barnett Run, or the Dodrill Cemetery at the mouth of Poplar Creek. One account (Sampson N. Miller's *Annals of Webster County*) says he settled at the mouth of Barnett Run when he first came to Birch River. Miller gives English Bill's surname as Doddridge.

For a certainty, he contributed mightily to the rich lore of upper Birch River, and perhaps started it all as the first white settler. There were other luminaries: Isaac Rose, the Revolutionary War soldier; Adam O'Brien, the wanderer and Indian fighter; Billy Barnett, who took on a bear and won; Christopher Baughman, the miller and landowner; George Mollohan, who, old and almost blind, lost his life in the wilderness between Sutton and Birch River; and Lise Sanson, the last of the legendary hunters of upper Birch.

Then there was the shootout at the Boggs store and post office. We can envision the Fleming brothers riding down the mountain at Barnett Run and following Birch upstream to their date with destiny.

And on a still night we may hear the creaking of the McCoy mill at the falls of Birch below Barnett Run, symbolizing, as it does, all the water mills that were so much a part of Birch River history.

Head of Skyles Creek looking south from the Mill Creek road

Three

Shay It Isn't So

Birch Locomotive Becomes a Museum Piece

Catch a logging train at Skyles, chug over the mountain to Erbacon, grab the B & O, and you're on your way to Chicago, a midwestern town that doesn't rival Skyles or Erbacon for native charm.

While the Chicago Connection seems apocryphal, in reality a traveler could have gone in any direction after reaching Erbacon and its passenger trains of long ago, and it conveys the point that Skyles, despite its remote location on upper Birch River, was a genuine mountain getaway in the early 1900s when logging railroads ran along Birch.

The railroad climbed up main Skyles Creek, then up Road Fork of Skyles, topped the mountain, and went down Missouri Run to Erbacon, with three switchbacks on each side. This is large country; the three above-listed streams total almost eleven miles in length. An 1865 Civil War Atlas refers to Skyles Creek as "Sciles River."

The route was named "the Chicago Connection" by Gerry Milnes, coordinator of folklore programs for the Augusta Heritage Center at Davis & Elkins College, who built a home on Skyles Creek at the forks and lived there from 1976 to 1989. Milnes is a musician ("anything with strings on it"), and played the fiddle in the movie *Matewan*.

The passenger trains of Erbacon history ran on the B & O spur line from Richwood to Erbacon to Burnsville. At Burnsville, they met trains from Charleston to continue the run to Grafton, where the B & O line ran east and west, hence the Chicago Connection.

In its logging days, which lasted from 1912 until 1927, Skyles was the Birch River counterpart of Cass, the town in Pocahontas County where Shay engines now carry tourists to the top of Cheat Mountain on the Cass Scenic Railroad.

The story of logging at Skyles is the story of a family operation known as Eakin Lumber Company. In 1989-1991, Ward Eakin, a Skyles native and son of longtime company president Pete Eakin, wrote a record of the company that preserves a remarkable chapter in Birch River, and indeed, West Virginia history.

In the seventy four years that have elapsed since Eakin ceased operations at Skyles and moved to Fenwick, all traces of the mill, company store, thirty-five houses, ice house, boarding house, the shop where the two Shay engines were serviced, three school rooms (where church services were also held when a preacher was available), and railroad track have disappeared. There were approximately thirty five miles of track in the Skyles operation, which is about equal to the underground track mileage in the Elk River Coal and Lumber Company mines at Widen, Clay County, to give an indication of the size of both operations in their time.

The Eakin logging train was called the E & S Railroad, or the Erbacon and Summersville. Ward Eakin pointed out that the train didn't come any closer to Summersville than the foot of Powell's Mountain on the spur line that ran up Powell's Creek, but that is probably where the Summersville part of the name came from. The "E" of course stood for Erbacon, which was the principal shipping center for Eakin Lumber Company, and the northern terminus of its logging railroad. In its time, the E & S was affectionately called "The Easy and Slow," or "Slow and Easy."

The Eakin mill and virtually everything else stood in an eighteen-acre bottom at the mouth of Skyles Creek, divided by the creek into an upper and lower town. Today, five families live at the mouth of Skyles. They are the Randy DeMoss, Jeff DeMoss, Rick DeMoss, Don Blankenship, and Mike Blankenship families. The Harry Love family lives on Skyles at the forks in the former Gerry Milnes house. In earlier times, this site was known as the Conley Hosey place.

A classic two-story farm house on the east side of the mouth of Skyles Creek, where Byrne Hoover lived in the latter part of his life, is vacant. Hoover, a teenager in Skyles when it was a lumber town, died in 1989. In the Eakin Lumber era, Okey Mollahan, a farmer and storekeeper, lived in the house.

The Skyles Elementary School closed in 1962, and is now used as a storage building by Randy DeMoss. Randy and his wife, Joy, live on the west side of the mouth of Skyles, and they are surrounded by Eakin Lumber Company history. "I'd love to sweep the area with a metal detector," said Randy, "but it would drive me crazy. There's so much here." Even without a metal detector, he plows out all manner of relics of bygone days every time he works his garden. The steam plant was located directly back of Randy's home, and when I visited there in 2000 he was in the process of removing the mammoth slabs of concrete that were the foundation for the dynamo.

During the 1999 drought, Don Blankenship was digging a pond for his cattle in a bottom on the south side of Birch, and unearthed several railroad crossties. Blankenship lives across the road from the mouth of Skyles. He was born in one of the Eakin company houses.

Skyles Creek today differs from the Skyles Creek of 1912 only in the absence of virgin timber. It is still forested, rugged, and uninhabited, with the exception of the cluster of houses at the mouth of the creek and the one at the forks.

Luther DeMoss, whose father worked for Eakin Lumber Company, took me up Skyles Creek one day to just below the forks. The watershed is so large that Road Fork of Skyles, which enters on the left about a half mile above the mouth, is the tenth largest of the forty two named tributaries of Birch River. Although not a direct tributary, Road Fork is included in the list of Birch tributaries shown elsewhere in this book, given its size and close proximity to the river. May Fork, Lick Fork, and Holbrook Fork are the other forks of Skyles.

Harry Holbrook, who died in 1998 at age one hundred, carried the mail on horseback up Skyles Creek He was also a teamster for Eakin Lumber Company. A grandson, Gary Dilley, lives at Boggs.

Little wonder that bears thrive in this big, remote watershed. There are probably not as many bears on Skyles now as when Bear-hunter Billy Barnett and his contemporaries were roaming the woods (see "Skyles and Boggs"), but there are many more than there were twenty five years ago when the West Virginia bear population reached a low ebb. "They [bears] put me out of the honey business," said Gerry Milnes.

Bear hunting legends are still being made on upper Birch. In 1991, Dee Kinslow, who lives between Skyles and Boggs, killed a bear on Skyles Creek that weighed four hundred and fifty four pounds field dressed. Boyd Cutright, Webster County conservation officer with thirty years' experience, said it was the largest bear he'd ever seen. Kinslow's bear was a product of perseverance. He had hunted hard for two weeks before making the kill.

Eakin Lumber had its beginning in 1891 on the Buckhannon River in Upshur County at Craddock. The company founder was Joceph (Ceph) Eakin, Ward Eakin's grandfather. Ward Eakin's father, Pete, began working at Craddock at age sixteen, and remained in the timber business for sixty eight years. For a long time, it was quite profitable. Pete Eakin once said he could write a check for $15,000 when he was seventeen years old. The company left Craddock around 1901-1902 and moved to Wainville, a flag stop on the B & O between Cowen and Erbacon, where they had a circular mill.

By this time the B & O had completed a railroad through from Flatwoods to Cowen and Camden on Gauley.

This was the beginning of the glory days of logging railroads in West Virginia. Much of the splendid virgin timber standing prior to 1880 had already been cut, and what remained required a railroad to haul it out. Upper Birch River was a textbook example of an isolated area where the only feasible way to get the timber out was to build a railroad. Ditto for West Virginia Pulp and Paper Company's storied operation at Cass, which necessitated a railroad to log the stands of virgin red spruce on Cheat Mountain. The logging railroad up "Cass hill" (*On Beyond Leatherbark*, Roy B. Clarkson), was begun in 1900, about the time that Eakin Lumber moved to Wainville. From there, Eakin shifted to Missouri Run near Erbacon, and logged there for eight or ten years before heading over the mountain to Skyles.

Ward Eakin was intrigued by the name Missouri Run. He wrote that it reminded him of the settlers out west (as in the song and movie, *Across the Wide Missouri*). He also vividly remembers the view down the mountain toward Erbacon where the railroad topped out. "You could see what appeared to be three railroads below you," he told me. "Actually, you were seeing three switchbacks of the same railroad."

Missouri Run begins near the top of the mountain between Erbacon and Skyles on what is known as Hickory Flats, and drains to the north to enter Laurel Creek at Erbacon. It is 3.38 miles in length. Laurel Creek, which starts near Cowen, is a picturesque stream with numerous rock ledges that create miniature waterfalls. From Erbacon, Laurel Creek continues northward to enter Elk River at Centralia. Laurel Creek is a major tributary of Elk; its drainage area of sixty seven square miles is exceeded only by those of Holly River, Birch River, Buffalo Creek, Big Sandy Creek, Blue Creek, and Back Fork of Elk.

Dencil Crites, a retired railroader with thirty seven years of service (B & O, Chessie System, and CSX), came to Erbacon in 1930 at age six. He remembers when Erbacon had two hotels, the Sigman and the Fleming. The two-story Sigman, run by May Sigman, operated until the mid-1960s. Ward Eakin always heard the story, probably not true, that

Erbacon got its name when the B & O Railroad was being built and crewmen and workers would take their meals at the hotel, a two-story building (probably the Sigman) in back of the depot. At breakfast, the waitress would always ask, "Do you want sausage 'er bacon?" After hearing this for several mornings, they decided to call the town Erbacon. A cute story, but Eakin believes the town was actually named for a railroad man. The Webster County Historical Society agrees. Its book, *Heritage of Webster County*, says the namesake was Edward R. Bacon, an attorney for the B & O Railroad.

Erbacon gave up Webster County's first casualty of World War II. Randall Thomas was a sailor on the battleship Arizona that went down in the Japanese raid on Pearl Harbor with more than a thousand of her crew trapped inside.

There are still many people living in and around Erbacon. In June 2000, Postmaster Betty Lewis estimated the community population at three hundred and fifty, based on the number of post office patrons. Coal trains still rumble through Erbacon, hauling coal from the Brooks Run Coal Company mine on Missouri Run, and from the Evergreen Mining Company loading facility near Cowen. The (sausage 'er) Erbacon depot was torn down many years ago.

Eakin Lumber Company began casting an eye on Birch River as the Missouri Run timbering wound down. The last years of the Missouri Run mill were occupied cutting ties, lumber, and large frame material for the upcoming Skyles job.

The Skyles operation, or at least the building of the "Easy and Slow" over the mountain from Erbacon, began in 1912, the year that Eakin Lumber Company bought a new seventy-ton Shay engine from Lima Locomotive Works of Lima, Ohio. It came to Erbacon partially disassembled to begin an illustrious career that, as we shall see, continues to this day.

Shay engines are synonymous with logging railroads. They were named for Ephraim Shay, a Michigan mill owner who, around 1880, devised a gear-driven, steam-powered locomotive that was slow but powerful; in other words, perfect for chugging up steep logging grades. Lima Locomotive Works produced over 3,000 of them during a sixty five year period that ended in 1945, and they were used in logging operations around the world.

Shays were said to be able to climb fifteen percent grades with ease. The steepest grade on the Erbacon to Skyles climb, or visa versa, was probably about ten percent. Later, when Eakin and its seventy ton Shay moved to Fenwick in Nicholas County, Ward Eakin wrote that a short section of railroad up Cold Knob in nearby Greenbrier County was, according to engineer Frank Harris, a thirteen percent grade. Contrast these steep climbs to present-day highways, where a six percent grade merits a warning sign for truckers (standard railroad practice limits main line grades to two percent).

Eakin Lumber also used a forty ton Shay at Skyles, which was designated No. 1 (the seventy ton was No. 2). When the Skyles operation shut down, No. 1 was sold to the Waggy Coal Company at Erbacon.

Prior to beginning its Skyles operation, Eakin had purchased over 7,600 acres of timberland. The largest single purchase was 6,500 acres of timber from Black Betsy Coal and Mining Company in 1911.

The Davis family of Clarksburg became a financial partner with Eakin in 1912, and the company was known as Davis-Eakin Lumber Company until about 1915, when the Eakins bought the Davis interest.

Domineck Rich of Weston was hired to build the "Easy and Slow" from Erbacon to Skyles. As was the case with the Elk River railroad between Charleston and Gassaway, including the trestle over the mouth of Birch River at Glendon, Italian immigrants were hired as workers. Building the railroad grade and laying track was arduous work that involved the use of mattocks, picks, shovels, and dynamite.

Ward Eakin wrote: "Horses were furnished by Eakin Lumber Company [for hauling materials], and of course the engine and railroad cars as they advanced over the mountain. I've heard Frank Harris, who helped supervise the building, tell the story of a runaway flat car loaded with ties. He told how the Italian workers yelled in Italian all over the mountain as the runaway car was careening down the mountain and the ties were flying off all down the mountain. Those mountains heard more Italian that day than they ever heard before or since."

Once the railroad was completed, and supplies could be brought in from Erbacon, work was begun on the lumber town of Skyles.

The mill was an eight-foot band mill, meaning its top and bottom wheels were eight feet in diameter (band mill wheels run from four and one-half feet to twelve feet in diameter; their saw bands vary from ten inches to sixteen and eighteen inches in width). In his classic book, *Tumult on the Mountains*, which helped stimulate interest in logging history in West Virginia and, by extension, the Cass Scenic Railroad, Roy Clarkson defined a band mill as "an endless belt of steel, having teeth on one or both edges, traveling at great speed around an upper and lower pulley. The latter is attached by belts to a steam engine which drives the saw. The logs are carried past the saw on a carriage which is run by a steam piston."

The Skyles mill also had a resaw, meaning another smaller band that could cut one-inch boards from slabs and small split logs, adding about a third to the mill's capacity. The mill was powered by twin steam engines, which were fueled by sawdust, shavings, and slabs. A steam driven dynamo provided electricity to the mill, store, houses, and other buildings.

Glenn Longacre Jr., who worked many years for Pardee-Curtin Lumber Company at Bergoo, Webster County, and now manages various coal and timber properties, said this of band mills: "The tension at the saw is very important, as the way the saw operates in cutting and the way it runs on the wheel are in a large part dependent on tension. This is where the men are separated from the boys as far as saw filing is concerned. If a saw is not properly tensioned, it will not cut properly. This (tension) is rolled into the saw blade by the filer." In *Tumult on the Mountains*, Clarkson wrote that "the saw-filer is the highest paid man on the job other than the mill foreman."

According to Clarkson, the first band mill in West Virginia may have been the one installed at Burnsville, Braxton County, in 1875, by the Burns brothers and J.R and A.E. Huffman. James Callahan's *Semi-Centennial History of West Virginia*, written in 1913, credits J.R. Huffman with inventing the band mill. Callahan, a professor of history and political science at West Virginia University, said the Deveraux Lumber Company's band mill at Charleston in 1881 was probably the first. The Mead-Speer mill on Strange Creek, Braxton County, in the early 1900s (starting around 1905) was a band mill.

Band saws could handle larger logs than circular saws, which preceded them in the evolutionary process of sawmills. Circular saws employed big disks with sawteeth on the circumference, usually being about five feet in diameter, driven by a belt from a steam engine. Circular

The Eakin Lumber Company mill at Skyles

mills had a carriage that moved the logs back and forth. They were more portable, thus were more commonly used in smaller operations, although quite large circular mills also existed. Said Longacre: "Almost all large circular mills had a top saw. This was a smaller circular saw which ran above and a little ahead of the main saw. This enabled them to cut a much larger diameter log."

The company store was the center of Skyles the lumber town, just as the company store at Widen was the center of that coal town. The two-story Skyles store opened early and closed late, had a Burnside stove in the middle of the first floor, old-fashioned glass showcases for candy and chewing gum and the like, a full basement for potatoes and canned goods, two sleeping rooms upstairs, attached feed room and hay house, oil lamps, and a post office. The mail came to Erbacon on the B & O, and then over the mountain to Skyles on the "Easy and Slow."

An ice house was later built across the railroad tracks in front of the store. The ice was packed in sawdust and shipped into thirsty Skyles in boxcars. Ward Eakin believes that ice may have been cut from Birch River during bad winters, which seemed to occur more frequently back then.

The boarding house was a large two-story building, with sixteen sleeping rooms upstairs and ten downstairs, a lobby with a Burnside stove on each floor, a downstairs dining room that seated about thirty five people, and a large kitchen with a sleeping room for the cook.

Drinking was sometimes a problem in lumber towns, although the Prohibition era of the 1920s made liquor difficult to obtain. However, where there's a will there's a way, and moonshine seeped into the social strata at Skyles every now and then. But drinking was not a great problem, because Pete Eakin, the company president, lived at Skyles and did not allow imbibing on the premises.

Ward Eakin remembers seeing his first movie at one of the school rooms, which was also used as a town meeting room. "The company got hold of an old film and a movie projector. I remember going with Dad and all our family. The room was packed, and Ebb Dean and Frank Gawthrop were the operators. More time was spent splicing film and rerunning than anything else."

Eakin recalls that the company doctor most of the time at Skyles was Ellis Frame. "He served through the flu epidemic of 1918, which was a very trying time for all," Eakin wrote. "There was so much sickness and death that there was hardly enough men to work the mill. The disease was so contagious that well people were afraid to go into a house that had the flu." Doctor Frame is credited in *Heritage of Webster County* with naming the Eakin railroad the "Easy and Slow."

Another company doctor was B.B. Sturdivant, who later moved to Cowen and lived in the former house of Doctor Dan Kessler, a Cowen legend (see "Origins of Birch").

Richwood lawyer Ralph Dunn believes his uncle, Hugh Dunn, made calls to Skyles while he was practicing at Birch Village. He recalls hearing his uncle talk about pumping a railroad hand car from Birch to Skyles to tend the sick.

Hugh Dunn later moved his practice to Richwood, where he became an obstetrical legend. He delivered 3,500 babies in his career, and developed an uncanny ability to predict the sex. In fact, he was never wrong, or so it seemed. Whatever he told the parents the baby was going to be, he wrote down just the opposite in his notebook. When the parents later pointed out that he had been wrong, he hauled out his notebook and said, "No, look here. Here's exactly what I wrote down."

Ward Eakin told about the circus coming to Skyles. "You couldn't imagine how the roads were from Sutton to Tesla, and over Crites Mountain to Skyles," he wrote. "This must have been about 1923-24. The first travel report to reach Skyles was that the lion truck had upset on Crites Mountain and the only lion in the circus was loose. Second travel report arriving: the lion was captured and back in the truck. The circus set up on the ball diamond at the lower end of the lumber yard. I remember going to the circus, but most of all I remember pushing the small 'push truck' on the railroad. It was dark and it was a challenge to push it and not run over people walking on the track and not to get your own foot under a wheel."

Skyles of the teens and twenties was like virtually every other coal and lumber town in West Virginia in that it had a baseball team. Games were usually played on Sundays. Companies hired good players and gave them jobs, with the expectation that they would play ball on Sunday. Eakin wrote that the captain and manager of the Skyles team was Frank Gawthrop (one of the movie projector operators). He said of Gawthrop: "He was also our second baseman and best fighter. The latter was very important as there was usually a fight. He once almost chewed a finger off a guy at Burnsville."

Some of the teams that Skyles played were Widen, Gauley Mills, Camden on Gauley, Little Birch, Big Birch, Rupert, Quinwood, and Cowen. If a big game was coming up, teams would borrow or steal players from another team.

Ward Eakin recalled some of the farmers who lived along Birch River during the Eakin Lumber Company era: Luther Bragg of Boggs, Leht Hoover of Skyles, Okey (Oke) Mollahan of Skyles, Jasper Collins, who lived below Skyles, and Big John Dodrill, who lived near Birch Village.

In 1927, the Skyles operation had run out of timber, and Eakin Lumber Company moved to Fenwick, Nicholas County, built a single-band mill, and logged, among other places, on Little Laurel Creek, a tributary of Cherry River. A skeleton crew was left at Skyles to grade and load the remaining lumber in the yard, dismantle the machinery, tear down the buildings, burn the trash, and, finally, "pull the steel," that is, remove the tracks. An era had ended on Birch River.

The Fenwick operation lasted until 1938, when Eakin Lumber was brought down by the Depression, which also bankrupted many other companies and individuals.

Pete Eakin, Ward Eakin's father and the heart and soul of Eakin Lumber Company, died in 1966 at ninety years of age. He is buried at Weston, Lewis County, where he was born. His wife, Elizabeth Woods Eakin, is also buried at Weston. Elizabeth Woods is believed to have moved from the Strange Creek area to Erbacon, where she met Pete Eakin.

The seventy ton Shay engine purchased by Eakin for the Skyles job went with the company to Fenwick and worked in the woods in Nicholas and Greenbrier Counties from 1927 until 1938. When Ely-Thomas Lumber Company (Ralph Ely and Wellington Thomas) bought the Eakin mill at Fenwick, they became the Shay's owner and used it into the 1960s.

But that was not the end of the line for the Shay. It was bought by the Penn-York Lumbermen's Club and moved to Pennsylvania around 1964. Penn-York donated it to the Pennsylvania Lumber Museum, where it went in 1972 and where it remains to this day.

During the time it was owned by Eakin, it was designated engine No. 2. Ely-Thomas designated it engine No. 3. The Lumber Museum changed its designation to No. 4. The museum also has on display the Barnhart log loader that was used at both Skyles and Fenwick. Barnharts were steam loaders that swung logs onto railroad flat cars, replacing the slow work of manual loading.

An excellent collection of pictures of the Shay at Fenwick is contained in the 1993 book, *West Virginia Logging Railroads*, by William E. Warden. One picture shows the Shay and Barnhart together.

The Pennsylvania Lumber Museum is located in northern Pennsylvania on U.S. 6, midway between the communities of Galeton and Coudersport in Potter County, and is administered by the Pennsylvania Historical and Museum Commission. It commemorates the logging history of that area. Whereas red spruce was the wealth and pride of logging in the mountains of West Virginia, in the northern Pennsylvania mountains it was white pine. Logging was essentially done in wintertime, when the bark peeled off easily and deep snow helped in skidding logs to water. The cutting time was from the dark of the moon in September to the dark of the moon in April.

I visited the museum, the Shay, and the Barnhart in September 2000. A neighbor, Denzil Baughman, accompanied me. Perhaps unwisely, we picked a day on which the West Virginia University football team was playing at Morgantown. We were escorted north on Interstate 79 by several thousand vehicles with WVU banners flying, or so it seemed.

From Interstate 48 at Cumberland, Maryland, we followed U.S. 220 north to Altoona, Pennsylvania, Interstate 80 from Mount Eagle west to Snow Shoe (Pennsylvania's, not ours), and then north through the mountains on Pennsylvania 144 to Galeton.

I'd never been in that part of Pennsylvania, only the western side through Pittsburgh, and the farther east side through Gettysburg, and it is lovely country: neat towns and farmland, with the mountains in the background. The towns are pure Main Street America. We knew we were in hunting country when we saw on a football schedule posted in a service station window at Renovo, south of Galeton, that the local high school is called Bucktail High.

Both Renovo and Galeton are former lumber towns that remind me of Richwood, Cass, Davis, and Thomas in West Virginia. I'm not sure why, perhaps a lack of space in the mountain valleys, but the houses of the early lumber towns were built almost uniformly two stories tall, and not very wide. I almost suspect that lumber companies of long ago awarded prizes to families who could fit the most people into the narrowest rooms. There were once 5,000 people living in Galeton, so there was a lot of fitting to do.

We drove west on U.S. 6 from Galeton to the Lumber Museum. I marveled at the twists and turns in life that had brought a Birch River logging locomotive, and me, to the northern mountains of Pennsylvania. We found the big fellow comfortably ensconced in the engine house adjacent to the museum. It ventures out once a year on the Fourth of July weekend for the annual Bark Peelers' Convention. A (very) heavy-duty tractor pulls it outside on standard gauge track for its two or three days in the sun.

I've seen Shays at Cass, including some bigger than this one, but they were outdoors. I wasn't prepared for the sight of one indoors in a form-fitted building, with room only to walk around it. The words mind-boggling seemed appropriately expressive.

After the walk-around, we climbed a platform and entered the cab. There is a wooden seat on the right for the engineer. I thought of Bert Brown, one of the engineers for Eakin Lumber Company, both at Skyles and Fenwick. Ward Eakin said this about Bert Brown:

"He was a great whistle blower. He could blow with the best of them and he practiced plenty on the mountain trip [Skyles to Erbacon]."

Other crewmen, as recalled by Ward Eakin, were Perl Barnette, fireman (his seat, when he wasn't shoveling coal into the ravenous boiler, was on the left of the cab, facing the engineer); George Dodrill, conductor and brakeman; and Herb Mollahan, tong hooker and brakeman. George Dodrill's son, Bert, lives at Richwood. He recalls riding No. 2 when he was eight years old.

I thought also of Mart Posey, who was with this Shay from beginning to end in West Virginia. He went to work for Eakin as a teenager, helped assemble the engine when it arrived from Lima Locomotive Works, stayed with Eakin until it went out of business, remained with the successor company, Ely-Thomas, at Fenwick, and helped load the engine onto a railroad car for its trip to Pennsylvania, thus ending an association of more than fifty years.

This engine (shop number 2598) was built expressly for Eakin Lumber Company and its Erbacon & Summersville Railroad, and came off the assembly line on October 14, 1912. It may have cost around ten thousand dollars. A 1905 Shay is known to have cost five thousand, and by the 1920s the cost had risen to twenty thousand or more.

The Shay engine used by Eakin

Following are the specifications for the Eakin Shay, obtained from the Internet (www.shaylocomotives.com). The notes in parentheses are the author's:

Class: 70-3 (seventy tons; three trucks).
Trucks: 3 (the drive mechanisms). Two of them were located under the engine, the third was located under the tender.
Cylinders: 3 - 12 x 15 (There are three cylinders, each of twelve inch bore, and fifteen inch stroke).
Gear ratio: 2.25 (comparable to the rear transmission in a vehicle; in this case, the shaft turns a little more than twice to one turn of the wheel).
Wheel diameter: 36 inches (a standard size in Shays).
Gauge: Standard (the width of the track; standard track is 56 ½ inches).

Boiler (style, diameter): E.W.T. - 50" (extended wagon top; fifty inch smoke box diameter).
Fuel type: Coal.
Fuel Capacity: 5 tons.
Water capacity: 3,000 gallons.
Empty weight (as built): 118,700 pounds.

A quick exercise in math shows that 118,700 pounds do not add up to seventy tons. However, seventy tons could have been the fully loaded weight of this particular Shay, or, more likely, it was custom built to Eakin Lumber Company's wishes to take into account the steepness of the grades, the sharpness of the curves, and other factors that it would encounter on the Skyles and Birch River runs, and thus its weight was increased. Fully loaded, it could have weighed as much as eighty tons, which Ward Eakin said that it did.

One of the great repositories of Shay engines is the Cass Scenic Railroad in West Virginia, which has seven of them, including the last one ever built (which was also the second biggest ever built). It was shipped to Western Maryland Railroad at Elkins, West Virginia, on May 14, 1945, for use on the nine percent grade on Chaffee Branch, a tributary of the Potomac River (this particular logging operation took place both in West Virginia and Garrett County, Maryland). Fully loaded, the huge Shay weighed one hundred and sixty two tons. The Cass Scenic Railroad obtained it in 1981 from the Baltimore & Ohio Museum in Baltimore, Maryland, designated it No. 6, and uses it on the short run to Whittaker Station.

One of the seven Shays at Cass (the scenic railroad also has a Climax and a Heisler) saw service on Birch River for the Birch Valley Lumber Company, and was involved in an accident on Powell's Mountain on February 12, 1941, that killed three crewmen and an official of Tioga Lumber Company when the engine hit a broken rail and toppled over.

A story in the February 13, 1941, edition of *The Nicholas Chronicle* tells the story: killed instantly were engineer Omer Fitzwater, and George Harrison, secretary-treasurer of Tioga Lumber Company of Wellsboro, Pennsylvania, who was visiting coal mines in the area that were owned by Tioga Coal Corporation, a subsidiary of Tioga Lumber. Harrison had hitched a ride on the train, which was hauling empties "over the mountain [Powell's] from Tioga." Tioga Lumber Company had formerly owned Birch Valley Lumber Company.

Fireman James Cox and brakeman Moody McCoy were not killed instantly, but died later the same day.

The engine was rebuilt at Richwood and sold to Mower Lumber Company at Cass in 1942, and became a part of the Cass Scenic Railroad in 1963. Its Birch Valley designation was No. 5; at Cass it is No. 4 and has been in regular service since 1963.

Appropriately, since they worked together at Skyles and Fenwick, the Barnhart log loader at the Pennsylvania Lumber Museum is kept in a shed adjacent to the Shay. Barnhart loaders were developed in 1887 by Henry Barnhart, co-founder of Marion Powel Shovel Company of Marion, Ohio. Lumber baron Frank Goodyear is credited with the idea of loading logs by machinery, as well as the basic idea of how the loader should function. Steam loaders replaced the slow, tedious job of manual loading, but whether done manually or with a steam loader, it was dangerous work.

The Pennsylvania Lumber Museum's description of its Barnhart loader from West Virginia: "[It is] equipped with a rotating cab [180 degrees in the case of Barnharts], stationary boom, pulleys and cable. At the free end of the cable were tongs, which were placed in the log at center. The log was raised by the cable, swung by the boom, and lowered in place on the log car."

Eakin's Barnhart log loader in action

Steam loaders such as Barnharts were mounted on railroad flat-cars when they were on active duty. In the Pennsylvania museum, this particular Barnhart sits on a concrete foundation; its railroad car sits just outside on track, as if awaiting a call to action.

When the Barnhart arrived at the museum, it was completely disassembled, restored to its original appearance, reassembled, and put on display in 1989.

In late June 2000, I attended the Eakin family reunion at Weston and met Ward Eakin and one of his sons, Paul, who works for Xerox and travels around the world. Paul's wife, Barbara, a retired high school history teacher, was also at the reunion. Paul and his brothers, Jim and Tom, all live in the Rochester, New York, area near their parents. Jim and Tom are contractors.

Eleanor Hinkle of Weston told me about riding the railroad hand cars at Skyles, and going up the mountain above Skyles for picnics. Her father, Ed Hinkle, worked for Eakin Lumber.

Mildred Fisher Burns of Flatwoods remembered that she visited Skyles during the 1918 flu epidemic. "I went back home and I think I gave everybody on Cedar Creek the flu." She and her late husband, Robert Burns, taught school in Braxton County.

I invited Ward Eakin to write a postscript to his Eakin Lumber Company history, and he chose to write about "The Giant Chestnut Tree at Skyles." His story follows:

> Around 1922-23, my dad asked me if I wanted to go to the mill and see them saw the largest chestnut tree that he had ever seen. I knew that he had seen a lot of chestnut trees. Naturally, I said 'yes.'
>
> The chestnut blight had struck all the chestnut trees in the state, and it certainly was a great loss to all. It was a fast growing tree, had good eating nuts on it, and made good lumber in building houses, barns, etc. So all sawmills, to save the lumber, were salvaging the best of them.
>
> Now back to the mill. As we got to the front of the millpond, the huge log was just being put on the jack-slip to be pulled up into the mill. It was so big that it didn't fit down in the trough of the jack-slip, so they had to fasten a big chain on it and then secure the chain to the jack-slip. It was the butt end of the tree, and a tall man could not see over it.
>
> As they pulled the log to the top, you could see that it was too big to get through the opening to get it into the mill. So they stopped pulling and had to take two or three boards off the sides and top of the mill opening. After they got it onto the mill and got the log kicker to start it down the skidway, it gradually rolled and was stopped with another good size log purposely left on the skidway to stop it.
>
> Now Uncle Jake Neal was the sawyer. He took another good chew of his Mail Pouch tobacco and went to work on the log, chewing and sawing [Jake Neal came to Skyles from the Mead-Speer mill on Strange Creek, where he was also the sawyer].
>
> The log was so high you could not see the two men on

the carriage. I don't know how long it took to cut up the log. I
do know that at noon it was still being worked on. Some log! I
would say that it was a good eight feet or more across the butt
end.

Among the men who came to Webster County with Eakin were
brothers Tom and Emery Reger. Tom Reger was described by Ward
Eakin as "over six feet tall, lean, and a good physical specimen." He
became woods boss for Eakin at Skyles; Emery was a tong hooker on the
Barnhart steam loader.

Tom Reger bought a farm at Little Birch in Braxton County in
1925 and lived there until his death at age seventy six. He is the father of
Roscoe Reger of Little Birch and Ruby Reger Spencer of Sutton. Roscoe
was born at Boggs, and Ruby at Skyles. Tom Reger and his wife, Blanche
Tinnel Reger, are buried at Selbyville, Upshur County.

Roscoe Reger remembers his father's skill with an axe: "He held it
down on the end of the handle, and if he hit three licks, he hit in the same
place every time."

Among Reger family pictures is one taken in the Skyles area of
an Eakin woods crew. It shows a mammoth pile of logs, three teams
of horses, and seventeen lumberjacks, including Tom Reger, who stands
slightly apart from the others with his hands on his hips. He was, indeed,
tall and lean.

- - -

Ward Eakin enlisted in the Marines on April 21, 1941, and was
stationed at Pearl Harbor, Hawaii, when the Japanese attacked on December 7, 1941. He was in a crew that helped shoot down the first of twenty
nine aircraft that were lost by the Japanese, either from ground fire or falling into the Pacific while attempting to land on aircraft carriers as they
returned.

When he came back from World War II, Eakin drove from his
home in Buckhannon to Birch Village, then up Birch to Skyles, and from
there to Fenwick and Richwood, where he saw a man he recognized and
spoke to him. It was E.B. Dean, son of Bracky Dean of Eakin Lumber days
at Skyles. "I saw that he didn't know me," said Eakin, "and I told him that
I was born and raised on Birch River, to which he replied: 'I still don't
know you, but I'll tell you one thing, you have some damned good blood
in you.'"

Eakin Lumber Company wasn't alone in operating on upper
Birch. Birch Valley Lumber Company had a mill at Tioga, Nicholas

County, or, in the local tongue, "Tiogy," and logged at least on Anthony, Poplar, and Powell's Creeks on the Birch watershed, and other places as well, including on the Gauley River drainage. Birch Valley logged all of the 11,000-acre Blair-Berthy tract on the Powell's Creek drainage of Powell's Mountain. (The surface owner of this tract is now Pardee-Curtin Lumber Company of Curtin, Webster County, and Philadelphia, Pennsylvania). Birch Valley closed its Tioga mill around 1941.

Charles T. Dodrill writes in *Heritage of a Pioneer* about Frank Dodrill, a native of Poplar Creek, cutting timber on Anthony Creek as a contractor for Birch Valley Lumber Company. Dodrill says he "moved the mill in, built tramways, cut over several acres of timberland and was sawing it into lumber when a dispute arose over title to the lands from which the timber was being removed." He was able to market some of the sawed timber, but not enough to salvage the cost of his investment. Dodrill continues: "He saw many years of hard work and a life's accumulation disappear. Weaker men than Frank Dodrill would have been driven to bankruptcy, but he directed his efforts to other lumber contracts in Braxton and Webster counties and paid his debts."

Paul Miller of Akron, Ohio, wrote in *The Nicholas Chronicle* (date unknown) about riding the Birch Valley Lumber Company logging train to school from Tioga to Allingdale, where they would catch the B & O passenger train coming from Richwood to continue on to Camden on Gauley and Cowen. Birch Valley allowed students to ride free. This was in the Depression days of the 1930s, and a free train ride was manna from heaven. Birch Valley bought out its predecessor, Tioga Lumber Company, in early 1915.

The community of Tioga is named for Tioga County, Pennsylvania, where the promoters of the Tioga Lumber Company lived. Tioga is closely linked geographically to Birch River. Powell's, Anthony, and Poplar Creeks of Birch all head within a few miles of Tioga; the head of Poplar is only one and one-half miles away.

- - -

There were coal mining and timbering operations sprinkled all along upper Birch in the early part of the century, and timbering has returned with a vengeance; there is hardly a hillside that hasn't been timbered in recent years.

In the early 1900s, there was a little sawmill town, with a store and several houses, located at the mouth of Two Lick Run in Webster County. Logs were pulled by cable up an incline to the top of the mountain on the north side, and then let down the other side, probably to the railroad near

Erbacon.

An "incline" was a track over which logs were pulled in cars. The hoist that operated the cable was located on the top of the hill; when the cars reached the top, the engine was reversed and they were let down the opposite side on an identical incline.

In the late 1930s and early 1940s, Cherry River Boom and Lumber Company had a large band mill at the mouth of Two Lick.

The early coal mines on upper Birch were mostly of the house coal variety; a 1916 report by the West Virginia Geological Survey lists at least a dozen such mines.

Skyles logging crew; Tom Reger is on the right
Photo courtesy of Roscoe Reger

Four

Birch Village

Route of the Presidents

The town of Birch River, or Birch Village, or simply Birch, is the only settlement of significant size on the entire thirty six miles of river. One could almost say the only settlement, although there were once post offices at Boggs on upper Birch and Herold on lower Birch.

According to the National Park Service, which studied Birch River for possible inclusion on the National Wild and Scenic Rivers System, Birch Village's population in 1983 was 300. It is more than that now, probably 350 or 400.

Birch Village (to distinguish it from the river for purposes of this book) is on the route of new U.S. 19, a four-lane highway that funnels an average of 10,000 vehicles per day past the town, according to West Virginia Department of Highways traffic counts.

Many, if not most, of these motorists are long-distance north-south travelers, but for some the destination is more localized. When Illene Cutlip Lewis, who attended Birch River Elementary, and now teaches at Frametown Elementary, tells her second graders where she went to school, they look puzzled at first, but then a light dawns. "Oh, yes," they say, "I know where that is. It's on the road to Wal-Mart." (The giant retail chain has a superstore at Summersville).

Birch Village sits about halfway along the river at an elevation of 1,130 feet. It is located in Nicholas County, 17.3 miles down from the start of the river near Cowen, and 19.3 miles above the mouth of the river at Glendon. It is also about halfway between Summersville and Sutton, the county seats of Nicholas and Braxton Counties, respectively.

In musty books, this "halfway house" is sometimes referred to as Birch Bottoms. Because of its broad river bottoms, the village does not have the hemmed-in appearance of many West Virginia towns, not even with 2,417-foot Powell's Mountain an imposing presence on its southern edge.

The bottoms, both at the village and below, are large enough that small airplanes have flown in and out of them, with mixed results. Paul Frame, Bailey Frame, Phillip Morris, and Jennings (Jink) Carte were perhaps the most frequent fliers. Paul Frame and Morris found that flying over the rugged local terrain was an excellent way to scout hunting territory, especially to locate side roads that could be used in deer season.

On one occasion, they didn't make it to the ground, at least not right away. They came down in birch trees along the river. But the gods of flight were with them. The trees cushioned their fall, and they walked away, although the plane was badly damaged. Ironically, both Frame and Morris were later killed in separate highway accidents.

Vernon Murphy Jr., who, with his son Mark, owns the Bluegrass Connection store at Birch Village, was an occasional passenger in planes piloted by Jink Carte in the 1950s. They flew in and out of the large bottom downriver from Birch Village. One time, Jink, flying alone, cracked up on landing, but was not seriously hurt.

Two future presidents of the United States walked or rode horseback through Birch Village, and maybe on the same day. Major Rutherford B. Hayes (he probably rode) and Private William McKinley (he probably walked) were part of the 23rd Ohio that moved along the Weston-Gauley Bridge Turnpike toward Carnifex Ferry in September 1861. Hayes became the 19th president, serving from 1877 to 1881, and McKinley became the 25th president, serving from 1897 to 1901. McKinley, who rose to the rank of captain during the war, was assassinated in office in 1901.

The 113-mile turnpike was built in 1851-52 for the same reason that U.S. 19 was built almost eighty years later: the need for a good north-south road in western Virginia (later West Virginia). From Weston, the turnpike went through Roanoke, Walkersville, Ireland, Falls Mill, Bulltown, Sutton, Birch Mountain, Birch Village, Summersville, Drennen, Lockwood, Belva, and, finally, to Gauley Bridge.

The turnpike became a focal point of troop movements and skirmishes around the time of the battle of Carnifex Ferry (see "Powell's Mountain"), and Birch Village shared in the action. In a 1993 article in *Goldenseal*, William D. Creasey wrote this about the movement of Union soldiers through the village:

> An army coming through remote Birch River was a
> most unusual event in the lives of everyone, especially the chil-
> dren and young people. Sally, my grandmother, had a calf her
> parents had given to her and of which she was duly proud; the
> Yankees killed her calf and ate it. She was eight years old at the
> time, and she never quite forgave them. Her religious beliefs
> did not permit her to hate, but she certainly had no love for Yan-
> kees.

In *September Blood: The Battle of Carnifex Ferry*, Terry Lowry wrote
that on August 11, 1861, a Union captain was captured by Confederate
cavalry at Birch River during the skirmishing for control of the turnpike.
The unfortunate captain was John W. Sprague of the 7th Ohio Volunteer
Infantry, who, along with four other soldiers, was enroute from Sutton to
Summersville. Even less fortunate were two of his men, who were killed.

The defining moment, however, for Birch Village's Civil War past
was the death of Henry Young on September 8, 1861 (see "Powell's Mountain"). Young was shot and killed by Union soldiers and is buried on the
mountain. The circumstances surrounding his death have been debated
ever since.

The story of buried Yankee gold lends glitter to the Civil War era
at Birch Village. Supposedly two Confederate guerillas robbed a Yankee
payroll and were pursued up Birch Valley. They buried the gold in a
small hollow near Rose Run, but both of them were killed and the gold
was never recovered. "All this turned into a ghost story that we were told
when we were growing up," said Michael Dilley, an upper Birch native.
"Needless to say, a lot of people went looking for this gold but never
found it."

The Weston-Gauley Turnpike of Civil War times was not the first
road into Birch Village. Nicholas County historian J.M. Hutchinson wrote
a series of articles in *The Nicholas Chronicle* in 1910 titled "A Brief History
of Nicholas County's Early Settlement." They were reproduced in the
book, *Nicholas County Heritage*, published by the county's Historical and
Genealogical Society, and provide a priceless record of Nicholas County's
past. Hutchinson told about a road that was built across Powell's Mountain:

> At the June term [of the county court] in 1822, it was
> decided to make a road across Powell's Mountain, and the ques-
> tion of the amount of work necessary to complete it was raised.
> After due consideration it was agreed that twenty men could

do the work in twenty days, and it was ordered that on the first day of September ten men from Muddlety and ten men from Birch, naming them, that is those nearest, begin and perform that work in twenty working days from that time. The equity of the court [its authority to enforce duties] was never questioned. Every one had to work on the roads the same number of days, for all used them.

Some accounts of early Birch Village have painted it as a bustling town with several businesses, and perhaps that was true in its Civil War heyday, but an eyewitness from the late 1800s doesn't necessarily paint it that way. *Nicholas County Heritage* contains a letter written by Emily Scott Horan to her granddaughter, Lois Wheeler, in 1943:

> I was born January 10, 1870, at Birch River, Nicholas County, West Virginia. I was the youngest child of my parents, Richard Scott and his wife Melcina Louisa, whose maiden name was Frame (daughter of William and Sarah Friend Frame). My father, while a young single man, came from Randolph County, West Virginia, where his folks lived.
>
> Birch River, on the main turnpike from Sutton to Gauley Bridge, consisted of one general store, my father's, in which the Post Office was kept, one small blacksmith shop, one mill for grinding wheat, and also for sawing logs. The mill was built by Col. John Brown and his son Rev. James F. Brown. A few families, mostly Frames, Browns and Hoovers, were living near the mouth of Powell's Creek where the store was located.
>
> The village lay at the foot of Powell Mountain and was entirely surrounded by rough hills. The river [Birch] and creeks wove in and out with many a crook and turn, dashing over rocks, roots, and fallen tree trunks to eventually form their crystal clear water into the larger river Elk. In the 70's, Powells Creek came rattling and bouncing down out of the mountains, clear and pure. We could and did take a drink out of a leaf cup, or by lying down by the creek and drinking directly from the clean water as it rolled over sand, gravel and rocks. No thoughts of germs disturbed us.

The origins of Powell's Creek are relatively undeveloped, even today. While the creek may not be as pristine as described in the above account, neither is it grossly polluted.

A relic of the fading days of the Weston-Gauley Turnpike is a concrete arch bridge in Birch Village that was built in 1916 by the Nicholas County Commission. It was probably the first bridge to span the river at the village. Records at the courthouse in Summersville tell the story: an entry for the commission meeting of March 23, 1916, said it was decided to receive bids "to construct a bridge across Birch where the Weston-Gauley Bridge Turnpike crosses said river. Bids are to be received by May 9, 1916."

A notation for the May 9 meeting said that six bids were received, and that upon examination of these bids and upon advice of the State Road Bureau, the contract was awarded to the Concrete Steel Bridge Company of Clarksburg for the sum of $6,464.00.

On September 20, 1916, was this final entry: "The court proceeded from the courthouse to Birch River, and after examination of the bridge, does conclude that the said bridge has been constructed according to specifications, and hereby receives same as complete."

The president of the commission was Granville Odell. His name and the names of the other commissioners are engraved on a plaque on the bridge. Upper Mill Creek enters Birch from the north at the historic and still sturdy concrete span. Some imaginative references to Birch River say it was once called "Bird River," at least at Birch Village, because Mill Creek and Powell's Creek, coming in from opposite directions, form a perfect bird's foot.

Records in the corporations division at the Secretary of State's office in Charleston show that the Concrete Steel Bridge Company was formed on January 23, 1914, and went out of business on May 27, 1932.

Historic concrete bridge over Birch

There is no listing of company executives, but they and their employees are recognized here and now for building a bridge that is still usable after eighty five years.

The concrete bridge is still owned by the Department of Highways, and is used by local residents. It was also scheduled to be used for construction traffic when a nearby 1929 steel bridge was being replaced in 2001. The latter structure is historic in its own right, having been part of original U.S. 19. Its steel truss design (bridges that get their support from an overhead steel frame, as opposed to piers underneath), is rarely seen anymore as ancient bridges are gradually replaced. There was once a sign near the steel bridge that said "Stonewall Jackson Highway," which was the designation of old U.S. 19.

The concrete bridge is the most visible, but not the only, evidence of the turnpike's existence in Birch Village. One day I visited Jack Mollohan, who lives near the concrete bridge. Across Powell's Creek in the yard of his neighbor, Jim Criss, is a slight but very discernible depression where the turnpike passed through. The roadway can also be seen on the left ascending bank of Powell's Creek as it approached Powell's Mountain. The pike followed the right side of Powell's Creek, crossed to the left side at about the present location of the Birch River Baptist Church, and then crossed to the right side again to follow Shanty Branch up Powell's Mountain.

A Birch Village antique of slightly more recent times is the former Gulf gasoline station built in 1937 by Roy Mollohan. Because of its lilliputian size, and a large electric clock that perches on its red tile roof, it eminently qualifies as a landmark. After Mollohan, subsequent owners and operators of the little station were Paul Frame, Jim and Nell Cook, and Sam and Betty Gibson, who ran it from 1966 until 1989. Sam Gibson died in 1994. His wife still owns the building and lives beside it.

The Little Gulf Station in Birch Village

Although quite small for a service station, the building is quite large in the memory of its former customers.

Jack Rose, who lives on old U.S. 19 on the road to Bays, was one year old when his family moved from Akron, Ohio, to the Birch area.

His father, Cleat Rose, managed the station for Roy Mollohan, and Jack pumped gas for Paul Frame in 1946 when he was sixteen years old. The term "pumping gas" literally meant just that. "You turned a handle to pump the gas into a glass bowl at the top," Jack recalls, "and from there it was gravity fed into the car's fuel tank."

In 1946, the first full year after the end of World War II, gasoline cost only eighteen cents a gallon.

One day I put the tape measure to the little station for the historical record. Scott Curry, Betty Gibson's grandson, assisted me. It measured sixteen feet by twelve feet two inches. Then I discovered it had been measured previously by Jack Coffman for insurance purposes. He has measured probably half the structures in a half-dozen counties in central West Virginia since he went into the insurance business in 1963.

Jack Coffman's father, Guy, who died in 1987, founded one of the longest running businesses in Birch Village in 1937 when he moved his fur and ginseng store from Little Birch, a nearby community in Braxton County. He previously worked for Eakin Lumber Company, which logged on upper Birch River from 1912 to 1927.

Jack Rose remembers his dad selling opossum and raccoon hides to Guy Coffman in the 1930s. "We had a dog," Jack recalls, "who may have caught every 'possum in Nicholas County, and probably Braxton, too."

Today, sixty four years after Guy Coffman came to Birch Village, the Coffmans (Jack and sons Tony and Gary) are still buying furs and ginseng, and have added a motel and a scrap metal business, as well as insurance. The fur industry has declined because of changing fashions, but the market for ginseng, a plant whose roots are valued in China for medicinal purposes, is still strong.

Jack Coffman, who was six years old when his family moved from Polemic Run to Birch Village, sang with the Pilots Quartet, a popular local gospel group, from 1967 until 1980, and he still sings at the Birch River Baptist Church. He played on the Little Birch baseball teams of the late 1940s and early 1950s.

The venerable red-brick Birch River Baptist Church was organized in 1882 by Levi J. Huffman, its first pastor. In the "charity begins at home" department, the church took up its first foreign missions offering on July 14, 1883, and the amount collected was one dollar and twenty-five cents.

The church was first located on Upper Mill Creek, and the builder was Marco McLaughlin. Wendell Dodrill now owns the property and lives where the church, as well as the former Birch River Elementary

School, were located on what is known alternately as old U.S. 19, the old turnpike road, or Mill Creek Road. The present Birch River Elementary School was built in 1953 to consolidate several small local schools. Its enrollment in school year 2000 was 160.

Howard Justus, who was born on Anthony Creek and now lives in Akron, Ohio, recalls attending school on Mill Creek in 1924. His father, James, had a farm between Skyles and Boggs, and was hired by Eakin Lumber Company to supply cider apple vinegar to the company store at Skyles.

The Birch River Baptist Church moved to its present location around 1939, which was the year it was dedicated. It was built of bricks obtained from a building that was being torn down at Sutton. The first pastor at the new location was L.T. Harvey. Major additions over the years were a parsonage, baptistry, and fellowship hall. Prior to the building of the baptistry, the church held its baptizings in Powell's Creek or in Birch River at the Bubbie Hole above the mouth of Anthony's Creek (the naming of the Bubbie Hole is explained later in this chapter).

Clara Mae Given, who lives on Powell's Creek and has attended the Birch River Baptist Church for fifty two years, recalls that in the 1970-74 period when new U.S. 19 was being built, the contractor agreed to move a large rock in Powell's Creek to enlarge the baptizing hole. That spot has gradually filled in, and creek baptizings are now held behind Jack Coffman's house. The baptismal candidate may also have his or her choice of the traditional church baptistry or the scenic Bubbie Hole of Birch River.

Trinity Baptist Church, also in Birch Village, began holding services in 1982 in a building owned by brothers Ophie and Gaylord Coffman, across the street from the Birch River Volunteer Fire Department. Its last use was by Ophie Coffman as a furniture store. The building burned in 2000, and the site is now a vacant lot beside the Bluegrass Connection.

The Bluegrass Connection, opened in 1998 by Vernon and Mark Murphy, sells musical instruments, tapes, and accessories. The building was formerly a game room (The Teen Center) and prior to that a restaurant.

The present Trinity Baptist Church was built in 1986. Alva Blankenship, who lives at Summersville and is an evangelist, was the first pastor. A striking feature of the church sanctuary is the knotty poplar walls, which came from the Widen High School gymnasium in Clay County. The Trinity pulpit is also made of knotty poplar from the same source.

Trinity is located on Powell's Creek near the site of the Bob Harrouff grist mill of the 1920s. Ches Coulter, a Birch Village resident, came to Powell's Mountain from Clay County in 1927 with his family, and he recalls riding off the mountain as a teenager to have corn ground into meal. Harrouff's fee was a gallon of corn, which he collected in a wooden box.

Harrouff was of German descent; his father migrated to this country from Berlin. Christopher Baughman, one of the early settlers on upper Birch (see "Skyles and Boggs") and also a miller, was likewise of German descent. Harrouff's grandson, Charles (Doc) Harrouff, lives in Birch Village, as does his daughter-in-law, Lola George Harrouff.

Morgan Tinnel operated a grist mill in Birch Village on the north side of the river. He lived "downtown" in a house diagonally across the street from the present Go-Mart. This house was vacant in late 2000; its last use had been as an antique shop. Jack Coffman recalls visiting Morgan Tinnel as a youngster and being shown a casket that reposed in an upstairs hallway. It had been made by Joe Tinnel, Morgan's brother. Joe Tinnel intended it for his own burial, and, Jack believes, he was indeed buried in it.

As a historical footnote, Daniel Boone became gravely ill while on a hunting trip with his grandson, James Boone, in Missouri Territory in 1817, and remained behind while his grandson went home to spread the news that the great frontiersman was dying. Daniel's son, Nathan, had a coffin made, but his father rallied and lived almost three more years. He didn't like the coffin, calling it "rough and uncouth", and had one built to his own satisfaction out of cherry wood, and was in fact buried in it when he died in 1820 (*My Father, Daniel Boone, the Draper Interviews with Nathan Boone*, edited by Neal O. Hammon).

Jack Rose recalls that when he was six or seven years old, he rode horseback from his home on White Oak Fork Road to the Tinnel mill. "They would put me on the horse, and then Morgan Tinnel would help me off, grind the corn, and put me back on the horse again."

The Harrouff and Tinnel mills were steam powered, but water-powered mills also existed along Birch, including the classic Barnett-McCoy mill at the falls below Boggs (see "Skyles and Boggs"). Such mills represented the first use of water power in West Virginia. They were the successors to the earlier hominy block mills, on which grain was pounded by hand into meal or flour, and later mills which consisted of two round stones turned by hand. "Going to mill" was an eagerly-awaited social occasion where people saw their neighbors and exchanged community news.

Prior to coming to Birch Village in 1921, Bob Harrouff had a grist mill on Meadow Fork, one of the two major tributaries that form Birch

River, and he lived on Back Fork, the other major contributor. Bill Armentrout, who owns the property where the mill was located, found two millstones at the site several years ago, and they are now decorations in his yard. Delma Justus Hickman of Camden on Gauley recalls that the mill was operated by Harrouff sometime around 1918.

Two trademark general stores in Birch Village early in the twentieth century were those of Ernest Tinnel and Roy Mollohan, which were located near where Trinity Church now stands, on the route of the turnpike. With the coming of U.S. 19, both stores were moved to new locations on the highway, although still in Birch Village.

The Trinity Church section, also called Mollohan Drive, is still referred to as "Old Birch," because that was where the businesses were clustered in turnpike days. "New Birch," which is the present center of the village, gradually evolved after the completion of U.S. 19 in 1929-30.

The Pop's Pizza building in "New Birch" was a movie theatre at one time, and musicians from Nashville performed there in the late 1930s or early 1940s. I was told that the attic of the building was made of wormy chestnut, and that it was probably still there and still beautiful wood. One day I went to Pop's Pizza and inquired about the wormy chestnut. The woman at the counter took my request in stride. She said she didn't have the faintest idea, but would look. She pulled up a chair and removed two pieces of ceiling tile. The results were inconclusive, but I wondered: what kind of reception would I get if I walked unannounced into a pizza place in Charleston and asked to have the ceiling tile removed?

It is possible that the attic of the Pop's Pizza building is indeed made of wormy chestnut, because there are, or were, other examples of this wood having been used in construction in Birch Village around the same time the Pop's Pizza building was being hammered and sawed into existence. The Roy Mollohan store, where the Birch River Post Office (zip code 26610) now resides, has some wormy chestnut, as did the Thurman Frame grist mill, which was torn down in the building of the Coffman Motel.

The Mollohan store was moved to its present location in 1930. The Tinnel store was moved, probably around the same time, to what is now a vacant lot in front of the Pro-Mart Sunoco Station. The final owners of the Tinnel store were Claude and Jean Criss, who were the proprietors from 1972 until 1992. Claude Criss bought the store from Virginia Tinnel Hickman, the daughter of Ernest and Daisy Tinnel.

There is no record of how the Mollohan store was moved, but the Tinnel store was pulled by a team of horses, using logs as rollers, and probably the Mollohan store was moved the same way.

A bit of Birch Village nostalgia has been preserved by Penn Frame. His mother, Cora Justice Frame, was postmaster when the post office was located in the Tinnel store. Around 1940 she had a post office built on the site of the present Sunoco Station. It is believed to have been the first separate post office in Birch. Prior to that, post offices were part of stores. When the post office moved across the street to its present location, the "Cora Frame Post Office" was moved to what at that time was a vacant lot, but is now the site of the Coffman Motel.

Former Birch Village Post Office

When Jack Coffman bought the property and built the motel in 1993, he gave the old post office building to Penn Frame, who moved it to his home just downriver from the village, where it still resides, a tiny relic of Birch Village's past. With its false front, it resembles something that might be seen on the set of an Old West movie. Frame lives in North Ridgeville, Ohio, but he has retained his Birch home.

It is possible, of course, that separate post office buildings may have existed prior to modern memory. But earlier in this chapter, Emily Scott Horan, who was born in Birch Village in 1870, recalled that the post office was in her father's store around that time.

The first Birch River Post Office was established in 1840. It presently has 1,240 patrons scattered over a large rural area.

Frame's Pennzoil Station and Garage is another Birch Village fixture. Wade Frame built the station in 1948, and he and his brother, Arthur, added the garage in 1952. Their brother, Kenneth, and Kenneth's son, Randy, are the present proprietors. Kenneth pumped gas and sold cigarettes, pop, and candy when he was ten years old, and began working in the garage at age seventeen.

He also worked at one of the seemingly ubiquitous grist mills at Birch Village, this one operated by his father, Thurman Frame, and Emil Brown. It was located on Powell's Creek at the east end of the present Coffman Motel. This mill was unique; it wasn't powered by water or steam; it was powered by a four-cylinder 1928 Chevrolet automobile engine.

Also at the motel site was the Matthew Justice barn. "It was the biggest barn I ever saw," said Jack Coffman. "We lived nearby, and we had a cow that we kept in the barn. It was turned loose in the daytime, and it was my job to find it in the evening. I chased that cow all over Birch Village." Matthew Justice was postmaster at Birch Village in the teens or 1920s.

Frames are synonymous with Birch Village. *In Heritage of a Pioneer*, Charles T. Dodrill lists seventeen Frames who were born on nearby Anthony Creek.

Supposedly, four Frame brothers came to Virginia from England in the late 1700s. One migrated to Frametown in Braxton County, one was killed by Indians, and one migrated to Birch River. There is no record of what happened to the fourth. Frametown is believed to have been named for James Frame, who built a grist mill there in the 1800s. He was also a justice of the peace, was fond of shooting matches in which a beef was the prize, and declined to hold court on days when shooting matches were being held (L.V. McWhorter's *Border Settlers of North-Western Virginia*).

William (Billy) Frame may not have been the brother who came to Birch Village from Virginia, but he was known to have operated a grist mill at the mouth of Powell's Creek prior to the Civil War.

Bernard Roy Frame Jr., who grew up on Anthony Creek, recalls hearing the story that his grandparents, Andrew and Molly Frame, placed logs on top of the hogpen at their home in Birch Village to keep out marauding bears. Andrew was in the Confederate army, and his brother, John, also a Birch Village resident, was in the Union army. Both survived the war, although Andrew was captured "in the north." His capture may have occurred either at Antietam or Gettysburg, which were Robert E. Lee's two invasions of the north.

A lifelong resident of the Birch Village area is Elmer Dodrill, who was born on Poplar Creek in 1914, the year that cars first began to show up in Birch Village. He now lives on the north side of the river across from the mouth of Anthony Creek, and owns five hundred and thirty acres which lie on both sides of the river. He is the great-great grandson of English Bill Dodrill, who is believed to have been the earliest settler on upper Birch River (see "Skyles and Boggs").

When Eakin Lumber Company operated a large mill at Skyles from 1912 to 1927, its logging train ran within ten yards of the back door of the house where Elmer now lives, and he and his brother would hitch rides to Birch Village. They also rode the Birch Valley Lumber Company train on the other side of the river.

When Elmer was in basic training at Camp Claiborne, Louisiana, in World War II, he had an early taste of why Omar Bradley, the camp commander, was so popular with the average GI. One day in training he addressed Elmer: "Soldier, how are you getting along?" Dodrill wasn't feeling well, and replied, "Not so good, sir." But at least Bradley asked. Bradley went on to command the U.S. 12th Army Group in Europe and attained the rank of four-star general.

While at Claiborne, Bradley invited Alvin York, the legendary hero of the Argonne in World War I, to address the troops. York's old outfit, the Eighty-second Division, was being reactivated at Claiborne. York had tried to persuade the army to give him a combat role in World War II, and in fact registered for the draft, but he was fifty five years old, overweight, and arthritic, and was denied regular military service (*Sergeant York: An American Hero*, David D. Lee, 1985, The University Press of Kentucky).

But the army, and certainly Bradley, eagerly embraced him as a symbol. Elmer Dodrill has one of those panoramic training camp pictures that shows York at Claiborne in front of a sea of faces. The date was May 7, 1942. York, a large man, had his right hand thrust in the pocket of his suit coat, and he wore a hat. Dodrill remembers that he talked about the use of the bayonet, and demonstrated the basic strokes: forward drive, slice, sweep, and butt stroke. York had no doubt received bayonet training in WWI at Camp Gordon, Georgia, but he marched into U.S. military history on that bloody morning of October 8, 1918, for his use of the Enfield rifle and Colt .45 pistol, when he was credited with killing twenty five Germans and almost single-handedly effecting the capture of one hundred and thirty two others.

One of Elmer Dodrill's ancestors was Big John Dodrill, said to have been a large and powerful man, hence the prefix to his name. He lived across from the mouth of Anthony Creek, and his farm is still referred to as "the Salt Works" because a salt well was drilled there sometime after 1850. John Dodrill died in 1933 at age seventy five.

The well was drilled to a depth of 1,300 feet with a spring pole, which consisted of a forked stationary pole, with a springy pole placed between the forks. The short end of the spring pole was fitted with a steel cylinder and drill bit. The drillers pulled down on the long end, and when they let go the steel thudded down with enough force to gradually drill a hole. But as it turned out, the well was not salty enough for commercial use.

Gerald Dunn, a native of Canfield, Braxton County, wrote in his 1987 book, *An Appalachian Boyhood*, that the driller may have been James McLaughlin, an ancestor:

"The family believes that Dennis McLaughlin came across to Richmond, Virginia, then migrated to Birch River. Apparently he suffered great financial hardship when his herd of cattle was lost with a ship at sea. It is thought that he married Elizabeth Hurley. Salt was discovered here, and it is said that James McLaughlin (a son of Dennis) drilled a salt well at Birch River thirteen hundred feet deep by hand with a spring pole."

There are five cemeteries on Elmer Dodrill's farm, and one of them contains the grave of Elizabeth Hurley, who was born in 1790 and died in 1858.

Just upstream from the salt well is the Bubbie Hole of Birch River. Probably every kid who ever grew up around Birch Village has sampled the waters of the Bubbie Hole, and it was also a popular spot for baptizings. It was named for James (Bubbie) Dodrill, son of Big John Dodrill. Bubbie was born in 1890 on the family farm across from the mouth of Anthony Creek, and died in 1954. He was a schoolteacher, and circuit clerk of Nicholas County for twelve years. He swam so often in the Bubbie Hole, both as a youngster and as an adult, that the local kids named it for him.

The Bubbie Hole of Birch River

The athletic high-water mark for Birch Village is the remarkable record posted by its Little League baseball teams from 1970 through 1974, when they won eighty nine games and lost only six. They won the Braxton County title in 1970, and the Summersville Little League title four straight years from 1971 to 1974.

Dave McCoy, who now lives at Rainelle and works for Green Valley Coal Company at Leivasy, was the manager, and Vernon Murphy Jr. was the coach. Most of the Birch River players went on to play baseball at Nicholas County High School. One season, eight of the nine Nicholas starters were products of the Birch River Little League teams. Mark Murphy played at Braxton County High School, and pitched that school's first ever shutout victory.

Several Birch River Little Leaguers played college ball, and one, Randy Bennett, a righthanded pitcher, was on his way to a possible shot at the major leagues, but injured his arm in a College League game at Winchester, Virginia, in 1980, and never pitched again. "I was called in from the bullpen," Randy remembers, "and on my first pitch I heard my elbow snap, and the pitch hit two feet in front of the plate. I threw two more pitches, with the same result. They wanted me to have an operation, but I decided against that and returned home."

Earlier, Randy played two years at Potomac State Junior College at Keyser, West Virginia, as did Tony Martin, another Birch alumnus. One of their teammates at Potomac State was John Kruk, who later played for the Philadelphia Phillies. Randy posted records of 4-3 and 9-3 at Potomac State, and had an impressive 1.67 earned run average his second year.

Los Angeles Dodgers scout Jim Garland was instrumental in obtaining a scholarship for Randy to play two years at East Carolina University at Greenville, North Carolina, and then, the deal was, the Dodgers would draft him. But before he ever pitched a game for East Carolina, the arm injury occurred.

One of his teammates in the College League was Jimmy Key, who later pitched for the Toronto Blue Jays and New York Yankees. Key was the winning pitcher for the Yankees in the sixth and final game of the 1996 World Series against the Atlanta Braves.

Randy is a Birch Village native. He presently lives in Dille and works for C.W. Wright Construction Company of Kingwood. In 1999, his son, Jason, then twelve, pitched and won the championship game in the Summersville Little League.

During the early 1970s, brothers Tony and Louie Martin played on the Birch teams. Louie was a pitcher who possessed an outstanding curve ball for a twelve-year-old. When Birch entered the Summersville Little League, the curve ball was suddenly outlawed. Dave McCoy still refers to this as "the Louie Martin rule."

One of the memorable sporting events at Birch Village in the late 1940s to early 1950s was the football rivalry between Birch and Dille, a small community in Clay County. The participants were of high school and college age, and they played without helmets or other padding normally associated with contact football. Junior Murphy was one of the Dille players, and his recollection of those rough and tumble games is that Dille always lost.

- - -

Postscript: A historical marker about Birch Village, "the route of the presidents," would be appropriate on the Powell's Mountain overlook of U.S. 19, as would another marker calling attention to the nearby Henry Young grave. Both are so much a part of the history of this corner of Nicholas County.

Aerial view of Birch Village nestled among the hills. Photo courtesy of Eddie Pinney

~ Five ~

Powell's Mountain

And the saga of Henry Young

I have been drawn to Powell's Mountain from the time I first heard my parents tell about driving over the mountain in a car with running boards, and a rattlesnake dropped from overhanging brush onto the running board on my mother's side. The forerunner of U.S. 19 over Powell's Mountain was very narrow and winding, and the overhanging brush was never far away.

The complete story of the building of U.S. 19 over Powell's Mountain is included at the end of this chapter for the historical record. It shows that the highway was designated State Route 4 in 1922; it did not become U.S. 19 until 1930.

The mountain has a very rugged, remote and inspiring look about it, so much so that the State Department of Highways included an overlook above Powell's Creek on the northbound side when new U.S. 19 was built in the late 1990s. The best view is near the highway crest on the west side, a view that looks out toward Widen and Clay. Unfortunately, because of the terrain, which drops off sharply, no overlook was built there. But it is one of the finest scenic vistas in the state, and marvelously expressive of the rolling hills of central West Virginia.

L.V. McWhorter in *Border Settlers of North-Western Virginia*, published a letter from William Connelley of Chenute, Kansas, written in 1903, who commented on this view: "I would give much for a photograph of the view from the mountain [Powell's] looking west; a finer view I have not seen."

The dominating presence of Powell's Mountain in the region is illustrated by the fact that the two principal streams draining off the west side of the mountain total over forty miles in length. Buffalo Creek, the stream that flows through Widen and ultimately empties into Elk River at Dundon, is 23.81 miles long and is the fourth largest tributary of Elk River; Strange Creek, which gained its name from the enduring legend of a lost member of a surveying party (see "William Strange"), is 19.96 miles long and empties into Elk at the village of Strange Creek.

On the east part of the mountain, which divides the Birch River drainage from the Gauley River drainage, the two major streams are Powell's Creek and Anthony Creek, which, combined, total almost eleven miles. Powell's is the largest at 6.08 miles; Anthony is 4.75 miles long.

Looking east toward the high point of Powell's Mountain

I wonder how this formidable mountain, with its deep hollows, rock cliffs, steep hillsides, and rhododendron thickets, must have seemed to William Powell, its namesake. To my knowledge, he left no written record of his thoughts, impressions, and hunting experiences. But we are indebted to J.M. Hutchinson, an early historian of Nicholas County, for what is known about Powell. Hutchinson was born near Summersville in 1835, fifteen years after that town was established as the county seat, and lived until 1934. In 1910 he wrote "A Brief History of Nicholas County's Early Settlement" that appeared as a series in *The Nicholas Chronicle*. He said of Powell:

> In the early days a man by the name of Powell, a
> noted hunter and pioneer, lived on Peters Creek near the Dren-

nen spring [Peters Creek heads at Summersville and flows into Gauley River]. He came up Bucks' Garden [the name of a large tract of land north of Gilboa], by the lick, followed the Buffalo trail that went to Bulltown, over on the Muddy Creek [original name of present Muddlety Creek] , and up Muddy Creek and Brushy Fork, then across the mountain and down the creek [Powell's]. There he built a hunting camp below the mouth of the creek, and went to it each fall for many years. This gave the name to Powell's Mountain and Powell's Creek.

There is no known record of when he settled on Peters Creek, or when he established his hunting camp at present day Birch Village, but it was most likely in the late 1700s or early 1800s.

- - -

William Powell might have envied today's travelers. Motorists today cross Powell's Mountain in a few minutes on a four-lane superhighway. Rattlesnakes had better stay clear of the thousands of vehicles that zip over the mountain every day going to or from Myrtle Beach and other southern destinations on a corridor that connects Toronto, Ontario, with Miami, Florida.

The fact that Powell's Mountain has rattlesnakes is a source of herpetological interest to me, and not just because of the running-board incident. Why do places like Powell's Mountain have rattlesnakes, and other areas do not, although the terrain is similar? For example, it would seem that the rocky hillsides of Birch River generally would appeal to any average easy-to-please rattlesnake. In *Amphibians & Reptiles in West Virginia*, N. Bayard Green and Thomas K. Pauley wrote this about timber rattler habitat: "The timber rattler is most frequently found in rough, mountainous terrain where brushy ridges and rocky hillsides with ledges abound." That description could have come straight off the Birch River hillsides around me, but I've never heard of any rattlers where I live, which is about ten air miles from Powell's Mountain.

And by the way, I am complaining. I consider the presence of rattlesnakes and other endemic species as cultural enrichment.

Inexplicably, the rattlesnakes of Powell's Mountain are picky even within the narrow confines of that range. Vaughn Davis, who lives on the Mill Creek-Erbacon Road, has never seen a rattler close to his home, but they are common three or four miles farther along toward Erbacon. Davis hunted rattlers for many years, either on main Powell's Mountain or along the logging roads on Anthony and Poplar Creeks, both of which are part of the Powell's Mountain drainage into Birch River. He has caught as many as eight rattlers in one afternoon.

A classic "man bites dog" story involving a rattlesnake occurred in the early 1900s on Anthony. Fred Roberts told about this incident in a September 16, 1986, interview with Gerry Milnes for the Augusta Collection, Booth Library, Davis & Elkins College. A man picking huckleberries on Anthony was bitten by a rattlesnake, and went home for treatment without attempting to kill the snake. Others returned to see if they could locate the snake, and found it dead!

In the same interview, Roberts told about stepping bare-footed on two rattlesnakes when he and his dad, Maston Roberts, were driving their hogs up Skyles Creek to feed on the abundant chestnut mast. Amazingly, he wasn't bitten, which proves what herpetologists have told us all along: that snakes have more to fear from man than the other way around. Roberts said the snakes felt like ice cubes on his bare feet.

On Powell's Mountain, old U.S. 19 is more likely to harbor rattlers than the new highway. Residents along Powell's Creek, which empties into Birch at the village, occasionally find rattlers in their lawns.

In the first quarter of the 20th century, people in the Powell's Mountain vicinity would turn their hogs loose in the fall to fatten them on acorns, confident that the rattlesnakes would not be a problem for the hogs, and they were right. In fact, it was just the opposite; hogs, being very thick-skinned and thin-tempered, were impervious to rattlesnake bites, but rattlesnakes weren't impervious to the pointed, slashing hoofs of the hogs, and often wound up being a meal. The wild boars stocked in southern West Virginia in 1979 likewise have nothing to fear from rattlesnakes or any other kind of snake.

Dana Carte, who lives on Powell's Mountain near the highway summit, next door to the Powell's Mountain Baptist Church, tells about a den of rattlesnakes being disrupted by the four-lane construction, and for a few days the crews had to watch their steps. The creeping, crawling reptiles even found their way onto equipment that had been parked overnight.

- - -

I grew up confident in my belief that Powell's Mountain was Powell's Mountain. I'd always heard it referred to in the first-person plural. Then the DOH erected a sign in 1974, when new U.S. 19 was completed, calling it Powell Mountain, first-person singular.

Perhaps the DOH is right. An agency that large should know what it's doing. A. James Manchin, Marion County's gift to the Mother Tongue, tells the story about his days as a wrestling coach and teacher

at Webster County High School when one of his students with the surname Cogar suddenly, in his senior year, changed the spelling to Coger.
Manchin asked him why, explaining that he was creating havoc with their
records. The boy had a very logical and unassailable explanation: "My
mom said that's the way Montgomery Ward spelled it on their catalogue,
and a company that large should know what it's doing."

Also, the DOH is dealing from a position of strength (remember
those thousands of Myrtle Beach-bound motorists who see the sign
saying Powell Mountain). The U.S. Geological Survey agrees with the
DOH, calling it Powell Mountain.

But too many people locally have called it Powell's Mountain for
too long to change now.

On the Powell's Mountain
sign, the elevation is given as 2,276
feet at the highway summit, which it
undoubtedly is. Determining elevations is a process that is built into surveys for new roads. But the highest

elevation on the mountain is 2,417 feet at a ridgetop about one mile east of
the highway crossing, according to the West Virginia Geological Survey.
From this true summit, near the head of Tug Fork of Powell's Creek, the
drainage on the eastern half of the mountain is to Birch River on the north
side, and to Muddlety Creek of Gauley River on the south side. A spectacular view of the summit opens up on the Frank Tinnel property near
Powell's Mountain Baptist Church. Tinnel was born at the mouth of Tug
Fork, which is part of the summit view.

Tug Fork was named by loggers after the Civil War. "Tug" is a
term used to describe the leather straps that are part of the harness placed
on teams of oxen or horses.

Two landmarks on Powell's Mountain are Flanders Camp and
Painter Rocks. Flanders is located on the head of the Left Hand Fork of
Brushy Fork of Muddlety Creek, about four miles east of old U.S. 19, and
is simply a rock formation where hunters have camped, and where moon-
shiners were said to have plied their trade during Prohibition days. There
was a camp of sorts there at one time, but it no longer exists. Painter
Rocks is an impressive collection of rock cliffs near the head of Strange
Creek on the west side of the mountain. Painter is a colloquialism for
panthers, or mountain lions, which roamed the area in the nineteenth century.

Another landmark is Noah's Ark, the large rock formation with
the crosses on top that is clearly visible to the east from the new highway.
Supposedly the formation has approximately the same dimensions as the

ark of biblical fame.

There is an aura of mystery about Powell's Mountain. On the highway summit is one of those very conspicuous green and white signs that says "Young's Monument Road," named for the nearby graves of Henry Young and his wife, Lucinda James Young. For one hundred and forty years, people have speculated about the events surrounding Henry Young's death on September 8, 1861. The graves are located on a little knoll a stone's throw from the intersection of U.S. 19 and Young's Monument Road on the western side of the highway. In the winter, when the leaves are off, the gravesite can be seen from the four-lane. In repose, Henry Young is a passing acquaintance to thousands of motorists every day. A cinderblock wall, painted white, encloses the graves and the single bevel-top monument.

There are many local versions of the demise of Henry Young, the most common being that he was a Confederate soldier on the way across the mountain to rejoin his outfit and was ambushed by Union soldiers. That's basically what I grew up hearing, and "ambushed" usually became "bushwhacked," which means the same thing but is a somewhat more derisive term. That fit the general sentiment of this area at the time of the Civil War, which was largely pro-South.

The same sentiment existed seventy years later when U.S. 19 was built. The proof of that pudding is that old U.S. 19 was named the Stonewall Jackson Highway. One of the landmarks on the highway was the Stonewall Jackson Grill at Summersville, which advertised "Southern Home Cooking" and always lived up to its billing. Butch Mullins was the restauranteur there from 1952 until his death in 1996. Early on, a sister, Ella Fulton, who now lives in Georgia, was his partner. Butch Mullins' grandson, Mike Mullins, recalls that his grandfather did the cooking at first, and even after he hired cooks he continued to sample the food. The landmark restaurant closed after his death.

Henry Young most likely was either a Confederate soldier or recently-recruited militiaman, probably the latter. That he was killed on Powell's Mountain by Union troops is agreed to by all accounts. The details are less clear, which is understandable given the situation and the passing of time.

Exactly where on the mountain he met his fate is unclear. One story has it that he was not on top, where his grave has long been located, but in a hollow on the western side near the head of Buffalo Creek. That story postulates that he was buried beside the log where he fell, and that later his remains were exhumed and reburied on top of the mountain.

Another version is that he was killed near the head of Shanty Branch, which drains off Powell's Mountain into Powell's Creek on the eastern side. This version relates that he was moved a few days later from the precise spot where he fell and was given a decent burial on top within the present intersection of Young's Monument Road and the northbound lane of U.S. 19. A certainty is that thirty six years later, on August 26, 1897, a service was held at the lonely gravesite that included the placing of a monument and enclosing the grave in a black wrought iron fence. According to published accounts at the time, this memorial service attracted about 1,500 people, who came from several surrounding counties on horseback, in wagons and buggies, and on foot.

Kitty Young Brown, a great-niece of Henry Young, died in 1993 at age 106. Over the years, she contended she was at the service, describing in detail the scene of the horses, wagons, and buggies, and the many people in attendance. She would have been ten years old at the time, so it's quite possible she was there and remembered.

Henry Young's wife, Lucinda, who was left to raise five young children when her husband was killed, died on July 26, 1898, and is buried beside her husband on Powell's Mountain. She had never remarried.

But this site was not to be the final resting place for Henry and Lucinda Young. When new U.S. 19 was built in 1970, their earthly remains were moved to the present location on the western side of the highway on the road that leads to the Clay County town of Dille. The original wrought iron enclosure did not accompany the remains, except for the gate. The gravesite is now enclosed by a cinderblock wall.

- - -

The aura of intrigue surrounding the death of Henry Young will not go away. One account is that he was on a clandestine mission for the Confederates. This version surfaced in a long-ago newspaper story, handwritten when I obtained it, minus the name of the newspaper, the date, or the author. The spy version:

> In Summersville lives 86-year-old Richard Scott McCoy, who is probably the only living man who knows the story, and he doesn't know it all. He remembers what his father, William McCoy, told him when he was living. The elder McCoy told what he knew because he was with Henry Young when the Federal soldier got him. Young, according to Mr. McCoy, was ordered by General Floyd (Brig. Gen. John B. Floyd, commander of Confederate operations in the Kanawha Valley theater) to spy out the Union General Rosecrans (Brig. Gen. William

Rosecrans, commander of the western Virginia theater for the North) and see what he was up to. Floyd wanted to know how many men they had, and something about their equipment.

McCoy's father, who was in his 20s, and had but recently become a part of Floyd's army, was ordered to follow Young and bring his report back to headquarters. He followed until he saw Young suddenly stop and hug up to a pine tree. McCoy jumped behind the nearest tree himself, and just then the bullets started whizzing from a nearby clearing. A sentry had evidently been around, and as the firing became increasingly abundant, he (McCoy) realized that other Union soldiers must have joined the sentry. All this time McCoy had his eye on Young. The spy was safe against enemy fire all the time, a fact McCoy could not understand when he saw Young step out from behind the tree, into full view and range of the Union firing. He stood there a minute or two. Then he fell dead at the foot of the tree. One of the Federal's bullets had found its mark. McCoy slunk into the woods, then ran to headquarters. Young's body was buried there where he had fallen, on top of Powell's Mountain.

The date of Young's death (September 8) is significant because it came two days before the battle of Carnifex Ferry, where troops under the commands of Floyd and Rosecrans clashed in one of the early Civil War battles for control of western Virginia. Powell's Mountain, being on the route of the Weston-Gauley Bridge Turnpike, was crossed by Union troops enroute to Carnifex. Rosecrans' forces had marched from Clarksburg in September, 1861. Western Virginia was important to the Union for political reasons; it wanted separate statehood for that part of secessionist Virginia, and, as we are well aware, got it on June 20, 1863.

The goal of Floyd, the Confederate commander, was to drive Federal troops out of Nicholas County and thus deny them use of the turnpike.

John D. Sutton, in his 1919 *History of Braxton County and Central West Virginia*, wrote this version of Henry Young's death: "Near the summit of this mountain, Henry Young, a southern soldier, was approaching the Turnpike from a path leading up the mountain, and as he stepped out into the open space in the road, he came in full view of a regiment of Federal soldiers coming up the pike. Young refused to surrender or save himself by flight; undaunted even in the presence of an entire regiment, he stood his ground until he fell. Some years since, his friends assembled at the lonely grave on the mountain where he fell and erected a monument to mark the resting place of this daring citizen."

A more detailed version of the death of Henry Young, and a less romanticized one, appears in *September Blood: The Battle of Carnifex Ferry,* a 1985 book by Terry Lowry. He wrote that Henry Young was a recently-recruited militiaman who was on picket (guard) duty when he met his death. According to this version, Floyd, the Confederate commander, had ordered Captain Henry M. Beckley's Logan County Wildcats (one of several local militia units formed in the spring of 1861) "to advance toward Sutton and down the Elk River to Strange Creek, where they recruited sixty one additional militiamen, including John Frame, L.M. Frame, Charles D. Keener, John Keener, Jack Knottingham, Henry Young, and Hie Young. The combined troops were ordered to Powell Mountain, immediately south of Big Birch (Bottoms), where they were to delay the advance (of Union troops).

"That night two spies from [Union commander] Rosecrans' camp, posing as farmers, encountered Confederate pickets. Expressing their wish to visit the Confederate camp (which later became known as the Robertson farm on Powell Creek at the foot of Powell Mountain), they were permitted into the camp. They stayed until midnight, learning the countersign for the next day: the word or letter "I." Indeed, this knowledge by the Yankees would prove fatal to Henry Young of the militia the following day.

"Shortly before daylight, the Wildcats and the militia had proceeded up the mountain to a point where the Old Turnpike crossed Shant(y) Branch. Here large rock formations were located on both sides of the road, behind which the men were placed in line of battle. John Keener and Henry Young were posted as pickets under a large hemlock tree beside the road.

"Just as anticipated, some eighteen or nineteen Union soldiers appeared on the road shortly after daylight, probably part of a reconnaissance... [the 13th Ohio Infantry with some Union cavalry]. Henry Young, not recognizing them as the enemy, yelled to them for the countersign, which they immediately gave. This prompted Young and Keener to foolishly leave the safety of their post. When close enough to realize their mistake, they quickly started back to the tree, but the Federals opened fire, killing Henry Young instantly."

Lowry wrote that Young's body "was located by friends a week later at the head of Shant(y) Branch, where the Yankees had moved it and thrown brush over it. Although his body was in no condition to be moved, his friends carried him to the top of Powell's Mountain, where he was buried."

Shanty Branch drains off Powell's

Mountain into Powell's Creek on the east side of present U.S. 19. The Shanty Branch Road runs just above the highway at the Young's Monument Road intersection, although because of the highway construction it now dead ends nearby.

The presence of the Logan Wildcats on Powell Mountain on the fateful morning of September 8 is confirmed by the account of a southern soldier in the book, *War Stories: Civil War in West Virginia*, by David L. Phillips and Rebecca L. Hill. The soldier wrote that his unit was sent to Powell's Mountain, where they found the Logan Wildcats valiantly defending against Rosecrans' army.

It was no doubt in this action, either before or after the arrival of the above unit, that Henry Young was killed.

The colorfully-named Logan Wildcats (which the Logan High School athletic teams carry proudly to this day) were ordered to delay the advance of Rosecrans' army to give the Confederates at Carnifex time to bolster their defenses.

The delay partially worked, according to *September Blood*. The Union soldiers returned to Birch Village, but resumed their advance the following day, September 9. Two militiamen, including Hie Young, who was recruited with Henry Young (relationship, if any, not known) opened fire on the Union soldiers, killing one and wounding another, slowing but not stopping the advance.

If Henry Young was recruited in the Elk River-Strange Creek area, it is plausible that his outfit traveled to Powell's Mountain either up Birch River or up the parallel Keener's Ridge Road. *The Official Military Atlas of the Civil War*, republished in 1978, and showing Civil War maps of 1861-65, indicates there were two roads parallel to Birch at that time, perhaps one on Birch and the other on Keener's Ridge. Oldtime accounts indicate there was a road of some sort on Keener's Ridge during the Civil War. Soldiers from both sides passed that way sporadically.

John Hymes Jr., Glenville State College history professor, wrote in a 1982 paper on Birch River that the Civil War atlas "mentions the existence of a road from Glendon to Little Birch that supposedly followed the path of Birch River." J.H. Colton's 1865 *Map of the State of West Virginia*, the first commercially published map of the state, shows one road along Birch, maybe on Keener's Ridge. Colton was a New York City mapmaker.

- - -

There's yet another version of the Henry Young saga, and in this one he is not just a militiaman, but an officer in the militia. Charles T.

Dodrill, in his *Heritage of a Pioneer*, writes that Young was recruited in the Elk Valley, that most of the recruits came from Wilson Ridge in present-day Clay County, and that Young was in charge of a contingent that was ordered to advance from Wattsville to Powell's Mountain. Wattsville is the name of a community in Clay County, probably a post office long ago, whose present-day existence even most local residents are unaware of. But it was located near the top of the Widen hill in the area where the road to Runion Ridge turns off Wilson Ridge. Dille, the gateway to approaching Powell's Mountain from the west, is just a few miles away. The correct spelling of Runion Ridge is open to honest debate. Eleven families listed in the Clay phone directory spell it that way, while four other families spell it Runnion. Others may prefer Runyan or Runyon. All of which proves the old adage that there is no proper way to spell a proper noun.

According to this version, when Young's men reached Powell's Mountain and saw approaching Union forces, the militiamen became excited and ran, leaving Young alone. He stood his ground , and was killed in the first volley. This version of Young acting heroically agrees with the John D. Sutton account. Later, after the Union soldiers had passed, he was buried where he fell. Dodrill says that a grave marker was placed years later by Hamilton Burton Hickman of Clay County, a son-in-law; another account says the marker was placed by Henry Young's oldest child, Mortimer.

Dodrill wrote that advance Union scouts were informed of the presence of Young's men by Union sympathizers, which partly coincides with the *September Blood* account of Union spies gaining the password in the militia camp the previous evening.

Despite all of the above versions, was Henry Young really a soldier or militiaman? One intriguing account says he was a civilian. This account is in the book *Border Settlers of North-Western Virginia*, by L.V. McWhorter, who wrote: "The Federals came upon Young near the summit of the mountain, then a wilderness, and disregarding the order to halt he was killed. A Federal officer appeared at the Young homestead and reported the particulars of the death [which would indicate that Henry Young lived near Powell's Mountain]."

Support for this version, or perhaps obtained from it, was an account that appeared in *West Virginia: A Guide to the Mountain State*, which was compiled in 1941 by workers of the writers' program of the Work Projects Administration. This account identified Young as "a Confederate sympathizer who was shot down when he refused to surrender to Union troops." It further said: "Young preferred certain death to surrender, and died in a one-man battle with the entire advance gard of General William S. Rosecrans's Union army."

Probably the most thorough file on Henry Young's life and family
has been assembled by Brenda Hickman of Gassaway, a great-great granddaughter. Her grandfather, Henry Preston Hickman, received a permit in
1963 to open the grave. He wanted to ascertain that Henry Young was
not running away when he was killed. Carl Wilson Sr., who owned the
funeral home at Clay and assisted in obtaining the permit, was there for
the grave opening, and he confirmed to me that Young had clearly been
shot through the right cheek, and that the size of the bullet hole indicated
the wound would have been instantly fatal. He had definitely not been
running away.

Ches Coulter of Birch Village, who lived on Shanty Branch near
the present highway overlook from 1927 until 1940, was told by Preston
Hickman that Henry Young was killed on the head of Cutlip Cabin, a
tributary of Buffalo Creek, within 200 yards of the present Young's Monument Road. This would tend to support the story that Young's outfit
approached Powell's Mountain from the western side, and would not
conflict necessarily with other accounts that he was killed near the head of
Shanty Branch. The head of Buffalo Creek and the head of Shanty Branch
are in close proximity. In 1935, Ches Coulter, age seventeen at the time,
was plowing a cornfield on Powell's Mountain and unearthed a sword,
obviously a relic of the mountain's Civil War history.

Henry Young was one of six children of Bazel and Agnes Pierson
Young, who were married in 1817 in what was then Kanawha County.
Bazel Young lived twenty three years after his son's death. He died in
1884 in Wirt County at approximately eighty seven years of age. The date
of Agnes Pierson Young's death could not be found.

Henry Young and Lucinda James were married on September 27,
1847, in Braxton County. They had five children. The eldest, Mortimer,
died in 1911 at age sixty four and is buried at Black's Chapel Cemetery at
Allingdale, Nicholas County, near Cowen. His obituary in the March 30,
1911, *Nicholas Chronicle* said: "Mort Young of Lanes Bottom, proprietor
for two or three years of the hotel near the B & O depot [probably the Clifton, which was across the street], died one day last week of heart trouble.
He was considerably past middle life, was a good citizen, and a son of
the man who sleeps in the 'Lone Grave' on Powell's Mountain." Lanes
Bottom was an earlier name for the town of Camden on Gauley.

Amanda Young Morton, second child of Henry and Lucinda
Young, died in 1923 at age seventy three and is also buried at the Black's
Chapel Cemetery. Her first husband was Francis G. Morton, who died
thirty nine years earlier on July 14, 1884. Later she married Pierce
Matheny. Francis Morton taught school in Webster County, but, after
marriage, came to Braxton County and farmed. He is buried in the woods

beyond Adams School on the road to the Blue Hole of Birch River, in an even lonelier spot than the grave of his father-in-law on Powell's Mountain. He and Amanda (Mandy) are believed to have lived at the head of Sugar Camp Run of Birch River near where he is buried. The site has always been known in the community as "the Morton place," although no house has existed in the memory of anyone now living.

The Black's Chapel Cemetery where Mortimer and Mandy Young are buried is a classic country cemetery located on a rounded knoll, with stately large white oaks and pines lending character to the setting. Nearby Black's Chapel was founded in 1857 and is named for Samuel Black, a Methodist circuit rider.

Jess, another son of Henry and Lucinda Young, died of a fever in 1876 at age twenty three and is buried in the Levi Cart Cemetery near Strange Creek. Levi Cart was a private in Company E of the 22nd Virginia Cavalry during the Civil War. A picture taken in 1915 at the Methodist church at Meadville on Strange Creek shows him wearing his Confederate uniform blouse and cap. He died in 1937 at age ninety two.

Mary Agnes Young Given, another daughter of Henry and Lucinda, died in 1917 at age sixty two, and is buried at the Middle Run Cemetery on the Herold-Frametown Road in Braxton County, as is her husband, Jasper Given. Middle Run is a tributary of Birch River.

The youngest child, Sarah Jane Young Hickman, died in 1951 at age ninety two in Roane County, and is buried at the Walnut Grove Methodist Church Cemetery on Wilson Ridge, Clay County. She and her husband, Hamilton Burton Hickman, were the parents of thirteen children, including the aforementioned Henry Preston Hickman, who died in 1975. Preston Hickman was a well-known miner and lumberman, and at one time was president of the Clay County Board of Education.

- - -

Where Henry Young was born and where he was living at the time of his death are, like the details surrounding his death, uncertain. The 1850 Braxton County census lists him as living in that county, and gives his occupation as farmer. His place of birth is listed as Nicholas County, but Braxton County did not exist when Henry Young was born on January 20, 1827. Braxton was created in 1836 from Kanawha, Lewis, and Nicholas Counties.

Tantalizing clues as to where Henry Young may have been living at the time of his death have been unearthed by Brenda Hickman. His estate included 335 acres of land on Strange Creek in Mumble-the-Peg Township (Mumble-the-Peg was a long ago name for present day Muddlety Creek). It was not until 1863 that townships became magisterial districts in Nicholas County. Mumble-the-Peg Township became Hamilton District, which covers the northern end of the county, including Powell's Mountain and the head of Strange Creek.

Nicholas Countian historian J.M. Hutchinson wrote in 1910 that Muddlety Creek was first called Muddy Creek, but surveyors changed its name to Muddlety to distinguish it from Muddy Creek on the Greenbrier River, where they had also surveyed. Later, Hutchinson said, it became Mumble-the-Peg when another group of surveyors played a game by that name while staying on Muddlety. In 1820, James McMillion was elected Nicholas County surveyor, and, deciding enough was enough, changed the name back to Muddlety.

But J.H. Colton's 1865 map of West Virginia calls it Mummelpeck Creek. Mummelpeck is a word of Dutch origin, perhaps a game or a family surname. Hence, Mummelpeck may have gradually evolved into Muddlety, perhaps a more likely scenario.

In any event, a deed in the Nicholas County Courthouse shows that in 1854 a David Young (relationship, if any, not known) sold Henry Young 350 acres on Strange Creek for six hundred dollars, which was a considerable sum at that time. On the side of the deed is written: "Deeded to Jasper Given and Burton Hickman, two of the heirs of Henry Young." The latter notation was dated June 12, 1877.

The Nicholas County records further show that in March, 1880, Mortimer Young and his wife Elizabeth, Francis Morton and his wife Amanda, and Jasper Given and his wife Mary, sold one hundred acres, more or less, of Henry Young's estate on Strange Creek to Hamilton Burton Hickman and his wife Sarah Jane Young Hickman for ten dollars. It is possible, then, that the Hamilton Burton Hickman place of later years, which was located on Runion Ridge, was the homeplace of Henry Young.

This would corroborate the versions that most of the militia that included Henry Young were recruited in Clay County, that they moved to Powell's Mountain from that direction, and that Henry Young was killed near the top of the mountain on the western side.

But another deed, dated June 4, 1869, and filed at the Nicholas County Courthouse, shows that Bazel Young, Henry's father, sold one hundred acres of land to John Elliott of Wirt County. The deed lists the parcel as being in Nicholas County and on the waters of Strange Creek where Lucinda Young was living at the time. Bazel Young was said to be living in Braxton County. The tract is described as follows:

Beginning on Fielding McClung poplar corner standing on a line of the lands on which Henry Young's widow now lives on the waters of Strange Creek, thence with said McClung's line to the line that formerly divides Braxton County from Nicholas County and with said county line to Grass Run and up Grass Run to where said widow Young line crosses it with said Young's line or lines to the beginning, containing one hundred acres more or less.

This indicates that in 1869, eight years after her husband's death, Lucinda Young was living on the head of Strange Creek.

- - -

The 1897 memorial service for Henry Young on Powell's Mountain was reported by a local newspaper:

Here on top of this beautiful elevation, at the western end, near the turnpike, Henry Young, a confederate, was shot by the Federal soldiers on September 8, 1861, and was buried a few days later by the citizens a short distance from where he was killed.

His grave designated as the 'lone grave' on the top of this high, desolate mountain, remained for nearly 36 years unmarked except for a few rough rocks, surrounded by growing timber, until a few weeks ago when his friends suggested that a monument be erected to perpetuate his memory.

The suggestion was followed by prompt action, and there now stands, and on last Thursday was dedicated to his memory, a beautiful marble shaft (manufactured by T.H. Hawkins of Sutton).

The sermon was given by Rev. M.V. Bowles, presiding elder of the Fayette District of the Methodist Church. His subject was "Unrealized Hopes of Human Life," and his text was from *Deuteronomy* 34:5-7. Henry Young was only thirty four years old when he died, hence the sermon on unrealized hopes was appropriate.

When Lucinda James Young died slightly less than a year after the memorial service for her husband, and was buried beside him, her service was conducted by her pastor,

Henry Young Monument

Rev. R.P. Fitch. A choir sang her favorite song, *When the Roll Is Called Up Yonder.*

The monument at the Young grave includes this inscription:

> Remember friends as you pass by, that all mankind are born to die. Then let your hopes on Christ be cast, that you may dwell with him at last

Although the precise details of Henry Young's death on that fateful Sunday in 1861 are not known for a certainty, he nevertheless lives on in local folklore. To enlighten those who see the highway sign and visit the gravesite, something more should be said about him. A West Virginia Historical Society sign at the nearby highway overlook would be appropriate. Perhaps it is because of the uncertainty surrounding his death that it hasn't been done. If so, let me suggest the following words:

> The death of Henry Young is one of the enduring sagas of the Civil War in West Virginia. He was a Confederate militiaman or sympathizer who was killed near here on September 8, 1861, by Union soldiers enroute to the September 10 battle of Carnifex Ferry. The remains of Henry Young and his wife, Lucinda, were moved to their present location in 1970 when a new U.S. 19 was constructed. The gravesite is located just off U.S. 19 on Young's Monument Road. Whatever the precise details of his death, he represents a tragic time in our history when state was pitted against state, and brother against brother.

- - -

The story of old U.S. 19 across Powell's Mountain:

> 1917: The State Road Commission (SRC) approves the location of a Class A road (one that connects county seats) from Sutton to Summersville. In October of that year, the Nicholas County Court also approves the location.

> 1922: The road is assigned the designation State Route 4. It was to begin at the state line at Bluefield, and then run through Beckley, Fayetteville, Gauley Bridge, Belva, Summersville, Muddlety, Birch River, Sutton, Weston, Clarksburg, Fairmont, Rivesville, Westover, Morgantown, Easton, and on to the Pennsylvania line.

> 1930: Route number is changed to U.S. 19.

1931-32: The SRC's annual report shows the Powell's Mountain stretch (Muddlety to Birch River) under state maintenance for the first time.

1933: Nicholas County map shows U.S. 19 as having been hard surfaced over Powell's Mountain.

1933: SRC takes over all roads formerly under individual county jurisdiction (West Virginia, Delaware, Virginia, and North Carolina are currently the only states in the nation that are responsible for all roads except city streets). As early as 1922, the SRC began taking over roads that were deemed in proper condition for takeover (having been hard surfaced). In the case of U.S. 19 in the Powell's Mountain area, it wasn't until 1931-32 that hard surfacing, or black topping, was done.

Contract by contract:

Hookersville to top of Powell's Mountain, unless otherwise noted:

February 1927: Grading is done on 5.43 miles by contractors George N. and O.J. Yoho; $60,493.51 authorized, $59,910.01 spent; closed August 1929; this was designated project 159-A, which ran from Hookersville, just south of Muddlety at Paddy Run, to the top of Powell's Mountain.

August 1927: Gravel surface applied by the above contractors on the same stretch; $47,223 authorized, $44,206.03 spent; closed December 1928.

February 1931: Gravel in preparation for surface treatment (black-topping) applied by Keeley Construction on a 19.53 mile stretch from Fockler School near Summersville to Braxton County line; $55,946.46 authorized, $55,308.37 spent; closed January 1932; projects 159-A, C, and D.

August 1931: Cold tar surface treatment applied by contractor R.F. Kirkham on a 21.57 mile stretch from Summersville to Braxton County line; $24,900 authorized, $24,672.78 spent; closed January 1933; projects 159-A, C, and D.

Top of Powell's Mountain to Birch River, unless otherwise noted:

February 1927: Grading is done on 2.9 miles by state contractor Keeley Construction and on 1.9 miles by a county contractor (unknown); state authorized $65,541.12, $55,439.89 spent; closed July 1928; project 159-C.

August 1927: Gravel surface applied on the same 4.8 mile stretch by Keeley Construction; $30,384.75 authorized, $27,979.77 spent;

closed July 1928.

February 1931: Gravel in preparation for surface treatment applied by Keeley Construction on a 19.53 mile stretch from Fockler School to Braxton County line; $55,946.46 authorized, $55,308.37 spent; closed January 1932; projects 159-A, C, and D.

August 1931: Cold tar surface treatment applied by state contractor R.F. Kirkham on a 21.57 mile stretch from Summersville to Braxton County line; $24,900 authorized, $24,672.78 spent; closed January 1933; projects 159-A, C, and D.

The above starting dates indicate when the various project segments were authorized; the closing dates were when the financial accounts were closed, and not necessarily when the work was completed.

Surprisingly, the above records show that contracts were much higher for application of gravel in preparation for surface treatment than for the actual paving of basically the same stretch. This shows a realization that the road foundation is the most important part of any highway.

- - -

Thirty seven years later, in 1970, construction was begun on new U.S. 19 over Powell's Mountain, and was completed in 1974. In 1996, work began on upgrading this section to four lanes, and was completed in 1998. The four-lane upgrade was, at the time, the largest earth-moving project in the nation.

Portions of old U.S. 19 are still in use for local traffic. The part that crosses Powell's Mountain is still as serpentine as a coiled rattlesnake, and partially follows the route of the 1800s Weston-Gauley Bridge Turnpike.

View of Powell's Creek and Tug Fork drainage from highway overlook

~ Six ~

Cora Brown

A Birch River Icon

Residents of Nicholas, Braxton, and Clay Counties never carry road maps nor have any use for them. They have the Cora Brown house and bridge. If further orientation is needed, they also have the Cora Brown hill, which begins just beyond the house and bridge.

"How do you get to Keener's Ridge?" "Go past the Cora Brown house, top the hill, and you're there."

"Where's Dille?" "Go past the Cora Brown house, top the hill, turn left and keep going."

"How do you get to Widen?" "Go past the Cora Brown house, top the hill, turn left to Dille, and don't look back."

"Where's Slabcamp Run?" "Just down Birch from the Cora Brown house."

"Where's Feedtrough Run?" "Just a little farther below the Cora Brown house."

"Where's Paris?" "Just over the ocean from the Cora Brown house."

"Where's Moscow?" "Just over the ocean from the Cora Brown house and turn right at Paris."

Well, you get the idea.

The Cora Brown bridge has its own special niche. It is likely that every document ever published by a state or federal agency about Birch River mentions the bridge. For example:

National Park Service: "The Birch River was authorized for study as a potential component of the National Wild and Scenic Rivers System under Public Law 96-199, which amended Section 5(a) of Public Law 90-542 to add the Birch River, between Cora Brown bridge and its confluence with the Elk River to the study category."

Farther along in the same document: "From Cora Brown bridge to its confluence with Elk River, [Birch's] descent is seventeen feet per mile."

Same document: "Downstream from the Cora Brown bridge, the valley floor narrows between converging inclines and the stream enters a gorge. Flow velocity increases and reaches Class III or IV difficulty at higher water levels."

State Natural Streams Preservation Act: "Birch River from the Cora Brown bridge in Nicholas County to the confluence of the river with the Elk River."

Cora Brown probably didn't realize that her house was becoming a road map, and she died before the bridge that also bears her name became common usage in state and federal documents. But she certainly took note of the bridge. One time its planking had become loose, and made a terrible noise when vehicles passed over it. She wrote a letter to the Department of Highways and told them the flopping planks were keeping her awake at night. The DOH sympathized, and came and put a new deck on the structure, or at least made repairs.

Her letter:

I am writing you about the bridge across Birch River up here in Nicholas County in front of my house. I don't think there is a single plank in the floor that is not loose. When cars go over it they make so much noise we can't sleep at night, & for a half mile away they tell me they hear it. It was an old bridge when it was put up years ago. It was knocked down once & put back up. I don't think it will stand up much longer anyhow. We went in to see the road commission about it & they referred us to A.S. Turner at Lewisburg & I wrote him & got no reply. Hope we don't have to stand the noise all winter. Cars go over all hrs. in the night. Please see what you can do. & oblige.

Mrs. Cora A. Brown
Birch River, W.Va.

There is no date on the letter. She wrote it in longhand and sent it to her daughter in Charleston to type properly and mail to the state agency. DOH records show that a new bridge was built in 1950. The new bridge was of "simple steel government surplus, pony truss [sides], and supported by concrete abutments." The 1950 structure may not have been built in response to her letter; repairs to the noisy planking could have been made many years prior to that.

But her daughter, Juanita, believes the 1950 bridge was built as a result of the letter. At least, she says, that was when it began to be referred to as "the Cora Brown bridge."

In 1987, the bridge was completely renovated by the DOH. The renovations included replacing the original stringers (floor supports), floor beams, and, for additional support, the bridge was enclosed with concrete cribbing. The DOH, perhaps less mindful of local history, doesn't call the structure "the Cora Brown bridge." It simply refers to it as "the Birch River bridge approximately two miles west of the town of Birch River." The official designation of the route is Secondary Route 1, also known as the Dille-Widen road.

Ches Coulter of Birch Village worked for Carl Morris Construction Company in 1936-37 when the firm was putting a rock base on the road. He worked at a stone quarry near the top of Powell's Mountain, swinging a sixteen-pound sledgehammer. The stone was broken into small pieces, and then run through a crusher. In those Depression days, his wages were forty cents an hour.

When the 1950 Cora Brown bridge was built, the site was moved a few yards upstream, but the west abutment of the old bridge is still there. Bill Murphy, who once lived at the Cora Brown house, was cutting grass on a riding mower and stopped to remove something from the yard. The mower kicked into gear and went over the abutment into the river. But Bill and a neighbor, Junior Murphy, pulled it out, and Bill straightened some dents and cleaned the engine, and the baptized, born-again mower gave many more years of good service.

Predating both of the bridges is the former county road that ran between Keener's Ridge and Birch Village and forded the river at the Cora Brown house. It is still visible where it curves down through the yard to the river.

Cora Given Brown was born on December 17, 1877, on Keener's Ridge near the Walker Cemetery. Her parents were Hamilton and Isabel Pierson Given. Her father, a Strange Creek native, worked in his younger years at the iron furnace at Strange Creek that was built in 1874 by brothers Jesse and William Savage (see "William Strange" chapter). She married I. Pat Brown on December 17, 1898, and in 1909 they built what is known today as the Cora Brown house.

They had five children: Virgie Brown Clifton, born in 1899; Berniece Brown Wadepuhl, born in 1905; Emil Brown, born in 1908; Juanita Brown, born in 1909; and Ozzie Brown, born in 1912. Ozzie lived eighteen months. On September 6, 1913, he wandered down to the river in front of the house and drowned.

Pat Brown, a school teacher and farmer, died in 1912 of blood poisoning at age forty two. He had smashed a finger, and infection set in. That was long before the time of infection-fighting drugs such as penicillin.

With one exception, Cora Brown lived on in the familiar two-story house from 1909 until her death on April 26, 1960. She went to Charleston in 1926 to stay with a daughter so her two youngest children could attend high school there. She bought her first and only car, a Chevrolet, sometime in the 1920s, and drove it to Charleston. Around 1933, she returned to Birch River.

She lived alone in her later years, although son Emil and his wife Beulah (now Beulah Brown Neil of Daytona Beach, Florida), lived just across the road. Emil was a school bus driver, insurance salesman, deputy assessor, and farmer. Beulah Mollohan Brown was a schoolteacher for thirty-four years, and "Hills of Birch River" columnist for *The Nicholas Chronicle* (see "The Poem").

Cora Brown taught school for a few years prior to marriage, possibly at Rose Hill on Keener's Ridge, although records aren't available that far back. She attended the New Hope Baptist Church at Morris. A church history compiled by Mildred Butcher includes this notation: "A bell for the church was purchased sometime in 1922. The committee for this project was Sister Cora Brown and Sister Clora Baughman." A family picture shows her leaving home on May 10, 1959 (Mother's Day) to attend services at New Hope. Slightly less than a year later she died at Sutton Hospital after a short illness.

Juanita Brown, the only surviving immediate family member, lives in Vero Beach, Florida. Although over ninety years of age, she walks a mile every morning. She is a 1942

Cora Brown, 1920s

graduate of Glenville State College, and taught school in Nicholas County prior to retirement. She sold the Cora Brown house in 1993 to Thomas Ward, a judge from Baltimore, Maryland.

The house had fallen into disrepair, and Ward was advised to tear it down. But he has a track record of restoring decrepit properties, including several townhouses in Baltimore that were scheduled to be demolished in an urban renewal project. He also restored a log house in Tucker County, West Virginia. "When I discovered its hand-hewn logs," he said, "I was hooked." The 1985 flood in Cheat River swept away many houses, but the two-story log house, which is over one hundred years old, survived.

"My first move [with the Cora Brown house]," Ward said, "was to try and find someone who would be willing to live there and take care of the place. I knocked on the door of the Murphys [Vernon Jr. and Anna], whom I had heard about. I told them I would like to make the house something that they would want to live in and would meet their standards in the restoration. We talked about the house at some length [the Murphys lived across the road, and still do].

"I knew when I heard from them in Baltimore not to make any decisions until later, because we seemed to be approaching an agreement."

As it turned out, Vernon and Anna's son, Mark, became the renter. He and his wife, Kathy, and their two teenage sons, Cody and Luke, moved into the house in 1999. It was a homecoming for Mark, because his parents were living there in 1960 when he was born. One day Anna pointed out to him the dresser drawer where she kept his diapers. Mark is a surveyor for Brooks Run Coal Company at Erbacon.

Ward obtained pictures from Juanita Brown and faithfully restored the house. "Among the most interesting features," he said, "were twin stone fireplaces. One was behind the wall in the downstairs bedroom. We opened that one, and it works. The other is in the adjacent dining room, and it could be used."

The sturdy old farmhouse has a "homey" look and feel, with its high ceilings, large rooms on both floors, and a fireplace in every bedroom. Oak flooring and an oak mantel were restored to their original finishes.

Dresser drawers in the downstairs bedroom are original, as is a dining room cabinet. The cabinet, made of poplar, was put together the old-fashioned way with homemade wooden pins called dowels. Holes were bored and the slightly oversized pins were driven into the holes.

They were less expensive than nails, and nails may have been difficult to obtain at that time. Juanita Brown recalls that the cabinetmaker was a man named Perrine, who lived in the Keener's Ridge community.

An auction was held after Cora Brown's death, and virtually all of the household furnishings were sold. The only remaining item is a

The house in the early 1900s

The renovated house of today

black iron teakettle which Junior Murphy bought and which he has since returned to the house. It sits on the hearth of the reopened fireplace.

One of Tom Ward's prized possessions is a sketch drawn by Juanita Brown which shows the outbuildings that existed in Cora Brown's time. There were a barn, grainery, sheepshed, chickenhouse, smokehouse, milk gap (a gate or wooden bars where cows were brought in for milking), drying house (a small building with racks and shelves for drying fruits and vegetables), woodhouse, coalhouse, and cellar. The barn, grainery, and cellar are still there. The cellar's foundation, made of hand-hewn stones, is as sturdy as when it was laid in place over ninety years ago.

The sketch also shows a potato patch, cornfield, fields of buckwheat and cane, pasture, meadows, and woodland. Bailey Walker of Birch Village recalls helping Emil Brown harvest potatoes one year in the rich river bottom soil. The potatoes were plowed out with a turn plow pulled by a team of horses; the patch yielded three hundred bags of potatoes. Emil Brown had a lifelong interest in farming the homeplace.

Cora Brown worked in the fields herself on occasion. A yellowed family picture shows her sitting on an old-fashioned hay rake, wearing a broad-brimmed straw hat and a long dress, and driving a team of horses. The picture includes a notation on the back by Juanita Brown: "I rode the horse that hauled the hay to the barn."

The fields were not being farmed when I visited them in late summer 2000, but the setting is as appealing as ever. They lie in a basin surrounded by the Birch River hills. One could not imagine a more scenic piece of river bottom.

Juanita Brown recalls the old country telephone of her childhood. "Our ring was one short, one long, and one short. One long ring would get us to the switchboard at Herold, and the switchboard operator [probably my grandmother, Isabel Young Johnson] would connect us to Sutton so we could talk to Grandpa and Grandma [Hamilton and Isabel Given]. We often listened in on other people's calls. I was listening in when I heard that World War I was over, and I ran down in the field to tell the workers."

The owner of the telephone service of that era was Hampton Pierson. Juanita remembers him coming to their home to work on the phone or line. Hampton and his wife, Kitty Cowger Pierson, lived on upper Middle Run.

A logging railroad, most likely the Birch Valley Lumber Company railroad, was located across the road from the Cora Brown house. It went up Madison Run, which enters Birch from the south at the Cora Brown bridge. The engineer was Granville Northcraft, who lived nearby.

The present owner of the Northcraft house is Harry English, who, like Ward, is from Baltimore.

In later years, Cora Brown wrote long, newsy letters to her children, and she went to Florida on three occasions to stay with Juanita for a few months at a time. But she was given a loom by her daughter-in-law, Beulah Brown Neil, and she spent her final years at home weaving. A family picture, taken in 1959 a few months before her death, shows her weaving on the Sears Roebuck loom.

Cora Brown and her husband, Pat, are buried at the Walker Cemetery on Keener's Ridge, near where she was born. Ozzie, the son who drowned in Birch, is buried beside his parents.

The Cora Brown Bridge

From the Cora Brown bridge, Birch River turns sharply north and enters its lower seventeen miles. This is the stretch that is included in the State Natural Streams Preservation Act, and which was also studied by the National Park Service for possible inclusion in the National Wild and Scenic Rivers System. The final seventeen miles are lightly populated and, for the most part, isolated. The National Park Service expressed it well: "Its shorelines are generally undeveloped, and it is generally inaccessible by road."

About a half mile below the Cora Brown house is the Henshelwood Eddy, the first large eddy on the river. J.V. Henshelwood, general superintendent for Elk River Coal and Lumber Company, built a camp there around 1936. It was a one-story structure of average size, and may have been the first camp on the river, with the exception, of course, of the hunting camp built near Birch Village in the late 1700s by

William Powell, for whom Powell's Mountain is named (see "Powell's Mountain"). Only a few foundation stones remain of the Henshelwood camp.

Henshelwood came to the Elk River Coal and Lumber Company at Widen in 1927. He is credited with helping the company survive during the Depression days of the 1930s.

My neighbor, Roger Tenney, remembers camping in the Henshelwood bottom with a friend, Randall Jones, when they were teenagers. "We had settled in for the night," said Roger, "when we were awakened by deer grazing and snorting around us."

One of the early residents below the Cora Brown house was Frank Given, a farmer who bought a tract of land in 1896 at the mouth of Big Run on the north side of the river (there are two Big Runs on Birch; this is the one in Nicholas County). A coal mine opening near the mouth of the run is still visible where Frank Given dug coal, probably for his own use. The one-room Big Run School that stood nearby is long gone. Oma Baughman Clifton, who later lived at Herold, taught at Big Run and boarded with Frank and Belle Given.

There are some very large cliffs, as well as individual rocks, in the Big Run locale that are characteristic of Birch from this point on. In fact, River on the Rocks more or less begins at the Frank Given Hole, which is a favorite of swimmers because it has an attractive sandbar that slopes gradually into deeper water like a city swimming pool. There are many splendid settings on the State Natural Streams section of Birch, and the Frank Given Hole is one of them.

The Graham family presently owns the Frank Given place. Wade Graham, who worked for Elk River Coal and Lumber Company, bought the property in the 1940s, and he, his wife Lula, and their children lived there for about ten years. "We were in the water [Birch River] more than we were on dry land," said Kenny Graham of Burnsville. The Grahams have a camp on the river just above the Frank Given Hole.

A county road once ran from Polemic Run on the north side of the river to Keener's Ridge on the south side. It forded the river at the present Graham camp, and is still visible where it entered the river, and again where it came out on the opposite side and wound its way up the steep hillside toward Keener's Ridge. Bailey Walker drove on this road in his first car, a Model A Ford roadster, for which he had traded a twenty-five dollar seven-jewel Elgin watch. One day when he was fording the river, the rear end of the car slid into a deep hole and became submerged momentarily, but the sturdy Model A kept going.

In July 2000, I took a deep breath and climbed on behind Mark

Frank Given Hole, where the rocks begin

Murphy for my quadrennial four-wheeler ride, and we headed downstream to visit Jack Johnston below the Frank Given Hole. Actually, Mark is a careful four-wheeler, and I knew that, and I knew also that he respects nature and a beautiful river.

On our way downriver, we saw two buck deer in velvet; they looked at us with curiosity, but without fear. I was tempted to stop and interview them. In fact, I believe I did say something to Mark about this, and he looked at *me* with curiosity.

Jack Johnston was born in Fayetteville, grew up in Sutton, and presently lives in Bradenton, Florida. But his heart is on Birch River. His camp, a lodge really, is so isolated that it would have cost over twenty thousand dollars to run electricity to it, and almost that much for a telephone. Jack solved these problems with a generator and a cell phone.

In river terms, he is located about halfway between Big Run and Feedtrough Run. His property consists of over two hundred acres that were bought by his father, Earl Johnston, in 1941 from Waitman Pierson, a logger and sawmill operator who lived near Herold and had a sawmill at the mouth of Feedtrough, among other places. Earl Johnston owned a feed store in Sutton.

Feedtrough is the most colorfully named tributary of Birch, among many colorfully named tributaries (see "Tributaries of Birch River"). The story is told that a long-ago horseback mail carrier ate lunch at a certain spot on Feedtrough. He cut down a tree, and hewed out a trough in which to feed his horse. Thus the tributary gained its name.

Jack's grandfather, Lee Johnston, once had a store and post office at Canfield. His uncle, Orva Johnston, lives on the Herold Road. On the wall of Jack's camp is a framed copy of a story I wrote for *The Braxton Citizens' News* about Orva walking and climbing hills, despite his more than ninety years of age.

Six years ago, the first time Jack stayed overnight at his camp, a pack of coonhounds treed something in his yard, and their incessant barking kept him awake all night. He believes the treed creature was a bobcat. On the second night, he heard a terrific racket downstairs. Pots and pans were literally flying off the walls. A bear had walked in through a doorway in which a door had not yet been installed. Jack decided to let the bear have its way with the kitchen, and in fact his options in the matter were rather limited. The bear eventually left, but not before it ate everything in sight. Jack's priority the next day was to install a thick door. That night he was awakened by a monumental thud. The bear was back, and in a foul mood because its way to the food was barred. But the door held, and the bear gave up and departed into the dark night.

Jack didn't find the bear encounter nearly as threatening as an experience he had while hiking up rugged and isolated Big Run. He was climbing over rocks, and suddenly fell into a crevice up to his shoulders in cold water. It may have been a mine shaft, or a hole worn out by the water, and for a few minutes he wasn't sure he could get out. But he saw light ahead and gradually wriggled his way to freedom.

The river in front of Jack's camp, a rugged setting with swirling water and big rocks, is known as the Dean Hole. Many years ago, John Dean, a sawmiller, lived there with his family. Two years ago, a pair of otters took up residence in the Dean Hole and were a prime attraction for Jack, his wife Roberta, and guests Bill Boggs, John Thomas, and Dale Cunningham of Sutton, and Charles Kelly, a Ravenswood optometrist. River otters were reintroduced into Elk River a few years ago by the Division of Natural Resources, and this pair may have migrated up Birch.

Below Jack's camp is Long Hole. Jack gave it that name because it is longer than the other eddies on this stretch of river, the Henshelwood excepted. By any name, it is a very idyllic setting. Jack, Mark, and I sat on a rock and watched the sun settle below the hills, and Long Hole become ghostly in the shadows. According to Jack, a few years ago a national outdoor magazine rated Long Hole prime walleye water. He isn't sure that it contains walleyes, and I too doubt that it does. Walleyes are more commonly associated with lower Birch. Still I found myself involuntarily reaching for the fishing rod that I didn't have with me. But Mark and I left Long Hole to the lengthening shadows, climbed back on the four-wheeler, and returned to "civilization."

Another time, Mark and I rode downriver from the Cora Brown house on the south side of the river. We parked the four-wheeler at trail's end and began walking through the rhododendron thickets that flourish on Birch hillsides. Then we crawled on our hands and knees. Finally, we were flat on our stomachs, inching our way through the stuff. I worried about coming face to face with a bear, but I didn't worry too much, because Mark was in front.

After many years of wrestling with rhododendron on Birch, and elsewhere, I have become convinced that this shrub that produces the state flower has a mind that is capable of reasoning, and that it doesn't want to be walked, crawled, or bellied through, and will reach out and take hold of anyone who is foolish enough to try. When I deer hunted on Otter Creek in Randolph and Tucker Counties, I detoured around a dense growth of rhododendron at the head of Devil's Gulch for a simple reason: I couldn't get through it.

I mentioned the belligerence of rhododendron to Mark, and he looked at me curiously for the second time that summer.

But he understands that rhododendron is formidable. He told me about three fishermen who were camped on Little Birch River. They became confused in the dense stands of rhododendron, and wound up on main Birch. They followed it upstream, thinking they were following Little Birch back to their campsite. Eventually they came to the Cora Brown house, tired and totally lost. I thought about William Strange of Strange Creek legend, who became confused as to which was Holly River and which was Elk River (see "William Strange"), and it cost him his life.

I also thought how fortunate we were to live in an area where, ten minutes from Mark's home, we could be in a virtual wilderness. We saw nobody else, nor did we hear anybody else, an experience that could be repeated almost anywhere on the final seventeen miles of Birch. The National Park Service had it right about the isolation.

Our destinations that day were Slabcamp and Coalbed Runs, two tributaries of Birch which drain down from Keener's Ridge.

We came first to Slabcamp, which approaches Birch through a large bottom where Ancel Brown, his wife, Sarah Frame Brown, and their daughter, Lela, lived in the 1930s. The remains of an old cellar, dug into the bank, are still there, as are chimney stones from a fireplace. The house preceded the Browns; who built it is unknown.

A path ran from the mouth of Slabcamp upriver to the Cora

Brown house. Remains of the path are still visible in places. There was also a wagon road on the other side of the river that was used when the river was low enough to cross.

Ancel Brown was a timberman, and he was quite adept at handling his end of a crosscut saw. Crosscuts were long, flexible saw blades with short handles on each end. Two men worked in rhythm (hopefully) to cut trees. Timbermen who used them called them "misery whips." Crosscuts came along about 1870, replacing axes. Without them, the big logging era of 1880-1920 probably wouldn't have happened. The present-day chainsaw didn't come into use in West Virginia until around 1950.

Bailey Walker married Lela Brown, and they lived with Ancel and Sarah Brown at the mouth of Slabcamp for about three years. The marriage ceremony was performed by Willie Lewis (see "The Doctor and the Preacher").

Slabcamp Run forks about a half mile above the river. One fork heads at the Strickland Low Gap near where John Beam lives, and the other fork heads near where Bailey Walker once lived. There was a sawmill at the forks prior to 1920 (a 1917 map lists the name of the tributary as Slabcamp Run). Presumably someone, maybe the sawmill operator, built a crude slab camp there.

A short distance downriver from the mouth of Slabcamp, a splash dam was built in the early 1900s by the Birch River Boom and Lumber Company to float logs to Glendon (see "The Big Timber Era"). A wall of logs was built across the river, and a sluice gate was raised to release water. But Warder Dean wrote that the dam was a failure because the water rushed out too fast and the logs were left behind, either lodged on rocks or washed onto the river bank. The dam was built in a shoal, and timbers can still be seen on the riverbed when the water is low enough, as it was on the day that Mark and I visited the site. The dam washed away, probably in the 1918 flood that claimed a garden and footbridge at the Cora Brown house (see "Floods of Birch").

Below Slabcamp and the splash dam is Coalbed Run, which heads near the Walker Cemetery. Doy Barnette and his wife, Dicey Burroughs Barnette, lived there in the 1930s. Port and Rachel Browning and their children lived farther up Coalbed from around 1930 to 1940 in the former Cornelius Baughman house. Okey Browning of Dille recalls walking to Doy Barnette's to listen to the Grand Old Opry and Joe Louis boxing matches (Louis, the "Brown Bomber from Detroit," was boxing's dominant figure in the 1930s and 1940s, and the radio broadcasts of his fights always brought neighbors together wherever a radio was located).

The Barnette house burned many years ago. James Searfoss, who grew up on Keener's Ridge and now lives near Centralia, built a camp at the mouth of Coalbed in the 1960s. Remains of his camp are still visible.

The origin of the name Coalbed Run is uncertain. George Beam's grandmother, Vina Mollohan, said that a large beech tree uprooted, turning up coalbucket-size lumps of coal. Certainly, there is coal on Coalbed. "You could see coal seams all along the run from our house down to the river," said Okey Browning.

Coalbed Run appears on a 1917 West Virginia Geological Survey map, as do Slabcamp and Feedtrough Runs.

Although upper Birch was logged extensively by companies using locomotives, it is doubtful if locomotives ever ran along Birch below the Cora Brown house. But there was a logging railroad of sorts. Ernest Tinnel, the Birch Village storekeeper, logged below Cora Brown's on the left descending side of the river in the late 1920s and early 1930s. He put down steel rails as his logging operation advanced, and logs were hauled out on a stripped-down railroad car that was pulled by a Fordson (a joint product of the Ford and Ferguson companies) tractor driven by George Beam's uncle, Ira Mollohan.

On frosty mornings, salt was sprinkled on the rails to melt the frost or ice. Ira Mollohan told the story that on one particularly cold morning, one of Emil Brown's buck sheep began licking the salt, and its tongue stuck to the rail, and the unfortunate animal had to be pulled loose. Well, the subsequent telling of that story probably enlivened many a cold morning.

The sawdust pile from Tinnel's mill in the bottom below the Cora Brown house was visible for many years, and more than one generation of local kids made use of it as a marvelous playhouse. Mark Murphy, his brother, Mike, and Tim Wood, who also lived nearby, liked to tunnel into the sawdust, but their parents weren't as enamored of the idea. One day, the boys turned up missing, and the tunnel had fallen in. Junior Murphy and Alden Wood dug frantically into the collapsed sawdust, all the while calling for the boys. They eventually answered from the woods, where they had gone to explore, but had delayed answering until they were back within permissible territory.

Mike Murphy's parents gave him a tricycle when they were living at the Cora Brown house. It was delivered by the mailman, Pat Brown (not Cora Brown's husband). Mike thought for years that the tricycle had been a gift from the mailman, and not his parents, and they couldn't convince him otherwise. Mike is now a project manager for Verizon in Arlington, Virginia, and lives in Clarksburg, Maryland.

Mark Murphy, a musician, singer, and songwriter, wrote a song about a stone fence downstream from the Cora Brown house that was built to enclose an orchard. In a sense, the song represents all the early homesteads along Birch River, most of which are now only memories:

In '34 my Grandpa bought the land
And cleared the brush and timber off by hand,
Then gathered up each stone to mark the line
And built a fence to stand the test of time.

Where the work was hard but the victory won
With the satisfaction of a job well done,
The pace was slow but the way was sure
Like a fence of stone made to endure.

We're living in a world that moves so fast
Where there's no time to make things built to last,
But pointing to the error of our way
Are the old stone fences built in yesterday.

If I could turn back time I'd never leave
The way of life an old man showed to me,
But trees are growing in the pasture field
They cover up the fence that Grandpa built.

Henshelwood Eddy below the Cora Brown bridge

Mountain laurel in bloom at the Jack Johnston camp

Seven

Little Birch

From Cat Heaven to Crites Mountain

L ittle Birch River begins on Hickory Flats west of Erbacon in the pure heartland of West Virginia. It is spawned in the rugged hills of Webster County, the home of wood-choppers and rattlesnakes. Just a few miles north of Erbacon lies Centralia, the closest named place on the map to the geographical center of the state.

Erbacon itself, a Webster County railroad village, is located on Laurel Creek of Elk River. The Erbacon Road in that vicinity is on the divide between the two drainages.

The area once had a reputation, well deserved, some longtime residents say, for making and drinking moonshine, dancing, and fighting; the latter two went together, because the dances usually ended in fights. The story is told that at one dance a local resident rode his horse onto the dance floor, and wouldn't leave. This, of course, precipitated another fight.

Little Birch flows northwest into Braxton County, and enters Birch River slightly over three miles above Herold where its mouth defines a corner of Braxton and Nicholas Counties. At 19.4 miles in length, it is by far the largest of Birch's forty one named tributaries.

Its drainage touches on place names that, like the origins of Little Birch itself, are pure West Virginia: Big and Little Coon Den Hollows, Painter Fork, the Lyda Wilson Ridge, Pilot Knob, Carpenter Fork, Ramp

Run, Seng Run, Crites Mountain, Tesla, Polemic Run, and Road Run.

Tesla, a community in Braxton County, was inexplicably named for Nikola Tesla, who was born in 1856 in Croatia, came to the United States in 1884, and invented, among other things, alternating current. That he was ever in Tesla, or ever heard of it, is highly doubtful. But in 1898 the U.S. Postal Service named the Tesla Post Office for him.

It is also highly doubtful whether Nikola Tesla ever heard of Two Lick and Cat Heaven in the community that is named for him. Unfortunately, the origins of these colorful names have been lost to antiquity, although there are two popular versions of the naming of Cat Heaven. One is that a woman who owned many cats once lived there. The other is that a family of bobcats once denned at the head of the hollow. The latter version was told to me by Charley Facemire, who has lived at the mouth of Cat Heaven Hollow for fifty six years.

- - -

As with any river, pinpointing the precise spot where Little Birch begins requires some geographical flexibility. I went to the head of Little Birch one warm day in early May of 2001 in the company of Vaughn Davis, the rattlesnake man, who lives on the Mill Creek Road. Vaughn's passion is hunting the timber rattler (see "Powell's Mountain"). He has caught as many as eight in one afternoon, and hundreds in his lifetime, and has returned virtually all of them to the wild.

We are familiar with deer crossings, but on the Lyda Wilson Ridge (pronounced locally as "the Lyd Wilson Ridge") heading east toward Hickory Flats is a rattlesnake crossing. Vaughn Davis has seen many of them slithering back and forth across the road there. I envisioned a highway sign being placed at the crossing, with the symbol on it of a coiled rattler with its tail whirring.

According to Goldie Carpenter Rose, who grew up on Hickory Flats, Lyda Greene Wilson was a long ago resident of the area that bears her name. Three years ago, Louie Martin, the former standout Little League pitcher (see "Birch Village"), was scouting for turkeys on Lyd Wilson Ridge and came across a coiled yellow rattler that was as thick as his pitching arm.

They tell the story about a resident of Hickory Flats who burned his woodshed and all the firewood in it because a rattler had taken refuge under the shed. Whether the fire consumed the snake is unknown.

- - -

The western end of the road to Hickory Flats is called the Mill Creek Road. A short distance from the start of the road on old U.S. 19 is a Smiley Face sculpted into a hillside meadow by brothers Sherman and Dale Dodrill that brings smiles to the faces of passers-by. The face is two hundred feet in diameter, its eyes measure twenty feet, and its mouth is one hundred feet long. The brothers created it with a farm tractor and liberal use of fertilizer.

Smiley face sculpted into a Little Birch hillside

East of the Smiley Face is the Rose Hill Methodist Church, and, just beyond the church, a splendid view of the Skyles Creek drainage to the south; Skyles Creek is a tributary of Birch River, and was the centerpiece of Eakin Lumber Company's logging empire in 1912-1927 (see "Shay It Isn't So").

The area was also logged in the early 1900s by Henry Waggy and his son, William. The Waggys' narrow gauge railroad, or at least a spur line of it, ran past where Esker Cutlip now lives, and the locomotive took on water at the head of Henry Long Hollow on Cutlip's farm.

Esker Cutlip is a man in the middle. His farm is bisected by the Nicholas and Braxton County line; he lives in Braxton, but he can throw a rock across the road in front of his home, and it will land in Nicholas.

Although Henry and William Waggy had sawmills at more than one location, the one most familiar to oldtime residents stood at the forks of the Mill Creek Road and the road that goes over Crites Mountain to Carpenter Fork.

The Waggy Post Office was located nearby, and was named for William Waggy, who was a delegate to the Republican National Convention in 1928. One of the postmasters was Homer Wines, the grandfather of Sebert Wines, who lives beside the Rose Hill Church. A horseback mail route went from Waggy to Skyles, and from there to Boggs and Cowen.

Another oldtime horse and wagon route in the area was the Greenbrier and Harrison Trail, which went north to Bays from the Mill Creek Road.

- - -

Hickory Flats begins in the vicinity of Pilot Knob, a 2,200-foot prominence in the area and the highest elevation in the Little Birch drainage. Two hollows near the Pilot Knob Road are believed to be the official start of Little Birch. They drain off what are known locally as the Clinton Humphreys and Rex Holcomb places, both named for long ago residents.

Hickory Flats School, one of the hundreds of one-room schools that once dotted the hills of West Virginia, was located east of Pilot Knob Road. Goldie Carpenter Rose went to school there. Brooks Run School, another institution of learning in the area, was located farther east on Spring Ridge.

The Brooks Run name is quite familiar nowadays: Brooks Run Coal Company has a large underground complex on Missouri Run near Erbacon, where Eakin Lumber Company logging trains once huffed and puffed their way over the mountain from Skyles to Erbacon.

Vaughn Davis is somewhat familiar with the Hickory Flats country. He coon hunted there and would become thoroughly lost, but he would simply go wherever the dogs went, and they always came out somewhere. Raccoons are well represented on the head of Little Birch: two hollows branching off Painter Fork are called Big Coon Den and Little Coon Den.

Delbert Perrine, a retired coal miner, lives at the eastern end of Hickory Flats where it becomes Spring Ridge Road. From his house you can go almost anywhere by following Spring Ridge: Wolf Creek, Bakers Run, Bug Ridge, or wherever your fancy leads you. The road to Erbacon also drops off to Missouri Run near his home.

- - -

Crites Mountain is located in Braxton County on the Carpenter Fork drainage, and was named for John Crites and his descendants. John Crites came to Braxton County in the mid 1800s from Upshur County. He and his wife, Margaret Skidmore Crites, were living in the Crites Mountain area at the time of the 1850 census, as were their eleven children.

The progenitor of the Crites's in central West Virginia is believed to be Phillip Kreutz, who came to Hardy County from Germany. His surname was pronounced Crites, and that is the way later generations spelled it.

John Crites' oldest son was Riley Crites, who was born in 1826. The tombstone at the Crites Mountain Cemetery for Riley Crites and his wife, Mahala, was put up long after their deaths, and there are no dates on it. Many of the graves are marked by field stones with no inscriptions, but on one is etched the initials "N.C.," which is probably Naham Crites, one of the sons of Riley and Mahala. He was called "Little Naham" to distinguish him from Riley Crites' brother, also named Naham.

The date of John Crites' death isn't known, but he was not living at the time of the 1880 census. Where he is buried isn't certain either, although Carlin Clifton, who lives about halfway up the mountain, has heard over the years that John Crites is buried in a cemetery in the woods on Clifton's farm. I went there in May of 2001 with Clifton. The cemetery is a large one, with perhaps three dozen graves marked by field rock with no inscriptions. The large number of graves is mute testimony to the fact that many more people lived on Crites Mountain in the eighteenth and nineteenth centuries than is the case today.

We walked to a spot in the upper left corner where field stones and sunken graves indicate two burial sites. One of those graves may be that of John Crites, and, if so, the other would probably be his wife, Margaret Skidmore Crites.

But there is a grave in the Crites Mountain Cemetery with the name John etched into a field stone marker. I could not decipher what was written underneath it. The possibility exists, of course, that this is the grave of John Crites.

- - -

Another prominent family name on Crites Mountain is Sartin. Their presence began in 1901 when Robert and Asenath Nesselrotte Sartin came to West Virginia from Missouri. They first lived in Jackson County, then lived near Sutton, and finally settled on Crites Mountain.

Robert and Asenath Sartin raised nine children, two of whom are still living: Mae Sartin Burge of Little Birch, and Juanita Sartin Facemire of Richwood. A brother, George Sartin, was pictured in the Braxton Democrat in 1973 above the headline: "Mother Sartin's Christmas Gift" (he was born on Christmas day). Some accounts say that George Sartin wore a waist-length beard in his later days, but in the newspaper photo his beard was of only average length. George Sartin's three brothers, Alva, Junior, and Marion, all served in World War II.

George Sartin died in 1975, and he and his wife, Myrtle Wines Sartin, are buried at the Crites Mountain Cemetery, as are Alva and Marion Sartin, and Robert and Asenath Sartin. Robert Sartin died in 1941, and his wife died in 1961.

There are still Sartins living on Crites Mountain. There were no Crites' living on the mountain at the time of this writing, but many Crites' still live in the general area.

The one-room Crites Mountain School, located in a low gap near the cemetery, closed in 1968. Its last teacher was Strosie Rose, who lives on Carpenter Fork.

- - -

The village of Little Birch is located in Braxton County about half-way between the headwaters and mouth of the stream. In Civil War days, Little Birch was on the route of the historic Weston to Gauley Bridge Turn-pike, and in places the turnpike is still quite visible where it crosses Little Birch Mountain.

I went there in July of 2000 with Harold Long, the founder and president of Product Distributors of Little Birch, and a former member of the West Virginia Legislature who was instrumental in getting Birch River included in the State Natural Streams Preservation Act. (He was killed on August 12, 2000, in a plane crash in Canaan Valley).

We climbed up a steep hill to the roadway, which is so well defined where it runs through the woods that I imagined I could still hear the sounds of men, horses, and wagons as they toiled their way uphill. The turnpike was the route of troop movement for Union forces in central West Virginia in 1861 prior to the battle of Carnifex Ferry.

A lithograph at the State Archives in Charleston entitled "Cross-ing Little Birch River" shows massed ranks of troops in the river, or begin-ning their climb up what is probably Little Birch Mountain. The artist was J.N. Roesler, a Union soldier.

David Jackson, great grandfather of Frank Johnston (see "Long Run"), owned a mill and boarding house where the turnpike crossed Little Birch, and the lithograph shows a log building on the south side of the crossing.

He was one of the early settlers in Little Birch, and the name Jack-son remains prominent in the area to this day. Little Birch School has had only two secretaries in its thirty six years of existence in the present build-ing: Angie Jackson, the current one, and her predecessor, Oleta Jackson.

Amos Jackson and his wife, Dottie Snyder Jackson, have lived on Little Birch below the village for over fifty years. Amos Jackson's first school was, appropriately, the Jackson School, located near the intersection of Polemic and Road Runs. His wife attended Laurel Run School, which, although vacant, still stands.

The Windy Run School, located on the Little Birch drainage, is one of the few remaining well preserved one room school buildings in central West Virginia, and is listed on the National Register of Historic Places.

The tiny, white painted school stands proudly at its original site on the Tesla Road just off U.S. 19. It was built in 1889 by a local builder, Jacob Huffman, and since its closing in 1963 has been remarkably preserved by the Windy Run Historical Association as a nostalgic example of the now almost extinct nineteenth century country schoolhouse.

The large single room with attached pump shed is very much like it was when the last classes were held there. Its furnishings include desks of various sizes, a table with small, cane-bottomed chairs, a blackboard, and framed pictures. And of course a pot-bellied stove stands in the middle of the room.

The historical group was formed in 1995 to maintain the school and its surroundings. The building has been painted, a new split rain fence surrounds the school yard, and the 1925 roof has been replaced.

A Windy Run homecoming has been held every Labor Day Sunday since 1948.

- - -

Upstream of the mouth of Little Birch, Polemic Run enters the river from the south side, and Road Run enters the same place from the north side. Oley Gregory, the grandfather of Jack Coffman (see "Birch Village"), carried the mail on foot from Polemic Run over Bear Run to Canfield, a distance of about five miles. The post office was located about a mile above the mouth of Polemic.

"He told me he didn't mind the walking, except at catalog time [the Sears Roebuck and Montgomery Ward catalogues were large and heavy]," Jack Coffman recalled. "He never delivered them all in the same day."

One time Oley Gregory grew weary of toting heavy parts that Jim Dunn of Bear Run had ordered for his mowing machine. "I think," Gregory grumbled, "he ordered the whole damn mowing machine."

The Polemic Post Office was established in 1916 and the first postmaster was Alpha Messenger, followed by James Cummings. The post office was discontinued in 1948.

There is an Indian mound located on Polemic Run near the home of Burl Westfall. He estimates that it is sixty to seventy feet in diameter, although not very high.

- - -

Below the mouth of Little Birch, the Bob Given Hollow comes into Birch River on the south side. It begins near Herold, probably close to the former Cleveland School (see "Herold and Wolfpen").

There is no record of where Bob Given lived, but he was one of the early settlers in the area. The deed to an 1868 land purchase by S. Clark Dean mentions that the four hundred acre property crossed "the Robert Given Run." S. Clark Dean was the first settler in Herold (see "Herold and Wolfpen"), and built a grist mill there.

A 1946 deed for the Phillip Gibson farm near Herold mentions "the Robert Given Hollow." Most likely, Bob Given lived either at the head of the hollow near Herold, or at the mouth.

Hardesty's History of Braxton County mentions a Robert Givens who settled at Sutton in 1796, and also mentions a Robert Givens who fought for the South in the Civil War in the 19th Virginia Cavalry as a volunteer from Braxton County. He could have been the son of the early settler, and perhaps the namesake of the Bob Given Hollow.

- - -

A Birch River landmark is the George Hoylman camp below the Bob Given Hollow. George Hoylman, a doctor at Gassaway who died in 1992, built the camp of river rocks on the site of the Simeon Dean house (see "The Big Timber Era"). He also built a five-hole golf course in the isolated river bottom, which in its time was a neighborhood conversation piece, and a challenging little layout. A slice would put you in the woods; a hook would put you in the river.

The camp was headquarters for Boy Scout activities in Braxton County for many years, and of course the scouts canoed, fished, camped, and swam in Birch River. Tom Uldrich of Frametown recalls the canoe trips: "Sometimes we'd go all the way from the Cora Brown Bridge to the mouth of the river [a distance of seventeen miles]. It was easy if there was a good water flow; if not, it was hard work."

He remembers one trip that included a flotilla of eight canoes, a stopover at the Blue Hole for swimming ("the boys liked the Blue Hole best"), and an overnight campout below the mouth of Diatter Run.

Uldrich was one of the scout leaders. Others were Bill Carr of Chapel, Page Singleton of Mill Creek, Fred James of Mill Creek, John Gawthrop of Gassaway, Jack Phillips of Gassaway, Loran Kniceley of Flatwoods, Richard Gibson of Flatwoods, Rodney Hickman of Sutton, and the late Harry Underwood of Frametown.

Doug Given, now a doctor at Gassaway (see "Leatherwood Country"), was one of the scouts, as was Ed Given, publisher of *The Braxton Citizens' News*.

Loran Kniceley (Kniceley's Insurance Agency) said that the outings at the Hoylman camp were not just summertime fun and games. "That was also where we held our winter camporees," he pointed out.

Another of George Hoylman's legacies is that he and his wife, Alta, who still lives in Gassaway, were strong supporters of Birch River's inclusion in the State Natural Streams Preservation Act.

- - -

Below the Hoylman camp, Birch begins the first of several large loops that are prominent geographical features of the lower part of the river.

The loop begins at the Bill Johnson Campground, where the "Jumping Rock" is located. The rock gradually rises to a peak from which countless swimmers have sailed off into the waters of Birch.

Farther downriver in the middle of the loop is the Wood Eddy, named for Tom Wood, who built a house there prior to 1900. His son, Wetzel, and grandson, Ray, also lived there in later years. Ray Wood caught a twenty nine inch walleye in the eddy in the 1940s. Ray's wife, Freda, has lived on the river since their marriage in 1934.

~ Eight ~

Long Run

All That Glitters Isn't Gold

James Long was seven years old when his father, Jacob, came from Pocahontas County and settled on Elk River across from the mouth of Little Buffalo Creek about 1810. Little Buffalo comes into Elk between Gassaway and Sutton.

The son later purchased land, and probably lived, on the head of an unnamed tributary of Birch River that came to be called Long Run.

A sliver of doubt as to exactly where he lived, however, arises from an 1860 deed when John Garee obtained title to five hundred and sixty one acres on Long Run, Coon Creek, and Buffalo Creek. The property description includes this line: "Being the same tract of land on which James Long formerly resided, and which belonged to him." Thus Long could have lived on any of the three watersheds.

But they are all closely connected, and if he didn't actually live on Long Run, he certainly owned land there, as well as quite a few other places. He bought and sold properties like kids of a later era traded marbles.

He received land grants totaling several hundred acres, and purchased more than that. His major transaction came on October 27, 1858, when he bought 1,504 acres "on Birch waters." Long Run is the only stream in the immediate area that drains into Birch, but perhaps some of the purchase spilled over elsewhere into the Birch drainage.

In any event, less than a month later, on November 24, 1858, he and his wife, Nancy, conveyed this land and several hundred additional acres to one of their sons, Felix, with the stipulation that he take care of his parents "in a good and comfortable manner."

James Long died in 1871 at age sixty eight, most likely as the namesake of Birch River's sixth largest tributary. He is probably buried in one of the graves marked only by field stones in the Long Cemetery on a knoll above U.S. 19 and the Herold Road. One of his sons, Asa, who died in 1905, is buried there, thus increasing the likelihood that his father is buried there as well.

Asa was the father of Dave Long, who lived on the east side of the present U.S. 19-Herold Road intersection. Dave was a beekeeper of considerable renown who never wore a veil, but he may have been better known for "the Dave Long Hill," which stalled many a motorist in pre-pavement days. He attended church at Long Run, and drove there in a Model T Ford with the gas pedal rigged to the steering wheel. He and his wife, Fannie, operated the switchboard for the local country telephone system of their time. He died in 1957 at age eighty seven, and is buried near his father in the Long Cemetery.

The 1860 land transaction by John Garee began a Garee presence on the head of Long Run that continued for one hundred and thirty five years. His son, also named John, lived there, as did his grandson, Ward Garee.

Their legacy continues with the Garee Low Gap, which lies at the intersection of the Herold Road and U.S. 19. I know it, as others do, as the fog capital of the world; the vapory stuff settles there as if it had nowhere else to go.

I've often thought that a sonnet should be written about the Garee Low Gap, and I promise to write one before this chapter ends. In addition to the fog, the road leading to the low gap from the Herold side has reduced many a driver to tears. In the old days it was mirey mud. "If you can make it up the Garee Low Gap hill," so the saying went, "you'll probably make it the rest of the way to wherever you're going." One of the low gap legends is that Byrne Dunn was driving a wagon and team of horses down the hill on the west side, hauling groceries to the country stores at Canfield and Herold, and his wagon bogged down in the mud and not even the horses could pull it out.

Nowadays the threat is snow and ice, assuming you're unfortunate enough to arrive ahead of the Department of Highways salt truck; a curve near the top of the hill makes it difficult if not impossible to maintain momentum.

The sonnet is beginning to form in my mind.

The low gap has been around since the formation of the earth, probably, but the earliest reference to it that I could find was in the 1860 deed. It says that "one acre near the low gap is excepted" (perhaps it was considered too foggy for human habitation, or more likely it was for the Long Cemetery).

The Garee Low Gap

The deed doesn't call it the Garee Low Gap, but that obviously sprang up soon afterwards. The original John Garee is believed to have lived on both the east and west sides of the low gap, as perhaps did his son, a farmer and schoolteacher, who in his later years lived on the west side on a flat above what is called "the Ward Garee fish pond." The pond has become filled in over the years.

Ward Garee, the son of the younger John, continued the Garee presence at the head of Long Run in a very visible way. He was born in 1893, and, probably upon marriage to Zela Baughman, moved across the Herold Road into a two-story house on the hill that he ordered pre-cut from Sears Roebuck. His family believes this occurred around World War I. It was the first pre-cut house in the community, and has been a conversation piece and landmark ever since.

Ward Garee was a farmer, mailman, and school bus driver. One of my memories of growing up at Herold was his car, which he drove on the mail run between Sutton and Herold. It was the longest and biggest car I'd ever seen. His son, Ward Jr., believes it was a Dodge, but it could have been a DeSoto, which also made a long sedan.

Ward Garee was a voracious reader. In later years, he and his wife moved to Sutton, and Patty Long, librarian at the Sutton Public Library, told me that his name appeared on a large number of books that he had signed out.

Ward Garee's sons had a talent for athletics. Ward Jr. and his brother, John, played basketball at Sutton High School, and another brother, Dale, was an outstanding baseball player in the Marines both prior to and during World War II.

In his 1987 book, *An Appalachian Boyhood*, Canfield native Gerald Dunn wrote this: "The best baseball players in Canfield were the Garee boys, Dale, Murrel, and John. Dale was an excellent pitcher with a hopping fast ball, and a good assortment of curves. All of us thought that he could have made the big leagues if he had had the chance. Murrel and John were good in the field, and often hit for extra bases.

"It was hard to find a field large enough for baseball in our area of Braxton County. Fortunately for us, Ward Garee had three bottom fields large enough to play on, and he always donated one for our use.

"The field we commonly used was fine in left and right field, but in center field the land started to rise about fifty feet behind second base [the sloping ground in front of the Garee house, which is now owned by Tim Tanner]."

Ward Garee was manager of the Canfield team when his sons played. Gerald told about a game they played at Sutton when Ward was managing:

"A brother of one of the Sutton players was umpiring, and we felt that he was cheating us. After a few innings of this, Mr. Garee said to us: 'Get your equipment, boys, we're going home.' By this time, he had a truck to haul us to games, so we loaded up and left in the middle of the game."

Dale Garee, the outstanding pitcher, was killed in an automobile accident in California in 1944 soon after returning from Guadalcanal in World War II, and was brought home to the family cemetery for burial.

John Garee served in the Air Force in World War II, and flew fifty missions in Liberator bombers over Germany. After the war he became a game warden in Braxton County, attended West Virginia University, and then reenlisted in the Air Force. He served with the occupation forces in Japan, and also served in Korea. He was one of the first enlisted men to attain the new rank of chief master sergeant. He died at the age of thirty nine. His wife, Naomi Cogar Garee, the daughter of Cecil and Clara Rose Cogar of Gassaway, lives in Ilion, New York.

Ward Jr. saw service in the Korean War and rose to the rank of lieutenant colonel before retiring from the military in 1972. He later worked for the Pennsylvania state government, and now lives in Pittsburgh. A brother, David, lives in Herkimer, New York. He was in the military also, and is retired from the Navy Reserve. A sister, Veda Garee Canfield, lives in Tucson, Arizona.

Several generations of Garees are buried in the family cemetery on the ridge on the south side of the Herold Road. The ridge is broad and the cemetery is virtually level. The graves are laid out neatly, giving it a dignified look. White oaks and shagbark hickories grow nearby. The cemetery overlooks the Garee Low Gap and the intersection of U.S. 19 and the Herold Road.

Among the graves are those of the two John Garees and their wives, and Ward ·Sr. and Zela Garee. The elder John Garee died in 1884; his son died in 1903. Ward Garee died in 1981, and his wife died in 1988. Zela Baughman Garee was the daughter of Cornelius Baughman (see "Skyles and Boggs").

- - -

The present owners of the Garee house are Tim and Christina Tanner. They live there with their daughters, Elizabeth and Laura. They bought the house in 1995 and renovated it, but, for the sake of historical authenticity, retained its original shape. It had been vacant for many years, and had gradually become hidden by pine trees, which have since been cut.

Tim made an interesting historical discovery during the inside renovation of the house. On the lumber is stamped these words: "Garee. Bison, WV." Bison was the name of the B & O railroad siding on Elk River at the mouth of Big Buffalo Creek. The lumber (southern cypress) was probably hauled from there to the house site by wagon.

- - -

The centerpiece of Long Run is Canfield, which was established in 1888 and named for its first postmaster, Benjamin T. Canfield. It sits at the junction of the Herold Road and Bear Run Road. Holly Fork, a small tributary, enters Long Run at the store. When Connie Furbee (see "Leatherwood Country") reopened the former Dunn Grocery at Canfield in 1997, she named it the Birch River Junction. The Birch River part of the name came from Connie's fond memories of swimming in Birch as a child.

There are no Canfields still living in Canfield. The last one was George Canfield, who moved to Sutton in 1981. George was a cousin of Harry Canfield, who died in 1982 at age ninety at the home of a daughter-in-law in South Charleston, and is buried in the Canfield Cemetery on the Carsel Hamrick farm. Harry farmed and worked for the Department of Highways; in earlier days he would walk from his home to Elk River at the mouth of Big Buffalo Creek, and boat across the river to the DOH garage.

Benjamin T. Canfield, the community's first postmaster, is also buried at the Canfield family cemetery. He died in 1908 at age seventy seven.

If Canfield is the centerpiece of Long Run, then Dunn Grocery was the centerpiece of Canfield for eighty eight years. It was opened in 1904 by Martin Dunn and sons James, Lewis, Dennis, and Byrne, and was called Dunn Brothers Grocery. In 1930 it became Dunn & Hines Grocery under the ownership of Byrne Dunn and his brother-in-law, Will Hines, who died in 1937. When Byrne Dunn retired in 1952, his son, Paul, became the owner, changed the name to simply Dunn Grocery, and ran it until his retirement in 1992.

In the last year, the store's chief function seemed to be as a gathering place for a local "Liar's Club," whose members sat around the pot-bellied stove to tell everything but the truth. Charter members were Carsel Hamrick, Fred Jarvis, Joe Pettit, Don Justus, Wesley Davis, Junior Hoard, and myself, and I'm proud of having belonged to an organization where the truth was irrelevant. But somebody had to keep the stove going, and we elected Paul on the basis of experience. In forty years he had fed seven hundred and twenty buckets of coal into the stove a year, for a total of twenty eight thousand eight hundred bucketfuls, which translates to one hundred and sixty tons.

Canfield and Dunns have become synonymous over the years. Someone once told Byrne Dunn that "Dunns and broomsedge are taking over the country." The progenitor of the Dunns at Canfield was J. Martin Dunn, who came there in the late 1860s from Monroe County and settled

Birch River Junction store at Canfield

in a hollow on the Bear Run Road near Canfield. He died in 1908 and is buried at the Dunn Cemetery on Bear Run, as are twenty six other Dunns in three neat rows.

At one time, there were eight Dunns on the roster of the local baseball team: Bill Dunn and his brothers Glen and Gordon, and Paul's brothers Gerald, Eugene, Howard, Lester, and Ralph (in spring 2001, Ralph and others in his 1951 class at the West Virginia University College of Law were honored by the West Virginia Bar Association on their 50th anniversary in the practice of law).

Paul Dunn was the last postmaster in the sixty five year history of post offices at Canfield, and his reign was brief. He became postmaster in 1952 and the post office was closed in 1953 when the Eisenhower administration launched a D-Day assault on fourth class post offices.

- - -

The Dunn Grocery wasn't the only game in town during the 1930s and 1940s. Lee Johnston also had a store at Canfield, and was postmaster for a time. He was a schoolteacher as well as storekeeper; grandson Frank, who lives in Staunton, Virginia, obtained a student roster kept by his grandfather when he taught at Little Birch School (later called Jackson School) in 1888. Renaming the school was a case of surrendering to the inevitable: twelve of the twenty six students listed on the roster were Jacksons.

One day a veterinarian from the State Department of Agriculture came to Lee's store to check on his cattle (a disease was going around). The vet was obviously a man of sensibilities, because at some point in the discussion he said he never brought up politics or religion while on the job, to which Lee replied, "By my soul, I'm a Democrat and a Baptist, and proud of it."

Another time a customer came into the store and wanted to buy a billfold on credit, but Lee refused. "Why," he asked with irrefutable logic, "would you need a billfold if you don't have any money to put in it?"

Lee Johnston's son, Orva, lives on the Herold Road, and, at age ninety seven, walks to church, a distance of a mile and a half; then he walks back home, waving off all offers of rides.

- - -

As did most rural communities in the early part of the twentieth century, Canfield boasted several commercial enterprises: store, grist mill, cattle scales, sawmill, and blacksmith shop. The sawmill sawed hickory into lumber and hauled it by wagon to Bison (the same railroad siding that received the Ward Garee house) for shipment to factories that made axe handles and such.

Canfield got an early leg up on school consolidation. At one time it had two schools, but in 1932 they were combined into one at the site of the present Nanny's Country Apple, owned by Betty Gibson. Her husband, John, grew up in Herold and is a member of the Braxton County Commission.

Mel Tucker was a farmer of renown in Canfield. He raised cattle, operated weighing scales that were a focal point of cattle and sheep farmers far and wide, and grew bountiful crops. In *An Appalachian Boyhood*, Gerald Dunn observed that "the Tuckers [Mel and his brother, Bill] were the best farmers in Canfield" (an accolade later won by Bill Dunn, Gerald's first cousin, who raised cattle, and had an uncanny ability to know when to cut hay so it wouldn't get rained on). Bill's wife, Bernice Dent Dunn, published two books of poetry, *Gems From Grandma's Pen*, and *Velvet Petals*.

But all that glittered at Canfield wasn't gold (a line from Shakespeare's *Merchant of Venice*, although the bard actually said, "All that glisters isn't gold)". Shakespeare tended to invent his own vocabulary, and even spelled Shakespeare many different ways.

A 1916 publication of the West Virginia Geological Survey reported: "A futile attempt was once made to mine gold from a heading driven a few feet into this ledge [Lower Freeport sandstone] in a crop exposure on the north bank of Long Run, one-fourth mile southwest of Canfield."

Frank Johnston, Orva's son, mined a rich lode of information on the "Canfield gold rush" in a 1962 conversation with Okey Jackson. The miners were Willis and Ward Beall, who lived at Locust Stump. Ward was the last to dig there in the 1930s (he was also said to have a salve that cured cancer).

Ore was hauled by wagon to the mouth of Big Buffalo Creek (Bison) and shipped by train for assaying. But there was to be no Canfield Klondike: the grade of ore was found not to be high enough to support digging and shipping.

The gold mine that didn't glitter was located across Long Run from the present Jim Pierson and Matt Gibson homes. Evidence of long-ago digging is still visible. At that time the road ran along the creek, therefore a knowledgeable prospector traveling the road may have seen the "signs" of ore that contained gold.

Across the hill on Bear Run was a lead mine. Randall Butcher's grandmother, Sally Kiger, said that early settlers chopped out huge chunks of the bluish-white metallic element with an axe and made bullets for their mountain rifles. The mine was located on property presently owned by Dale Hamrick, near the Dunn Cemetery. I went there in late February 2001, and found what I suspect, and what Dale suspects, is the mine. It is located on a knoll between two ravines that drain off the hill behind Dale's house, and clearly has the appearance of having been hand dug long ago.

- - -

A tale of gold coins was told to me by Randall Butcher. An old Indian medicine man came to John Q. Harris' house on Long Run in the 1800s, and was invited to spend the night and share the family meal. The next morning, to repay the kindness, the Indian drew a map on the ground, supposedly pointing the way to where an iron kettle containing gold coins had been buried on a drainage of Long Run. The story was that the Indians had "taken the gold from soldiers," although what soldiers, or when the heist occurred, is left to the imagination.

Randall once tramped around the area with a metal detector, and became excited at a strong signal, but it turned out to be buried barbed wire (try saying "buried barbed wire" three times rapidly; the gold coins could be found more easily).

John Q. Harris was born in 1854 and died in 1937; he and his wife, Glorvina, are buried at Middle Run Cemetery. His son, Aubrey, and Aubrey's wife, Dorothy, are also buried at Middle Run. Harris descendents still live at the homeplace on Long Run.

- - -

The Indian medicine man was kind and generous, but no more so than Ira Jackson, a stocky, hard-working, gentle man who lived on the head of Holly Fork of Long Run. He was never known to have a bad word to say about anybody or anything, and one time at the Dunn Grocery he was put to the test. The conversation had drifted around to the community drunk who had recently died, and someone challenged Ira to say something good about the fellow. "Well," Ira replied, "he was a good whistler."

Ira once spent six months making a stone chimney flu, one painstaking chip at a time with a hammer and chisel, and just when the flu was almost finished, he made a mislick and broke it. His only comment was "Oops!" or words to that effect.

He was obviously a man of resilience, and so was Hilliard Skidmore, who fought for both the North and the South in the Civil War, according to the *History of Skidmore Family* by Warren Skidmore. Hilliard moved to Canfield around 1857 and lived on Hungry Spring Run of Bear Run. In 1862 he enlisted in Company I of the 17th Virginia Cavalry, but Confederate renegades stole his cattle and all but one horse, and he joined a home guard unit that was formed for protection against the renegades. Supposedly this unit fought for the North in the October 13, 1863, Battle of Bulltown.

Hilliard Skidmore had a habit of preceding a statement with the words "tut tut." One time George Chamberlain was plowing a corn field for Hilliard with a young horse, and he didn't want to sink the plow too deep into the ground. Hilliard, who was furrowing the corn rows with a hoe, noticed this and said, "tut tut, George, you're just scratching the ground; let down on them plow handles a little." To which George replied, "Hilliard, if you'd spend more time diggin', you wouldn't be noticing how I'm doin' plowin.'"

- - -

The Long Run Baptist Church was organized in 1885 by James F. Brown and L.J. Huffman, and Brown was its first pastor. Martin Dunn, the original Dunn settler in Canfield, gave the land on which the church was built.

In a 1993 article in *Goldenseal*, William D. Creasy wrote that Brown, who was born in Birch Village in 1845, enlisted in Company A of the 14th Virginia Infantry and fought through a number of Civil War battles, including Gettysburg and Droop Mountain, and was present at Appomattox when Lee surrendered to Grant.

After the war, he and his wife, Sally, lived on Mill Creek at Birch Village, where he farmed and timbered. Creasy wrote: "Some of their choice walnut logs were floated all the way to Charleston via the Birch and Elk Rivers."

He became a minister in 1882, and continued to preach the gospel until his death in 1920. In addition to preaching, he also pulled teeth. Creasy said his record for separating tooth from gum was thirteen teeth at one sitting. Often he would seat the patient on a log in the field where he was working, and begin wielding the forceps.

Brown served two different stints as pastor of the Long Run Church for a total of twenty one years. He was also pastor of the Birch River Baptist Church (see "Birch Village") for fourteen years.

The longest-serving pastor at Long Run was James H. McLaughlin, who was called four different times for a total of twenty three years. In more than sixty years in the ministry, "Preacher Jim" baptized over 3,000 souls, conducted more than 1,500 funerals, and assisted in the ordination of fifty five ministers, and over one hundred deacons.

He was almost, but not quite, the equal of Willie Lewis (see "The Doctor and the Preacher") in reciting Bible scripture verbatim. Sometimes he'd ask those in his congregation to quote a verse of scripture, and most of the time he would quickly identify the book, chapter, and verse number.

A solidly-built man who was proud of his physical fitness, he once challenged a group of boys at Long Run Church to a foot race. This was after he had walked several miles from his home on Upper Mill Creek. "I'll bet I can beat all of you to the church steps," he said to the boys who were playing in the lower churchyard. They accepted the challenge, and "Preacher Jim" won by a wide margin.

- - -

The largest tributary of Long Run is Buck Fork, which begins near Coon Knob and enters Long Run one mile west of Canfield. When Interstate 79 travelers top out near Coon Knob and Exit 57, the grand view to the south begins on the head of Buck Fork.

Early 1900s deeds refer to this tributary as Plantation Fork; U.S. Geological Survey maps call it Buckeye Fork; and local residents call it simply Buck Fork. The present Charles Groves farm lies at the head of Buck Fork.

For seventy years, Starbucks lived on Buck Fork, although it is unlikely that the name originated with them, otherwise it would have been called Starbuck Fork, and it isn't listed that way on any documents that I came across.

The Starbuck presence is a story that had its beginning on Nantucket Island off the coast of Massachusetts. One of the seven purchasers of Nantucket Island was Edward Starbuck, who came to America from England in 1635 and died on Nantucket in 1690, a man of wealth and influence.

A great grandson, Paul Starbuck, became a whale oil dealer, and in 1720 is said to have sent the first shipment of oil from Nantucket to England. A great great grandson, Mathew Starbuck, was a crew member on Continental Navy officer John Paul ("I have not yet begun to fight") Jones' ship, the *Bonhomme Richard*; he moved to North Carolina in 1795, where a son, Benjamin, was born in 1798.

Benjamin moved to Indiana in 1830, but when his first wife died, he and his second wife came to Sutton around 1850. Two of their sons, George and David, purchased one hundred acres of land on Buck Fork on November 29, 1902, from B.F. Baughman, thus beginning the Starbuck connection on Long Run.

David Starbuck and his wife, Martha Barnett Starbuck, lived the remainder of their lives there, as, for the most part, did four of their seven children: Mary, Edna, Lydia, and Jimmy, none of whom married.

They were a familiar sight, walking single file along the Herold Road; Mary, Edna, and Lydia attended Long Run Church, and they would carry extra pairs of clean shoes and put them on before approaching the church, leaving their muddy "walking" shoes alongside the road, where they would retrieve them after church.

Every Memorial Day, they would walk eight miles to the Skidmore Cemetery in Sutton, where their parents are buried, to put freshly-picked flowers on the graves, and then walk back home.

Among the twelve Starbuck graves at the Skidmore Cemetery are those of David, who died in 1933; his wife Martha, who died in 1942; Mary, who died in 1954; Lydia, who died in 1962; Edna, who died in 1970; and Jimmy, who died in 1977.

A stone's throw from the Starbuck graves is the grave of John D. Sutton, the founder of the town of Sutton, who died in 1839.

David Starbuck's brother, George, died in Colorado Springs, Colorado, in 1927.

- - -

Long Run was hit by huge floods in 1994 and 1996. Roger and Peggy Tenney and their children took refuge in the woods when waters from the 1996 deluge circled their home near the mouth of the creek. The Tenneys are gospel singers, and they waited out the floodwaters by singing the song, *Put It In God's Hands*, which may be a good way to conclude this chapter, because the Garee Low Gap weighs heavy on my mind.

I am tormented by the anguished wails of all the drivers who have rolled in the mud, snow, ice, and fog, putting on chains, and who, perhaps, like the ill-fated captain in Whitman's poem *O Captain! My Captain!*, may not make it to the port where bells are ringing and people exulting.

But it was told to me in a vision that one car did. This vision inspired the promised sonnet, which follows:

If one foggy night, perchance
I would fall into a dreamlike trance,

I fear my fate would be to see
Cars stretching into eternity.

Dozens of drivers on bended knee,
Imploring the heavens for help, you see.

Tuckers, Stonestreets, and Dunns, galore,
Canfields, Duffields, and Dunns, some more.

Tales of gold I do not hear,
Although their words are very clear.

For none have stopped to take a nap,
All are stalled on the Garee Low Gap.

There'll be Dodges, Durants, and Duesenbergs, too,
Stutz and Pierce Arrow, though far and few.

And even an Auburn designed by Cord,
And, good lord, there in the middle a Model T Ford !

The only car of that vast array
To mount the gap by the end of the day.

Although this a sonnet may not be,
The moral here is plain to see.

Thus we learn, if truth be told,
All that glitters isn't gold.

- - -

Author's note: Peter and Elizabeth Silitch participated in creating the above "sonnet."

Scenic Birch River sign at the mouth of Long Run

Bridge over Birch above Herold

~ Nine ~

Herold and Wolfpen

Interludes On the Way to Elk

An 1895 map confirms that Herold, the "capital" of lower Birch, is very close to Bliss, which its dozen or so residents knew all along. But in this case, Bliss is a place name on the 1895 map, which shows it was located just southwest of Herold. Exactly where is unknown, as is the origin of the name.

No mystery about Herold, though. It came into being in 1891 when George A. Herold, a native of Muddlety, Nicholas County, opened a general store at the village that is located 9.7 miles above the mouth of Birch.

George A. Herold, of German ancestry, never lived at the tiny hamlet that bears his name, but he came there frequently, and usually brought a bag of candy for the local children, who called him "Uncle George."

Jim Comstock's *West Virginia Encyclopedia* says of him: "A state legislator of Webster County, was born in Nicholas County, where his parents operated a farm on Muddlety Creek. His brother, Henry, became sheriff of Nicholas County. He was reared on the farm and later became a school teacher, before engaging in business in Hookersville [near Muddlety]. Later he moved to Herold, Braxton County [doubtful], and still later moved to Webster County where he owned a huge estate. For ten years he was president of the First National Bank of Webster Springs. He served on the County Court for six years. In 1920 he was elected a member of the House of Delegates, and there introduced the so-called Eugenics bill, requiring a certificate of health before the issuance of a marriage license. He married Viola Hill, of Nicholas County, and had three children."

George A. and Viola Hill Herold lived at Cowen for many years and owned a general store there (see "Origins of Birch"). Their home, although vacant and crumbling, still stands. They continued to own property on Birch near Herold until 1923, and their heirs still own an interest in mineral rights in the area.

- - -

Polk's Directory of 1895-96 says of Herold the village: "Banking and shipping point. Mail semi-weekly. G.R. Pierson, postmaster. George A. Herold, general store. J.H. Stavis, shoemaker; S.C. Dean, flour mill.

The reference to banking is curious; never to my knowledge did Herold have a bank or anything that resembled a bank. Neither was it a shipping point, except that local trappers would bring their furs to my grandfather Louis Johnson's store for shipment.

Where the furs went is a question I never asked, although I recall my grandfather telling a story that involved New York City fur buyers. My recollection mainly involves entering the back room of the store and looking with wide-eyed fascination at the stacks of fox, mink, opossum, skunk, and muskrat pelts, and imagining that I was a mountain man of the 1800s with my winter's catch.

- - -

Louis Johnson was born on Keener's Ridge and came to Herold in 1894 to work for George A. Herold. He initially lived downstream at a place known locally as the Big Eddy, a stretch of water that includes the second largest rock in Birch (see "The Rocks"). Foundation stones from the house in the river bottom are still there.

In 1902, Louis Johnson and his wife, Isabel Young Johnson, moved to Herold proper and built a large two-story house with a full porch and white columns that was a community landmark until it was torn down in 1960. The only remnant is the cellar

Louis Johnson, circa 1900

house, which was built on hand-hewn stones in 1906. That year, Louis Johnson bought the store from George A. Herold, and ran it for approximately forty years. Also around 1906, the store was rotated to face the road. Previously it had faced downriver.

A 1905 picture that accompanies this chapter shows the store building still facing downriver. It also shows a mystery horseman, perhaps an early mailman, and a mystery "woman in white." Weeds are growing profusely along a picket fence, something that would not be allowed to happen in Herold today. Butch Gibson, a Herold native who has returned to his roots, is known as the "the mad mower" of Herold because of his insistence that everything be neatly cut, especially near his beloved horseshoe pitching grounds.

George R. Pierson, the first postmaster, served from 1891 until 1901; George S. Johnson served from 1901 until 1906; Louis Johnson served from 1906 until 1940; Carolyn Gibson Johnson served from 1940 until 1955; and Mabel Gibson served from 1955 until 1980. Service was suspended on April 23, 1982, and the post office was discontinued on December 23, 1984.

The Herold store and post office burned in 1948, and with it the small brown house where my two brothers and I were born. After that, the post office was located for a time in my grandfather's house, and later in a cinderblock building that is now Connie Duffey's garage. Connie, a native of Wayne, New Jersey, bought property at Herold in 1993, and moved there in 2001 after retiring from Wesleyan University in Middletown, Connecticut.

"It wasn't so much the house that sold me," Connie recalled. "It

The Herold horseman, circa 1905

was when I walked out on the deck and heard the river murmuring. I said to myself, 'this place has my name on it.'"

- - -

The first resident of Herold was S. Clark Dean, who was born in 1836, the year his parents, John and Elizabeth Teeter Dean, moved from Pendleton County to Braxton County. The year of S. Clark Dean's arrival in Herold is not known, but it was probably after the Civil War (he was a Confederate soldier in the 60th Virginia Infantry). One account says he was captured by Union forces near Winchester, Virginia, and spent some time in a prisoner of war camp; another account says he served throughout the war, although technically both could be true.

He built a grist mill on the river at the lower Herold bottom, and later a two-story mill near my grandfather's store that served as a garage in Model T days. The mill dam washed away in a flood in the early 1900s, and nothing remains of it today. The garage was torn down in 2001.

S. Clark Dean died in 1908 and is buried near Herold in a cemetery in the woods above Wofpen Run, as is his wife, Irena.

- - -

Another miller at Herold, according to a 1982 article by Glenville State College history professor John Hymes Jr., was J. Clark Dean, nephew of the original. Hymes wrote that he built and operated a roller mill at Herold [in the early 1900s] that was powered by a steam boiler plant and used machine-made parts to grind wheat into what was called "graham flour." He later became postmaster at Glendon at the mouth of Birch.

The last miller was Henry Baughman, grandson of Christopher Baughman, one of the early settlers on upper Birch (see "Skyles and Boggs"). Henry came to Herold in the 1920s from upper Keener's Ridge.

His mill was gasoline powered, and its broad belts, large churning wheels, and the "putt, putt, putt" of the engine intrigued me. This "last of the Mohicans" mill fell silent in the late 1940s, and the building no longer exists.

Henry Baughman fascinated me as much as his mill did. He chewed plug tobacco, and, sitting in my grandfather's store, he would carefully slice a "chaw" of the good stuff with a small black knife that I always suspected was razor sharp. He paid for the tobacco with coins from a small black purse, carefully selecting the precise amount.

His wife, Cynthia, operated the switchboard for the community telephone system from their home, and the myriad of cords were of more interest to me than NASA's control center at Houston would be today. Earlier, my grandmother was the switchboard operator. The local telephone system connected the Herold community with far away (ten miles) Sutton.

Sometimes the really momentous news was better delivered in person than by phone. When World War I ended on November 11, 1918, my grandfather walked two miles to the home of Ellet and Belle Carte on Adams Ridge to read the newspaper account of the war's ending to them. Their son, Elmer, was in combat in France.

- - -

Early mail carriers at Herold included Warder S. Dean, Floyd Johnson, Willis Keener, Charley Keener, Curt Walker, and Ward Garee (see "Long Run"). Orva Johnston carried the mail in the late 1930s and early 1940s. He lived in the house where I was born, and one of his sons, Frank, was born there as well.

The early carriers faced a daunting horseback ride to Sutton. Before a bridge was built over Birch in 1921, they forded the river above Herold. The road wound in and out of Long Run, and can still be seen coming through the woods across from Bill Dunn's house near Canfield.

Of equal rank with the mail carriers were the doctors. The first physician in Herold was Irving O'Dell, who arrived in 1900; the last was Thomas Walsh, who arrived in 1910 and returned to his native New Jersey in the mid 1920s.

Doctor Walsh lived with my grandfather and grandmother. During the flu epidemic of 1918 he rode day and night through the community on horseback, and no doubt saved many lives. In the 1920s, he "traded" his horse for a Model T Ford, which had the distinction of being the first car in Herold.

Among my memorabilia is a postcard mailed to "Dr. Thomas M. Walsh, Harold, West Va." from his brother, Jim Walsh, in Brooklyn, New York. Herold was misspelled, but it probably wasn't the first time and certainly wasn't the last. Even a Department of Highways road sign near Sutton spells it "Harold." But the card arrived at its intended destination, and in that simpler time no box number, route number, or zip code was required.

Like Norman Goad (see "The Doctor and the Preacher"), Doctor Walsh made the best of circumstances that would be unthinkable today. Once he operated on Kate Chamberlain, a Canfield resident, for a ruptured appendix. The "operating table" was the kitchen table at her home; a neighbor, Ida Dunn, supplied blankets and hot water, and the patient recovered nicely.

He was helpful in ways other than practicing medicine. Alma DeMoss of Keener's Ridge told me that when he delivered her mother, Walsie Craft, the parents hadn't yet picked a name for the new baby, so he suggested Walsie, a variation of his surname, and Walsie Craft she became.

Blair and Emma Dixon lived in Herold during the Doctor Walsh era, and when their son, James, was born in 1921, they named him James Walsh.

- - -

Louis Johnson was quite a traveler for his time, primarily because of Doctor Walsh, who invited him to his home in New Jersey for visits. From there they took trips to surrounding states and Canada. My grandfather wrote about these trips in the Braxton Democrat, for whom he was the Herold correspondent.

I have a seashell that he obtained somewhere on the New Jersey coast. A boyhood fascination for me was "listening to the sound of the ocean" when I put the shell to my ear. I'm not a traveler, but I have "visited" the ocean many times that way.

Another memento is a ticket stub to a baseball game at Yankee Stadium on April 29, 1926. The signature on the ticket is that of Jacob Ruppert, president of the Yankees (it would have been nice if Babe Ruth had personally signed it). The 1926 Yankees won the American League pennant but lost the World Series to the St. Louis Cardinals. The following year, 1927, was the benchmark year for the Yankees of the Ruth era; they won 110 regular season games, swept the Pittsburgh Pirates in the Series, and Ruth hit sixty home runs.

As a baseball fan, my grandfather ranked among the most avid in those days of listening to games on radio. The reception tended to fade it and out, but he would put his ear against the speaker so he wouldn't miss a play. He kept a scorecard, with hits, walks, runs, and other highlights carefully entered.

He attended the Chicago World's Fair in 1934, which included exhibits of the forerunners of the DC-3 and B-17 airplanes, diesel trucks, and plush railroad passenger cars.

He played the piano at home, "cording" the bass notes. A favorite family song was "Precious memories, how they linger, how they ever flood my soul; in the stillness of the midnight, precious sacred scenes unfold."

Betty Clifton Pilegge recalls going to my grandfather's house and hearing him play. "We'd sit around the piano on a summer evening, and he'd play with his arthritic fingers. One of his favorites was *The Big Rock Candy Mountain.*"

- - -

The original mail road into Herold was located on the north side of the river, and is still visible today. It was there when Herold was established in 1891, and it is mentioned in a 1917 report on coal activity by the West Virginia Geological Survey. When the river was high and could not be crossed to the store, the mail was pulled across the river on a cable.

The mail road to Herold was switched to the south side of the river in 1921 when a bridge was built about a mile east of Herold. Soon after that cars began to come on the scene, and the era of the horseback mailmen ended, just as the train had earlier replaced the Pony Express in the Old West.

But not everybody owned a car. Jennings Fast of Charleston recalls spending the summer of 1925 at the home of my maternal grandfather, Hampton Riffel, and accompanying him to Sutton and back on a wagon pulled by a team of horses. "I was asleep long before we got back," said Jennings, who was thirteen at the time.

A cousin, Carmel Johnson, worked on the original Herold bridge. He once told me about the workers going on strike because they were being paid only fifteen cents an hour. The unhappy bridge foreman

Herold in 1941. The original road can be seen across river on hillside.

walked to Sutton to consult with the Braxton County Commission, which agreed to a raise to twenty five cents, and the work resumed.

In 1993, the Department of Highways replaced the seventy two year old structure with a new bridge. Some of the original bridge's steel supports the Silitch house on Keener's Ridge. During the construction phase, it was like a throwback to old times for those of us who lived on the Herold side. To get across, we waded the river. My nephew, Rob Johnson, carried my first computer across the river that summer.

The road into Herold was rock based in the fall of 1941. Denzil Baughman, who grew up on a nearby farm, caught the school bus at Herold. He recalls watching the workers knapping rock on the little hill that leads into Herold. The rock basing was a Works Progress Administration (WPA) project. This federal program was begun in the 1930s as part of the nation's effort to climb out of the Depression. The road was hard-topped in the late 1940s or early 1950s.

- - -

At the north end of the Herold Bridge is a sign commemorating the inclusion of seventeen miles of Birch in the State Natural Streams Preservation Act by the 1975 West Virginia Legislature. It was a close call all the way. The first attempt failed in 1974, but Delegates Billy Burke and Harold Long reintroduced the bill in 1975, and it passed the House, but stalled in the Senate when efforts were made to add additional rivers.

Carl Gainer, the bill's principal supporter in the Senate, fought these efforts, and was successful on all but New River, which at that time was being studied for the Blue Ridge power project. New River's friends in the Legislature saw addition to the act as a wedge against that project.

The House refused to concur in the New River amendment, and the bill went to a conference committee. The committee released the bill, with both rivers attached, on the final day of the session.

But time ran out when the Legislature became stalemated over a dog racing issue, and the Birch bill appeared to be doomed again. However, it was given a reprieve when the lawmakers voted to extend the session by one day. Birch's chances seemingly died a second death when the lawmakers voted to consider only budget items, but a second resolution broadened the scope of the session to include bills in conference. With that, both Birch and New River sailed through.

There have been no more streams added in twenty six years. The act still includes only Greenbrier River from Knapps Creek to its mouth, Anthony Creek from its headwaters to its mouth, all of Cranberry River, Birch from the Cora Brown Bridge to its mouth, and New River from its confluence with Greenbrier River to its confluence with Gauley River.

The act preserves these segments of streams in their free-flowing condition, meaning without impoundments or other modifications or diversions.

Billy Burke, who lives at Sand Fork, Gilmer County, and works for the U.S. Department of Agriculture, recalls that opposition on upper Birch stymied the bill in 1974. He suggested a compromise: include only the final seventeen miles. This gave the bill the impetus it needed to pass. The seventeen mile segment includes four miles in Nicholas County and thirteen miles in Braxton County.

Harold Long, who died in a plane crash in Canaan Valley in August of 2000, confirmed to me just weeks prior to his death that there was considerable opposition on upper Birch. He also recalled that the late Sarah Neal, delegate from Greenbrier County, was helpful in getting the compromise bill passed.

Carl Gainer, who lives in Richwood, played the key role in the Senate as chairman of the Natural Resources Committee and as a member of the conference committee that took up the bill in the final hours of the regular session.

In August of 1975, the Herold Homemakers Club erected a sign that commemorates the addition of Birch to the Natural Streams Act, and a dedication ceremony was held at the home of Carmel and Mabel Johnson.

This ceremony is still known as "the day the helicopter landed." Dick Benson, a state senator who supported the bill, flew in from his Elkins home and landed in Carmel and Mabel Johnson's front yard.

Benson was a legendary pilot who flew in the Air Transport Command in World War II, and knew Ernest Gann, the author of *The High and the Mighty* and other classic books about flying. During his days in the legislature, Benson performed one of the great feats of flying in West Virginia history. He made a "dead stick" landing at night in a snowstorm on I-79 at Big Otter. He was flying home after a legislative session when an oil line ruptured and sprayed oil over the windshield. He shut off the engine, honed in on the lights at the Big Otter exit, and landed safely.

- - -

Herold has always had its "summer" population. The earliest summer camp, called Restawhile, was owned by Orlan Carte, a Charleston banker who grew up in Nicholas and Braxton Counties. The camp was built by Henry Baughman, who used stone from the S. Clark Dean chimney for the Restawhile chimney.

Two of the summer people were Betty Jo Clifton Pilegge, who lives in Tuscaloosa, Alabama, and her sister, Pat Clifton Stolzman, who lives in Waterford, Michigan. I asked them to share their memories of summers in Herold.

Betty: "I was very young when we began to visit Birch River. We would go to Uncle Louis' store [Louis Johnson], and offer to sweep. Our pay would be a little brown bag of candy that we would select from the candy case. We would take the candy down by the river and sit on the rocks and eat it.

"Every spring and summer, the first thing daddy [Joe Clifton, former Herold resident] would do at the camp would be to clean out the fireplace, because sometimes hunters would use the place, and sometimes blacksnakes would build in there, and that just scared me to death. He'd shovel the ashes out, and usually get five snakes with it.

"They built bunk beds in the corners to have enough space for the sleepers. The most popular beds were the top bunks, because if you slept on the bottom you got an eye full of sand. Kids would come up from the river and sit on the top bunk and play cards, and the sand on their feet would sift down on the lower bunks.

"I remember the ball games we played in the grass. Daddy worked at the rubber plant at Institute, and he would carve out a rubber ball, and somebody would get a stick or limb off a tree, and we'd carve the handle where you could hold it, and that was our equipment.

"One of the things we enjoyed most was fresh corn on the cob from Ray and Freda Wood's garden. Harry Truman [a family friend, not the former president] always bought about four dozen ears because he ate a dozen at a time. Merle [his wife] would wash dishes in the water she had boiled the corn in, and we all went 'yuck,' but water was scarce because we had to carry it from Aunt Cynthia's."

Pat: "We stayed in the river most of the time. I got big blisters on my back because I would be out in the water and sun all day long. Mabel Gibson [the last Herold postmaster] would float down the river singing 'Rye whiskey, rye whiskey, rye whiskey I cry, if I don't get rye whiskey I think I will die.' Then she'd dunk in the river and come up spitting and sputtering.

"Once us girls decided we'd go skinny dipping; it was early evening, and Merle said she would go with us to make sure everything was okay. So we got out there and took off our bathing suits. We were all swan diving and having a good time, and all of a sudden some country boys came up the river. Well, Merle told them to get out of there. We got our suits on really fast. We thought we were really something, going skinny dipping. The water was so nice and warm; it was wonderful. [Merle Truman died in May of 2001 at age ninety nine].

"Something I loved and dreaded at the same time was when we would take a 'trip' down Birch and its rocks. I mean, it was big stuff. We would pack food and supplies, and go maybe an eighth of a mile down the river. I was scared to death because of the rocks and how you had to jump them, or crawl across them. I can still smell the rocks today. They had a different smell. Eventually we would sit on the rocks and eat our food."

- - -

Camp Restawhile is now owned by the family of Fred and Anna Fisher. "We were introduced to Birch River about 1946," recalls a daughter, Phyllis Fisher Myers of Ronceverte, and we bought the camp in 1952.

"Dad would sing songs that he made up about Birch [Fred Fisher played the guitar and mandolin]. He loved playing with the Gibson boys, and we would all sing by the campfire. I spent the best years of my life on Birch.

"This property [Restawhile] has been the tie that binds the family. It is the one last thing that remains of our roots. Mother and dad lived to see their grandchildren learn to swim in Birch; the grandchildren helped pick blackberries and watched as Nanny [Anna Fisher] created those wonderful cobblers she was well known for.

"Now we return to 'our' river and still find the quiet peace that four generations of our family have found. As long as Birch flows clean and clear, I hope our children, their children, and their children's children will be able to go there and love Birch as we have. My prayer is that it remains a refuge for their lives."

One of "the Gibson boys" referred to by Phyllis Myers was Mike, the youngest of the brothers. Mike made fishing history in Birch at the Fisher camp when he caught a duck. He was casting a lure which attracted a duck that was floating happily nearby, and the air was filled with feathers and squawking for a few minutes until the lure came loose.

- - -

My niece, Rebekah Johnson, now eleven, won the Young Writers Award among fourth graders in the Kanawha County schools system in 2000, and I asked her to speak for the younger generation of our family about Birch River:

"I love the river because it is a pretty place. It has beautiful surroundings. One of my favorite things to do is skip stones with my mawmaw and pawpaw. I love to go fishing. One of the most beautiful places are the Falls [below Herold]. I had never been there before, but my dad said it is very pretty. The last time I was there I went with my dad to take pictures.

"When we would take my dog up there he loved to chase sticks and dig in the sand. I'll never forget that when I was little, my brothers [Justin, now seventeen, and Travis, now fourteen] and I went up on this big rock and jumped in the river. It was so much fun. I'll always remember the river as it is.

"I know Birch River is not one of the most common rivers in the U.S., but after everyone reads this book they will know it should be one of the top ten most beautiful places in the U.S."

- - -

My brother Walt remembered the gasoline pump on the porch of our grandfather's store. It had a crank handle that pumped the gasoline into a glass bowl, from where it was fed by gravity flow into the automobile gas tank. He also recalled the coffee grinder in the store, the letter compartments in the post office section that were a source of childhood fascination, and our grandfather's Delco plant with its large glass batteries. I still find pieces of that glass today.

Walt has brought three generations of his family to Herold for visits, starting with his own children, then his grandchildren, and now his great grandchildren. "I've visited Chicago, St. Louis, Miami, Washington, D.C., Los Angeles, Atlanta, and many other cities," he told me, "and, sure, the Washington Monument, Statue of Liberty, Queen Mary, and so forth, are impressive, but I can barely remember them today. However, it seems I can remember every day at Herold."

- - -

Brother Bob insists that our grandfather's yard and garden were bigger than the present space, and that the configuration is different. He recalled something I had forgotten: a large wooden wheel in the yard that was used for a flower bed. We have no idea where it came from, or where it went.

Although younger, he has a more vivid memory of the Henry Baughman grist mill: a long, red building with a big wheel at one end, a small wheel at the other end, and a large conveyor belt running between them (perhaps the larger wheel became the flower bed).

He recalls that our grandfather would "play Santa Claus" at Christmas by changing his voice so that we thought he was, indeed, talking in the next room to the man from the North Pole with all the goodies.

Our grandfather had a large male cat named "Old Moon," which Bob would place on the piano so the cat would "tickle the ivories" as he walked across the keys.

Naturally, all the kids of Herold gravitated to the candy showcases in the store. The sights and smells linger in our minds to this day. Bob remembers a diamond shaped, flat piece of candy with chocolate on the outside and brown filling inside that he has never found anywhere else, and which he still considers the best candy he ever tasted.

His memory of Birch is that "it was always there" as part of the Herold scene, although a specific recollection is of bullfrog hunting when he was quite young. He is convinced to this day that we were trying to drown him by sending him into watery rock crevices after bullfrogs.

- - -

Wolfpen Run enters Birch from the south about a half mile below Herold. The origin of its name has been lost to antiquity, but in early times settlers would build pyramid shaped log structures that wolves could enter but couldn't exit, and perhaps one of those structures gave the little stream its name.

Among the early residents (long after wolves disappeared) were Hugh Wood, a blacksmith; Tyburtis Butcher, a fisherman and ginseng hunter; Edmund Murphy, a blacksmith, barber, carpenter, and veterinarian; Curt Walker, a farmer and mailman; and Fannie Dodrill, a housewife.

Tyburtis Butcher, born in 1857, was a man of Birch River. "He lived to fish, hunt, and dig genseng," said grandson Glenn Brown. "Even after he left Wolfpen Run to live in Richwood, he came back in the summer to fish." But apparently Hugh Wood caught the largest fish, a fifty inch muskie (see "If We Were Counting").

At one time, a large number of Murphys lived on Wolfpen, among them Edmund Murphy. Edmund's son, Leonard Murphy of Cottle, recalls that the original Murphy house was located on the ridge above the head of Wolfpen, but was later moved downhill to the county road by eight teams of horses.

Curt Walker was one of the early Herold mailmen. He rode a mule, and one day when Hale Hamrick was the substitute carrier and the river was high, the stubborn animal laid down in the middle of the river while crossing to Herold. Hale's thoughts about this episode have gone unrecorded.

Fannie Dodrill lived in a log house across from where Gene and Jane Nauman now live. Patty Long, librarian at Sutton, recalls her grandmother: "She was born and raised in that house. She was a tall, strong woman who could pick up a sack of potatoes and carry them in one arm. She was a woman of deep religious faith, and on Sunday she would put whatever money she had in the collection. Her kids occasionally would tell her she shouldn't put in all her money, but she would reply, 'No, it's the Lord's money.' She was a strong willed person, and although she believed that the husband was master of the house, she did whatever she wanted to do."

Fannie Dodrill's father, Israel Brown, fought for the South in the Civil War. When he came home to see his wife, Sarah, he didn't come all the way, fearing capture if word got out that he was home. So he and his wife would meet at the overhanging cliff near Herold (see "The Rocks").

- - -

A Wolfpen icon is "The Schoolhouse," which sits on the bank near the little iron bridge over Wolfpen. Neal Gentry, a native of Bel Air, Maryland, now owns the property and lives there.

It was called Cleveland School, and was probably named for Grover Cleveland, the 22nd and 24th president of the United States (1885-89 and 1893-97). Originally it was located on the ridge above Wolfpen, but in 1909 was moved off the hill to the house on Wolfpen.

The hilltop Cleveland School began in 1889, according to an article by J.E. Baughman that appeared in the Braxton Democrat in 1935. He wrote: "The Cleveland school house stood on the mountain back of Dean's Mill next to Nicholas County and this [1889-90] was the first school taught in the building.

"At that time, Dean's Mill [Herold] was one of the most important centers in Braxton County. People for fifteen miles around went there to the mill, and Hon. G.A. Herold, now of Cowen, operated a large, well-stocked general store."

J.E Baughman told about representing a Robert Johnson in a lawsuit over timbering. "Lawyers were scarce," said Baughman, "and Mr. Johnson got me to look after his side of the case. It was tried before some Justice over on the head of Strange Creek, whose name I do not remember. It was really some law suit. However, I had some kind of a law book, and with that I persuaded the Justice that Bob was right and won the case.

This was my first and last time [to appear] as an attorney."

Bob Johnson may have been the same timberman who cut a poplar at the Lower Turn Hole in the early 1900s that measured six feet in diameter and was fashioned into a dugout canoe for use on Elk River (see "Leatherwood Country").

The Cleveland School continued for six years after moving off the hill. Its final roll call came in 1915, when the teacher was Chris Ballengee. By 1916, he was teaching at Adams, another one room school in the community that lasted until 1956. Chris Ballengee's daughter, Winifrede Ballengee Tyree, lives in St. Albans. A son, Ray Ballengee, built a camp on Birch below Herold in the 1930s and called it "Camp Porcupine," which was the first camp in the Herold area, and one of the first on Birch.

- - -

Many people have lived at The Schoolhouse over the years. It was a private dwelling prior to 1909, when it became a school, and after 1915 there was a "musical chairs" multitude of residents.

At one point it became a camp, and was called "Camp Wesley" for Wesley Carte, who lived there in the 1920s.

The present owner, Neal Gentry, acquired the property in 1996. "I became familiar with the area through Mick Curtis," said Neal. "I grew up in Maryland with Mick and his son, Clint. I moved to Morgantown for grad school, decided to live in West Virginia, and bought the schoolhouse from Mick."

The Schoolhouse, a.k.a. Camp Wesley, bears no resemblance today to its former one hundred year old self. Neal Gentry has remodeled it extensively, beginning by sandblasting the paint off the native chestnut walls, and then basically restoring it back to its original layout, with the addition of an office. He has a digital media production business called Wolfpen Digital.

- - -

Long before Wolfpen Run became a high-tech corridor, it was home to an underground moonshine still.

Braxton County realtor Jack Butler, who was born where Neal Gentry now lives, tells the story about his Uncle Charley turning out the good stuff in a nearby coal mine during Prohibition days.

Jack's parents lived at The Schoolhouse for three years, and his father dug coal and traded it for corn, wheat, and other items. Uncle

The Schoolhouse today (Photo courtesy of Neal Gentry)

Charley helped dig coal, and also operated the still.

Word of this got out, and revenue agents showed up at the mine entrance one day just as Uncle Charley was emerging. He told them, "okay, boys, let me go back in and get my dinner bucket, and I'll go with you." They waited and waited and waited, but Uncle Charley never returned. He had exited the mine through an air shaft on the far side.

Uncle Charley was never collared by the revenue agents. "They were always after him, but never caught him," said his nephew.

- - -

Another business of a slightly different stripe in the Herold area in the 1930s was the Louis Lombard stave mill in the river bottom at the Falls. Lombard cut white oak and turned it into staves, which were used as casks for aging fine bourbon, Scotch, and wine.

Louis Lombard stopped at my grandfather's store, and he would always buy Milky Way candy bars. My mouth watered as he ate them, and Milky Ways are my favorite candy bar to this day.

~ Ten ~

The Rocks

Birch's Footprints in Time

"From the end of the earth will I cry unto thee,
When my heart is overwhelmed:
Lead me to the rock that is higher than I."

-- The Psalmist David

The rocks of Birch River in its middle and lower sections are numbered as grains of sand in the ocean, and many are immense.

But Bill Gillespie, my geologist friend from Charleston, didn't so much as raise an eyebrow when I asked him to weigh some of the largest. Well, he may have smiled slightly. I suspect he had not previously entertained such a request.

Bill is a scholarly and versatile fellow whose interests range from the first to the last page of the Encyclopedia Britannica, and weighing rocks that are as much as twenty five times heavier than the seventy-ton Shay engine that once pulled logging trains on Birch River was a challenge of the sort he would not turn down on a day that ends in "y."

In May 2000, I met Bill at the Tidewater Grill, a fine seafood restaurant at Charleston Town Center, to discuss River on the Rocks. I was accompanied by Peter and Elizabeth Silitch, my neighbors and editors of this book. We talked about not only the immensity of the rocks but also the geology of the river in general.

There are other rivers in West Virginia with admirable collections of rocks, of course. New, Gauley and Meadow Rivers come immediately to mind. But for size and numbers, Birch is unique. I don't have to look far from my home to see them. There are two impressive boulders in my front yard, not to mention an incredible array of rocks in the river within my view.

The large rocks of Birch occur on a stretch of about eight miles, starting near the mouth of Big Run in Nicholas County and ending above the Raven Eddy in Braxton County. Because of the proliferation of rocks in and around the river, wading and fishing this stretch is no walk in the park. The river lays down a challenge.

Over lunch, Elizabeth, who as a child lived with her grandparents in New England, pointed out that large rocks in that part of the country are called "Pudding Stones." Her grandmother, Mabel Warren Bradley, once told her: "The giant made big cauldrons of pudding, set them off to cool, and they finally turned to stone." The geologic version is that these rocks were deposited by glaciers. I considered naming this book "River on the Pudding Stones," but somehow it didn't seem to fit Birch.

By the time coffee arrived, Bill had assured us that, indeed, there is a way of weighing rocks that would take us to within reasonable hailing distance of their actual weights. Since we were talking about objects that weigh in the hundreds or thousands of tons, "reasonable hailing distance" seemed close enough.

My goal included not only weighing a representative number of large rocks, but also asking questions that have intrigued me since I was old enough to admire and appreciate the rocks of Birch as the natural treasures that they are: How did they get there? Why Birch? Why are they found only on part of the river and not all of it? How old are they? The list soon covered a parchment the size of an Old Testament scroll.

Of course all of this involves geology in general, or, as Webster defines it, "a science that deals with the history of the earth and its life, *especially* [author's italics] as recorded in rocks." Therefore, of necessity, this chapter will discuss the geology of the river in concert with its rocks, or, to broaden our geographical horizons, its "Pudding Stones."

Soon after our Charleston meeting, Bill came to my home and we went downriver on one of those top ten spring days when nature is feeling quite good about itself. Bill wanted to get a first-hand look at what he had agreed to weigh. Bill is a native of Webster County, and is Webster County large. He is six-foot-three and weighs 235 pounds. I have always associated him with the mountains and woodchoppers of Webster County, and indeed he has a farm on Point Mountain and emcees woodchopping contests. When I saw him approach one of the signature rocks of Birch, I saw Paul Bunyan attacking a giant sequoia with a double-bitted axe.

This signature rock is located fifty seven yards below the Falls, a well-known, picturesque setting about half a mile downstream from Herold. The rock is spectacular not only because of its size, but also because it chose, about a thousand years ago, to tumble down into the river where it would more or less stand alone as one of the great marvels of nature in West Virginia or anywhere else.

The region through which Birch flows was never invaded by glaciers. As geologists say, it is "unglaciated," as is all of West Virginia (the closest the Ice Age glaciers came was slightly north of the Northern Panhandle). Therefore the rocks either fell from the hillside cliffs that abound in middle and lower sections of the river, or they were already there and the river gradually cut down to them. The smaller ones have been moved around over the years by floodwaters. The cliffs of Birch are as impressive in size as the rocks they have contributed to the riverbed, and, in time to come, the process of weathering and cracking will continue and will bring down more "Pudding Stones."

On the steep hillside immediately above the Falls Rock is one of those impressive cliffs, which undoubtedly was even more impressive about a thousand years ago. Looking up at the cliff, there is a very large void in the stratum to the right, where the Falls Rock obviously once resided. We can only imagine the resounding crash that must have occurred when it calved off and rolled or somersaulted down into the river. The distance from the cliff to where it now sits is only thirty two yards, so it would have been a short-lived, if awe-inspiring, spectacle.

I have difficulty describing rocks. Perhaps the dictionary definition will suffice: "A cliff or mass of stone." I will add that they are firm, dignified, solid, unchanging, and eternal. Patrick Hemingway, middle son of Ernest Hemingway, wrote in his father's last published work, *True At First Light*, that one word is worth a thousand pictures. I read that book while writing this one, and I would certainly agree, if the writer of that "one word" was Ernest Hemingway. But to portray the Falls Rock, and other behemoths of Birch, I have relied heavily on pictures.

I do, however, love the poetry and inspiring grandeur of biblical references to rocks:

"I will stand before thee upon the rock" (God to Moses).

"Speak ye unto the rock" (God to Moses again).

"Neither is there any rock like our God" (Hannah's song of thankfulness).

"As the shadow of a great rock in a weary land" (Isaiah's prophesy).

"Upon this rock I will build my church" (Jesus to Peter).

Rocks have become famous. Some thirty four hundred years ago, Moses was denied entrance into the Promised Land because he impatiently smote a rock instead of commanding it to bring forth water; one of the revered sites of the Christian, Jewish, and Islam religions is the Dome of the Rock Mosque in Jerusalem at the supposed site where Abraham was prepared to sacrifice Isaac, where Solomon built his temple, and where Mohammed sprang to heaven. The Rock of Gibraltar, a British possession on the coast of Spain, is a landmark on the eastern end of the Strait of Gibraltar. The Pilgrims landed at Plymouth Rock on the southeastern coast of Massachusetts. Alcatraz prison in San Francisco Bay was called "the Rock." The Rocky Mountains of western North America are celebrated for their majesty. The Blarney stone in Blarney Castle, near Cork, Ireland, is said to reward those who kiss it by giving them skill in flattery, or "blarney." Finally, the Rosetta stone, found in 1799, gave the first clue to the deciphering of Egyptian hieroglyphics.

Of course there are rocks, and then there are rocks. Ayers Rock, an outcrop in Australia's Northern Territory, is one and one-half miles long, and 1,143 feet high, and is estimated to be four-fifths underground. Neil Boggs, a Clay County native who now lives in New Mexico, travels extensively, and one of his recent trips was to Australia. He describes Ayers Rock thusly:

"More than just its immensity distinguishes Ayers Rock: there's its color. Or I should say colors. They constantly change, depending on the light at various times of day, red to gold to umber and all variations in between. But what startles is that the great rock truly pulsates with light and color regardless of the time of day. No wonder the aboriginal Australians, then and now, make it central to their spiritual heritage."

- - -

The Bible describes a flood of biblical proportions, and, according to local legend, the less-than-biblical 1936 flood in Birch River moved the Falls Rock (see "The Floods of Birch"). Bill Gillespie sized up the rock and suggested that, if anything at all happened, it wasn't actually moved, but was tilted by the floodwaters. The rock is extremely undercut, and from certain angles one could envision a giant hand grasping it and spinning it like a top.

An impressive collection of driftwood, including large logs, nestles under its upriver side. This has been true for as long as I can remember. One large flood may send them on their way downstream, but the next flood will begin a new collection. This is typical of a changing river environment.

Hemlock trees and squaw huckleberry grow on the crown of the rock, as they do on other large rocks of Birch. The Falls Rock is locally known as "Huckleberry Rock." Huckleberries are a shrub of the heath family, as are rhododendrons, azaleas, mountain laurel, and mountain teaberries, all of which are found along Birch River. Squaw huckleberry is not a true huckleberry because its berries are sour and inedible. The plant is also called deerberry and buckberry. Mick Curtis of Bel Air, Maryland, and Herold, who has a camp at the Falls, calls the Falls Rock "Crosby Rock" for his grandmother, Sarah Crosby Curtis.

Among the driftwood that has accumulated under the rock is a log about twenty feet long and three feet in diameter, jutting out from the bottom.

"It has remained in the same spot ever since I can remember and has served as a springboard to a rite of passage," said Mick. "This lodged hardwood is the only foothold leading to the only way up the rock, and the hand and footholds that allow ascent and descent (that is, under control) are a challenge to all but experienced rock climbers.

"Naturally, there are those who have felt the urge to view the Falls and the river from the top. There is a ledge that juts out just before

Falls of Birch below Herold

reaching the top that stops the faint of heart, thus the climb has become known as one that 'separates the men from the boys.' I have a picture somewhere of one of Clint's friends [Clint is Mick's son] flexing his muscles at the top of the rock, and an hour later he was putting ice on his broken ankle, so the descent is as perilous as the ascent."

It is a tribute to nature and its marvelous ways that vegetation, including trees, can gain a toehold on rocks. I asked Gerald Dunn, a Canfield native and retired professor of botany at the University of New Hampshire, to comment on this phenomenon. He said:

"Any plant which spends its life on a rock has a hard row to hoe. Two very important essentials for plant growth are water and nutrients, and both are practically non-existent on the surface of a rock [especially river rocks, which are nurtured only by floodwaters; their cousins in the woods have a slight edge in the buildup of nutrients]. Plants, be they grasses, mosses, shrubs, trees, weeds, or others, are forced to send their roots into every crack and cranny of rocks in their attempt to reach the soil for these essentials.

"The slow accumulation of organic matter on the rock may allow the plant to survive or even grow reasonably well. This is why the plant appears to, and does in fact, cling most tenaciously to the rock for life itself.

"Over time, the growth of the roots, plus the action of freezing and thawing, may gradually shatter the rock into fragments, which might provide some additional nutrients to the plants."

Gerald added: "All this reminds me of an old New England joke. A city slicker came into the country to buy a farm. A realtor took him to a very rocky farm, and the buyer said, 'How could I farm this?' Realtor: 'But these rocks provide heat, and conserve moisture (he put his hand on the rock, noting how warm it was).' He lifted one up to show the moisture under the rock. The buyer said, 'No, I'd rather see another farm.'

"So the realtor took him down the road to another farm, where two men were picking up rocks and hauling them off. The buyer observed, 'I thought you said rocks were good?' Realtor: 'I'll be damned. This farm belongs to Mr. Jones, and he is in Florida, and these men are stealing his rocks.'"

- - -

Bill Gillespie returned to Birch in the summer with an associate, Jim Brown of Mount Nebo, to measure rocks. I had mixed feelings as we approached the Falls, a.k.a. Huckleberry, a.k.a. Crosby, Rock. To me, it was like opening King Tut's tomb; both had lain inviolate for a thousand or more years. I thought of the hundreds of times I had appreciated the splendor of the rock and had fished in its looming presence without having to know its weight. Nevertheless, it didn't seem the time or place to bring up King Tut's tomb, or my secret love affair with the Falls Rock. The tape measure was applied, numbers were jotted down, height was determined, allowances were made for the contours of the rock, and only the flow of the river could be heard when Bill began to scribble in his notepad. He looked up after what seemed like an eternity, and asked us what we thought. Guesses in the hundreds of tons were tossed about like leaves in the wind, all of which fell short. His preliminary figure was eleven hundred tons. Later, in his office in Charleston, the official determination was made that the Falls Rock weighs one thousand and eighty tons. That ranks it as only the third largest among the five rocks we weighed that memorable day. But it is perhaps the most spectacular, given its blockhouse shape, and the Falls setting.

Downriver about an eighth of a mile is the largest rock on the river, known as the Fast Hollow Rock. Between it and the Falls is a long stretch of water called the Plains, named for its flat-rock river bed. The Fast Hollow begins on the Frametown Road and is named for Waitman and Delia Fast, who lived there from 1886 until 1917. One of their nine children was my grandmother, Launa Fast Riffel.

Like most Birch tributaries, the Fast Hollow is deep and rugged, and is much easier to write about than to walk in. One bright winter day, Denzil Baughman and I decided to hike up the Fast Hollow from mouth to head. On the way there, we enjoyed the grand view looking down Birch from the Frametown Road, which is one of the finest river vistas in West Virginia; we enjoyed 1,300-foot Fast Knob; we enjoyed seeing deer, since they weren't eating our gardens at the moment; we enjoyed the view of Birch from Vulture Tree, which sits on a large rock cliff above Herold and is a favorite roosting place of turkey vultures; and we enjoyed going up the Fast Hollow for the first twenty-five yards.

Then the hollow grew deeper and more imposing and the boulders grew bigger.

"Am I imagining this," Denzil asked, "or are the rocks growing as we speak?"

"And the hollow getting deeper?" I replied.

"And more imposing?" Denzil summed up.

Without saying more, we headed up the hillside, pulling ourselves from bush to bush and tree to tree, and mercifully found an old logging road, from which we enjoyed the Fast Hollow.

At the river, there is a cluster of large rocks near where the hollow enters, the second largest of which sits in the middle of the river at the lower end of the pool. Viewed from a certain angle, it resembles an alligator, which are not otherwise found on Birch, to my knowledge. Warder Dean wrote about enticing an enormous smallmouth bass from under Alligator Rock, but the bass declined to take his lure.

The biggest of the cluster, the Fast Hollow Rock, is a sleeper. It sits mostly on the river bank, where trees tend to obscure its bulk, but it weighs two thousand and twenty five tons. I called time out in a fishing trip one day and studied this rock, and I came away convinced that, indeed, it is the heaviest on the river. A large dead hemlock leans on top of the rock at its left corner, where it peaks thirty feet above the river, and the rock easily handles this intrusion without appearing at all overshadowed. The same can be said for the presence of the live hemlocks and rhododendrons that grow on it.

The Fast Hollow Rock was rewarded for contributing part of itself to the river floor. A piece had obviously fallen from its right front corner, and was counted as part of its weight. But this calved piece represents only a tiny fraction of the rock's overall weight.

I have studied pictures of the Fast Hollow Rock, and one angle, in particular, is striking: it appears to be the prow of an ancient, sunken ship; it very much resembles the ghostly underwater images of the Titanic, and indeed this rock is a titan of Birch. If it was sitting in the river, rather than on the edge, it would be stunningly impressive.

The Fast Hollow Rock was home, in the 1940s, to the largest smallmouth bass ever hooked on Birch, in the estimation of Don Hamric, a Glendon resident who fished both Elk River and Birch River extensively. He was fishing with Monty Wickline, who hooked the bass on a fly rod where the river flows deep past the rock. Don told me many times, and offered to swear on a stack of Lucky 13's (his favorite lure), that the bass weighed fully five pounds. Certainly it broke the fly line with relative ease.

In more recent times, my Herold neighbor, Sam Gibson, caught a twenty nine inch flathead catfish (mudcat) at the Fast Hollow.

This largest of Birch's rocks posed somewhat of a challenge to Bill. It sits sixty three yards from the nearest stratum that might have spawned it, which would be a long way for it to tumble down what is a relatively gentle slope. Bill chuckled, and said almost to himself: "Maybe it got a running start."

Which brought us to the Big Eddy and the same puzzle, only more so. The Big Eddy Rock is just around the bend below Herold, and is an imposing chunk of sandstone if there ever was one. I always thought it was the largest of Birch's rocks, and I have misled enough people on that score to fill the Manhattan telephone directory. But it weighs "only" sixteen hundred and ninety nine tons, or three hundred and twenty six tons less than the rock at the Fast Hollow.

The dilemma is that it sits squarely in the middle of the river at a point where the river is forty nine yards wide. There is a broad bottom on the north side, so the rock couldn't have come from that direction, and on the south side there is no cliff that is close enough to have obviously been its geologic progenitor. Bill suggests that both the Big Eddy and Fast Hollow Rocks may have been there first, and the river cut down to them. After all, Birch was once on the ridges that now surround it, and over eons of time it cut deeper and deeper until it arrived at its present valley floor location.

This cutting process creates river gorges and the "hollers" that flow into rivers. The Royal Gorge at Herold is a splendid example. It is an isolated canyon-like stretch above and below Herold, interrupted only by the Herold bottom. In places, the river is almost two hundred vertical feet below the county road. Bill Gillespie named this stretch Royal Gorge because of the abundance of Royal ferns, a water-loving plant. The botany books say the Royal should be found in most counties of the state, but Bill considers it rare. "In fact," he says, "it is doubtful if I see specimens more than two or three times a year, and I am in the field a lot."

Consider a river as a cutting torch. The moving water washes sand and gravel downstream with it. This material grinds its way through more solid sediments such as sandstone and cuts a narrow channel. The young river then reaches into softer, looser, sedimentary soil, widening its bed under the solid strata, which later collapse under their own weight and become large boulders in the river bed.

These boulders in turn become the river's major earth-moving abrasives and are eventually broken into smaller and smaller pieces, which in older river beds are seldom larger than one or two feet in diameter.

All this material inexorably migrates to the river mouth. Thus what may have begun its river life as part of an East Lynn sandstone stratum on Birch may end as a small rock or a bit of sand under a New Orleans graveyard.

Birch continues to cut. In five to ten thousand years, if the world as we know it still stands, the river channel will be much deeper than it presently is, and its rock floor will be seen as cliffs on either side high above the new floor, and the missing material may have contributed to a yet larger Mississippi Delta.

The scenic Abner Hole of Birch

The geologic possibility that Birch once flowed up near the ridgetops requires a leap of faith to embrace. A further leap is required to consider the possibility that Birch has reinvented itself three or four times. But geologists believe the Appalachian area has been flattened by erosion, then uplifted, then flattened again, and then uplifted again. After the last uplifting, Birch and other streams began cutting down to form the rivers as we know them.

"This could be the third Birch," says Bill Gillespie. "Or could it? I'm sure no one really knows. Regardless, it took probably one hundred million years from when the first sand grains were swept aside by the first drops flowing together to start the first Birch, and for the river to reach its present level."

We must make yet another leap of credulity to accept that there is movement underneath the floor of Birch. The crust of the earth moves up and down each day, but the movements are relatively small, and, since they coincide with the earth's rotation, we have no point of reference and we don't notice them. Bill casually mentioned this one day on the river. I could not help myself: I looked down. I saw no movement. But Bill insisted it is there, an average of three to four feet each day under the sand and rocks of the river floor, and indeed under all of the earth's surface.

He explained further: "Look upon the earth as an elastic ball, with an inner molten core. Outside that core, the rigidity of the earth is about twice that of steel. Yet there is periodic movement caused by the same forces that produce ocean tides [the sun and the moon, primarily the latter]. Thus, although the earth is twice as rigid as steel, it is also more elastic."

- - -

The fourth ranked of the five Birch rocks we weighed that spring day was the Margaret Johnson Rock at Herold, which is shown in "The Floods of Birch" chapter with a large hemlock log resting on top of it, deposited there by high water in February 2000. Like the Big Eddy Rock, it is surrounded by water, which tends to make any such Birch rocks more impressive than their peers which are situated on the edge of the stream. This rock is named for my sister-in-law, who has written the book, so to speak, on fishing there. Her specialty is continuing to fish with serenity while kids and dogs splash and swim happily around her. Bill found that the Margaret Johnson Rock weighs seven hundred and sixty nine tons.

Chris Kent of Peralta, New Mexico, visited Herold and became determined to spend the night on the Margaret Johnson Rock. He carried his sleeping bag to the river and in fact did spend the night there. The river raised several inches that night, and he slept through it all.

The fifth was the Freda Wood Rock, upstream from Herold, which weighs two hundred and sixty one tons. Freda has lived on the river since 1934; the rock at her home is a familiar landmark to fishermen, swimmers, and picnickers, and, because one end connects to the bank during normal summer water flow, it is very accessible. It's a river's version of a walkway leading out over the water.

In early fall, Bill and Jim returned to measure two more rocks, both at Herold, to complete the representative lineup. One was the Leaning Hemlock Rock (see "The Floods of Birch"). The hemlock, which fell in 1994, grew between its namesake rock and another of slightly smaller size. Jim and I crawled through thick rhododendron to reach the larger rock and measure it. Below us, the water glistened in the autumn sunlight. Bill would conclude that it weighs seven hundred and fifty eight tons. In the winter, the Leaning Hemlock Rock can be seen from the road high on the hill above the river, especially when snow-covered, and it never fails to impress.

The final rock was the Royal Gorge Rock just upstream. It sits in the bend where the river begins to straighten out to flow past Herold. Like the Falls and Fast Hollow Rocks, it has an impressive array of hemlock and huckleberry on its crown. With Jim's help, I climbed it for the

first time in ages. I remembered an incident from years ago when a canoe-
ist came to my home with a dislocated shoulder, or some such injury,
sustained when the current swept him against the undercut side of the
rock. Birch is threatening to boaters only at high flows, which was the
case that time. Bill calculated again and concluded that the Royal Gorge
Rock weighs two hundred and ninety two tons, not including a plastic
container that had been left on top of it by a previous flood. That would
have required a raise in the water level of at least twelve feet.

Following are the seven selected rocks, listed in order of size,
along with the width of the river at normal summer stage:

Fast Hollow Rock	2,025 tons	26 yards
Big Eddy Rock	1,699 tons	49 yards
Falls Rock	1,080 tons	33 yards
Margaret Johnson Rock	769 tons	26 yards
Leaning Hemlock Rock	758 tons	26 yards
Royal Gorge Rock	292 tons	40 yards
Freda Wood Rock	261 tons	35 yards

(The seven average 983 tons)

All of these weights are, of course, estimations, but they are based
on a mathematical formula, which Bill explains as follows:

> I drew sketches and recorded the lengths, widths, and
> heights as we measured the overall rock and any projections.
> Then I lined the sketches into geometric outlines, used the mea-
> surements to calculate the volume in cubic feet for each outlined
> section, and added them to get the total number of cubic feet.
>
> This total was multiplied by 95, the weight per cubic
> foot of that sandstone, to get the total number of pounds, and
> divided by 2,000 to get the weight in tons.
>
> I had to accept that the rocks are 'as seen' on the river
> floor. If they have buried corners, the weight will increase.
> Maybe they will wash out a bit one day and we can be more
> certain.

On one of his visits to my home, Bill began scrutinizing a small
rock above the patio. This time I didn't see Paul Bunyan; I saw Sherlock
Holmes, the fictional detective creation of Conan Doyle, examining evidence with a magnifying glass. I almost expected to hear him exclaim,
"Elementary, my dear Watson." He was looking for, and found, pebbles
embedded in the rock.

"When pebbles are found in sandstone," he explained, "the rock is called a conglomerate [rock composed of various materials rolled together]. These conglomerates started when water was moving fast enough to move pebbles as well as sand. They were then cemented together into a conglomerate instead of just a sandstone. The pebbles are commonly rounded due to rolling against one another on the trip."

"The trip" was of short duration, in the case of this small rock, which probably came from one of the cliffs just upriver from my home. The astonishing part is that the river had to have been at least seventy five yards above where it now flows. In other words, one thousand years ago I couldn't have lived where I do now.

I now look at this modest rock with new respect, and I wonder exactly how long ago it started the trip that was destined to deposit it in my backyard. At the very least, I'm more patronizing when I trim grass and weeds around it with one of those buzzing, angry machines with strings protruding from the cutting head that resembles the whiskers of a Birch River catfish.

- - -

The rocks of Birch are from the East Lynn and Homewood sandstone strata. East Lynn, the most prevalent, was named after the town of

Rocks in the vicinity of Jack Johnston camp

East Lynn in Wayne County, and gained geologic prominence in a 1913 report by the West Virginia Geological and Economic Survey.

The rocks that broke away from cliffs and cascaded down to the Birch floor are from the East Lynn; those that may have been in place from the beginning (the Big Eddy Rock, for example) are from the Homewood.

A 1917 report by the West Virginia Geological and Economic survey says this of the East Lynn sandstone: "Makes great cliff at Herold." The report doesn't specify which cliff, although the answer would probably be all of them.

Underneath the East Lynn stratum is a layer of coal, once locally mined at several places along Birch, and beneath the coal seam is the Homewood sandstone. Coal seams are a common occurrence in West Virginia sandstone strata.

The Homewood comprises the riverbed foundation on part of Birch. The riverbed rock at the Falls below Herold, for example, is Homewood. It seems to outcrop only in the gorge area; elsewhere it is below drainage. It is known to be below drainage in the Diatter Run area, and there are no large rocks in the river from a point well above Diatter Run to the mouth of the river. This would answer the previously-posed question as to why the big rocks occur only on part of Birch, and not all of it: they are found only where the Homewood strata outcrops.

Also, they are found only where Birch is lined with massive cliffs, as it is on its middle and lower sections. As we've noted, these cliffs have contributed many large rocks to the riverbed over the eons of time.

The East Lynn stratum is prominent all along the rocky section of Birch, but a more convenient way to see it is to drive over Powell's Mountain on U.S. 19 and view the massive highway cuts. Sedimentary rock (rock such as sandstone which is formed of sediment) always comes in layers. Many layers can be seen on Powell's Mountain across the highway from the overlook.

Birch is a river of moderate fertility because of its sandstone origins. Streams that flow through limestone country have a higher calcium content, and are therefore more fertile, and fish grow faster and in greater numbers.

The most recent water quality data for Birch was obtained in 1997 by the state Division of Environmental Protection, and showed a moderate fertility reading of 190 near the mouth of the river. By comparison, Greenbrier River, a classic limestone stream, consistently has fertility readings in the 300 to 500 range.

- - -

Cliffs like this one at Herold are common on lower Birch

The cliffs of Birch are as impressive as the rocks. A cliff is defined by Webster as "a very steep, vertical, or overhanging face of rock." We know from history books, television, and the Internet about the cliff dwellers, those ancient people who built their homes on rock ledges or in the recesses of canyon walls. But a trusted everyday favorite phrase is cliff-hanger: the game was a cliff-hanger until the very end (when presumably one team fell or was shoved off); the election was a cliff-hanger; and the successful completion of something in doubt (like this paragraph) can be a real cliff-hanger.

Cliffs abound in the Herold area. The most prominent one is located at the western end of the village. The exposed part of this monolith is five hundred and seventy feet long and fifty feet high. It once hung out over the road, but sometime in the 1940s or 1950s the Department of Highways blasted off the overhanging part. The remainder is still a very impressive cliff, especially in winter when spectacular columns of ice form on it. In extremely cold weather, large blocks of ice collect underneath the cliff in piles that would have made the old North Pole Ice Company in Charleston covetous.

This cliff, in all probability, was the one visited in the early 1900s by I.C. White, state geologist and a superb coal authority whose findings are still studied today. He gave its location in the 1917 West Virginia Geological Survey report as "south edge of Herold," and referred to it as "a great pebbly cliff."

Bill Gillespie sees cliffs as overlooked habitat for various kinds of plants, birds, reptiles, amphibians, invertebrates, and mammals. A case in point is the Herold cliff, where ravens nest on one of the ledges; they use the same nest year after year, reinforcing it with more sticks each year prior to nesting season. Bill, Jim Brown, and I were there in January 2001, and two ravens showed up and squawked long and loud at our intrusion.

A cliff across from my home spawned the large rocks that lie in the river there, including those shown on the front cover of this book. This formation extends more or less all the way to the lower end of the

Herold bottom, where a huge cliff rises above the river. It has two large "rooms" that are connected by a narrow passageway that must be wriggled through. I have done this, as has probably every kid who ever grew up at Herold, and I always imagined that snakes, rats, and other fearsome creatures lurked there. The second "room" has a nice view of the river about fifty feet below.

We always referred to the "rooms" as caves, but in reality there are no caves on Birch. In the true sense of the word, a cave is an underground cavern.

Chad Gibson, a neighbor, remembers this cliff unfondly. When he was twelve years old, he was attacked there by a swarm of yellowjackets. He slid and tumbled down the hill to the river, but the angry insects followed him into the water. He ran home, ripping off his clothes as he went because his unsocial attackers clung to his shirt and pants. They followed him inside the house, but in fewer numbers than had begun the pursuit, and he may have hid in a closet until these final ones gave up and went away.

There may be a "thing" with yellowjackets and the north side of Birch at Herold. In the summer of 2000, Lowell James was stung about thirty times when he ran across a nest with a wheelbarrow while working at his camp. The same day, a hammer slid off a ladder and hit him on the head, bringing him to his knees. Simultaneously, his wife, Janie, was whacked across the forehead by a rhododendron limb and knocked down. It wasn't their day, obviously.

The Gibsons (Sam and Sandra and their children) have a cliff for a backyard. In a fissure in the rock is a large spring that has never gone dry, even in the drought years of the 1930s. The tenth commandment tells us not to covet our neighbor's house, but it doesn't mention our neighbor's spring.

- - -

I made a unilateral editorial decision not to weigh cliffs, but probably the largest of the large protrudes from the steep hillside just upriver from my house. I crawled through the rhododendron thickets on a decent day in February 2001 to marvel once again at its impressive bulk. Its "dome" room, or principal overhang, would accommodate a tractor-trailer. The river flows perhaps one hundred feet below it. Exhibit A of the case for cliffs as overlooked habitat was a nest that had been built in a crevice; the occupant or occupants had carried hundreds of acorns into their "castle."

In summer 2000, Benjie Nichols and I renewed a walking acquaintance with the Devil's Backbone, a long, spiny ridge on lower Birch (see "Big Run Meets Lower Keener"). We'd both done that before, but it had been a while. On the way, we found a nest of ferns that had been built in the crevice of one of the numerous Devil's Backbone rocks. The inhabitants were probably field mice, which like to nest under rocks.

Bill Gillespie makes the point that cliffs are about the only habitat that man hasn't succeeded in destroying or altering, the reason being their relative inaccessibility. "Who," he asked rhetorically," wants to slide down a rope and face a rattlesnake eyeball to eyeball?"

Cliffs, like rocks, are difficult to describe because they don't adhere to any particular shape or pattern. As to definition, that's somewhat easier. Bill settled on "an extremely steep or overhanging mass of rock," although he conceded that high and steep are subject to interpretation. "Perhaps," he offered, "it means more or less ninety degrees, and the heck with the rest."

My definition of a cliff is something that I will not climb, will not be lowered over, will not place my hands in its crevices, will not ever again wriggle through, and will not stand under its overhang for more than ten seconds. Will not.

- - -

The Brady Rock below the mouth of Little Birch is a hidden treasure; it cannot be seen from the river, but it is a very awesome cliff. The local legend is that it was named for two Brady brothers, who hid there to escape serving in the Civil War. Remnants of shoes and other articles left by the brothers were supposedly found long ago. The rock is large, and certainly someone could have lived under its overhang quite uncomfortably, all the while hoping the war didn't last too long. In rainy times, a stream of water from the Brady Hollow spills over the rock.

A few miles down Birch at the Lee Jack Plout is the "huge cliff" that I referred to in my rain-smudged notes during a fishing trip (see "If We Were Counting"). I returned for a closer look in early March 2001, and immediately regretted it. I didn't want to wade the icy river at that time of year, so I approached from the north side, which required a long walk (that was okay) and a long crawl on my stomach through the rhododendron (that was not okay).

But the cliff is indeed huge. A giant hemlock stands guard at the lower end, its branches waving in the breeze on the day of my visit. Farther along, an ancient beech presses against the cliff face, having moulded its shape to fit the contour of the rock. Everywhere, stunted rhododendrons cling to the miniscule amounts of nutrients that have collected in crevices of the cliff.

The rock is honeycombed by nature's relentless work over the eons, reminding me of post office boxes; I was tempted to deposit a page from my pocket-sized notepad asking for help in getting out of that god-forsaken place, but I suspected I'd already missed the 3:10 to Yuma.

Under one overhang, a mammoth piece of rock, weighing tons, had calved off the cliff and had found its eternal resting place on the ground, surrounded by smaller pieces of similarly calved rock. Water dripping from the cliff had formed sheets of ice on the branches of a small hemlock where the sun had not penetrated.

But it was decision time: the position of the sun told me that the day was well stricken in hours, and I didn't want to spend the night curled up under the icy hemlock. I followed the cliff to its more or less ending, and headed straight up the hill, pulling myself from one tree to another until I reached the "Old Passway," a former wagon road on the top of Middle Ridge.

I saw fifteen deer that day, none of them in the rhododendron thickets anywhere near the Lee Jack Plout, which told me that they did not have the same burning desire to see the place that I'd had earlier in the day.

There are cliffs at many other places along lower Birch, most notably at the Abner, the Raven Eddy, the Smith Eddy, the Lower Keener Eddy, and the Martha Butcher Hole; the entire south side of the Raven is a cliff that slopes sharply to the water.

Perhaps the most spectacular of them all, from the standpoint of river view, is the cliff on the Devil's Backbone above the Martha Butcher Hole. A large stretch of Birch can be seen from this cliff (see "Big Run Meets Lower Keener").

The most unique rocks away from Birch are Pillar Rock on the lower end of Middle Ridge (see "The Blue Hole"), and Pinnacle Rock on the south hillside above the Lower Keener Eddy. Pillar Rock is supported precariously by a pillar of layered, crumbling rock; Pinnacle Rock is a very large formation of layered rock that sits on the river bluff; below it is "the old log run," where in the early 1900s logs were slid to the river for rafting.

- - -

BILL GILLESPIE is a native of Webster County who now lives in Charleston. He is the owner of Gillespie Forestry Services, a consulting firm with offices in Charleston and Webster Springs, and William

H. Gillespie and Associates, a plant bio-
stratigraphical-geological consulting firm
of Charleston. He is former director of
the West Virginia Division of Forestry, and
former deputy commissioner of agriculture. He is a 1952 and 1954 graduate of
West Virginia University, and is currently
an adjunct professor in WVU's Department
of Geology and Geography. From 1974
through 1996, he also worked as a research

paleobotanist for the U.S. Geological Survey. He has received numerous
state and national awards, including having two genera of plants scientifi-
cally named in honor of his research achievements. He is credited with
finding and helping to describe and name the world's first seed plant, one
that lived and was fossilized near Elkins, Randolph County, some 350 million years ago, when all other plants were still reproducing via spores,
as ferns still do. He has published or had accepted for publication two
hundred articles, abstracts, leaflets, and books. In 1998 he was inducted
into the West Virginia Agricultural and Forestry Hall of Fame, one of only
sixteen foresters inducted since initiation of the hall in 1975. His hobbies
are woodworking, photography, and fishing.

JIM BROWN is a native of Nicholas
County, and lives at Mount Nebo. He is a
1995 graduate of Glenville State College with
a degree in forestry and bachelor of science in
biology. He became a registered forester in
October 2000, and his company, Brown Forestry, is a contractor for Gillespie Forestry Services. His hobbies are hunting and fishing.

Bottlenose Rock above the mouth of Long Run

The Sulfur Springs Hole below Herold

~ Eleven ~

Big Run Meets Lower Keener

Remembering a Burial Procession and More

According to local legend, the last mountain lion in the Keener's Ridge area was killed on Big Run in the 1880s. "Uncle Johnny" Young , a well-known Keener's Ridge resident who died in 1953 at age seventy seven, was said to have been a member of the hunting party as a young boy.

Perhaps the ghost of that big cat still haunts Big Run. It would not be too fanciful to imagine that its deep and boulder-strewn hollow may yet, on a dark night, reverberate to the roar of a cougar on the hunt.

Sometime around the same period, Cynthia Cart, a young girl, was visiting Francis and Amanda Morton and their three children at their home on the head of Sugar Camp Run of Birch River, and saw what she believed was a mountain lion. Sugar Camp heads across Adams Ridge from the origins of Big Run.

Big Run begins in a marshy area on the farm of Dale and Ruth Lewis, and winds its way toward Birch. I chose an appropriate day in late March 2001 to walk down it to the river; the day was overcast and threatened rain, and seemed to fit the gloomy recesses of Big Run.

I followed a logging road, then an old wagon road, then a deer path, then a fresh logging road, then a wagon road again, and finally the path of a squirrel or rabbit through the mountain laurel and hemlock, and was grateful for it. I slogged in and out of the run, sometimes climbing steep hillsides to escape the boulders. The river always seemed just around the next bend. I decided that Big Run is the longest 2.4 miles in North America.

But finally, the river appeared quietly. Big Run enters at the Lower Keener Eddy, six miles above Glendon. Here, in an isolated setting, it meets one of Birch's longest eddies, and one rich in river lore.

Lower Keener is most closely identified with Warder S. Dean, who built a house there sometime between 1913 and 1917, and lived there most of the next thirty years. He was tall, an inch or so over six feet, and wiry. He was at various times a farmer, carpenter (two different stints for Elk River Coal and Lumber Company), log-rafter, and road worker.

He left the Lower Keener fifty six years ago, but his house on the river still stands as a reminder of earlier times on Birch. Hemlocks surround the downriver corner of the house, which is now a camp. The owner is Steve Gibson of Hurricane, whose father, Forrest, bought the property in 1953.

Warder Dean's trademark was a military-style salute, and I gave his house my soldierly best when I departed to climb the hill another way back to Dale and Ruth's. I followed "the old log run," which curves gently uphill above the Lower Keener

Warder S. Dean

and tops out at Brad Nettles' farm. In the early 1900s, an incline was built of posts and boards, and logs were "shot" down to the Lower Keener and rafted down Birch.

- - -

The Lower Keener is, as the name implies, an extension of the Upper Keener Eddy, which begins two river bends below the mouth of Diatter Run. The two eddies are linked by a shoal of about one hundred yards in length, where, in the 1960s, enterprising beavers built a dam all the way across Birch that lasted until the first high water. During the same period the Army Corps of Engineers also considered building a dam on Birch (see "A Much Studied River").

Together, the two eddies extend for about seven-tenths of a mile of mostly deep water, with the exception of the upper half of the Upper Keener, which is fairly shallow. The south hillside, starting about midway between the two eddies, is steep and covered with dense stands of rhododendron that defy passage. Oldtimers appropriately called such rhodo-

The Lower Keener Eddy

dendron thickets "a hell."

Both eddies contain sunken logs and rock cover that once made them very fine eddies for catching large muskies, but reports of such catches are becoming increasingly rare.

Ten years ago, Steve Gibson hooked and lost a large muskie in the Lower Keener that he estimated to be over forty inches long. A friend, Tim Naylor of Hurricane, was visiting at the time, and Steve paddled back to the camp, told Tim about the muskie, handed him his fishing rod, and Tim rowed to the same spot; he didn't catch a muskie, but he did catch a thirty inch, eight pound walleye.

A lingering question about the two eddies is the origin of the name. One possibility is Andrew Keener, who may have lived at the Upper Keener after his marriage to Julianna Rose, the daughter of William Rose, a War of 1812 veteran who is buried nearby (see "The Blue Hole"). Andrew Keener, who died in 1907, was one of the founders of the Middle Run Baptist Church.

Another possibility is Samuel Keener, whose daughter, Delila Keener Butcher, lived downstream from the Lower Keener prior to 1920. Whether Samuel Keener and his wife, Sarah, lived on Birch is unknown.

- - -

Warder Dean, the patriarch of the Lower Keener, was born on the river above Herold in 1876, the son of Simeon and Mariah Dean. The place of his birth was known as the Simeon Dean bottom, but in more recent times has been called the George Hoylman bottom. The late

George Hoylman, a doctor at Gassaway, built a camp there of river rock.

Warder married Sarah McMorrow in 1905 at Herold. Their wedding day picture shows them seated in a buggy drawn by a team of white horses. Their daughter, Valeria Dean Strickland of Summersville, believes the buggy was owned by my grandfather, Louis Johnson.

They lived at several places, including the Perry Riffel (now Eddy Grey) place on Adams Ridge, before moving to the Lower Keener. Valeria was born at the Lower Keener in 1917, and her memory of the river remains keen.

She told me about her sister, Alta, who was ten at the time, seeing a procession cross the river at the Perrine Ford below the Lower Keener carrying the remains of my great grandfather, William Johnson, for reburial at the new Johnson Cemetery on Keener's Ridge. Ola Johnson Martin, a daughter of William Johnson, was part of the procession; she rode a black horse and wore a black dress. The procession wound its way up the hill to the ridge and to the cemetery.

My great grandfather, a Confederate soldier in the Civil War (Company G, 10th Virginia), died in 1875 and was buried at the Robert (Robin) Given Cemetery on the north side of the river. Great grandmother Jane Given Johnson lived for another forty one years; when she died in 1916 she became the first person buried at our family cemetery. Soon afterwards, William Johnson was reburied beside his wife.

- - -

Perrine Ford was a name that resonated with me for another reason. I was fishing one summer day at the lower end of the Lower Keener Eddy, drifting in a rubber raft which was not designed for fishing in the first place but which had the advantage of being light and could be stuffed into the back of my Jeep. Its disadvantage was that sitting in it and fishing from it brought on slow but sure paralysis of the legs. It was probably designed by the same people who hit upon the idea of Chinese water torture.

My legs had long since ceased to exist when I hooked a smallmouth bass of about fifteen inches. I brought it in and released it, since legs are not required to do that, but by then I was in the shoal's dreaded grasp.

I began to bump against the rocks. I struggled to my knees, or where I thought my knees were, and sure enough they were there. They banged on the rocks too. Had I been able to stand or move in any way, I would have jumped or rolled into the river. So the Perrine Ford, where the shoal ended, was a welcome sight.

The Perrine Ford

The ford was named for Lewis Perrine, who lived on the Camden McMorrow farm near the river. Perrine was a voracious buyer of land in the 1800s; old deeds show that he was obtaining property on Birch and other watersheds as early as 1847, and was still buying land in 1887. An 1867 deed revealed that he bought two hundred and twenty seven acres from Patrick and John Duffy for almost two dollars an acre, which was an astounding price in an era when, typically, land was selling for five or ten cents an acre.

- - -

Bernard Given operated a sawmill at the Lower Keener in the 1920s just above the Warder Dean house. He sawed crossties, which were fastened together and floated to the railroad at Elk River. Crossties were cut from hardwood, usually oak, hickory, or beech, were either hand-hewn or sawed, and are eight and one-half feet long, seven inches high on the sides, and six to nine inches in width, depending on the soil conditions where they were being placed on the railroad bed.

In the late 1800s, before the railroad arrived, crossties were floated all the way down the Elk to Charleston. Bill James of Gassaway told me about his grandfather, Ellott James, taking crossties to Charleston and selling them to Charleston Lumber Company for ten cents apiece.

Valeria Dean was more attracted to the sights and sounds of the Bernard Given mill than to the crossties, but the proprietor, fearing she would get hurt, would blow the steam whistle as a warning when he saw her approaching. She would take the hint and retreat back home. Later, when the mill was no longer in operation, she would play in the sawdust pile, which also served another purpose. Her father and Bernard Given built an ice house from sawmill slabs, and cut ice from Birch that, insulated in the sawdust, kept into the summer.

- - -

Valeria's brother, Doyle Dean, once caught a forty two inch muskie across from their home, and called for her to bring a washtub. "I yelled back," she said, "and asked him how he expected me to get a washtub across the river when he had the boat. So he paddled back across the river with one hand, and towed the fish with the other hand, while I waited at the bank. We flopped the fish into the tub, and it stuck out on both sides."

In later years, Doyle became superintendent of the Elk River Wildlife Management Area for the Division of Natural Resources. He wrote articles about local lore for *The Braxton Citizens' News*. His "office" was often the Century Inn Restaurant at Sutton. He sat at a table, ate breakfast or lunch, and wrote longhand on a yellow legal pad. He died in 1995 at Stephens City, Virginia, but his columns remain as a nostalgic record of an earlier time on Birch.

When he was a young man, Doyle lost a leg in a southern West Virginia coal mine when he was a young man, but he continued to enjoy the outdoors and Birch River. One day he was sitting on a sloping rock across from his home at the Lower Keener with his three year old nephew,

Dean Strickland, who, engrossed in shelling peanuts that Doyle had brought from town, tumbled into the deep water. With difficulty, Doyle reached out his hand, and the little boy grasped it and was pulled to safety. Dean Strickland now lives in Glenville, and works for a trucking firm in Summersville.

Long Shoal below the Lower Keener

- - -

The stretch of Birch below the Lower Keener all the way to the Sand Hole is Devil's Backbone country. The Devil's Backbone is a long, spiny ridge that creates one of the loops of lower Birch, and is quite impressive when viewed from the air.

The name Devil's Backbone, although appropriate, isn't unique to Birch. It may have originated in Sonora in northwest Mexico as the appellation given to a rugged region where the Apache warrior Geronimo took sanctuary on his flights from the San Carlos reservation in Arizona.

The Willis Long Plout at the end of Long Shoal marks the approach to the Devil's Backbone. The Oxford English Dictionary quotes the famous preacher and theologian, Spurgeon, to the effect that "plout" means "to splash about in the water," in essence a place that isn't large enough to qualify as an eddy, but is big enough to splash around in.

The Willis Long who had a plout named for him lived there in the teens and early 1920s.

Two sycamore trees and an overhanging birch announce the start of the plout. There are river birches all along Birch River, hence the name, but as a canopy over the river they are perhaps most prevalent in the section from the Willis Long Plout to the Upper Turn Hole, a distance of a mile or more.

- - -

Below the Willis Long Plout is a modest shoal filled with small, rounded rocks that Benjie Nichols affectionately calls "the hatchery" because it constitutes a great spawning bed for white suckers and other fish. Fortunately for the fish, the proliferation of rocks made the spawning fish difficult to gig (the practice of spearing fish with a two- or three-pronged long-handled spear called a gig). The fish took refuge in the crevices between the rounded rocks and were almost impervious to gigging.

Benjie lives on Birch across from the mouth of Leatherwood Run. He is a native of Clay County and spent part of his growing-up years in Fayette County, but came to Birch with his parents, Woody and Jean Nichols, at a young age and has lived on the river ever since. He once caught a forty seven and one-half inch muskie and a twenty eight and one-half inch walleye at the mouth of Birch.

- - -

The "hatchery" leads to the Dudley Nottingham Plout and its centerpiece, the Reynolds Rock. Reynolds Given, a farmer and logger, lived on the north side of the river, and left his signature on Birch in a very explosive way. After his log rafts hit the rock two or three times, he drilled into it with a turn drill, and dynamited it. A turn drill is a hand-held rod, sharpened on one end and shaped like the head of a Phillips screwdriver. One man holds the drill, and another hits it with a sledgehammer (which requires a high degree of trust in the man wielding the sledgehammer). The bar is turned after each blow from the sledgehammer, and water is put in the hole each time to soften the rock. Eventually, a large enough hole is drilled in which to place dynamite. John Henry drilled the rock in the Big Bend Tunnel this way in the 1870s.

The rock shows the effects of the blasting. It rises only about two feet out of the water at normal summer flow, and is broken into misshapen crevices out of which water willows grow. Several slab-like rocks lie in the river surrounding the rock, but it is impossible to know whether they are a product of the blasting or are just simply there. Rocks are

The dynamited Reynolds Rock

everywhere along Birch in that area; not the large ones of farther upriver, but many rocks.

The river makes a very slight bend that apparently was just enough to sweep log rafts into the offending rock, although there are a hundred places along the river where the same thing might have occurred, since Birch is a small, rocky, and twisting river.

Reynolds Given, the rock blaster, was called "Big Reynolds" because another Reynolds Given, a cousin, lived in the area at the same time. The cousin, a surveyor and school teacher, was called "Little Reynolds."

- - -

The Dudley Plout is named for Dudley Nottingham, a farmer and timberer who lived on the hillside above the plout, among other places. In the early 1920s, he helped build the iron bridge across Strange Creek upstream from the village of the same name. Another bridge worker was Charley Nottingham, father of Fred Nottingham (see "The Doctor and the Preacher").

Cleo Teets bought the Dudley Nottingham farm in 1939. He and his sons, Medford and Merlin, cut four boxcar loads of pulpwood and sold two calves to pay for the farm. The five-foot pulpwood logs were peeled, trucked to Strange Creek, and shipped out by train. The hillside is so steep that occasionally a peeled log would slide all the way into Birch. Their horse, Mac, had bumps on his knees from jumping across the sliding logs. Medford recalls them singing *The Great Speckled Bird*, the song that made Roy Acuff famous, but he stopped short of claiming that the horse joined in.

- - -

Below the dynamited rock, Birch flows through a small, curving shoal and enters the Martha Butcher Hole, which brings up the question: when does a plout become a hole? In the context of water, the Webster New Collegiate Dictionary defines a hole as "a deep place in a body of water."

The named "holes" of lower Birch are, in descending order, the Blue Hole, the Martha Butcher Hole, the Upper Turn Hole, the Sand Hole, and the Lower Turn Hole. The Sand Hole may be miscast; it is a sandy stretch of water without any deep places that I can see.

Among the early residents at the Martha Butcher Hole were Andy and Delila Keener Butcher, and, later, Theodore and Ivy Given (not the preacher Theodore Given). Fred and Laura Sampson lived just across the river. Ivy Given and Laura Sampson were pregnant at the same time, and their babies were born close together. Laura named her baby Rosalie, and Ivy named her baby Rosalie. To avoid too much confusion, Ivy prounced the name of her daughter "Rosala."

Ernie and Martha Butcher lived there in later years. Ernie was an electrician and plumber for the Elk River Coal and Lumber Company. Occasionally the river was high and he couldn't wade or drive across at the Perrine Ford, so he attached cables and pulleys to trees on each side of the river, built a cedar box with a crank inside, and cranked himself across. Perhaps he grew tired of cranking, but this arrangement didn't last long.

He may also have been the only person to produce hydroelectric power on Birch. He installed a water wheel on the river that generated enough current for electric lights. In that respect, he was years ahead of his time. In 1966 the Army Corps of Engineers considered the feasibility of developing hydroelectric power as part of the Birch Reservoir, but the Federal Power Commission concluded that development of the power potential of the Birch project wasn't economically feasible at that time.

Martha Butcher lived on the river longer, from 1927 until 1954, hence the name of the hole. A daughter, Thelma Butcher Teets, remembers: "All seven of us kids grew up on the river, and nobody ever had so much as a broken bone. We did use a lot of Vick's salve, as I recall."

Martha Butcher died in 1980 at age eighty four, and is buried at the Baughman Cemetery on Upper Keener's Ridge.

The house on the river is no longer there. Like the abandoned one-room Adams School building on Adams Ridge, it just gradually fell down. The present owner of the property, Roger Randolph of Teays Valley, Putnam County, has a camp near where the house once stood.

- - -

Below the Martha Butcher Hole the river becomes shallow and flows over a series of underwater rocks. On the left descending side, a seam of coal, probably the Upper Kittanning, outcrops underneath a cliff. Medford Teets and James Butcher dug coal there during low flow, and Medford used it to fire his blacksmith shop and make pony-size horseshoes. "Every kid on Keener's Ridge had ponies," he said. "There must have been ten or twelve of them."

Many years ago, some men came from Pittsburgh and gathered a few sacks full of the coal for analysis, but there is no record that anything ever came of this.

A farm animal of great renown is memorialized at Pig Shoal Plout below the Pittsburgh coal cliff. I've camped there in the past while boating and fishing lower Birch, and more recently my nephew, Rob, his daughter, Rebekah, and I had lunch there while canoeing and fishing.

I'm an admirer of pigs. I find them tenacious, irascible, intelligent, and possessed of a grunt that borders on arrogance. Brenda Pin-

Pig Shoal Plout below the Martha Butcher Hole

nell and I trade pig cards like kids trade baseball cards. I worked with Brenda at *The Charleston Gazette*; she now lives in Charlotte, North Carolina, and works for *The Charlotte Observer*. I was delighted when Valeria Dean Strickland mentioned Pig Shoal, a narrow, modest shoal that flows out of the plout of the same name. But delight turned to sadness when she related the rest of the story. Many years ago a hard-scrabble farmer was driving his pigs across the river, and several of them drowned at the crossing, or so the story goes.

I asked Benjie Nichols for a second opinion. He hadn't heard about the pigs drowning, but didn't discount the possibility. He was told that in the late 1800s or early 1900s, local farmers would conduct pig drives. They drove their swine across the river at the shoal and left them to their own devices in the hundreds of acres of rugged hardwood forest on the north side of the river that abounded in chestnuts, acorns, and beechnuts. Then in late fall they would return for the fattened porkers.

The end of Pig Shoal is the beginning of a long stretch of water of more overhanging birches that leads to Fingerstone Rock. Fingerstone supposedly got its name from marks on top of the rock that look like they were made by giant fingers. When it comes to imagining that rocks resemble everything from killer whales to the man in the moon, my imagination is as vivid as the next person's, but I was never able to see fingers on Fingerstone Rock. But no matter; it is a very nice rock in a very nice pool of water in a very scenic and isolated stretch of Birch.

On the right descending side below Fingerstone are the Cedar Cliffs, a series of rock ledges on a rugged hillside where cedar trees grow. The legend of Cedar Cliffs is that there is a deep hole among the rocks where raccoons would take refuge when being pursued by hounds. The ill-fated hounds would follow in after them, but couldn't get out.

- - -

Lurking in the vicinity of all of this is the Devil's Backbone. The "Bone" is about a mile long, and is aptly named because it drops off precipitously on each side, although more so on the upstream or Martha Butcher side, where the river's loop around the Backbone begins.

One of the great cliffs of Birch runs along this side, offering glimpses of the river almost vertically below. This grand view takes in a stretch of river from above the Martha Butcher Hole to Pig Shoal, with the Roger Randolph camp in the middle.

The loop ends at the Sand Hole. In between are Pig Shoal, Fingerstone Rock, and the Upper Turn Hole. The end of the Backbone,

The Devil's Backbone

if extended on a straight line to the river, would arrive at a point about halfway between Fingerstone and the Upper Turn Hole.

The Backbone is not high in elevation (around 900 feet), and nestles below the surrounding ridges, which rise to 1,300 feet, a geographical feature that actually makes it stand out in the crowd when viewed from the air or from higher terrestrial vantage points.

It is unique in another way: it is owned entirely by one person, Skeeter Pletcher of Gassaway. He acquired the property in 1987, including the camp on the river at the Sand Hole.

One day, two men came into Pletcher Pontiac Company and mentioned that they had looked at property on lower Birch, and described the difficulty they encountered getting their vehicle back out. For that reason, they decided not to buy the property. "I thought to myself," said Skeeter, "that's what I'm looking for: a place you can't get out of." So he bought the Devil's Backbone.

The isolation is very nice, but not inviolate. Randy Riffle, a friend of Skeeter's son, Jon, was spending some quiet time alone at the camp, and stretched out on a blanket in the yard to soak up some sun, clad only in his underwear. He drifted off to sleep, and was awakened by noises; he looked up, and four men on horseback were looking down at him. It turned out they were local residents who like to trail ride, and had picked that day to ride down to the river at the Sand Hole. So much for isolation.

The Backbone begins above Skeeter's camp, and we hiked it on a warm, sunshiny day in early April 2001 that reminded me of similar weather a year earlier when Bill Gillespie and I walked down Birch to begin "weighing" rocks (see "The Rocks").

Although the Backbone rises well above the river, nature simply moved the rocks up with it; a large rock marks the entrance, moss-covered rock ledges signal the beginning of the path along the top, the cliffs offer a spectacular view of the river, and a large rock sits at the end of the Backbone.

My introduction to "the Bone" occurred many years ago on a deer hunt, and for a change, nothing had changed. Many of the special places I revisited in writing this book have been severely timbered in recent years. On the day of our walk, we saw several fresh deer beds; deer like to lie on the narrow ridgetop, with its steep hillsides offering quick escape from danger (a hunter, for example). Not surprisingly, we saw only beds, and no deer; they had obviously heard us before we had a chance to see them.

There was also fresh turkey scratching where a flock had fed its way along the ridge, seeking the variety of foods that are available in and under the leaves: bulbs, roots, insects, salamanders, snails, and dozens of other delicacies that are hidden under the leaf cover.

Later, we sat on the deck at Skeeter's camp, enjoyed the sun and the river, had our own lunch (but none of the above), and then walked upriver to Pig Shoal, where I closed my eyes and envisioned great herds of swine splashing and squealing in the water.

On the way back downriver, we enjoyed the arrival of Spring Beauties, those early woodland wildflowers that love sunshine and absolutely will not unfold on dreary days (their scientific name, Claytonia virginica, honors Dr. John Clayton, a pioneer American botanist). We also took special note of the many piles of rock in the bottom where long-ago farmers had tilled the ground and planted corn. One of them was Dudley Nottingham, who lived in the early 1900s where Skeeter's camp now stands. He died in 1940 at age eighty one, and is buried in a nearby hilltop cemetery.

- - -

My brother, Walt Johnson, and Glenn Carte were leaders of Boy Scout Troop 20 in Charleston, and one memorable day they led eighteen kids up Birch from Glendon to Herold, an outing that including climbing over the Devil's Backbone. This is a daunting task, because "the Bone" is vertical on the downriver side, and seems to get steeper than that on the upriver side.

But on a topo map it looked like a great idea to bypass the long river loop by simply going over it rather than around it. To this day, that climb is referred to as "Walt's Shortcut," but the scouts only took it as a grand challenge. They have no doubt faced greater challenges in their adult lives.

That night the tired and hungry "Lost Battalion" camped at a rock overhang on the north side of the river, the exact location of which has become, well, lost in their memories. They built a fire at the entrance, and the next morning the kids in the front emerged with hands and faces blackened. But a swim in the river soon cured that.

Throughout the trip, they crossed and recrossed the river many times in an effort to find "easier" going. "At first," Glenn recalled, "I would take my boots off and put them back on after reaching the other side. Finally, my feet became so sore that I just left my boots on and sloshed through the water with them."

Over lunch twenty five years later, I asked if they fought their way through any of the rhododendron thickets that line the river hillsides. "Only one," they replied in unison. "The one that starts at Glendon and ends at Herold."

- - -

The two-story Henry and Martha Davis Frame house is a landmark near the Devil's Backbone. The last residents were Pearl Frame, who cooked at the Widen clubhouse for many years, and Sarah Frame Walker Jucovich, who was a schoolteacher. Sarah died in 1997 at one hundred and one years of age, and is buried at the Eureka Church Cemetery.

The premier view of Devil's Backbone country is from a high, rounded knoll on veterinarian Ross Young's farm. I went there one day with Ross' mother, Marjorie Young, who remembered the knoll when it was in trees; now Ross cuts hay on it.

Marjorie and her late husband, Carl, bought the property in 1940, and she helped him clear the land.

We took in the sweeping panorama, one of the most splendid of any on the Birch watershed: Interstate 79 glimmering in the distance at Coon Knob, the Middle Run drainage, the former Jerald Shawver farm, Birch's loop around the Backbone, the mouth of Leatherwood Run, the old road that went over the hill from Leatherwood to the mouth of Birch (perhaps a continuation of "the old buffalo trail" that skirted the river high above the Smith Eddy), and the Henry Given farm. We could see across Elk River to the north, and into Clay County to the west.

- - -

On a late June day in 2000, my nephew Rob and his youngest son, Travis, came up from Charleston to fish the Lower Keener Eddy with me. The obligatory rainstorm that seems to always precede fishing trips also came up, but we headed for the river anyway. By the time we arrived at the Lower Keener over one of the roughest roads in the history of the western world, the sky showed some slight indication of clearing. Our aluminum canoe slid over the muddy bank into the river with great ease. We slid down and got into it with great unease.

I was mindful of muskies, and perhaps Rob was too. Travis was mindful, but not very, of trees along the bank. His favorite was pawpaw and their unripe clusters of fruit. His lure sailed easily into the pawpaws, from which it was retrieved with great difficulty. At other times he preferred witch hazel, or ironwood, or, for variety's sake, a sunken log or a limb protruding from the water.

We had a rubber raft in addition to the canoe, and I all but took out an ad in the paper declaring, in the manner of Chief Joseph at the Bear Paw Battlefield on the high plains of northern Montana in October 1877, that where the sun now stood I would ride no more rubber rafts forever. Twenty years had elapsed since my ride through Long Shoal, but I have a memory like an elephant about anything that involves pain. Travis tried the raft in the eddy, but soon decided he preferred the friendlier canoe with its rigid bottom and sides. Rob, who is trim and athletic, nevertheless climbed into the raft from the mucky river bottom with all the grace of a wallowing hippopotamus on a bad hair day. After about a half hour, he asked if anyone had seen his legs. I chuckled, but not too loudly.

We drifted down the eddy, catching a few small bass but none of the muskies that are so much a part of Lower Keener lore. The rule of thumb of crazed muskie fishermen is that you catch one muskie for every eight hundred casts, and we still had sixty or seventy casts to go by the time the shoal came into sight. At this point, Travis, in his mysterious thirteen-year-old way, decided he wanted to fish from the bank. Rob reluctantly accepted the prospect of leaving the despised rubber raft.

"Are you sure, Travis, you want to go to the bank and give up your seat in the canoe, even though the bank is lovely in June and you'd probably catch more fish there?"

He was sure.

We approached the shoal. I was paddling, Rob was fishing. But first we received an announcement from upstream that Travis was in the trees, or rather his line, hook, and bobber were in the trees. We backpaddled and surveyed the situation. His line was draped like a giant spider web through the limbs of a large sycamore tree that guards the river in front of the former Warder Dean house. We took care of this, and again approached the shoal.

I suggested a spot where a rock slopes down gently to the river. It was the same place I'd caught the fifteen inch bass years before, but I didn't divulge that right away, in the hope of appearing later to have the gift of reading a fish's mind. Rob's lure plopped into the water at the edge of the rock, and faster than I could say "See, I told you so" he had a smallmouth on. I always marvel at how quickly smallmouth and brook trout react to a lure hitting the water. It's almost as if they see it coming. Combined with the tugging current of the shoal, this fish was a rodful. It was eighteen inches long and weighed over three pounds.

We took its vital statistics, admired it, and released it.

- - -

His interest in the river renewed, Travis stretched out in the rubber raft and headed over Long Shoal to ride the rapids. The river was running swifter and fuller than when I went over, and it was a great ride, I'm sure, although I still have no interest in small, spongy rubber rafts or their children or their children's children.

The thin pale rays of a setting sun illuminated the Lower Keener and surrounding hillsides. The rhododendron was in full bloom. It was a gorgeous evening to be alive and on a river.

Back home, we almost ran to the grill, dumped in a bag of charcoal, and slapped on thick hamburgers. Rob and I toasted his Lower Keener smallmouth with a Jamaican brew. Then followed brews from California and Mexico. Rob observed that we had been to three foreign countries without leaving the patio. The coals glowed in the gathering darkness, and Birch River talked to us as it came out of the Herold Canyon. The cat and dog eyed the hamburgers with undisguised glee.

I've read that some food critics cavalierly dismiss food grilled outside as not tasting any better than food cooked inside on a stove. Technically I would agree, but the critics must first ride to the Lower Keener Eddy over a god-awful road and slide down a bank muddy from rain and retrieve lures from pawpaw trees and lose all feeling in their legs in a rubber raft and loop a line through a sycamore tree and hope to catch a muskie and catch an eighteen inch smallmouth and ride Long Shoal in gorgeous water conditions and see the sun setting on a lonely river and visit three foreign countries without leaving the patio and then eat food cooked outdoors.

- - -

The lower end of the Lower Keener came through for us that day, but it isn't always so. I was fishing there another time with Rob and his daughter, Rebekah, and we climbed out of the canoe to lead it through Long Shoal. They climbed out, anyway. I got one foot on top of the canoe and tipped it over. I went completely under, my orange baseball cap floating away in the current.

- - -

A neighbor, Dale Lewis, has bittersweet memories of Long Shoal fron his teenage days. He and others were coon hunting on Big Run when Jack Butler's redbone hound chased a coon to the river. Dale and Royce Teets were convinced that the dog was barking across the river, so they stripped off their clothes in twenty degree temperatures and waded the icy water. Dale stepped on a slick rock, dropped one boot, and fell as he grabbed for it. He was swept downstream and washed onto the opposite bank. As it turned out, the hound had been barking on the Big Run side all along; a curve in the river had conveyed a false sense of direction.

Royce later served in the Marines in Vietnam, came home, and was killed by lightning while fishing in Ohio in 1972; he was twenty four years old.

- - -

Dale Lewis, who lived on Adams Ridge, and Walter Pierson, who lived on a remote hilltop above Herold, were the last of the mountain men on Birch, or, in Dale's case, the last of the teenage mountain men. They trapped from the Falls below Herold to the Blue Hole, and had a gentleman's agreement that Dale would trap the south side and Walter the north side. They caught mink, raccoon, muskrat, beaver, opossum, skunk, and gray fox. Mink pelts were the most valuable in those days (mid 1960s), bringing from ten to twelve dollars.

Once Dale saw a skunk swimming the river below the Fast Hollow in late January. This is very rare, but Dale believes it was a male answering the call of mating season. I believe the skunk could no longer stomach its own odoriferous self, and was washing off.

- - -

In the fall of 2000, Rob and I returned to the Keener Eddies. The rhododendron bloom had faded into memory, and leaves had collected in the lower end of the Lower Keener. We slid the canoe into the water and paddled to the shoal that connects the two eddies. Our companion was a great blue heron which would fly and alight, fly and alight, never too far away but never too close. The great blue heron is the largest of our common wading birds, and a solitary bird except at nesting time. I see them on Birch, but never more than one at a time. They are quite adept, as they must be, at spearing small fish with their long necks that lash out with the rapidity of a king cobra.

We pulled the canoe through the shoal and paddled through the Upper Keener, and turned and began floating back down. We caught a few small fish, but the smallmouth that Rob had lost in the Upper Keener on a previous trip either had been caught or wasn't hungry. We preferred to think it was the latter. There are few more mortal enemies to a bass stream of moderate fertility, such as Birch, than fishermen who keep their catches.

We pulled through the shoal again and entered the Lower Keener of Warder Dean's domain. I put on a Jitterbug, a surface lure that plops and gurgles and twitches, and which was introduced in 1934 by the Fred Arbogast Company of Akron, Ohio. It wasn't particularly the time of day to use a Jitterbug, but a lure that has been around that long deserves to be tried occasionally. We could measure our progress through the eddy by the trails of bubbles left on the water by the lure.

A few dozen plops, gurgles, and twitches later, something struck at the Jitterbug with a vengeance, but missed it twice. They were, however, very spectacular misses of the kind that only fishing with a surface lure can produce. Fred Arbogast knew what he was doing , and so did this fish. We turned around, paddled upstream, and came back again, but there was no vengeance this time, and not even a cursory look. The moment seemed right to leave the Lower Keener Eddy to the great blue heron, to the vengeful mystery fish, and to the memory of Warder Dean.

- - -

At least we left it until spring 2001, when we returned for some early fishing. It soon became evident that the water wasn't warm enough for smallmouth, and we did not raise a walleye or muskie. But there were other compensations. We heard the gobble of a wild turkey upriver, and saw a gaggle of Canada geese on the water. At one point, the honking of the geese triggered the turkey's gobble, and later, below Long Shoal, four or five turkeys sailed across the river.

- - -

Postscript: Warder Dean left the Lower Keener in 1945, and died in Gassaway in 1964 at age eighty eight. He and his wife, Sarah McMorrow Dean, are buried at the Mount Olive Church Cemetery on Keener's Ridge, as are daughters Alta Dean and Phala Dean Given.

The celebrated Falls Rock below Herold

Fast Hollow Rock, the largest on the river

The Big Eddy Rock weighs a "mere" 1,700 tons

The sixteen foot falls of Birch near Boggs

End of the rocks above the Raven Eddy

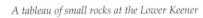

A tableau of small rocks at the Lower Keener

Jumble of rocks ushers in the Lee Jack Plout

Day lilies brighten the Birch riverside

Royal Fern Rock above Herold

A cluster of large rocks at the Fast Hollow

The scenic falls below Herold

Swift water above the Abner Hole

Twelve

If We Were Counting

Fishing and Other Misadventures

In 1939, Warder Dean ("The Big Timber Era") canoed down Birch River from Herold to the mouth of the river at Glendon, fishing along the way, or at least part of the way. He wrote about this trip many years later, and believed that it was the first canoe trip down Birch, which it probably was.

"There had been trips made by small wooden john boats," he wrote, "mostly beginning at what was known as the smooth water of the lower reaches of the river, usually from the Raven Hollow Eddy."

Reading his account, I savored every word. He was a good fisherman, and he knew the river. To my disappointment, looking back over time, I never had the opportunity to fish on Birch with Warder. But I did fish with him in later years on Elk River, and he gave me a canoe paddle which he made and which I still have.

His account was written in 1974, and was accompanied by a hand-drawn map of the river from the mouth of Little Birch to Glendon, listing the tributaries and other prominent features. To my knowledge, it is the only such sketch ever made of the final thirteen miles of Birch, and is therefore a valuable link to the river's past. As this chapter proceeds, I will mention instances where his names for eddies and other places on the river differ from what I know them to be today.

My nephew, Rob Johnson, and I set out in 2000 to fish the same stretch of river that Warder fished sixty two years ago, and we did, although not at one time, and, depending on water conditions, not entirely by canoe. Sometimes it was easier to walk, although easier is a relative term on a river as rocky as Birch. I've never waded Birch that I didn't wish, for a few fleeting moments here and there, that I was somewhere else, like climbing the Matterhorn at night in the dark of the moon.

But canoes have their golden moments too. I'd already been dumped into the river previously at the Lower Keener Eddy when, another day, we came to the peaceful looking Martha Butcher Hole downstream. Rob took the river pictures for this book, and on our trips he was never without a digital camera dangling from his neck. Suddenly he saw a very large water snake stretched out on the trunk of an oak tree that had fallen into the deep part of the hole, and the camera quickly came into play and a picture was taken. Resting against the tree trunk in front of the snake and adding natural appeal to the picture was a forked limb whose points had been freshly and neatly cut by beavers.

But photographers always want "just one more," and they always want it closer to the subject. Adult water snakes are ill-tempered by nature, and this one had attended no charm schools. As the shutter snapped for the close-up, the snake lurched, and so did Rob. My nephew is close to six feet tall, weighs one hundred and eighty five

The snake that upset the canoe

pounds, and is very athletic. When he lurches, he does a good job of it. The canoe tipped over and both of us joined the fat, ugly serpent in the river. The Martha Butcher Hole is lovely in September, but I prefer to enjoy it from within the canoe, rather than under water with the canoe on top of me.

As I came up sputtering, I thought I heard Rob say, "Damn a snake that doesn't want its picture taken."

I noticed that his hair wasn't wet, and maybe I only imagined that he said something about being able to walk on water, given the proper motivation, which in this instance was the presence of a three-foot snake in the water. *Easy Identification Guide to North American Snakes* by Hilda Simon says this about our common water snake: "Seeks refuge in the water when disturbed." Perhaps Rob had read the book.

My main concern was for my fishing rod, or more precisely the Rapala lure that was attached to it. I had grown to love and revere this three and one-quarter inch piece of balsa wood, which had come off the bench to perform well after I'd lost two similar lures during a season of fishing on Birch. But Rob's main concern, selfishly, I thought, was for the three hundred dollar Olympus digital camera that had gone under with him. At least that was his main concern after he had determined that the snake was nowhere to be seen. But the camera survived quite nicely, as did the close-up picture of the grouchy snake, which is shown elsewhere in this book in happier times (a split second before the picture was taken). The four dollar and ninety five cent Rapala survived as well.

We collected life jackets, paddles, fishing rods, and a small ice chest containing our lunches and a couple of soft drinks, and ferried the overturned canoe to the opposite side of the hole, where, as far as we knew, the snake wasn't.

In the post-mortem, there was an animated discussion about who had offended the snake, and who was primarily responsible for capsizing the canoe. I thought the close-up picture ticked off the snake big time; Rob thought that the canoe had nudged the beaver limb, thus alarming the snake, which implicated me, since I was paddling; I thought Rob's lurch in reaction to the snake's lurch brought us into the drink; he thought all three of us lurched, and, in an imperious manner, I thought, for someone who had just turned the canoe over, quoted Sir Isaac Newton's third law of motion, "For every action there is an equal and opposite reaction." I was not in a mood to argue with both Rob and the English philosopher and mathematician, especially when I was wet and chilled at the Martha Butcher Hole, so the discussion ended.

Throughout the year, we had hoped for a picture of deer on the river. We'd seen many tracks, but no deer. The irony of that day was that a half hour later, below Pig Shoal, we came upon three deer at the water's edge. At the time, the camera was still soaking wet, so we were deprived of a deer picture.

The presence of the digital camera was another manifestation of the advent of high-tech on lower Birch. Earlier we were drifting through the Willis Long Plout, the quiet disturbed only by the light plops of our lures hitting the water, when Rob's pager beeped. It was such an historic moment that I asked him for the time (I have an ironclad rule that if I get into a canoe, my watch doesn't). He told me: 10:54 a.m. Eastern Daylight Time, September 19, 2000 Anno Domini. The Willis Long Plout (see "Big Run Meets Lower Keener") is on an isolated stretch of Birch, and I doubt that it had heard a pager beep previously. The caller, it was determined later, was Phillip Pfister, who was building a house near Charleston and wanted to confer with my nephew, who works for American Electric Power Company, about electrical service.

Warder didn't mention either the Willis Long Plout or the Martha

The Willis Long Plout

The Martha Butcher Hole

Butcher Hole in the account of his 1939 trip, the reason being, as he put it, that "the day was almost spent" by the time he and his partner fished through the Lower Keener Eddy, which is six miles above the mouth of Birch. So they "beat it out before dark." He mentioned having taken a second trip later, starting at the Smith Eddy, three miles below Herold, and said that he would write about it, but perhaps he never did.

Warder's fishing and canoeing partner was his brother-in-law, Kenny Canfield, who died in October 2000 in California at age eighty five.

One day, Rob, his ten-year-old daughter Rebekah, and I had reached the Leatherwood Run area, about two and one-half miles above the mouth, when I realized that although the day wasn't almost spent, I was. We put our fishing rods away and paddled out to Glendon. And we hadn't started at Herold, as Warder did; we had started at the Smith Eddy. But I have made the Herold to Glendon float, and it is an ordeal if the river is low. Warder wrote that the water level on the day of his trip was normal for summer, so I suspect they were dragging their canoe as much as they were paddling, but, if true, he didn't mention it. His canoe was a seventeen-foot canvas Old Towne; ours was a thirteen-foot alumi-num Grumman.

The Grumman is a story in itself. It was Rob's high school gradu-ation gift in 1977, but for various and sundry reasons he sold it in 1985. Immediately he sensed he'd made a mistake, and finally, in 1998, was able to buy it back, but for more money than it had cost originally. It is perfect for two people on a small river like Birch, is lightweight, and seems to roll with the punches as far as the rocks are concerned.

Warder wrote that their only portage, that is, carrying the canoe overland, was at "Diatta Falls" about a half mile below Herold. I'd never heard this well-known place on Birch (see "The Rocks") called anything but the Falls. Diatter Run comes into Birch more than two miles down-stream, so that tributary could not be the namesake of the Falls. A small tributary of Wolfpen Run near Herold is called, in old deeds, Diadda Spring Run, but it is somewhat removed from the Falls, too, so the mys-tery continues.

But confirmation of the historical authenticity of the name cropped up in 1981 and 1985 deeds involving property transactions at the Falls. References were made to "Diada Falls" and "Diado Falls," the latter prob-ably a misspelling. My favorite misspelling occurred in another deed where Wolfpen Run was called "Woolfpen Run."

Upstream from the Falls, and just around the bend below Herold, is a place called the Big Eddy, or the Big Rock. The eddy is not big. It was called that long ago because it is larger than any other eddy from

Herold to the Raven Eddy, a distance of about two miles. But the rock is definitely big. It sits in solitary majesty in the upper end of the eddy, and weighs almost seventeen hundred tons (see "The Rocks"), which makes it the second largest rock on the river. A lone hemlock tree grows on its downriver end, accentuating its size.

Warder said this about the Big Eddy and its rock:

> The first place of interest after casting off was the Big Eddy [which tells us it was called that at least sixty-two years ago], a deep pool with an enormous boulder in the middle of the river with deep water surrounding it. This was a favorite spot for bass and pike. When the river was in proper shape, you rarely failed to connect. Since the river was normal and clear that day, we were not disappointed. I might add in passing that it was here many years before the date of this float trip that Hugh Wood, a muskie fisherman of the old school, who lived on Wolfpen Run, caught a muskie in the fifty inch class.

This catch probably occurred around 1909 to 1914. Pershing Keener, who lives on the Herold Road, is Hugh Wood's grandson, and he remembers that his father, Charley Keener, saw the fish when he was in his early twenties. Charley Keener was born in 1889, thus it was most likely somewhere in the 1909-1914 period that Hugh Wood caught what might have been the largest muskie ever caught that far up Birch (nine miles). Such statements must remain in the "might have been" category, because nobody really knows. For example, some large muskies have been caught in the Freda Wood Eddy near Herold, and probably elsewhere, for which there is no written or verbal record.

Hugh Wood was fishing with a young boy named Johnny Dean, a Herold resident, when he caught the big muskie. Wood, a large man and a blacksmith who made, among other things, plowshares, lived where Leonard and Emza Brown lived in later years. He and his wife, Lydia, are buried at Maysel, Clay County. Johnny Dean was the son of Clark Dean, who is believed to be the first settler in Herold.

Rob and I didn't catch a muskie of fifty inches or any other size during our considerable time on the river in 2000. That isn't to say they aren't there, but certainly their numbers have diminished because of fishing pressure. Still, we could have spent the same amount of time on Elk River, a renowned muskie stream, and we might not have caught a muskie there either. But I doubt it.

- - -

One day we came to the Lee Jack Woods Plout. I got there first because I had detoured through the woods to save energy for the mile or so still ahead before we would reach Paul Roche's home at the Falls, where we had left our vehicle. I was not unmindful that my neighbor, Denzil Baughman, had seen a bear in this woods earlier in the year. It was raining lightly when I reached the Lee Jack Plout, named for the man who lived there in a two-story house early in the century in what was and is a very isolated river bottom. The remains of his house were visible as late as the 1960s, but all traces of it have since disappeared.

The mystery continues with Lee Jack himself. Determining when he lived on the river, when he left, and where he went, proved elusive. One clue was unearthed in the following story recalled by Denzil Baughman: Lee Jack and Wesley Carte were neighbors, and they liked to banter good naturedly about their corn crops. One time Lee Jack was bragging on his corn, and Wesley spotted a puny-looking ear. He shucked it back, revealing a cob with few kernels. "Look," he exclaimed, "a nubbin'." "That's right," Lee Jack replied. "This ground is so good that the corn couldn't keep up with the cob."

Wesley Carte lived on the property adjacent to Lee Jack from around 1890 until 1925, when he sold the farm to his grandson, Ed Baughman. So it was somewhere in that time frame that Lee Jack lived on the river.

The Lee Jack Plout

A death certificate for a Lee Jack Woods is on file at the Clay County Courthouse. It states that he died at Harrison, Clay County, on December 14, 1947, at age seventy eight, and is buried there. His parents were William and Sally Pardue Woods, and his wife, who gave the information for the death certificate, was listed as Sarrah (perhaps Sarah) Woods. It gives his birth date and place of birth as October 2, 1869, at Widen (or what later officially became Widen; the town as we know it wasn't formed until the early 1900s).

One cold day in early December 2000, I visited his grave in the White Cemetery on Paddy Ridge. The cemetery is wedged on a knoll between two houses, and commands a grand view of the rolling West Virginia hills to the south toward Powell's Mountain and Summersville. An icy wind ruffled the dead grass and weeds. On the gravestone, his surname is spelled Wood. His year of birth is given as 1871, which differs from the date given on the death certificate. His wife's name is spelled Sarah, and her year of birth is given as 1881. There is no date of death. A son, Lee Roy Wood (1901-1971) is buried nearby.

The Lee J. Wood buried on Paddy Ridge is, in all probability, the Lee Jack Woods (or Wood) who once lived on Birch River, but in the course of researching for this book I was unable to find anyone who could tell me that for an absolute certainty. Carl Wilson Sr., retired Clay funeral home director who grew up on Paddy Ridge, remembers Lee Jack, but he never heard whether he once lived on Birch.

- - -

I arrived at the plout named for him, took shelter from the sprinkles under an overhang of brookside alder and rhododendron, and waited for Rob. I began to scribble notes with a red ballpoint pen on a single sheet of yellow legal pad that folded nicely into a plastic freezer bag. A similar freezer bag and similar piece of paper survived the snake incident at the Martha Butcher Hole on a later day. Drops of rain soon smudged my notes, but they were as follows:

> Lee Jack. Huge cliff. Spiders on water. Bugs about so long. Sprinkles of rain. Water gurgled. Tall, thin-bladed grass in clumps. What a marvelous thing an unspoiled river environment.

Well, it wasn't Vincent van Gogh sitting down to paint, or standing, whichever he did, but the Dutch master did favor doing nature. Of his 1887 *Sunflowers* he wrote: "I forget everything in favor of the external beauty of things, which I cannot reproduce, for in my pictures I render it as something coarse and ugly, whereas nature seems perfect to me."

So it was with the Lee Jack setting: a perfect river environment on a perfect day. Rain only enhances the sensual experience. Let's face it, you're wet anyway; being in water tends to have that effect. But the smell of a clean river in the rain is exhilarating. It is like the smell of fresh rain on dry leaves in the autumn woods.

The "spiders on water" of my notes were water striders. They are seen everywhere on the river's surface, skimming and skipping along, literally walking on water. The "bugs about so long" were coffee bugs, little black bugs shaped like coffee beans that also walk on water. The "huge cliff" is one of the many marvelous cliffs on lower Birch. For more about this one, see "The Rocks" chapter.

I heard Rob slogging toward the Lee Jack Plout. He didn't see me, and he called out. I stuffed my smudged notes back into the freezer bag and into the hip pocket of my jeans, and emerged from the overhang and began fishing. Moments before, Rob had caught a Kentucky spotted bass, a species that inhabits Birch but in far less numbers than smallmouth. He also caught a twelve inch rock bass that was the largest I'd ever seen in Birch. It measured from his elbow to his wrist.

On my third cast, the Lee Jack Bass came out of the depths of a dark green pool of swirling water, near where flecks of foam washed back and forth in the calmer water on the opposite side. It missed the lure, and disappeared, but it wasn't finished. It flashed again, and missed again, perhaps by design. I think smallmouth tend to do this if they aren't particularly hungry. It didn't return, which meant that for the rest of the day, and days to come, and months and years and decades and generations and eternity to come, I could exaggerate its size. But it was a very nice smallmouth.

- - -

Warder Dean didn't take note of the Lee Jack Plout, either in his narrative or his sketch, but he did include the Abner, the next hole upstream, which, according to river lore, was named for a man who drowned there while helping take logs downriver. This could have occurred anytime from the late 1800s to the early 1900s. Any further knowledge of him remains locked in the mists of time. Warder apparently didn't know, because he didn't mention anything more than the name of the hole, and the fact that he caught a small muskie there. But I have long been haunted by the man named Abner who met his fate on one of the roughest and most isolated sections of Birch.

There are three large rocks guarding the upper end of the hole, with a narrow passage of water between the two on the right. Was it there that he drowned? Immediately below the Abner Hole is a maelstrom of swift water and rocks. Was it somewhere in this stretch?

I think about this; Rob thinks about copperheads. We were fishing there one year when he was a teenager, and perhaps on that occasion doubted that he would ever see twenty. We encountered two copperheads on the driftwood-strewn trail that runs above the Abner, and another time I stepped over a copperhead that was lying in the cleft of a rock. All of them escaped, a fact that is not lost on Rob each time he returns to the Abner.

Below the Abner, in the maelstrom, lives the Abner Bass. It was the largest I saw during our year of fishing, with the possible exception of the Lee Jack Bass, and with the likely exception of an eighteen-inch smallmouth that Rob caught at the Lower Keener Eddy. The Abner Bass appeared magically about a foot behind my lure in clear, quiet water, which is uncharacteristic of a large smallmouth. Generally they are found in fast-moving water with cover. Like a wary shopper at an upscale store, this fish looked but didn't buy. But I thought: how lifeless a river would be without the Abner Bass and its kin.

Warder Dean wrote about a small island immediately below the Abner that he called Piney Island because of a lone pine (hemlock) tree

The Abner, named for a man of mystery

that stood on it. That was in 1939; today Piney Island is covered with hemlocks and shrubs.

- - -

One day I walked the river from the Lower Keener Eddy to Leatherwood Run, accompanied by Benjie Nichols, who has lived near the mouth of Leatherwood most of his life. We reached the Upper Turn Hole, an idyllic setting in the shadow of the Devil's Backbone. We met three campers there, all of whom work for coal companies: Doug Morris, a foreman for A.T. Massey; his wife, Emma, who works for Evergreen on the head of Birch; and Joe Morton, who also works for A.T. Massey. They were enjoying a week of camping and fishing.

I mentioned to Doug that my nephew and I had been fishing on Birch a lot that summer, and he quietly asked: "Do you keep your catches?"

My answer was no. My nephew and I release everything we catch.

Almost equally important, we doubted that we had lost a single fish in the process of releasing them. Birch is a small stream in a relatively infertile watershed, which makes it, and streams like it, particularly susceptible to over-fishing, or, more to the point, over-keeping.

- - -

One of the storied fishermen of Birch River was Guy Bragg, who lived at Birch Village and fished not only Birch but other rivers, including Elk, Gauley, Cranberry, and Cherry. He was unique in that he was almost exclusively a fly fisherman.

"He would fish all weekend and then spend the rest of the week repairing his tackle," said a daughter, Judy Bragg Brooks of Falls Church, Virginia. "I can still see him applying fingernail polish and thread to his double-built bamboo fly rod."

She recalls that among his Birch haunts were the Blue Hole and the mouth of Birch. "He walked and fly-fished," said his daughter. "When he came to a hole the length of a football field, he would fish it two or three times."

He was well ahead of his time as a conservationist. "He would measure his catches and then release them," his daughter remembered. "He would occasionally keep enough for a 'mess,' but no more."

Guy Bragg worked in the coal mines at Widen and Tioga; he died in 1980.

- - -

The Upper Turn Hole (Warder called it the "Little Turn Hole") is located about three miles above the mouth of the river. Its counterpart, the Lower Turn Hole, is located farther downstream, a precursor of the Mouth of Birch Eddy. The upper reminds me of a gigantic bathtub. It is deep and oval-shaped, and has a sandy bottom that contributes to its appeal as a classic "old swimming hole," of which there are many on Birch. A wire cable hangs from a tree to launch swimmers out over the water.

Below nature's bathtub the river narrows into a small shoal that leads to the Sand Hole, a long, shallow stretch of water at the lower end of the Devil's Backbone. Skeeter Pletcher of Gassaway (Pletcher Pontiac) has a camp at the Sand Hole. Naming the Sand Hole was an easy choice for someone. In its marvelous and mysterious ways, nature decided long ago to deposit half the sand in Birch River there. But it compensated in another way: the smallmouth and rock bass don't seem to mind; we found them in the pockets of cover along the shoreline, although they weren't large fish.

Below the Sand Hole lies a puzzle in the form of an eddy that is probably the longest in Birch, unless the Upper and Lower Keener Eddies are counted as one, which they normally aren't. The puzzle is whether this eddy is the Riffel or the Leatherwood, or both rolled into one. This enigma of lower Birch is discussed in the "Leatherwood Country" chapter.

But sufficient unto the day is the evil thereof: could I wade and fish in the River on the Rocks from the Smith Eddy to Herold without falling and breaking my neck?

The Smith Eddy is located almost precisely three miles below Herold at the mouth of Diatter Run. It is named for Alonzo (Lon) Smith, who farmed, had a mustache, raised watermelons in the river bottom, and traded in mules and horses. He would ride one of his mules to services at Middle Run Baptist Church.

A footbridge once crossed the eddy and was used by personnel of Hope Natural Gas Company (Dominion-Hope since a 2000 merger) in walking their pipeline. Pipeline surveillance is now done mostly by helicopter, and the bridge planking has been removed. The only physical reminders of this lower Birch landmark are the cables to which the planking was attached. Generations of daring swimmers once jumped into the river from the swinging bridge. They still swing out over the river and plummet in from a wire cable attached to a tree near the north end of the bridge and which has been there for as long as I can remember and which isn't my cup of tea and neither was the swinging, swaying bridge.

Rob and I were accompanied by James Tenney, teenage son of Roger and Peggy Tenney of Long Run. James brought along an impressive collection of crayfish, or crawfish, or crawcrabs, or crawdads (the list of colloquial names continues into infinity; Australians call them "bugs") that he had caught in Long Run. These crustaceans are to smallmouth and rock bass what a mouse is to a cat. The same can be said of hellgrammites and spring salamanders, or spring lizards, their colloquial name. My brother Bob has a phobia about crayfish, but he admires hellgrammites, those leathery aquatic insects, for their belligerence. "When you feel a tug on the line," he says, "it's the hellgrammite telling you that he has a fish on."

As for my bro's phobia, we must all admit that crayfish inspire a certain loathing, except among fish, which see them as the main course at a four-star restaurant. Their formidable pincers wave menacingly in the current; their legs (four on each side plus the pincers, which are counted as legs) are misshapen and end in forked little feet; their antennae are long and sinister looking; and their beady little eyes protrude grossly. If you look long enough at a head-on picture of a crayfish, you too will develop a phobia. And make no mistake, both crayfish and hellgrammites can pinch until it hurts if they get hold of a small enough chunk of skin to bring the full force of their pincers into play.

There are nineteen species of crayfish found in West Virginia, and Bob isn't fond of any of them.

James had not previously fished lower Birch, and the interminable shoal between the Smith Eddy and the Mouth of Middle Run is not a good place to start. It is long and shallow and devoid of cover. So we approached Middle Run in anticipation that our real day of fishing was about to begin. I know this hole, perhaps unimaginatively, as the Mouth of Middle Run. Warder called it Shaver Eddy for the Henry and Margaret Butcher Shaver family, who lived just upstream at the Blue Hole in the early 1900s.

The name Blue Hole is so ingrained in the consciousness of anyone who is familiar with lower Birch that perhaps Warder didn't want to tamper with it; he may have simply assigned the name of the family that lived at the Blue Hole to the eddy immediately below it. In any event, only a small curve in the river separates the Blue Hole and the Mouth of Middle Run, a.k.a. Shaver, Eddy. This curve is where old automobile tires go to spawn and die, or so it seems. The hydraulics of the river deposit many of them there. Birch is not badly littered, but it does have its share of tires thrown into the river by people with the I.Q. of a groundmole.

We began to catch fish at the Mouth of Middle Run and Blue Hole. James caught a nice bass on a crayfish (earlier in the year and farther upriver he had caught two seventeen inch smallmouth on crayfish), but he switched to lures because they are better suited to fishing on the move, and he was very efficient with them.

My principal contribution that day was to coin the phrase "the Called Shot" as applied to fishing on Birch. Babe Ruth made it a part of sports lexicon in the 1932 World Series with his called shot home run against the Chicago Cubs. I began to call my shots (predict that I would catch a fish on a specific cast, based on a gut feeling and reading the water), and actually did quite well with it for a time, but overall the numbers weren't adding up. It was like one of those election night maps where states are colored for a particular candidate; more and more of them were being colored for Rob and James.

But I hadn't fallen in the river, and I had caught the largest bass, a fourteen incher at the Blue Hole. Then we came to the Fast Hollow. I sat and rested and admired the two thousand and twenty five ton Fast Hollow Rock (see "The Rocks") while Rob and James fished. When I got up, I stepped on a sloping, slick underwater rock and fell every which way, thus answering the question I posed eleven paragraphs earlier: could I fish River on the Rocks from the Smith Eddy to Herold without falling and breaking my neck? The answer was no and yes. No, I didn't make it without falling, but yes, I did make it without breaking my neck.

- - -

Looking back at our fishing outings in 2000, it was interesting to compare them with Warder's account of his trip. He wrote:

> Some thirty five years ago [1939] Birch River provided some of the finest fishing water to be found in West Virginia. This was before the advent of the spinning reel and rod on this stream. The tackle then consisted of the bait casting rod, both bamboo and steel, and the bamboo fly rod with single action fly reel. The casting line was silk and the fly line was enameled silk. The lures were wooden plugs and bass flies tied in various colors with trade names like "terror fly" and "fuzzy wuzzy" (a real bass killer when worked behind a spinner). The pikie minnow is about the only lure still a favorite with fishermen.

> This kind of a trip could still be made, but I would suggest some changes to suit this day and time [he wrote his narrative in 1974]. To anyone interested, don't go with the expectation of catching many fish. Road construction and erosion upstream has about ruined the fishing with extreme sedimentation. We made the mistake of trying to cover the distance in one day. We should have camped one night about midway. This would have allowed a more leisurely trip and given more time to fish the good spots.

> The trip would be worthwhile even if not a fish be caught. The boulders are still there. The many pools and foaming rapids have changed very little. The towering hemlocks and the fringe of rhododendron and white honeysuckle line the shore, along with the stately oak, maple, poplar and hickory trees standing farther back. The wild flowers still bloom in profusion such as the white and purple trillium, violets, wild geranium, jewelweed and many others. The birds still sing the sweet song as of old, and the gray squirrels still come down from the hillsides morning and evening to drink at the river's edge. The huckleberry bushes still grow on the huckleberry rock [the Falls Rock]. Cool spring water still gushes from the bank at the sulphur spring near the falls. The falls still roar when at tide, but when the river is low, a softer sound is produced. That, along with the call of the whipporwill and the croaking of the frogs, would lull a camper to sleep even on a pile of stones on the shore.

He concluded:

> Here I will add one sad note to this otherwise pleasant tale, and that is the prospect of all this beautiful scenery being covered up by a manmade lake if the U.S. Corps of Engineers

at Huntington have their way about it. Along with it would go the last free flowing river in Central West Virginia. Many hearts would be saddened if this should come to pass due to the fact that many of our ancestors settled here and raised large families of sons and daughters who went out to make good in the world.

- - -

His mention of sediment from road construction was a reference to the 1970-1974 building of new U.S. 19, part of which crosses the Birch drainage in Nicholas and Braxton Counties. The river was muddy a lot during that period, and undoubtedly suffered from it. By contrast, the 1996-1998 upgrade of U.S. 19 to four lanes produced very little muddy water, the result of more stringent regulations required of contractors by the Department of Highways to control erosion.

I do not think the amount of sediment existing in Birch today is affecting the smallmouth fishing significantly, but I believe that the walleye fishing has declined, whether for this or other reasons. People familiar with lower Birch have told me the river has filled in considerably over the years, which is probably true to a degree, and this may be affecting the walleye migration up Birch from Elk River, and their spawning. Or the problem may be the walleye population in Elk itself.

But while the bass fishing is undoubtedly not as good as in Birch's heyday (the same can be said of almost any river), it's not bad, either. Rob and I walked and fished the river a lot in 2000, and we weren't walking just for walking's sake.

The proposed Birch Reservoir mentioned by Warder in 1974 never came about (see "A Much Studied River").

- - -

There is a hidden plout in lower Birch that I named "the Comeback Hole" because I caught several smallmouth there on one of our outings when I was scrambling to catch up with Rob's catches.

"If we were counting," I asked, "what would the score be?"

That line caught on.

"I realize we aren't counting," one of us would say after a catch, "but if we were, what would the score be?"

"Of course we aren't counting," the other would reply, and would then go on to recite exactly who had caught what and how many.

For two people who weren't counting, it was like we were working for the U.S. Treasury and keeping track of the national debt.

So how many fish did we catch?

Well, if we were counting....

- - -

Birch River - Summer for the Ages

I asked my nephew, Rob Johnson, to write his thoughts on our year of fishing in Birch in 2000. They follow:

Birch River has been an important part of my life for all of my forty one years. As a young boy, I would spend hours on end looking for crawdads and then fishing until I ran out of bait. Even if the fish weren't biting, crawling on and over the many rocks of Birch River and exploring its banks were great ways to spend a day.

My fishing experiences on the Birch has pretty much been concentrated in the Herold area, with occasional side trips to the Falls, which are located about one mile below Herold. It was always an adventure, especially when I was younger, to cross the river at the Fisher Camp and to then walk the old jeep trail down to the Falls.

You would always hear the Falls before you got there, which was a part of the trip I always enjoyed. We would fish the river the entire way back to Herold, sometimes having good luck and sometimes not catching many fish at all. No matter how many times that trip was made, it was always a different and enjoyable experience. It could be catching fish, enjoying the walk along the river or just experiencing the majesty of the changing seasons, but that is always a trip that I have loved and have never turned down.

So when the opportunity came this year [2000] to practically fish Birch from just below the mouth of Little Birch to its confluence with the Elk River at Glendon, I couldn't wait to start.

We planned our initial trip in late June. It was decided to fish the stretch of river from the ford above the Smith Eddy all the way back to Herold. This would require us to walk the river for approximately four miles. That sounded good to me. This first trip consisted of my Uncle Skip, Jamie Tenney, and myself. Jamie is a family friend and a resident of the Herold area. He had never fished any of this lower stretch of the river, and I had only a little more experience there. Skip has fished this area before, but of course we won't get into ages or the opportunities that come with age.

The ford where we began this trip brought back a memory of my grandmother, Carmine Johnson, Skip and myself at this very ford thirty-some odd years ago. Skip has a picture of me in the river at this ford tucked away somewhere in his archives.

But I digress. We had an excellent day for walking the river and fishing back to Herold. The fishing was good enough to keep our interest throughout the day. However, the best experience for me was seeing a part of Birch River that I had never had the opportunity to see before. I have canoed from Herold to Glendon a number of times but I had never fished during any of those trips. Birch, especially in this area, is best fished by doing exactly what we were doing: walking and taking our time while fishing each inviting looking hole of water.

As on any fishing trip, the big one always gets away and this one was not any different. Skip raised the nicest fish of the day (or at least he said he did) just below the Abner. That by itself would give us the incentive (like I would need any) to make this trip a yearly event.

One week later we were at the same ford, but this time our destination was Glendon, about six miles downriver. I had brought along my thirteen foot Grumman canoe as well as my ten year old daughter, Rebekah. It was another perfect day to fish on Birch, as it was not too hot and was slightly overcast. We fished the Smith Eddy and both of the Keener Eddies, and we were not disappointed with the results. The biggest fish of this trip flopped off my lure before I could handle it. It was every bit as big as the bass I had caught on an earlier trip with Skip and my thirteen year old son, Travis, at the Lower Keener Eddy. Travis was farther up the bank fishing, while Skip and I were fishing from the canoe. When I landed that fish, I hollered at Travis to come and see it. Travis has caught a few fish in his day, but he had seen nothing like this bass. The look on his face was priceless, as I thought his eyes would bug out. Skip had pretty much told me to throw my plug in a particular spot on the basis that he had once caught a nice bass there. So this was another of his 'Called Shots' of the 2000 summer.

But getting back to the trip at hand: we fished the deeper holes and pulled the canoe through most of the shoals. Well, Skip pulled the canoe through the shoals while I fished. The river's flow this day was just short of what was needed for an uninterrupted float to Glendon. Rebekah probably had the worst ride of all because she was sitting on a makeshift seat in the middle of the canoe. But she never once complained, and I think she enjoyed seeing this part of Birch River that was brand new to her.

The beauty of Birch River, and especially this stretch that we were on, is the lack of roads and houses along its path. With the exception of the road at Herold and a few other jeep trails, most access is only by walking or boating. Likewise, this trip leads to very few homes or camps until you get to the last couple of miles of the river. We were enjoying our trip and time had kind of passed us by as we approached the Leatherwood Shoal. We knew that if we didn't hurry, Denzil Baughman, who had agreed to pick us up at Glendon, was going to have quite a wait. We decided to quit fishing and just paddle through the last two miles of our journey. It was a nice end to a perfect day as we glided through the eddies of lower Birch River.

We encountered our first human contact of the day at the Lower Turn Hole. Two groups of fishermen were at this distinctive eddy where Birch makes an abrupt ninety degree turn toward Elk River. After we greeted our fellow anglers, we entered the last eddy of Birch. The log boom islands passed by, and the train trestle that signals the end of Birch came into view. This last eddy was home to the state record muskie caught in the 1950s. We floated under the blackened train trestle and entered Elk River. It was noticeably different in width and flow from what we had grown used to that day. We paddled across, and another great day on Birch was now another valued memory.

The last trip of the summer began a little differently from the previous two. Instead of driving down to the river, we drove to the mountaintop home of Walter Pierson. From there, a steep path leads downhill to the Brady Rock, which is a huge overhanging rock cliff. Brady Run flows over this and makes a spectacular waterfall rivaled by few. However, Brady Run runs dry for the majority of the year.

Just fifty yards below the Brady Rock lies Birch River. This area is about three quarters of a mile below the confluence of Little Birch and Big Birch, and about four miles above Herold. The fishing in this stretch of river was consistent with the fishing we had on the other stretches of the river. But the hard part of this fishing trip was this walk itself. This stretch of river is characterized by numerous boulders of various sizes, and small eddies separated by swift water and rocky shoals. I took a number of pretty good tumbles, but my only injury was a bruised behind from landing on too many of Birch's rocks.

I was fishing alone this day, and since I had never fished this area before I was having quite an experience. Everything was brand new to me, and I was in my own little world.

Something new waited behind every rock and just beyond each bend of the river. I had been up the road that parallels the opposite side of the river that I was on, but I had never fished this area like this.

I fished the entire stretch back to Herold in about seven hours. It was quite a day for me, and I was anxious to share my experiences with my family as I entered the yard from the river at Herold. I was thirty yards from the house and I heard footsteps as someone ran through the house. Unbeknownst to me, Skip and my Mom and Dad had decided that I should have been home at least three or four hours ago. Mom met me at the porch and demanded to know where I had been. I started to reply, but before I could she hugged me and started crying. She then told me that everyone thought that I must have gotten hurt somewhere along my trip because Skip thought I should have been home hours ago. Gee, thanks Skip. Skip and my Dad were walking down from Walter's with the idea that they would eventually find me along the river. Mother drove me to the Johnson Campground, and against her better judgment she let me out of her sight as I crossed the river.

I walked over to the road and began to hunt for my search party. I found them just below the first shoal below the Brady Run Eddy. It's kind of funny when you find someone that is looking for you. I couldn't tell if it was relief when they saw me, or maybe they were just a little ticked off that they had just walked off of that steep mountain down to the river for nothing. Regardless, it was an unforgettable end to my unforgettable summer of fishing on Birch River.

They say that the fishing on Birch, as well as many other small streams, is not quite what it used to be. Well, what is? Fishing pressure, floods, and extended periods of muddy water have had an effect on Birch. Never before had I fished Birch as much or fished that much of it, but rest assured I'm already planning my trips for next summer.

~ Thirteen ~

The Blue Hole

And Middle Run, Smith Eddy, and Diatter Run

The proverbial story about highway curves so sharp that you meet yourself coming back can also be applied to the curves of lower Birch River, particularly those at the Devil's Backbone and the Lower Turn Hole.

But there are other loops as well. Birch makes a sweeping turn above Herold, another at the Falls and Fast Hollow, another at the Blue Hole, and one at Leatherwood Run, for a total of six.

In actuality, these six could be expanded to eight or nine. Readers may want to make their own count from the map that accompanies this book, but suffice it to say, the river can't decide in which direction it wants to run from above Herold to the mouth.

The largest of the six is the Blue Hole loop, which is located 7.5 miles above the mouth of the river. The Blue Hole is to Birch River what the enigmatic smile on Mona Lisa's face is to the Leonardo da Vinci painting: everybody who knows the painting knows the smile; everybody who knows lower Birch River knows the Blue Hole.

The loop that derives its name from the hole is shaped like a large morel, those edible mushrooms that grow in the spring: place a ruler on the bottom of the loop on a topographic map, and the mushroom takes shape. It begins at the upper Blue Hole bottom, and ends at the Upper Keener Eddy, a distance of over a mile, and includes the mouth of Middle Run, the Smith Eddy, and the mouth of Diatter Run.

The storied Blue Hole

At one stretch on the dirt road that runs from Adams Ridge to the Smith Eddy, the river lies on both sides, so pronounced is the loop.

I went there on a frigid day in December 2000 when the temperature never got above twenty five degrees. A chilling wind blew snow flurries across the road, and I heard the piercing cry of a red-tailed hawk, but could not locate him in the gray winter sky. Some two hundred feet below us the Blue Hole and Raven Eddy were visible in the leafless landscape, with the Anderson Davis Knob prominent just to the southwest. I envied the hawk's better view of this panorama of lower Birch, but mine wasn't bad either. There is a raw and natural quality about a river environment in winter: the starkness of naked trees, the green of hemlocks, the white of sycamores, the cold, the deer tracks frozen in the sand, and the river itself glimmering far below in the paleness, its every turn so much more clearly defined.

I returned with a friend in late February 2001 for a clearer look at the ending of the loop; there were no snow flurries, and the river wasn't frozen as before, but the wind still had a bite that spoke of winter hanging on. We saw two loops: the conclusion of the Blue Hole loop at the Harry Nettles property (south side of the river), and a smaller but very pronounced loop that comprises part of the Upper Keener Eddy and all of the Lower Keener. On the north side of the river near the end of the larger loop is a thick growth of hemlocks on a steep river bluff that stands out as the perfect signature of lower Birch in wintertime.

The steep hillside above the Upper Keener on the south side is a tangle of rhododendron. Looking at it, I thought of the story of the Leaning Beech Coon. Dale Lewis and Ray Teets were hunting there on a night that was pouring rain. Their dog treed a coon and Dale climbed the Leaning Beech and began blowing on a "coon squaller," which makes a distress sound that irritates coons big time. Suddenly a cavity in the beech above Dale was filled with the Leaning Beech Coon, the largest he'd ever seen. It bolted down the tree, eluded the dog, gained refuge under a rock, and for all we know may still be there, gnashing its teeth in anger.

- - -

The Blue Hole is the only hole on Birch that is mentioned on U.S. Geological Survey maps, and in fact appears in type size that is otherwise reserved for the major tributaries. I'm not sure why, but perhaps it's simply because the Blue Hole is said to be deeper than any other hole on Birch, and has therefore gained a certain aura of mystery.

But exactly how deep is a question that will not be answered here. It would, of course, be an easy matter to drop a weighted line into the hole and determine the depth, and probably this has been done many times. But not all of nature's secrets need to be known; it was intrusion enough that I had the largest rocks on Birch weighed (see "The Rocks").

When the National Park Service studied the river for possible inclusion in the National Wild and Scenic Rivers System, it assigned a depth of thirty feet to the Blue Hole. I doubt, however, if it's anywhere near that deep at normal summer flow; twenty feet, maybe.

The Blue Hole makes a very abrupt turn at its lower end, somewhat like the abruptness of a bent elbow, but not before it eddies out into a large, round pool that swirls at high flows, perhaps producing a scouring effect that causes the deepness. Because of its configuration, the pool resembles a pond, lacking only lily pads and bullfrogs (the latter have become scarce, and Birch never had lily pads in the first place).

Bullfrogs were once plentiful on Birch. Burton Pierson told about camping at the Blue Hole with John Blake, Berkley Keener, Charles Wilt, and Wilbur Blake, and catching "a bucket full of frogs." I hadn't heard a bullfrog's bellow in Birch for at least ten years, until summer 2000, when I heard one just after I had gone to bed. It was like a ghost from out of the past. For the next several nights, I heard it again, but more faintly, and then no more. I mentioned this to Tom Pauley, associate professor of biology at Marshall University, who has written extensively about amphibians of West Virginia, and he chuckled. "Perhaps," he said, "it was a male seeking to attract a female, but got no answer, and moved on." Pauley speculates that bullfrogs and their eggs may be more sensitive to environmental changes than some other frog species (not all are in trouble).

- - -

There is another attribute of the Blue Hole: it's so well known that it serves as a point of reference for almost everything else on lower Birch, just as the Cora Brown bridge does for the middle section, and the falls at Boggs do for the upper part.

For example, the mouth of Middle Run is not just that; it's the mouth of Middle Run below the Blue Hole; and the Raven Eddy could never stand on its own except among a few intimates of lower Birch; it's the Raven Eddy above the Blue Hole. And so it goes.

The Blue Hole comes by its name honestly: the water really is a striking indigo blue when seen from above river level in the wintertime during low flows. Its bluish tint is most pronounced at the narrow neck where it enters the rounded pool. In terms of an ocean, blue water means deep water. There is a line in the movie, *Message in a Bottle*, when Kevin Costner is heading out in stormy waters in his sailboat, and Paul Newman yells from the shore, "Are you going out into the blue water?" (Costner's movie character drowned in the blue water).

There are probably Blue Holes or variations thereof on half the rivers of the western hemisphere. There's a Blue Hole on upper Elk River, a Blue Hole on New River at the top of Gauley Mountain, a Blue Hole on the Fajardo River in eastern Puerto Rico, a Blue Hole on the Macal River in Belize, and a Blue Bend on the Greenbrier River; the list goes on.

Paul Roche, who lived in Puerto Rico before he came to Birch River, remembers fondly the Blue Hole on the Fajardo, which drains out of the Yunke rain forest. That Blue Hole has a natural rock slide into the water, and a rock from which to jump. The Birch River Blue Hole has a small "jumping" rock on one side of the river, and a combination wire cable and rope dangling from a tree on the other side.

Denzil Baughman and I once swam at the Blue Hole without really intending to. We borrowed a leaky johnboat that had been left there, and were in the middle of the hole when the boat sank. It was dark and we didn't realize what was happening until it had happened. But we got a nice campfire going, and dried our clothes around it.

The offending johnboat may have been the last of a breed. I don't recall seeing another one on Birch, and they have disappeared from Elk and other rivers in favor of lightweight aluminum boats or canoes. John-boats were made of poplar wood for buoyancy, they were mostly flat bot-tomed, narrow and square-ended, a dream to paddle, and a descendent of the Indian dugouts that were hollowed out of logs. But a craftsman was required to build and maintain one that wouldn't leak. Our "Titanic" on that dark night at the Blue Hole had no doubt served its owner well in its time.

One of the best known, and perhaps last, johnboat builder in West Virginia was Tom Cole of Gauley Bridge, who built fifty of these boats over the years. His grandfather, James B. Cole, began this family tradition that continued with Tom's uncles, Jim and Ed Cole, and his father, Walter Cole. A few years ago, Tom filled the most unusual johnboat order of his career: a 12-footer for a whitewater rafting firm at Ames, Fayette County, for a salad bar at its restaurant.

There are more fishing tales connected with the Blue Hole than with any other place on Birch River. Audrey Baughman caught a large walleye early one morning at the upper end of the Blue Hole when the mists were still rising from the water, and I was still curled up in a sleeping bag underneath the Blue Hole rock ledge. The fish was twenty six and one-half inches long and was caught on a River Runt, one of the classic old lures made by Heddon. Years later, Raban Young caught a twenty eight inch walleye at the Blue Hole on a Flatfish, also a classic lure.

The rock ledge is another Blue Hole attribute. It is quite large and has sheltered more than its share of fishermen and campers from rainstorms, and provided a place to spend the night that is not quite out under the stars. My neighbor, Peggy Tenney, once declined to sleep out under the stars with her son and daughter. "I was afraid I'd wake up in the morning and something would have built a nest in my hair," she explained.

On the north side of the river, opposite the rock ledge, is the bottom where Henry and Margaret Butcher Shaver and their children lived in the early 1900s. Yucca plants, with their long, rigid, fibrous leaves, are the telltale signs that someone once lived there. An army of yucca salesmen must have toured the countryside in the early twentieth century selling these plants, because yuccas are still found at many old homesites. The bank around my grandfather's circa 1906 cellar at Herold is dotted with yuccas, and I have wrapped many a weed-eater string around them.

Foundation stones from the Shaver house are visible on the edge of a high bank above the river where it makes its abrupt turn and heads toward the mouth of Middle Run. We can only speculate why the house was built so close to the riverbank, but perhaps it wasn't that close originally; the river may have cut into the bank and edged closer to the house site over the years.

Henry Shaver was of German descent; his great grandfather was a Hessian (those who came from a region in southwest Germany) who may have served with the British forces in the American Revolution. Henry Shaver's grandfather was born in America in 1795; his father, James Shaver, was born in West Virginia in 1834, probably in Braxton County, because he is buried at the Middle Run Cemetery.

The Shavers came to the Blue Hole in 1903, the year they were married. All four of their children were born there between 1905 and 1909: sons Marvin and Howard, and daughters Minnie and Maysell. Henry Shaver died of influenza in 1911 at age twenty nine; his widow married Al Murphy in 1916, and they lived at the Blue Hole until around

1923. Retta Faye Murphy Tyree of Summersville remembers her dad putting her in a washtub and pushing her around the Blue Hole.

Al and Margaret Shaver Murphy later lived at the Waitman Fast place on the Frametown Road, and at the Thomas Dixon place on upper Keener's Ridge (see "The Poem"). The Dixon family held a reunion there in 1938, and Bill Dixon recalls Al Murphy walking around the yard on his hands, which Bill's father had requested him to do because he knew he was good at it.

The Shaver sons, Marvin and Howard, moved to Widen in the 1920s and worked for the Elk River Coal and Lumber Company. Howard is the father of David Shaffer, a Widen native and administrator of the Stonewall Jackson Hospital at Weston. The descendents of Henry and Margaret Shaver still own the Blue Hole property.

Henry and Margaret Shaver are buried at Middle Run Cemetery. Margaret Shaver was the daughter of Andrew and Delila Keener Butcher, who were among the early residents at the Martha Butcher Hole on Birch. Delila Butcher was blind; Valeria Dean Strickland, who was born at the Lower Keener Eddy, remembers seeing Andrew and Delila walking along the river, with Delila holding to her husband's suspenders for guidance.

Thurman and Antonia Frame may also have lived at the Blue Hole. Pershing Keener recalls visiting them in the late 1920s. The Frames were supposedly living at the Blue Hole in 1930 when a son, Harry, died.

- - -

Both Middle Run and Diatter Run head near Coon Knob, the 1,818-foot prominence on Interstate 79 one mile west of the U.S. 19 interchange. The highway crosses the south side of Coon Knob, and one of the superb views of the rolling hills of central West Virginia is from I-79 looking south toward Long Run. Birch is well connected to I-79: the superhighway runs under the Leatherwood Run Road, and brushes close to Long, Middle, and Diatter Runs.

Northeast of Coon Knob, across Coon Creek, is a phenomenon of nature: holes in the ground where geothermally-produced steam rises from rock crevices. Randall Butcher, the property owner, took me there in late December 2000 in the company of Peter and Elizabeth Silitch, the editors of this book. The ambient air temperature was twenty five degrees, but not near the crevices; I placed a thermometer above one of them, and within minutes the reading had climbed to forty seven degrees! I warmed my hands over the crevice.

The colder the outside temperature, the more visible the steam, of course. Randall told us about visiting the crevices one clear morning during the winter of 1995-96 when the temperature was twelve below zero, and the steam rising from the hole was probably visible from the interstate about a half mile away.

Geothermals, or steam rising to the surface from the earth's molten inner core, are not unique; Yellowstone National Park in the western United States is famous for its geothermals, which include hot springs and geysers, and there are many other examples. But "taking the waters" on Coon Creek may not become medicinally popular, since there is no water associated with the Coon Creek geothermal.

Ken Ashton of the West Virginia Geological Survey told me that although the geothermal on Coon Creek might be unique to the area, geothermals in general are not unique to sandstone formations. "That's probably where you would find them," he said, "because water percolates up through sandstone. Although limestone seems super hard, it is more likely to dissolve."

- - -

Middle Run starts about three hundred feet below Coon Knob at an elevation of 1,500 feet, and flows in a southwesterly direction to Birch River. It crosses the Herold-Frametown Road at the site of the former Middle Run School, at which point it is slightly more than halfway toward its meeting with Birch.

Among the early settlers on Upper Middle Run were Peter and Nancy Davis Cowger, the great-great grandparents of Sam Cowger of Herold Road and Patty Cowger James of Gassaway. Peter is believed to have migrated here from Pennsylvania. He died in 1907, and his two-story log house with board siding still stands near the head of the run. His great grandson, Junior Cowger of Baltimore, owns the ancestral property. Peter and Nancy Cowger are buried at Middle Run Cemetery.

There are many Cowgers buried at Middle Run, reflecting the numerous presence of this family in the area at one time. Some of the graves date back to the late 1800s. In some instances, their surnames on tombstones are spelled "Cauger" or "Couger." The original Germanic spelling was "Gaugar." (In another cemetery, I noticed a man's name spelled differently on two different tombstones: his own tombstone and the tombstone of one of his two wives).

The defining property on upper Middle Run is the Alfred Cowger farm, which can be seen from Interstate 79 near Coon Knob. Alfred, son of Peter, lived there with his wife, Mariah Duffield Cowger, and farmed the sprawling, rolling ridgetop in the late 1800s and early 1900s. He had a small store on top of the hill which was patronized primarily by local residents who walked back and forth between Middle Run and and Long Run, and he was also a constable.

More recent owners of the Alfred Cowger property were Virgil and Faye Cowger Bail; Faye, the daughter of Alfred, was born there. She married Virgil Bail in 1933, and they lived on the isolated farm for fifty seven years. Virgil worked at Libbey-Owens-Ford in Charleston, and farmed; Faye was a schoolteacher, and was the last teacher at the one-room Middle Run School, which closed in 1959. The school building was eventually moved farther up the run, and remodeled, and is now a private residence.

Virgil Bail died in 1990, and Faye died in 1992; both are buried at Middle Run.

There is a splendid view of the lower Birch watershed from the farm, which is now owned by Vaughn and Patty Cowger James. Coon Knob and I-79 lie to the northeast; James Knob to the northwest toward Frametown; Long Run, Road Run, and Polemic Run to the south; and the Anderson Davis Knob at Eureka Methodist Church to the southwest.

James Knob is named for early settler Scott James and his son, Freeman. The probable namesake of the Davis Knob is William Anderson Davis, who lived in the vicinity of the Eureka Methodist Church at the time of the 1880 census. He was probably related to "Squire" George Davis, who owned the knob in later years.

Sam Cowger, who grew up on the Virgil Bail farm, remembers the view at haying time: "Everybody put up hay more or less at the same time, and you could see people in the hayfields a great distance away, for example at the Waitman Pierson and Oscar Clifton farms, and across Road Run."

A recent nighttime sight is the lights from the cell phone towers on Powell's Mountain.

- - -

A companion piece to Middle Run for its entire journey to Birch River is Middle Ridge, which raises the question: is the run named for the ridge, or the ridge named for the run? In the long ago, waterways were usually named first, so the latter sequence may be the correct one.

Middle Ridge is a commanding presence on the U.S. Geological Survey's Herold Quadrangle topographic map, being well defined by Middle Run, Long Run, and Birch River. It appears in the shape of a large running animal, its front feet being the loop the river makes around the Falls, Fast Hollow, and the Abner Hole, and its head being where the ridge narrows as it approaches the Blue Hole and mouth of Middle Run.

The lower end of Middle Ridge covers over five hundred acres of uninhabited woodland, with a Jeep road bisecting it. This road follows the top of the ridge and is called "the Middle Ridge Passway," or simply "the Old Passway." Its origin dates back to the early 1900s when the owner or owners of the upper portion granted, in writing, a right-of-way to the few families who lived downridge.

The existence of the Passway is academic now because one person owns virtually all of the lower ridge, including the old road, and, anyway, nobody lives downridge anymore.

George Marshall, a Sutton native who lives in Huntington, began buying land on Middle Ridge in 1986, and in winter 2000-2001 his ownership embraced five hundred and fifty two contiguous acres. He owns another one hundred and sixty five acres on nearby Diatter Run, for a total of seven hundred and seventeen acres.

His Middle Ridge property includes about a mile and a half of remote Birch River frontage on the north side from Herold downstream to the Raven Eddy. It touches the river again at the mouth of Middle Run below the Blue Hole.

George's camp on Middle Ridge has become a mecca for hunters, most of them from New York and Pennsylvania, who join him for pursuit of deer and turkey. The regulars include Ralph Snodgrass and Robert Joins of Stewartstown, Pennsylvania; Lon Ricci of Greenwood, New York; Tom Richardson of Utica, New York; Phil Batterson of Gaines, Pennsylvania; Steve Cochran, Jim Zengerle, and Charlie Sullivan of Galeton, Pennsylvania (where the Eakin Lumber Company's Shay engine is on display; see "Shay It Isn't So"), and West Virginians Arnold Keaton of Glasgow, Dick and Kenny Nance of Lesage, Larry Abbott and John Sexton of Huntington, and Jim Marshall of Ripley.

One family that benefitted from the Old Passway was the Hillard (Dick) Jackson family. The Jacksons lived on the lower end of the ridge at a low gap on the Birch River side. The hollow below the house enters Birch at the Lee Jack Plout (see "If We Were Counting").

Although she never lived on Middle Ridge, Arlene Jackson Kimberling of Columbus, Ohio, daughter of Dick Jackson, recalled that one of her brothers, Arlis, was born there in 1911. He died tragically in 1918 at age seven when playmates rolled a rock down the hill that struck him (this occurred in the Middle Run area, but not on Middle Ridge). Dick Jackson later lived in Clay County, but returned to Braxton County and lived on the Frametown Road until his death in 1957; his wife, Bertha, died in 1965; both are buried at Middle Run Cemetery.

George Marshall's mother, Erie King Marshall, remembers her mother, Clara King, telling about carrying her in her arms to visit the Jacksons when they lived on lower Middle Ridge. Erie was about two years old, and the date was about 1915.

Later occupants of the Jackson house were Hampton and Nettie Keener and their children. Hampton was the son of Andrew Keener, one of the founders of the Middle Run Baptist Church. Hampton later moved to Bergoo, Webster County, and worked for the Pardee-Curtin Lumber Company. Pershing Keener, a nephew, tore the old house down sometime prior to World War II, had the lumber trucked out, and used it to build a chicken house at his family's farm on the Frametown Road.

Pershing's wife, Bobby Meadows Keener, remembers the house from the 1930s when she accompanied her mother, Maude, on ginseng hunting trips on lower Middle Ridge. It was falling down by that time.

The house figured in a manhunt in the mid-1930s. Three jail escapees were believed to be hiding in the area, and lawmen swarmed into Herold. Someone thought they may have taken refuge in the vacant house, and although it turned out they had left ahead of the lawmen, the fugitives confirmed upon capture that they had stayed there a night or two.

At that time, the Willie Lewis family (see "The Doctor and the Preacher") lived at the Waitman Fast place near Middle Ridge, and the lawmen arrived there about the time that Fannie Lewis called to her husband to come inside because it was starting to rain. The lawmen, thinking she was calling to the fugitives, quickly surrounded the house, and came inside and searched it. Jim, the youngest son of Willie and Fannie Lewis, was lying on the floor reading and looked up to see policemen wearing guns enter the house. There were no fugitives in the house, nor had there been.

In late January 2001, during respite from snow, Denzil Baughman and I walked down Middle Ridge to the site of the Dick Jackson house. All that remains is a pile of foundation rocks, and a dug-out place where the cellar was located. A grizzled old cedar tree stands at the house site; two small cedar trees nearby had been rubbed by buck deer during the fall. We could see the faint traces of an old wagon or sled road that led to the house.

The low gap lies in a gently-sloping cove that was cleared and farmed many years ago; the predominant tree species is yellow poplar, which is the tree of succession on cleared land. An ancient fence post stands as a reminder of long-ago farming, and here and there barbed wire protrudes from white oak trees.

A mystery of the low gap is a mound of dirt in a classic grave configuration that lies on level ground at the top of the low gap. Somewhat larger than a normal grave, it has been there for as long as I can remember, and always gave us something to talk about when we hunted there as teenagers.

- - -

Beyond the low gap, on a river bluff overlooking the Blue Hole and Raven Eddy, is the most unusual rock formation in the Birch watershed. I call it Pillar Rock because it sits precariously on a pillar of layered rock that appears to be totally incapable of holding up anything so heavy (it probably weighs in the hundreds of tons).

A more intriguing question is how it gained its precarious perch in the first place. But it did, and I suspect that if this marvel of nature was located within easy walking distance of a road, and if public access was available, it would be featured in West Virginia travel brochures.

Pillar is the largest of several rocks in the formation, and stands out sharply in wintertime when seen from across the river on the Adams Ridge Road. There is a passageway between the two largest rocks that adds to the allure.

I visited Pillar Rock on a gray, dreary day that carried a hint of rain and a bite in the air. I sat on a log surrounded by rhododendron, mountain laurel, holly, hemlocks, and oaks, and listened to the silence. The breeze began to ruffle the pages of my pocket-size notepad, and I felt drops of rain on my face. Reluctantly, I rose; it was time to leave this decidedly remote place, where all I saw were deer and a lone grouse, and all I heard was the river far below nestled in the hills of lower Birch.

- - -

Middle Run enters Birch a few hundred yards below the Blue Hole. A log cabin stood at the mouth of the run for many years, but it has since disappeared and its foundation rocks are covered with moss. A rusting coal bucket, bed springs, and stove remain as relics of former occupants, and a large gnarled pitch pine still stands guard at the house site, as it has for generations, as if awaiting another family.

Mouth of Middle Run

Several families lived in this house, in all probability, but I was able to identify only two for an absolute certainty: the Elmore and Nida Riddles, and the George and Mabelle Knights. The Riddles lived there in the 1930s, and the Knights lived there for about a year in the 1940s, and were probably the last.

Dreama Nichols Young believes that her grandfather, Bennie Nottingham, lived there prior to 1920. Certainly the house existed when the Riddles moved there in the 1930s. A 1924 map of Braxton County shows two houses at the mouth of Middle Run, one on each side of the creek, perhaps two or three hundred yards apart. There is a large, level bottom below Middle Run which was probably the site of the second house, although its occupant or occupants are unknown.

A wagon road came down the hill from Middle Ridge to the mouth of Middle Run. There are piles of rocks on the hillside above the mouth of the run, indicating that the land was once cleared and farmed. Elmore Riddle was one of those who farmed this hillside, according to his son, Park, who lives in Winter Haven, Florida. Park was a teenager when his family lived on Birch at Middle Run.

Nora King Murphy remembers visiting the Riddles. "She [Nida Riddle] kept the log cabin immaculate," Nora recalls. Probably Nora's favorite memory is that Mrs. Riddle always offered to make cookies, an offer Nora couldn't refuse. She carried them home in a brown paper bag, the grease from the cookies gradually seeping through.

One time Nida Riddle ordered a brood of biddies (young chickens), and brought them in around the fireplace when the night turned cold. Years later, I warmed myself at the same fireplace. I was hunting on Middle Ridge on opening day of deer season, and an unexpected storm brought in several inches of wet snow. I took shelter in the deserted cabin and built a fire, and spent the morning there.

Gaylord Riddle, one of the sons, was an improviser. Medford Teets, who lived downstream at the mouth of Leatherwood Run, recalls listening to the Grand Old Oprey at the Riddles' on a radio that was hooked to an automobile battery that Gaylord charged with a one-cylinder Maytag washer engine. He also built a steam-powered sawmill at the mouth of the run, and used it to grind corn as well as to cut lumber.

Gaylord lived with his parents at the mouth of Middle Run for a time after he was married, and another son, Oley, may also have lived there or in the vicinity after marriage.

Medford's sister, Marjorie Teets Young, visited the Riddles with her mother, Leota. They walked upriver from Leatherwood, detouring above the river and perhaps following "the old buffalo trail" that supposedly skirted the river high on the hill above the Smith Eddy. Erman Smith, grandson of Smith Eddy namesake Lon Smith, remembers hearing talk of such a trail, and I came across a deed whose property description referred to "the buffalo path." It may be one of the two roads shown on Civil War maps that ran along Birch (one of them being the present Keener's Ridge Road). The trail was said to have been large enough for wagons to use it.

The thirty two acre tract that comprises the mouth of Middle Run property is one of the most well-traveled properties on lower Birch from a standpoint of ownership. Twelve different parties have owned it since 1913. Its present owner is George Marshall.

- - -

The Smith Eddy downstream is named for Alonzo (Lon) Smith, a Ritchie County native who came to Braxton County in the early 1900s, and bought property at the Smith Eddy in 1912. He was a farmer and blacksmith, and a trader of horses and mules. A brother, Adam, lived on the north side of the river at the mouth of Diatter Run, and owned property there.

The Middle Run Baptist Church, which Lon attended, held its baptizings at the Smith Eddy for many years. Freda Wood, who lives on Birch near Herold, was baptized there in 1932.

Erma James Kuhl remembers being ridden across Birch at the mouth of Diatter on one of Lon's mules named Fannie. "She was the sweetest thing," said Erma.

Erma taught school on Keener's Ridge, probably at Rose Hill, prior to her marriage in 1932 to Virgil Kuhl, a native of Gilmer County. She walked from her home on the Frametown Road across country to the mouth of Diatter, forded Birch either by mule or johnboat, and walked up the Adams School road to the home of Ellet and Belle Carte, now owned by Eddy Grey, where she roomed during the week.

Virgil and Erma Kuhl, both in their nineties, had been married sixty eight years when I visited them in late 2000 at their home on Lower Mill Creek. Their son, David, works in the Braxton County assessor's office.

Lon and Arimetha Smith had eight sons and a daughter. "Grandfather didn't allow his sons to fish on Sunday," recalled Erman Smith, who was born at the Smith Eddy and now lives on Leatherwood. "But one time my father [Spurgeon] sneaked off and caught a bass of about twelve inches. He tied it up near the swinging bridge, hoping to bring it home on Monday, but that night a large muskie swallowed it, so he brought the muskie home."

Erman was two years old when his father and mother, Spurgeon and Dolly Smith, and his grandparents, left the river in 1941. Lon Smith died in 1945, and his wife died in 1950. Both are buried at Middle Run Cemetery.

Spurgeon Smith was a partner with Glenn Coulter in Smith and Coulter Lumber Company, a familiar name in the Leatherwood community from the 1940s to the 1960s. Spurgeon died in 1986 and is buried at Sugar Creek Cemetery. His wife, Dolly, still lives on Leatherwood. Glenn Coulter died in 1980. He and his wife, Madge, are buried at the Given Cemetery on the north side of Elk River near the Elk River Baptist Church.

Lon Smith

- - -

The swinging bridge was a Smith Eddy fixture for many years. Hope Natural Gas Company installed an eight-inch line from Frametown to Richwood in 1927-28 that crossed the river just above the bridge, and the building of the bridge followed sometime after that for the use of pipeline maintenance crews.

Adventuresome swimmers jumped from it over the years, but pipeline surveillance is now done mostly by helicopter, and the bridge planking has been removed. Only the cables remain as a reminder of this Smith Eddy icon.

David Bail of Summersville recalls that his grandfather, Bryan Bail, who lived at Morris, Nicholas County, was a member of the crew that installed the line. The workers were paid by ten-foot sections of ditch.

If they needed to bend the pipe, they built a fire, wedged the hot pipe between trees, and pulled on it with horses. Working on the pipeline has come full circle in the Bail family: David, the grandson, helped install new sections of pipe in summer 2000 in the Adams Ridge area as a contractor for Dominion-Hope Gas Company.

Joe Clifton, a Middle Run native, was a cook for the 1927-28 pipeline crew. He bought chickens, eggs, and other items from community farmers as the line progressed. He once told me about buying chickens from my grandfather, Hampton Riffel.

Almost as familiar as the swinging bridge is a wire cable that has propelled many a swimmer into the Smith Eddy. I didn't see it when I visited the eddy in late 2000, but if it's missing, I'm sure a replacement will soon appear. The last cable was installed fifteen or twenty years ago by Erman Smith and Howard Carpenter. Howard, who was elected sheriff of Braxton County in November 2000, was living in the Leatherwood Run area at that time.

- - -

The Lon Smith property on Birch River was bought by Roscoe and Goldie Bragg in 1944. I knew the large, rounded field above the river, which is part of the property, as "the Bragg field." It extended to a large rock on the ridge overlooking the Blue Hole. The Blue Hole lies on a straight line, and almost straight down, from this rock. A yellow Piper Cub landed and took off from the Bragg field in the early 1950s, and we all thought it was the equivalent of Lindbergh flying the Atlantic.

The present owner of the Smith Eddy property is the Dolan family. The family also owns land across the river at the mouth of Diatter Run. The Diatter tract was acquired in 1953; the Smith tract in 1957.

The Dolans built a two-story beige and brown camp on the Smith Eddy that has become as much of a landmark as the swinging bridge before it. Two long fire engine red benches decorate the front porch. Over the years, the camp has acquired the name "Ponderosa." "I'm not sure how that got started," said Wayne, a State Farm agent in Proctorville, Ohio. "I suppose someone jokingly called it that, and it stuck."

A brother, Dan, lives in Clifton Park, New York, and is an executive of the Troy-Bilt Manufacturing Company, and another brother, Jimmy, lives in Madison. A fourth brother, Kenny, of Madison, died on June 2, 2001.

A few months prior to his death, I discussed the quality of the fishing on Birch with Kenny, a retired dentist, and I thought he expressed it perfectly when he said, "It's a moody river. Some days the fishing is quite good, but other days you can't catch anything." Perhaps the same can be said of any river, but Kenny and I agreed that Birch is especially moody. The best time to fish it is when it's almost too high to fish, and the water is almost clear, but not quite.

- - -

Across Birch from the mouth of Diatter Run, on a high riverbank, are three graves marked by field rock with no inscriptions. Supposedly one of the people buried there is William Rose, a veteran of the War of 1812. If we accept that supposition, we can also speculate that another of the graves contains the remains of his wife, Martha Persinger Rose. The spacing of the graves suggests that all three contain the remains of adults. The third grave may contain the remains of an Indian girl who, according to legend, the Roses took in and raised.

Isaac Rose, the Revolutionary War soldier who died in 1829 and is buried on upper Birch River (see "Skyles and Boggs"), had six children, one of whom was William Rose. According to *The Descendents of Isaac Rose*, a 1993 genealogy by Elizabeth Wiggins Sanders, William Rose once lived at Twistville. "From there," the Sanders account says, "they (Rose and his wife) moved to the Birch River area, two miles from Twistville, where they lived to a ripe old age." Twistville was located about two miles from the mouth of Diatter Run.

William Rose was the grandfather of William R. Pierson, the Twistville postmaster, whose mother was Sarah Jane Rose. Leo Boggs, granddaughter of the postmaster, recalls visiting the Diatter Run graves, which she believes to be the graves of William Rose and others of his family.

In some accounts, Rose is called "Captain Rose," although the 1993 genealogy said he attained the rank of corporal.

Andrew Keener married Julianna Rose, one of the daughters of William and Martha Rose, and it is possible that Andrew and Julianna lived downriver from the mouth of Diatter Run and gave the Keener Eddies their name. The Upper Keener begins about two hundred yards below the mouth of Diatter.

- - -

Diatter Run enters Birch at the Smith Eddy shoal below the swinging bridge. It heads near Coon Knob, as Middle Run does, and presents another Birch River guessing game: is it Diatter, or Diadda, or Diatta?

Officially, it's Diatter. That's what the Department of Highways sign says where the Frametown Road crosses it, and lending historical integrity to that spelling is a 1917 West Virginia Geological Survey map assembled from U.S. Geological Survey sheets, which also calls it Diatter.

But Ray Reip, who wrote an article about this tributary in *The Braxton Democrat* around 1965, called it Diadda Run, as do early property deeds. Occasionally in other references the spelling becomes Diatta.

Ray's account was fascinating as he told his version of how the little tributary came to be called, as he says, Diadda. His story follows:

> About 1814, my great-great grandfather, Jonathan Pierson, and his brother-in-law, Jesse James [not the outlaw], came over the Alleghenies from Virginia and settled on Leatherwood Run. There were a few people scattered along Elk River, and of course the little settlement at Sutton.
>
> Great-granddad and Uncle Jesse were busy clearing their land for their first crop, and getting their log cabins built, when one day they had a visitor. An old grey bearded man, dressed in buckskins and carrying a strange flintlock rifle, called on them. He spoke with a strong French accent, and when he became excited or angry he spoke no English at all.
>
> I have no documents or material matter to verify this tale, just by word of mouth as it has been handed down through the years by my ancestors.
>
> When the English took Fort Duquesne (Pittsburgh) from the French in 1758, there was a young French private named Frank Diadda, who, instead of retreating back to Canada with the rest of the French, deserted and headed down the Ohio River in a stolen canoe.
>
> Three years later this man had wandered to the mouth of the Great Kanawha, up it to the settlement at the mouth of the Elk [Charleston], and here he tarried for about six months and then ascended the Elk to the mouth of Birch, and ultimately to a peaceful Indian village on what we now know as Diadda Run.
>
> From the description handed down, this was probably one of the last villages of the Adena Indians, or mound builders as they are known today. Their village was a permanent one, not typical of the roving Indians who frequently hunted through what is now West Virginia. They had a ceremonial mound on a little rise overlooking their village. This mound can still be seen. It is on the Frank Duffield farm at the mouth of Rich Fork.
>
> While Frank [Diadda] was out hunting one day a war party of some strange Indians discovered the peaceful settlement. When the hunter returned, there was not a man, woman

or child alive. He was so incensed by the massacre that he took
out on the trail of the marauders and overtook them somewhere
on Steer Creek. He said the party numbered about fifty heavily armed savages, some of which possessed rifles. He did not
reveal his presence, but returned to the valley he had called
home so long.

Great-granddad said the first time he saw Frank
Diadda and heard his tale, that he was a very old and feeble
man. He would visit the new settlers every week or so, because
he was a very lonely man. Suddenly after about three years, the
visits abruptly ceased. Great-granddad and Uncle Jesse went
over to Diadda to see about the old man, but he was not to be
found. As far as anyone knows he was never seen or heard of
again.

Generations have looked for the old man's bones with
his strange French rifle lying beside him, but all in vain. All
that is left of Frank Diadda and his Indian friends is the mound
on the Duffield farm, and a little stream in Birch District named
Diadda Run.

Well, maybe not all. There are two gravestones (flat field stones
with no inscriptions) on the Bob Napier farm where, according to one
account, Frank Diadda and his wife are buried. Rita Napier's uncle, Leonard Tyo, who was interested in local history, related this story years ago.
He said the stones marked the graves of "General Diadda and his wife."
The Frank Diadda of Ray Reip's account was a private in the French army
when he deserted; how he may have risen to the rank of general is a
matter of conjecture.

Bob and Rita Tyo Napier live on the Frametown Road where Diatter Run crosses. Their house is one hundred and ten years old, and was
built by George Craft, an oldtime preacher and stonemason. The Napiers
bought the property from John Pierson in 1970. John once summed up
the Bible's mysteries as well as anyone I've ever heard. He said he was
immediately mystified when he read the first three words: "In the beginning...."

The Indian mound of Ray Reip's story is located about a mile
up Diatter from the Napiers on the Peck Allen farm. Allen lives in the
shadow of Interstate 79 (milepost 55) and within sight of the head of Diatter. He is a World War II veteran who was captured by the Germans
during the Battle of the Ardennes (Battle of the Bulge) in December 1944,
and spent the final five months of the war in a German prisoner of war
camp.

Allen and his five brothers were all in World War II, and all survived. Harry and Peck were in the Army, Marland and Forrest were in the Navy, Clarence was in the Navy and Army, and Harold was in the Air Force. Another brother, Travis, was too young for service. A cousin, Rufus Byrne, who was raised by the Allens' parents, Wirt and Margaret Allen, also served in World War II, for a total of seven servicemen from one home at the same time. Peck, Forrest, Travis, and a sister, Treva, are still living, as is Rufus.

One day Peck Allen took me to the Indian mound, which lies a stone's throw below the northbound lane of I-79. It is small as Indians mound go, but has the neatly rounded, gently sloped appearance of having been man-made. A gnarled apple tree grows on top of it. Near the tree there are signs that someone once dug into the mound. Whether they found anything isn't known.

Allen told me that arrowheads and other artifacts have been routinely found over the years in the creek bottom below the mound.

In 1981-82, John Hymes Jr., then associate professor of history at Glenville State College, wrote a paper on Birch River for the National Park Service when the agency was studying Birch for possible inclusion in the National Wild and Scenic Rivers System (see "A Much-Studied River"). Hymes is presently an instructor in the Department of History at Horry Georgetown Technical College in Conway, South Carolina, near Myrtle Beach.

He said this about the Diatter mound and others:

There are several prehistoric sites located in Braxton County. Mounds of either the Woodland or Adena period have been uncovered in the areas of Grannies Creek, Kanawha Run and near Birch River.

A survey of the mounds in the Diatter Run area of Birch undertaken by Broyles [Betty Broyles, former state archaeologist and one of the first woman state archaeologists in the nation] noted that these were partially uncovered and measured seven feet in height and twenty feet in diameter [which conforms to the approximate dimensions of the mound I visited]. This report describes the recovery of several flint chips and a projectile point and notes that area residents have collected various artifacts from these sites as well.

To date, however, there has been no scientific archaeological documentation of these mounds in the Birch River area. One can conclude that the Birch River and surrounding areas were probably utilized by Archaic peoples but most likely not to the extent that such cultures existed along the arteries of the Ohio and Greater Kanawha River Valley areas.

Hymes mentioned mounds (plural) in the Diatter area; I have never heard of more than the one on the Peck Allen (former Frank Duffield) farm, but there may be others. Donna Reip, in her Historical Society article, said there are four major artifact locations, although not necessarily mounds, in the area.

There was an Indian mound, or at least we always thought that's what it was, located about ten miles away near Adams School on the head of Big Run in Braxton County. It was considerably larger than the Diatter mound, but unfortunately a former property owner bulldozed it.

- - -

Livestock scales, an artifact of a different stripe, are being restored on Diatter Run near the Indian mound by Harold Gandee, the grandson of Peck Allen. The 1930s vintage scales were owned by Frank Duffield. Cattle and sheep were brought there from miles around, and usually Duffield or another livestock dealer would buy them.

Allen recalls taking part in cattle and sheep drives in the 1930s before trucks came into wide use. The animals were driven separately to Frametown and loaded on railroad boxcars for shipment to Pittsburgh and Baltimore, and perhaps other eastern cities.

There were two other sets of livestock scales in the community at about the same time, one on the road to the Martin and Newton Reip farm near Diatter Run, and another at Canfield on the Mel Tucker farm.

- - -

The Twistville Road, a horse and wagon road of the 1800s and early 1900s, is synonymous with the Diatter Run community.

Its centerpiece, the Twistville Post Office, was located in the now-vacant Grover Pierson house on the Frametown Road. Leo Boggs of Sutton, daughter of Grover and Ocie Given Pierson, grew up there, and is the present owner of the property. The Twistville postmaster for forty years was her grandfather, William R. Pierson, a Confederate soldier in the Civil War with Company I of the 17th Virginia Cavalry. In addition to being postmaster, he was also a justice of the peace, and held court in the living room where the post office was located (miscreants could get their mail and be tried at the same time).

There were two one-room schools in the area, neither named Twistville. The Banner School, which Leo Boggs attended, was located on Diatter Run near the present Bob Napier home, and the Dry Fork School was located on the road to the Reip farm.

Most of the Twistville Road in the Diatter and Middle Run communities was obliterated by the construction of I-79, but one clear segment remains. It can be seen coming through the woods toward the northbound lane just before the highway tops out near Coon Knob and approaches exit 57. A cell phone tower that was partially complete in early 2001 is located near the path of the old road.

The road began in Sutton. A portion of it is still there, and is still called Twistville Road. It is located on the south edge of town where old U.S. 19 begins climbing "Old Town Mountain" and heading south toward Tesla and Little Birch. Twistville Road parallels 19 for a short distance, and then makes a wide loop to the west, coming down onto the present Herold Road where Keith Shaver, Glenn Brown, and Robert Freeman live. It is very visible in the winter as it approaches the Herold Road across from Keith Shaver's, and again where it takes to the hill just west of Glenn Brown's and Robert Freeman's.

It ran west along Buffalo Creek for a short distance on what is now the Herold Road before fording the creek and climbing the hill in a northerly direction to the former Locust Stump School and Hoover Post Office, which were located in close proximity. Present-day remains of the road end abruptly at I-79 at about milepost 58, but reappear later in the Coon Knob vicinity.

From Locust Stump the road swung west toward Coon Knob, passed southward below the present Coon Knob Interstate Maintenance Garage, and came to an intersection, appropriately, at the present exit 57 interchange of I-79 where Raymond Gibson, a State Road Commission employee, lived in pre-interstate days.

The road headed in three directions from there: one fork went south to the Garee Low Gap, where the Herold Road presently enters U.S. 19; a second fork dropped into Little Buffalo Creek; and the main Twistville Road continued west to Coon Knob, meandered through the heads of Middle and Diatter Runs, and Buckeye Fork of Long Run, came down Diatter to the present Frametown Road, and from there went north a short distance to the Twistville Post Office.

The road is shown on an Outline Map of Braxton County that was published for *The Braxton Democrat* in 1924. Glenn Brown, Braxton County Circuit Clerk from 1966 to 1988, has a copy, and one snowy day in January 2001 we spread it out on the kitchen table at his home and traced the entire route. We computed the mileage from Sutton to Twistville P.O. as eight to ten miles. Its many twists and turns, which may have given the road its name, made a more precise figure difficult.

Larry Brady of South Bloomfield, Ohio, who grew up on Coon Creek, remembers walking the road from the Raymond Gibson house to Diatter Run. "It was a horseback road mainly," he said, "although in later years a few cars traveled it."

Twistville (the post office) was still listed on Braxton County highway maps as late as 1937. It is shown on a map of that date on the wall at the Braxton County DOH Maintenance Headquarters on W.Va. 4 between Sutton and Gassaway.

Obviously the Twistville Road didn't end in the middle of nowhere at the post office, although it may not have continued under that name. Erman Smith believes it turned left, climbed the hill to the present Leatherwood Road, followed Leatherwood Run to the ford on Birch River, and from there went on to Strange Creek. In a local version of Old West cattle drives, livestock is said to have been driven over the Twistville Road to Strange Creek, and on to Charleston.

Bill Byrne gives this belief credence in *Tale of the Elk*. He wrote: "One of the main roads from Sutton to Strange Creek traverses this Twistville and Diadda Run section." He told about riding it often on horseback, and stopping frequently to visit his friend, Burton Pierson, who lived on Leatherwood where Erman now lives. Byrne, a lawyer at Sutton, traveled this road on his trips between Sutton and Clay Court House (he began practicing law at Sutton in 1885 and was there for about ten years).

The Burton Pierson of Bill Byrne's acquaintance was the great grandfather of the Burton Pierson who lives at Frametown, and who thinks that after crossing Birch at the Leatherwood Ford, the road went down the left side of the river, climbed the hill at the present Henry Given farm, and dropped down to Strange Creek.

There is a contradiction between Byrne's account of where his friend, Burton Pierson, lived, and present-day belief. Byrne wrote that "his residence was on the hillside overlooking the Birch River." His great grandson is certain that he lived at the present Erman Smith place, which doesn't overlook the river. But perhaps in 1885 or thereabouts he did live on a farm that overlooked the river.

The Twistville Road served the community well in its time, and continues to serve. Mention any cowpath in the eastern United States, and someone with a burning desire to appear knowledgeable is bound to say, "Oh, yes, that's the old Twistville Road."

Former Twistville Post Office

The Raven Eddy above the Blue Hole

The Smith Eddy at the mouth of Diatter Run

Fourteen

Leatherwood Country

Gateway to the Mouth of Birch

L eatherwood Run comes into Birch River slightly over two miles above the mouth, and about a mile above where the Army Corps of Engineers planned in the 1960s to build a dam on Birch, a project that didn't come about (see "A Much-Studied River"). If it had, Leatherwood Run Camping Area would have become the major recreational development on the reservoir, thus forever changing the face of Leatherwood Country.

But today Leatherwood Run meanders in a leisurely fashion, as it always has, 2.27 miles from its origin near I-79 where the interstate crosses the Birch drainage to its meeting with Birch at what is known as the Leatherwood Ford. On the south side of the ford, the road climbs to Keener's Ridge at the Eureka Methodist Church.

Thousands of people go under the Leatherwood Road every day without realizing it. The road crosses over Interstate 79 between the U.S. 19 and Frametown exits at approximately milepost 53.

According to local lore, Leatherwood Run got its name because an ingenious farmer or logger of long ago, somewhere in the Leatherwood vicinity, used the bark of a leatherwood bush to repair the broken harness on his team of oxen.

It's a nice story, and entirely believable. Leatherwood bark is tough enough that it can be used for emergency repairs to barbed-wire fences, not to mention oxen harness. The story of the naming of Leatherwood is attributed to Benton Given, a farmer who lived on the north side of

Birch on a hillside overlooking Leatherwood Run. The
foundation stones from his
house are still visible. He
died in 1941 at ninety six
years of age, and is buried in
a hilltop cemetery near where
he lived.

Benton was sixteen
years old when the Civil War
began. According to a 1973
article by Donna Reip in the
Journal of the Braxton Histori-   *Birch near the mouth of Leatherwood Run*
cal Society, he served later with the Confederacy's 17th Virginia Cavalry.
He always contended that plantain, the scourge weed of lawns and gardens to this day, was introduced into the community from the manure of
Union cavalry horses.

Below the Benton Given Cemetery to the south lies the Leatherwood Eddy of Birch River. It is arguably the longest on the river, rivaled
only by the Upper and Lower Keener Eddies upstream, and the Duffield
and Mouth of Birch Eddies downstream. It begins below the Sand Hole
near the Skeeter Pletcher camp and continues all the way to the ford, a
distance of three quarters of a mile or more.

But is this the real Leatherwood Eddy?

Most of the people I interviewed who are familiar with lower
Birch were resolute in insisting that the eddy above the ford is the Leatherwood Eddy. But the existence of a hand-drawn map of the river (see
"If We Were Counting") casts doubt on this popular belief. Warder Dean,
who drew the map as a follow-up to a 1939 fishing trip, called it the Riffle
Eddy. He placed the Leatherwood Eddy below the ford, apparently referring to a stretch of water that leads to the Duffield Eddy.

If he was right, we are left to wonder who the Riffles were who
gave the upper eddy its name. Pearl Frame, who was born in the area in
1906 and lived there until age eighty nine (she now lives in Coshocton,
Ohio) did not know of any Riffles who ever lived there, nor did anyone
else that I could find.

The spelling of the family surname is open to question as well,
although admittedly there is no proper way to spell a proper noun. Families often spell it differently from one generation to the next, or even
within the same generation. For example, my great grandfather John Riffle's name is spelled just that way, Riffle, on his 1856 marriage certificate,
and in an 1857 deed, but by 1900 his descendents were spelling it Riffel.

For purposes of this book, I will spell it the latter way to conform with the 1900s version.

It is possible that my great grandfather lived on Birch River, but I have no knowledge of that. After 1857 he lived on Adams Ridge at the present Jim Lewis farm, which is on the Birch drainage but about five miles above the Riffel Eddy. He died in 1882 and is buried at the Riffel-Lewis Cemetery. His name on the weathered tombstone is spelled Riffel.

I grew up hearing about the Riffel Eddy, so obviously Warder didn't pull the name out of a hat. I romanticized that it was long and deep and harbored large muskies, which at one time it did. Elliott Butcher, who lived where Benjie Nichols now lives on the south side of Birch across from the Leatherwood Ford, caught a muskie in the 1930s that was in the fifty inch class.

Maybe both the Riffel and Leatherwood Eddies lie above the ford. There is a modest shoal about halfway through the eddy, marked by three or four small rocks that protrude above the water only at normal summer flow. But it is very definitely a shoal; no bass fisherman would miss it, with its rocks and shallow water nestled in the middle of a long stretch of deeper water. It may be the divide between two eddies of different names.

Benjie Nichols believes that the upper half down to the small shoal, or "shallow," is the Riffel Eddy, and that the lower half is the Leatherwood Eddy. His great grandfather, Dudley Nottingham, who lived upstream at the Sand Hole, always referred to the upper half as the Riffel Eddy.

Perhaps a simpler explanation is that the entire eddy was known long ago as the Riffel, but in more modern times has come to be called Leatherwood for the nearby tributary of the same name. Nevertheless, this mystery of lower Birch continues. The Apostle Paul said: "For now we see through a glass, darkly; but then face to face." Thus it may be with the Riffel and Leatherwood Eddies, if on a less apocalyptic note.

Regardless of what the eddy is called, it has the distinction of being home to the last large rock on Birch, which stands on the left descending side just above the small shoal. It is not large in comparison with other rocks farther upstream, but it is large in comparison with everything else on lower Birch below Fingerstone Rock (see "Big Run Meets Lower Keener"). It is called the Curt Rock for Curtis Frame, brother of Pearl Frame.

When Curt Frame married, he and his wife, Nimmie Tanner Frame, lived on the north side of the river across from the rock. It was in this area around 1914 that Birch River's own "Bigfoot" legend was born. Harry Long, son of Willis Long, was returning home from visiting a family in the Leatherwood area, and came upon a hairy, man-like creature at a deep ravine. It spoke to him, saying, "Its been a long time since I've seen you." For the remainder of his life (he died in 1970 at age seventy four), Harry insisted that he saw the creature, and that it spoke those words. A hoax perpetrated by someone who knew he would be taking that isolated path? Harry never thought so, and, equally telling, in the remaining fifty six years of his life nobody ever came forward and admitted to a prank. But neither were there any more sightings of hairy creatures.

In later years, there was a sawmill in the river bottom where the "Birch River Bigfoot" legend surfaced. The sawmill operators were Spurgeon Smith and Glenn Coulter, and the logger was Bennie Nottingham, who logged with a pair of large black horses. One would tend to suspect that one of the horses was the "Bigfoot" of Harry Long's experience, except that horses usually don't talk ("Mr. Ed," the horse on the popular 1960s television show, was a Hollywood created exception), and also the time frame doesn't fit.

Elmer Dodson, the mayor of Charleston from 1967 to 1971, was a prominent camp owner on the Leatherwood/Riffel Eddy from 1973 until his death in 1982. He and his wife, Polly, and their children, including sons Ray and Denny, and daughters Mary and Nellie, spent a lot of time there. They frequently brought church groups and kids from the Shawnee Hills Center in Charleston to Birch River.

The Dodson family continued to own the property until November 1997, when they sold it to Tim and Dawn Lucas of Newfield, New Jersey.

- - -

Early residents at the mouth of Leatherwood were Eldridge and Allie Mollohan Given, who lived there on two different occasions in the teens and 1920s. Later occupants of their house were the Jim Paintiff family, the Cleo Teets family, and the Cecil Cash family. The Teets family was living there in 1932 when waters from the flood of record in Birch River (see "The Floods of Birch") lapped under the house.

Eldridge and Allie Given's granddaughter, Eleanor Pardue of Gassaway, has pictures of the house. It was a one-story structure with an attic, horizontal siding, and a picket fence in front. A large boulder behind the house is the only physical reminder of where it once stood. The house was located about seventy five yards from the river, thus the 1932 flood was indeed one for the books.

Evidence of another huge flood, probably that of 1918, can be seen in a picture of Eleanor's mother, Pearl, sitting on a rock in front of the house. The picture was taken in the 1921-1923 period. Numerous rocks are visible that give the appearance of having been left there by raging floodwaters.

- - -

Leatherwood Run forks about a mile above the mouth. The right fork parallels the county road and heads near Interstate 79; the left fork goes past the home of Bobby and Willa Coulter Brown and heads near the George and Cynthia Given Keener Cemetery and the Glenn Coulter fish pond. The pond was built in the 1940s as one of the earliest examples in the community of farm ponds built for livestock watering and recreational purposes under the auspices of the local Soil Conservation District and the U.S. Soil Conservation Service, and is still a very appealing pond.

A landmark at the forks of Leatherwood was the one-room Leatherwood School, where Mike and Andrea Smith Posey now live. The former school playground is their front yard.

Leatherwood School may have held the distinction in the 1930s of being the first in Braxton County to serve hot lunches. The students brought food from home, and Rosie Harris cooked it. Some of the boys made small chairs for the lunch table. "This [the making of the chairs] went on simultaneously with classes, and without interruption of the classes," recalls Medford Teets, who attended the school when he was living at the mouth of Leatherwood.

Barrett Johnson (no relation to the author of this book) was one of the Leatherwood teachers, and occasionally he would arrive late after having fed his cattle on the way to school (a reminder of an era that is long gone). But there was no rowdiness in his absence, Medford recalls. "School simply took up and lessons started." On time or late, Barrett was regarded as an excellent teacher.

Betty Dent Reip attended Middle Run School when Barrett taught there, and she said this: "If a kid had any learning ability, and if he or she wanted to learn, then Barrett was a teacher who could bring out this ability and desire."

He thought that recreation was as important as classroom work, and when Betty was in the fourth grade she invoked his displeasure by declining to participate in sled-riding down a steep hill near the school. Her punishment was staying in school during the noon hour, learning the poem "Lazy Ned" from *McGuffey's Third Reader*, and reciting it after classes resumed:

"Tis royal fun," cried Lazy Ned,
To coast upon my fine new sled,
And beat the other boys.
But then, I cannot bear to climb
The tiresome hill, for every time
It more and more annoys.

So, while his schoolmates glided by,
And gladly tugged uphill to try
Another merry race,
Too indolent to share their plays
Ned was compelled to stand and gaze,
While shivering in his place.

Thus, he would never take the pains
To seek the prize that labor gains,
Until the time had passed;
For, all his life, he dreaded still
The silly bugbear of uphill,
And died a dunce at last.

McGuffey's Third Reader, one of a series of the McGuffey Readers that were wildly popular in the 1800s and early 1900s, stressed industriousness. For example, poor Ned wouldn't pull his sled uphill, an analogy to those who are indolent in life, and therefore died a dunce, or a failure. W.H. McGuffey, a college teacher, wrote his series during the period 1836-1853. Between 1870 and 1890, the series sold sixty million copies, and were the basic textbooks in thirty seven states. McGuffey died in 1873 when he was teaching at the University of Virginia.

While at Leatherwood, Barrett and the Leatherwood mailman, Norman Cunningham, had a contest on the order of John Henry and his sledgehammer taking on the steam drill, with a similar result. The teacher pitted his paper and pencil against the mailman's calculator, and the teacher won, as, according to legend, John Henry did against the steam drill.

Cunningham delivered mail on horseback. His route took him on a wide circuit, starting at Frametown and encompassing Diatter Run, Leatherwood Run, Middle Run, Painter's Fork, Mill Creek, and back to Frametown. Painter's Fork is better known today as the road to the Reip farm. One of the Reips who lived there in the days of horseback mailmen was Bland Reip, who made brooms and repaired shoes, despite being completely blind.

Norman Cunningham rode the mail circuit six days a week. During the Christmas season he would have a pack train of from three to five horses to deliver packages that had been ordered from firms such as Sears Roebuck and Montgomery Ward. One horse, a bay, would run from one mailbox to another and wait for Norman and the rest of the pack train to catch up.

Betty Reip remembers the excitement that attended the Christmas season and the arrival of packages. "When we came home from school," she said, "we'd yell to mother, in unison and running the questions together, 'supper ready any packages today?'"

- - -

I visited many cemeteries in the process of writing this book. In some cases, cemeteries are superior to libraries in resurrecting local history, because they bring to life, in a sense, people we've heard about all our lives, but never knew. One for me was my great grandfather, William Johnson. He is buried at the Johnson Cemetery on Keener's Ridge, but that was not his first burial place (see "Big Run Meets Lower Keener"). He was first buried at the Robert (Robin) Given Cemetery on a farm above the Perrine Ford of Birch River. I had never been there, and didn't know exactly where it was, and in fact didn't even know the name of the cemetery until I began researching *River on the Rocks*.

One warm, bright day in October 2000, I met Bobby Brown and Roy James at Bobby's home on Leatherwood Run, and we set out on a walking tour of Leatherwood Country. Bobby is a native of Strange Creek, and a farmer and logger. Roy is a Leatherwood native, and is retired from IBM. It was on this outing that I came to "know" my great grandfather better.

We parked near the forks of Leatherwood and walked uphill to the former Beldon Shawver place. The property is now owned by Henry Becker, an Arizona resident. Beldon was a farmer, as was his son, Jerald, who lived nearby. I remember seeing Jerald Shawver and his wife, Mildred, selling eggs at Herold, where I was born. They also sold eggs and produce at the Clay County coal town of Widen.

Mildred and Jerald Shawver were the aunt and uncle of Connie James Furbee, proprietor of the Birch River Junction country store at Canfield. "I remember the chickens, millions of chickens, it seemed," said Connie. "I went with them to Widen on Saturdays in their old green Jeep. They'd be up in the early morning hours killing and dressing chickens, and gathering eggs and garden produce. I loved to help grade eggs, and I still have one of the graders."

A hand-operated egg grader was a metal box with a hole in one end. Inside was an unfrosted light bulb, and behind the bulb a concave-shaped reflector to make the light more intense. The egg was held up to the hole, and the light illuminated the inside of the egg to check for flaws. This process was called "candling."

A cellarhouse is the only remaining vestige of the Beldon Shawver place. A fallen down barn and a rubble of rocks where the house once stood are all that remain of the Jerald Shawver place. Among the vanished buildings is the chicken house, which was long, and, as Connie Furbee recalls, a compact two stories high.

Roy James described Jerald as "a quiet man and a good farmer." He died in 1984 and is buried at the Middle Run Cemetery, as is his wife, who died in 1998. Beldon Shawver and his wife, Fannie, are also buried at Middle Run.

The views from Leatherwood Country are as scenic and pastoral as any in West Virginia. Looking south across Birch from the Jerald Shawver farm is a splendid view of the Anderson Davis Knob near the Eureka Methodist Church. At 1,366 feet, it is one of the highest elevations on the lower Birch drainage (although part of it drains into Strange Creek). Another nice view is of Adams Knob near the former Adams School, and the site of the Francis Morton grave (see "Powell's Mountain").

For the most part, I've known Leatherwood Run and its neighbor, Middle Run, from a distance. Just as Bobby, Roy, and I admired the view from Leatherwood looking toward Adams Knob, I grew up on the opposite side of Birch and my views were from the Adams Knob area looking toward Leatherwood and Middle Run. The subject would always come up: is that the Jerald Shawver place just to the left or right of something or other? Where was the Beldon Shawver place? Did Ernest Beall live just beyond that knoll?

Ernest Beall was, like Beldon and Jerald Shawver, a farmer long associated with that area. He and his wife, Winnie, are both deceased, and are buried at the Beall Cemetery. They lived on the ridge between Leatherwood and Diatter Runs. The Bealls were the grandparents of Connie Furbee.

- - -

We walked toward Birch from the Shawver farms to the supposed Robert Given Cemetery where my great grandfather was buried in 1875. None of us were sure it was the right cemetery. It was overgrown with multiflora rose, but we spotted a tombstone that was lying face down on the ground just inside the briery bushes. Bobby pulled it out, we cleaned it off, and there was the proof:

Robert Given, was
Borned Sept. 1800
Died Feburary l8
In the year 1877

The "v" in Given had been inadvertently omitted when his name was chiseled on the stone, and the inscriber had quickly corrected the error by inserting a tiny "v." February was misspelled, but in the grand scheme of things it doesn't matter. Some of the graves in other cemeteries I visited were marked only by rocks with no inscription on them, which brings us back to the grand scheme of things. Surely God must be no less mindful of the occupants of those unidentified graves than He is of the ones who lie beneath ornate tombstones and flowery words.

I was hoping there might still be a depression in the ground to indicate the original burial site of my great grandfather, and there may be, but the multiflora rose prevented us from looking. Perhaps, after the passage of one hundred and twenty five years, that was a forlorn hope anyway. But we had found the right cemetery.

We left the Robert Given Cemetery and climbed the hill toward the Benton Given Cemetery. On the way, we had a lively discussion about the locations of the Blue Hole and Cedar Cliffs, both well-known features of Birch River and both of which lay somewhere below us in the October sunshine. I don't recall who "won" the discussions, but we did identify both places in the serpentine twists and turns of lower Birch.

Among those buried at the Benton Given Cemetery, in addition to Benton himself, are his wife, Araminta, and his brother, Reynolds, who left his calling card on Birch River in a big way by dynamiting the "Reynolds Rock" (see "Big Run Meets Lower Keener"). Reynolds Given died in 1930 at age seventy nine.

We descended to Leatherwood Run at an abandoned two-story farmhouse known as the Dave Evans place, which is now owned by Andrea Smith Posey and is the last house on the Leatherwood Road prior to the ford. Dave Evans is the great grandfather of Jill James, the librarian at Braxton County High School.

- - -

Leatherwood Ford is located 2.4 miles above the mouth of the river, and represents decision time for anyone who may be considering boating and fishing the remainder of the way; the road that crosses at the ford is the final one that enters Birch before the end of the river at Glendon.

Below the ford is a series of plouts, more or less connected, where the river curves and straightens into the long Duffield Eddy. Early in the 1800s, there was a grist mill or sawmill located just below the ford. Its timbers were still visible for many years. A local legend has it that the mill owner was found drowned and floating face down in the mill pond, and his death was supposedly placed under the category of "mysterious circumstances."

I was wading and pulling the canoe over the "mysterious circumstances" shoal in summer 2000, with my fishing rod and lure dangling from the back of the canoe, a situation that may well have contributed to the saying about "Murphy's Law": if anything can go wrong, it will.

The lure caught on something (I gave it enough rope and it hung itself), the line fed out before I realized what was happening, and of course broke, and the lure floated away in the swift current. I gathered up hundreds of thousands of feet (or so it seemed) of monofilament line, dumped it by the armload into the canoe, and mourned the loss of a favorite lure.

Earlier in the year, at the mouth of Middle Run, I sailed a lure into an ironwood tree that stretched out over the water, and lost it too. Lures tend to sail, or take off into the stratosphere, if released at too high an angle during the forward motion of the fisherman's arm, usually the result of becoming tired or careless, and the two usually go together.

Casting a fishing lure with accuracy is an art; not as much of an art as hitting a baseball thrown at ninety five miles an hour from a distance of sixty feet six inches, but nevertheless an art that requires good hand and eye coordination, and ideally should be learned at an early age so it becomes second nature. The accuracy part is important when it comes to dropping a lure into the midst of cover, such as snags, limbs, and logs, where fish tend to lurk. Don Hamric, the muskie man of Glendon, was as good as anyone I've ever seen at doing this. His specialty was sailing a lure under the willow bushes that are prevalent along Elk River near his home, and extend out over the water.

Once I wrote a column for *The Charleston Gazette* about what happens to the millions of lures that fishermen contribute to the watery depths, and concluded that they're still down there somewhere, staring up at us with their beady little eyes, plotting to overthrow the government. Frighteningly, a reader wrote and agreed with me.

- - -

I first began fishing the Duffield Eddy more than thirty years ago.

I'd borrow a boat from Woody Nichols, and fish the eddy down and back. It was there that I caught my first muskie in Birch. The date was June 20, 1963, the centennial anniversary of statehood for West Virginia. The fish was about thirty inches long, and I released it, although I would have done that anyway had it been fifty inches.

This Centennial Muskie was one of several I subsequently caught in the Duffield Eddy, along with two or three elsewhere in Birch. But my nephew and I did not raise a muskie anywhere during our summer and fall 2000 trips.

I've heard it said that the Duffield Eddy, and other places on lower Birch, have filled in considerably over the years, and that is probably true from a long-term perspective. Benjie Nichols believes that parts of it have filled in, and since he has lived there for over fifty years, he should know. But the Duffield Eddy looks no different to me today than it did when I caught the Centennial Muskie thirty eight years ago. It wasn't very deep then, and it still isn't, but its saving grace from a fishing standpoint is that it contains several sunken logs that provide the kind of cover that muskies like.

The Duffield Eddy below Leatherwood

The Duffields who gave the eddy its name lived on both sides of the river, but mostly on the north side, and owned land that bordered the river. Lower Birch from Leatherwood to the mouth was once called "Duffield Country," and that is a fair assessment. There was a Duffield presence in the area from the 1800s until the death of Rose Duffield in 1971 at age ninety one. She lived in a familiar two-story house on the south side of Elk River above the mouth of Birch. The house burned in the 1980s.

There was a Duffield house long ago on the hilltop above the
Lower Turn Hole of Birch, and a cemetery nearby that is enclosed by an
impressive wall made of hand-hewn stone. Stone steps on the lower left
corner lead to the top of the wall, and another set of steps gives access to
the enclosure. Inside, there is a large polished granite tombstone that says
"Duffield." On top of it is another polished piece of rounded granite.

But apparently nobody is buried there. In September 1955, four
Duffields were moved to the family plot at Sunset Memorial Park in South
Charleston; slightly sunken places in the ground indicate where at least
three of the four were once buried. Those moved were Earl, who died
in 1914; Samuel, who died in 1919; his wife, Mary, who died in 1938;
and Richard, who died in 1941. When Rose Duffield died, she was also
buried at South Charleston. There are a total of eight Duffield graves in
the family plot.

Outside the stone wall are the graves of Florence Duffield, who
died in 1885, and Rhoda Duffield, who died in 1906. Three other graves
are marked only by field stones.

The "Nehemiah" who built the wall in the 1930s was Elliott
Butcher, a well-known stone mason and carpenter of his day who at that
time lived near the mouth of Leatherwood Run (the same Elliott Butcher
who is mentioned earlier in this chapter for having caught a large muskie
in the Leatherwood Eddy).

Obviously he was a craftsman, because the cemetery wall is a
work of art. There were several such craftsmen in the Birch community
long ago: old cellars, chimneys, and walls still stand as mute testimony
to their skills. They would draw a line on a chunk of stone, and, with a
small pick, make a hole or groove along the line. Then they gently tapped
wedges into the holes or groove; one mislick could waste hours or days of
work. The final product was a nicely shaped slab of sandstone. A stone
mason of Elliott Butcher's capability would likely have built the cemetery
wall in a summer.

The ancient Israelites were great stonemasons, and remains of
their quarries are widespread. Stones were hewn for boundary markers,
doors of burial caves, the Jerusalem temple foundation, and walls, among
them the famous Jewish Wailing Wall. The Nehemiah referred to above
was an Israelite leader who led the rebuilding of the walls around Jerusalem in the period 440-420 B.C.

The stone used for the Duffield Cemetery enclosure was plentiful
nearby. A 1916 report by the West Virginia Geological Survey speaks of
a quarry owned by Austin Long that was located "on an east hillside of
Birch, 0.3 miles southeast of Glendon." The report identified the rock as
being from the Upper Mahoning sandstone strata, and the quarry face as

ten feet high, one hundred to one hundred and twenty five feet long, and driven fifteen to twenty feet into the hillside.

This quarry probably produced the stone that was used in the construction of the abutments for the railroad trestle over the mouth of Birch around 1900-1905, the first large structure to span Birch. Italian immigrant workers were employed here, as they were in the building of the Eakin Lumber Company railroad over the mountain from Skyles to Erbacon (see "Shay It Isn't So"). These men also built the Davis Memorial Presbyterian and St. Thomas Catholic Churches in Gassaway.

The foundations of two houses remain on the road leading uphill to the Duffield Cemetery, and at one site an impressive use of stone can still be seen: stone steps leading up the steep hillside to the house, and basement walls made of large slabs of stone. Martin Rollyson, Glendon postmaster in 1922-1924, lived there, as did others over the years.

The Army Corps of Engineers proposed in the 1960s to build a dam on Birch above the Lower Turn Hole (see "A Much-Studied River"), and among construction materials would have been 1,300,000 cubic yards of sandstone "quarried from the massive Freeport sandstones which average about 100 feet in total thickness in the area of the dam site."

- - -

The Lower Turn Hole sits in the final loop on Birch, and is a very picturesque hole of water, rounded like the Blue Hole, except larger. It is popular for fishing, which means it is over-fished; fishermen can reach it easily by motoring or paddling through the Mouth of Birch Eddy, and wading a shoal, or they can walk up from the mouth; the path is narrow in places and pitted with many deer tracks, and was probably once also walked by buffalo and Indians; the Indians followed buffalo trails, just as we now follow deer trails.

My nephew and I visited the Lower Turn Hole in March 2001 to photograph this appealing hole of water and the stretch of river immediately above it where the dam would have been built. It was a bright Sunday afternoon that we shared with four wood ducks that were cavorting at the Lower Turn Hole, and with the biggest, fattest grouse we'd ever seen that flushed from a rhododendron thicket at Davis Run.

One Lower Turn Hole legend has it that a local logger, Bob Johnson, cut a poplar tree there in the early 1900s that measured six feet in diameter. From this mammoth log he hewed out a dugout canoe that was three feet wide and sixty five feet long to transport goods to and from Charleston (John Hymes Jr., 1982).

A half mile up the hill on the south side, Doug Given, then eigh-

The Lower Turn Hole

teen years old and now a doctor at Gassaway, killed a deer in 1976 that held the state typical (symmetrical rack) record for eighteen years. The deer's antlers scored 182 3/8 in the scoring system established by the venerable Boone and Crockett Club. Doug was walking home around noon in a snowstorm to eat lunch, when the buck appeared out of the snowflakes.

The state record muskie was caught in 1955 at the mouth of Birch, so for eighteen years both the deer and muskie records were held at lower Birch.

Doug Given's record fell in 1994 when Junior Bailes killed a deer in Nicholas County whose antlers measured 185 4/8; however, the Birch muskie, caught by Lester Hayes Jr., still holds the record length of fifty two and one-half inches. The weight record was broken in 1997 when Anna Marsh caught a muskie in Stonecoal Lake that weighed 49.75 pounds.

- - -

The earliest sighting of a deer after this animal began its comeback from local extinction was near the mouth of Birch in 1939. Burton Pierson, then twelve years old, was walking over the hill from Glendon, accompanied by Elliott Samples, and saw the deer, its tail bobbing up and down in the brush on the Scott Duffield farm (Scott Duffield was one of the early settlers on lower Birch in the 1812-1840 period). "It was quite a thrill for a twelve year old boy," Burton said of the deer sighting.

The deer may have migrated to lower Birch from the Elk River Wildlife Management Area near Sutton, where a remnant herd existed, and where deer were trapped to be stocked elsewhere, beginning around 1939.

It seems hard to believe now, with deer so plentiful, but there were so few of them in the early days of hunting seasons in West Virginia that bucks were given names. Three that I remember from our locale were the Tilden Buck on the Tilden Keener farm, the Dixon Buck on the Blair Dixon farm, and the McMorrow Buck on the Cam McMorrow farm.

- - -

The Mouth of Birch Eddy (as opposed to the mouth of Birch) is, I always thought, uninspiring fishing water, but it has history: in the early 1900s the Birch Boom and Lumber Company built a sawmill on the north side, and a boom across the river to snare logs. It received its certificate of incorporation on September 20, 1909, and began with twenty five thousand dollars in capital stock; the seven incorporators were Enoch Tetrick and Charles Short of Shinnston, West Virginia; Thomas Walsh of Grafton, West Virginia; S. Wineman of Fannettsburg, Pennsylvania; G.S. Basnett of Amos, West Virginia; J.C Remage of Sutton, West Virginia; and R.H. Pembroke of Gassaway, West Virginia.

The company was authorized to "charge such tolls and boomage as is lawful" to those who floated logs downriver (the fees were for collecting the logs and gathering them together for rafts). The company was also authorized to build splash dams in Birch all the way to the headwaters to provide additional water flow for logs, but the only one known to have actually been built was located near the mouth of Slabcamp Run in Nicholas County (see "Cora Brown" and "The Big Timber Era"). It never worked properly, which was probably why only one was built.

Operation of the boom at the Mouth of Birch Eddy is described in some detail by Warder Dean in "The Big Timber Era." Mounds of rock that held the boom have survived countless floods over the years, and are still visible.

There is no record in the Secretary of State's office in Charleston of when Birch Boom and Lumber went out of business, but certainly it did not survive the fifty-year life of its certificate of incorporation. Most likely it closed shop when the era of floating logs down Birch and Elk ended around 1920.

Doyle Dean wrote in a 1987 article in *The Braxton Citizens' News* that the sawmill was purchased by "a fellow from Pittsburgh," who hired Doyle's uncle, J. Clark Dean, to dismantle it and load it onto railroad cars. "The boiler was so large," Doyle wrote, "that they had to roll it, and each time it turned over they had to dig a hole in the ground for the steam dome, so they could roll it over again. The job lasted for several days, even with two teams of horses. The man gave them a check for $350, and it bounced."

- - -

The last house on Birch is a two-story farmhouse that sits on the south side near the former log boom. It was built in 1904 by J. Arthur Given, great uncle of Henry Given. Arthur Given later moved to Charleston and was elected sheriff of Kanawha County. Subsequent owners or occupants of his house have included W.T. Williamson, S. Austin Smith, Carl Butcher, Elliott Butcher, Warning Butcher, Corbett Samples, Billy and Suzanne Kuhl, Joe and Teri Kelford, and the current owners, Mike and Judy Nidiffer, who have lived there since 1982.

The house has the high ceilings that are trademarks of houses of that era, and fireplaces upstairs and down; its flooring and other woodwork are original, and still solid, and two upstairs rooms are paneled with wormy chestnut.

Elliott Butcher, the stone mason, and his wife, Rose, celebrated their fiftieth wedding anniversary there in 1950. A daughter, Dolly Butcher Slaughter of Gassaway, recalls taking hot lunch to her father when he was building the Duffield Cemetery wall. At that time, the Butchers were living on the south side of the Leatherwood Ford. Five of their sons were in World War II, and one, Freddie, was killed during the November 1942 Battle of Guadalcanal when Japanese fire struck his ship.

Savina Samples Allen of Frametown, the granddaughter of Elliott and Rose Butcher, was also present for the fiftieth anniversary.

- - -

Glendon, where Birch enters Elk, was once located on a little flat at the upper end of the railroad trestle; two foundation stones mark the spot. In later years, the post office and store were moved across Elk to the highway.

Records at the U.S. Postal Service archives in Washington show that the post office was originally established as Morley on July 31, 1889, and that the first postmaster was Samuel Duffield. The name was changed to Glendon on February 2, 1905; the postmaster at that time was Lillie Duffield.

There is no record of the origin of either name, although the arrival of the Coal and Coke Railroad at the mouth of Birch occurred around 1905, thus the name Glendon may have originated with railroad personnel. According to *Kanawha County Images* by Stan Cohen and Richard Andre, the Elk River railroad was chartered in 1890 by a group of Charleston businessmen, and was first called "the Black Jack Line," and then the Charleston, Clendenin and Sutton Railroad. It became the Coal and Coke when it was purchased around 1904-1906 by Senator Henry Gassaway Davis. The B & O acquired the Coal and Coke RR in 1917.

Where the post office was located in 1889 isn't known, but it was located at the mouth of Birch in 1905 when the railroad came through, and remained there until 1932 when Curg Hamric, the postmaster, moved it across Elk to the highway (W.Va. 4 had just been built through Braxton County). The year 1932 is carved on one of the foundation stones where the store and post office stood on the edge of the highway.

Don Hamric, the muskie fisherman, became Glendon postmaster when his father died in 1942, and served in that capacity for thirty seven years, the longest tenure of any Glendon postmaster. For a time, the mail still went out by train to be sorted on board; Don or his wife, Irene, walked the swinging bridge across Elk and hung the mail bag on an L-shaped hook located just above the mouth of Birch trestle, where it was snatched up by the passing mail car. The Glendon Post Office was closed in 1985, thus ending another chapter of small rural post offices.

Don died in 1979 and is buried in the family cemetery on the Tate Creek Road, as is Irene, who died in 2000.

- - -

The mouth of Birch is a legendary fishing spot, perhaps too legendary. Numerous walleyes, ripe for spawning, are caught there every winter and early spring, and this relentless pressure over the years may be contributing to a decline in walleye fishing in Birch, the major walleye spawning stream of Elk tributaries.

The most famous catch at the mouth of Birch was not a walleye, but the muskie caught on a blustery March 26, 1955, that still holds the state length record. The angler, Lester Hayes Jr., was standing on a sandbar on the downriver side, casting a small Lazy Ike lure. This sandbar has eroded away over the years, and fishermen now congregate on the other side under the railroad trestle.

Mouth of Birch and the railroad trestle

When I was there in late February 2001, it was business as usual at the mouth of Birch: a fisherman had just caught a 28 ½ inch walleye, and another was fishing from the swinging bridge into the larger waters of Elk.

- - -

The swinging bridge is still a mouth of Birch icon. It crosses Elk about thirty yards above the mouth, connects the highway side of Elk with the railroad side, and provides access for those who fish at the mouth of Birch.

In his 1987 article, Doyle Dean wrote that it was built by Birch Boom and Lumber Company for access to its store, post office, and mill, which would place its date of origin as around 1909, when the company was incorporated.

Responsibility for maintaining the bridge, or even its ownership, apparently rests with nobody. When the issue came up in 1986, as it does occasionally, the Department of Highways wrote a letter to the prosecuting attorney of Braxton County stating that "there is no evidence that the bridge is or has ever been a structure maintained or owned by the DOH." A spokesman for the agency reaffirmed this position to me in March 2001.

There is a public right-of-way to the bridge granted by former property owner J. Clark Dean. In the musty Road Record Book No. 1 at the Braxton County Courthouse is this entry for March 8, 1922: "J.C. Dean doth dedicate for public use a strip of land five feet wide extending from the north end [of the footbridge] to the public road. But it is understood that if said footbridge shall cease to be used as a bridge, then said strip of land so dedicated to the public shall revert to the owner of the land out of which this strip is dedicated."

That was seventy nine years ago, and the bridge is still being used by the public. Dana Corley, the landowner for the past sixty years, has never sought to deny access to anyone wanting to use it, and many people do.

- - -

I visited Dana Corley and his wife, Dolsie Ramsey Corley, on a bright March day in 2001. Both are in their nineties and have lived near the swinging bridge in the familiar two-story white house since around 1940, when they bought the property from J. Clark Dean, a brother of Warder S. Dean of the Lower Keener Eddy.

J. Clark Dean was the Glendon postmaster during 1915-1918. The 1918 flood, one of the largest on record in both Elk and Birch Rivers (see "The Floods of Birch"), left water a foot deep inside his house.

From their sun porch, which faces Elk and Birch, we watched the afternoon sunlight glisten on Birch. I noticed a cluster of rocks on the rail-road side of Elk, and remembered the large muskie I raised there without really trying. Don Hamric and I were fishing from his canoe, and Don's reel had malfunctioned, as it often did. While he was attending to it, the canoe drifted into the rocks. I swished a lure in the water, killing time, when the largest muskie I've ever personally encountered swirled up and lunged at the lure. It missed, and didn't come back, but for that matter, neither did I. For reasons that had nothing to do with anything, I never returned to that particular spot to fish.

Swinging bridge over Elk at Glendon

*Lester Hayes Jr.'s 1955 muskie catch and Doug Given's record deer from 1976
(Muskie photo courtesy of Ferrell Friend)*

Aerial view of the Lower Turn Hole. Photo courtesy of Eddie Pinney

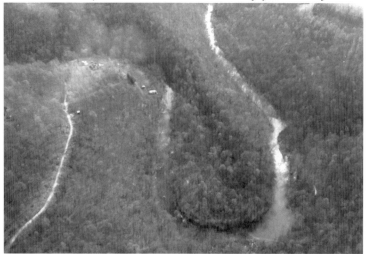

Fifteen

The Floods of Birch

1932 and Other Angry Waters

There is a large rock in the river in front of my home. Five generations of our family have fished from it or jumped off of it. On the morning of February 19, 2000, I looked out the window toward the river, as I always do. It had rained hard the previous twenty-four hours, and the river had flowed with a muffled roar during the night.

What I saw that damp and chilly February morning was a large hemlock log resting precariously on top of the rock. It hadn't been there the previous evening. The lower end was swaying in the water. I watched, fascinated by the power of the natural forces that had transported this big hemlock to my doorstep.

But this particular flood in Birch wasn't the highest I had ever seen, and in fact didn't even come close. Many have exceeded it.

At normal stage, Birch is a mild river. It is difficult for people seeing the river for the first time to envision that a particular spot where they might be standing would be, at times, under several feet of water, much less that very large rocks are occasionally completely under water.

Yet Birch floods have never been known to do any substantial damage in comparison to what occurs on other streams around the state. The reason is the terrain. The river corridor along the lower section, where Birch is largest, is narrow and V-shaped, and floodwaters cannot spill out to any great extent.

Upstream at Birch Village, which is the only sizeable settlement

Birch is a river of many moods: mostly tranquil as seen at the Margaret Johnson Rock (left) at Herold.

But a little over a year later, a raging torrent when viewed at the same rock.

on the river, flood waters have spilled into the broad river bottoms on many occasions. In particular, several homes periodically received flood waters where Powell's Creek enters Birch, but a joint effort by the Elk Valley Soil District, Birch River Ruritan Club, and the Nicholas County Commission helped ease this problem.

The most recent flooding at Birch Village occurred in 1996, when water backing up Powell's Creek from Birch River spread over the bottomland and reached the Trinity Baptist Church. The summer 1996 flood was the largest in Birch since the 1930s.

- - -

There has been no systematic gauging of water flow in Birch, with the exception of seven years when the U.S. Geological Survey had a gauge underneath the Herold Bridge below the mouth of Long Run. This gauge measured flows from September 1, 1974, through October 30, 1975, and from September 1, 1979, through October 30, 1984, as part of a larger basin study. None of the historic floods of Birch occurred in the 1970s or 1980s when the gauge was in place.

But more systematic measurements exist for Elk River, and they give a fairly good, if not precise, picture of the largest floods of the twentieth century in Birch, a tributary watershed.

To begin in another millennium, the largest flood ever recorded in Elk at Sutton occurred on or about September 28, 1861, when the flow was estimated at a whopping 50,000 cubic feet per second (cfs), and 848.2

feet above mean sea level (the level of the sea at a middle point between its extremes). The elevation of Elk at Sutton Bridge during normal flows is 811.50 feet, therefore the 1861 flood was 36.7 feet above normal. Overall, it wasn't a good year for Sutton. Three months later, on December 29, Confederate troops under the command of Captain John S. Sprigg of the 19th Virginia Cavalry were accused of capturing and burning the town (some of it, anyway), with the help of the Cowen militia, although local Confederate sympathizers were convinced that Union forces had burned Sutton.

To put the 1861 and other floods in further perspective, normal flow in Elk at Sutton is 1,000 cfs, or 49 times milder than the 1861 flood.

On September 29, 1861, the Kanawha River crested at 54.3 feet above normal at a point three and one-half miles below the mouth of Elk. This is still the highest reading ever recorded there.

In case anybody is wondering who was measuring in 1861, the answer is probably nobody, at least not in an official way. The Sutton figures are mathematical calculations, or reconstructed data, compiled by the Corps of Engineers or USGS, or both, and can be considered reasonably accurate. Some local records of flooding were kept in the middle to late 1800s, among them the 1861 Elk flood, thus aiding in the calculation.

An example of local records is the following notation in the USGS publication Water Resources Data 1998 for its gaging station on Elk River below Webster Springs: "Flood in 1861, probably in September, reached a stage of 26.34 feet (above normal) from floodmarks pointed out by a local resident."

The USGS had the first continuous-record streamflow gaging sites in place on Elk River from 1909 through 1916 at Webster Springs, Gassaway, and Clendenin, and, starting in 1929, at Queen Shoals, four miles above Clendenin. The latter is the longest-operating continuous gauge on Elk, and therefore provides the most comprehensive data. Around 1930, collection and documentation of flood data became more systematic with the initiation of a comprehensive state and federal streamflow gauging program by USGS.

The first station at Sutton did not go on line, however, until 1939. But there were stations at Webster Springs below the Back Fork of Elk from 1930 through 1934, and at Centralia from 1935 through 1963.

At present, the USGS has water-gaging stations in place on Elk at Webster Springs, Sutton, Glendon, Clay, and Queen Shoals.

The unfortunate gaps in collecting flood data in the early part of the century were a result of lack of funds. Unlike most federal agencies, USGS is not fully funded by Congress; much of its money comes from matching funds provided by state or other federal agencies.

The technology for gauging water flow has changed over the years, but not as dramatically as the method of collecting and receiving data. Early stations measured flow with a float driven recording graph wrapped around a drum housed in a box. The drum was powered by a clock set on a weekly or monthly cycle. At the end of each cycle the graph was removed, flattened and filed. Later gauges had punch tape that measured flows electronically, but the tape had to be retrieved manually and run through a machine at a USGS office. Now, flow information is radioed by satellite to USGS offices. Approximately every four hours a new chunk of information is available at the click of a computer mouse.

- - -

But some of the big floods of Elk River didn't wait for satellites and other high-tech surveillance. Based on reconstructed data and historic floodmarks, the second largest flood at Sutton occurred on March 13, 1918, when the flow was 49,000 cfs, and 845.2 feet above sea level. Old pictures show Elk River running down Main Street. John D. Sutton, in his *History of Braxton County and Central West Virginia*, said this of the 1918 flood:

> At Sutton, the water stood ten inches deep in the court house and nearly all the buildings on Main Street and Skidmore Addition were flooded. [The misery continued, according to Sutton's account]. The floods were followed by five or six heavy frosts in succession.

Warder P. Dean, who lived on Elk at Strange Creek in 1918, wrote many years later that the 1918 flood was "the biggest since the war tide of 1861." He described it as "halfway up the windows" of his home.

The 1918 flood was widespread, and followed three to six inches of rain. The Little Kanawha, West Fork, Tygart Valley, Cheat, Elk, Gauley, and Greenbrier River basins all flooded.

Then came the big one, as far as Birch River within memory is concerned.

If you tend to think it always rains on your Fourth of July picnic, you were certainly right if you happened to have been around on July 4, 1932. That was the date of the third largest flood ever recorded at Sutton, when the water reached 842.7 feet above sea level (Army Corps of Engineers data), with an estimated flow of 42,700 cfs (the latter a mathematical computation for purposes of this book, based on data from other floods for which precise numbers were available).

In a 2000 publication, *Significant Floods and Flash Floods in West Virginia since 1900,* Ken Batty of the National Weather Service in Charleston called the July 4, 1932, event "a rare summer river flood." This summer occurrence resulted from a storm that dumped from four to eight inches of rain in the Elk and Gauley River watersheds. West Virginia floods are normally the result of either a major frontal system in winter and early spring, or spillover from a tropical storm in late summer or early fall. A prime example of the latter type of storm occurred in October 1954 on upper Birch River, and caused the highest water there since 1932.

The July 4, 1932, washout on Elk and Gauley is further documented by the records from the USGS gaging station at Camden on Gauley, which is located near Cowen and near the head of Birch River. This station operated from 1909 to 1916, and has operated continuously from 1930 onward. The flood of record occurred there on the above date in 1932, when the flow reached 42,500 cfs.

In summary, following are what are believed to be the floods of record in Elk River at Sutton:

> 1861 - 50,000 cfs.
> 1918 - 49,000 cfs.
> 1932 - 42,700 cfs.

The "Last of the Mohicans" flood in Elk at Sutton occurred in 1957, with an impressive flow of 34,200 cfs, topping everything from 1932 on. Comparisons became no longer valid after 1961 with the completion of Sutton Dam.

There are no eyewitnesses around to tell us how Birch fared in 1861, but in all probability it also saw extensive flooding. Certainly it did in 1918. Juanita Brown of Vero Beach, Florida, was nine years old at the time, and she remembers that the river took away their garden and footbridge. The Browns lived in the familiar two-story house downstream from Birch Village which is still known today as the Cora Brown house (see "Cora Brown").

But the judgment call for the flood of record in Birch in the twentieth century, based on Elk data and Birch eyewitnesses, points to the Fourth of July, 1932, flood. The July 31, 1996, flood came close, as did those of 1936, 1937, and 1939. The January 26-28, 1937, flood was better known elsewhere; it was the greatest known flood in the Ohio River below the mouth of the Kanawha.

Giving validity to the severity of the 1932 flood is this note in

Corps of Engineers archives: "Observer (in the Webster Springs area) stated that this flood was the highest since 1896." The Gauley River at Belva, Nicholas County, reached its highest level ever on July 5, 1932.

Flows at Queen Shoals on Elk River four miles above Clendenin reached a record 72,000 cfs on that same date, which far exceeded anything recorded before or since.

For comparison purposes, here are the measurements at Queen Shoals for the other major 1930s floods:

> 1936: 30,000 cfs.
> 1937: 22,009 cfs.
> 1939: 59,001 cfs.

Army Corps of Engineers records for the same floods at Sutton (in elevation above sea level) give them the same ranking:

> 1936: 835.7 feet.
> 1937: 821.9 feet.
> 1939: 839.2 feet.

Obviously, the February 3, 1939, flood was a very large one on Birch as well as elsewhere.

The reasons for the devastating floods of the 1930s were that the timber had been cut wholesale from the late 1800s to 1920, and farming was much more prevalent then than it is now. Both activities denuded the hillsides, leaving them incapable of absorbing rainfall. Yellowed pictures from that era are striking for their absence of trees.

Medford Teets, who was born on lower Birch River, believes the 1932 flood was the biggest. His family was living about seventy five yards above the mouth of Leatherwood Run. He recalls that the floodwaters lapped under the house, and they had to enter and exit via the back door. The family dog was trapped on the front porch and saw a rare glimpse of the inside of the house as he was escorted out the back door to safety. They watched from the house as cornshocks floated down the river.

Thelma Butcher Teets was living with her parents, Ernie and Martha Butcher, on the river below the Lower Keener Eddy in 1932. The single-story house with full front porch faced the river, which normally was about 150 feet away. On that memorable Independence Day, 1932, the floodwater swirled and eddied up against the porch. "We put our feet in the water from the front steps," Thelma remembers. Her father cabled the house to trees and the kids went to bed at the usual time.

One major difference in floods then and now: then there were no plastic containers riding the waves to be caught somewhere, marring the beauty of the river.

During the 1932 flood, local residents gathered on the old Herold Bridge, and, using poles, pushed away logs and other debris that were threatening the structure that had been built eleven years earlier.

This same flood ravaged other streams in the area. The flooding on Buffalo Creek in Clay County was so severe, according to the 1979 publication *Widen: An Appalachian Empire* by the art department of Clay County High School, that all means of communication to and from Widen were cut off for four days.

Elmer Dodrill, who was born on Birch about a mile upstream from Birch Village in 1914, believes the 1932 flood was the largest there, too. The broad bottoms in the area were flooded to a greater extent than at any other time in his memory.

- - -

But large floods are in the eye of the beholder. On October 16, 1954, Hurricane Hazel caused flooding on several West Virginia watersheds, including upper Birch. Ruby Boggs Roberts, who was born at Boggs in 1912 and lived there all her life, was quoted in an article by Robert Bowers in *Wonderful West Virginia* magazine that 1954 was the only time she ever saw Birch overflow its banks.

Gary Dilley, a Boggs resident, points out that the Walnut Grove United Methodist Church near Boggs no longer sits on the riverbank. It washed away in the 1954 flood. The church was rebuilt, but farther away from the river.

The 1954 flood earned the sobriquet "the hog flood." Ella Hollandsworth of Boggs kept a hog in a pen near the river, and the high water washed the porker about one and one-half miles to just above a sixteen-foot falls, where it was rescued by Guy Holbrook. Ella Hollandsworth's daughter, Lorraine Hawkins, still lives at Boggs.

The 1954 flood washed out wooden bridges over Birch at Skyles Creek and Barnett Run.

Downstream at the Bubbie Hole (see "Birch Village"), Burl Tinney and Carl Dodrill had pulled their car to the edge of the river, and soon found themselves surrounded by floodwaters. They managed to escape, but the car was washed downstream about a quarter of a mile and left stranded on an island near the present Birch River Elementary School. The road that led to the edge of the Bubbie Hole is no longer there. A part of it washed away in the 1954 flood.

Okey and Joy Browning of Dille lived about a year in Birch Village, and it happened to be 1954, when the Hurricane Hazel flood occurred. The water was three feet deep, or more, in their home on Mollohan Drive, reaching the top of their kitchen sink.

Mention is made of a large flood on upper Birch at Skyles in 1926 in an article on Eakin Lumber Company written by Ward Eakin. Virtually all of the lumber company houses at Skyles were on the north side of Birch along Skyles Creek, but one, the Byrd Jackson house, was built across Birch on the south side. Eakin wrote:

> Dad took me with him to see what could be done to get the family [Byrd Jackson family], as the raging water was right up to their front door. In normal times a swinging bridge was used, but the water had taken some of the floor out and it left them in a bad way. The steel cable was still stretched across the river, and a small flat boat was tied to the cable and then a couple of men pulled themselves and the boat across the water to get the family. About three trips were necessary.

- - -

But for lower Birch, the 1930s and 1990s floods reigned supreme.

The contributing presence of Little Birch River is a major reason for the swelling floodwaters downstream. At 19.84 miles in length, Little Birch is a significant watershed in its own right. Of the 753 streams totaling 2,110 miles on the Elk River watershed, only six are bigger than Little Birch. They are main Birch, Left Fork of Holly, Back Fork of Elk, Right Fork of Holly, Buffalo Creek, and Laurel Creek.

An intriguing bit of folklore about lower Birch floods is that the 1936 flood moved an immense rock weighing 1,080 tons (see "River on the Rocks") that sits in the river in a picture-postcard setting about a mile below Herold. This rock has been photographed countless times, including by Arnout Hyde Jr., for a picture that appeared in a 1975 issue of *Wonderful West Virginia* magazine. The rock is considerably undercut, and therefore would be buffeted by floodwaters from underneath. But if it was moved in 1936, it hasn't happened since.

The same March 17-19, 1936, storm that may have moved the photogenic rock produced the flood of record on the Ohio River at Wheeling, where the river crested at fifty five feet above flood stage.

The 1936 flood wiped out some history on Birch's neighboring watershed of Strange Creek. It destroyed the remnant houses and mill at Meadville, the Mead and Speer Lumber Company town of the early 1900s that was located in what is presently known as the Cindy Woods bottom. Downstream a short distance was the Jennings Post Office, another Strange Creek artifact. Meadville and Jennings were located close enough together to be considered one and the same.

Meadville, as a lumber town, operated from 1904 or 1905 until at least 1915. The company logged quite a distance up Strange Creek, perhaps to Big Run, which enters Strange Creek about two miles below Dille. The logs were hauled to the mill on a narrow gauge railroad. (Narrow gauge track was, as the name says, laid closer together than standard track, and was often used by logging railroads, which were temporary in nature, and often operated in places where space was at a premium. Narrow gauge track was about three feet in width, compared to about forty two inches for standard gauge).

Overall, March of 1936 was a very stormy month. Four cyclonic storms passed over the Northeastern United States during March 9-22, producing severe flooding. The flood crests on the Cacapon River near Great Cacapon in West Virginia's Eastern Panhandle are still the maximum of record there, according to USGS records.

- - -

One of the biggest floods of the century in Birch occurred on July 31, 1996, six decades after the watery assaults of the 1930s. Freda Wood, who has lived on the river near Herold since 1934, says the 1996 flood topped any others of her remembrance, with the possible exception of one of the 1930s floods. The 1996 flood was the largest I can remember.

Ecclesiastes 11:3 says: "If the clouds be full of rain, they empty themselves upon the earth: and if the tree fall toward the south, or toward the north, in the place where the tree falleth, there it shall be." These are words of spiritual truth from the Preacher in *Ecclesiastes*, but in the realm of nature and Birch River, trees don't necessarily remain where they fall. In late August 1994, a landmark leaning hemlock tree on the river at my home fell with what must have been a resounding crash. It was ninety five feet tall and over three feet in diameter. Its precarious toehold had been more in rock than dirt, yet it had stood firm against the fiercest of storms. It fell on a day when there was no rain or wind. Four generations of our family, maybe five, had marveled that such a large leaning tree could stand so long. It had become a family icon, towering over our swimming hole, and we hoped it would at least remain as a foot bridge and a memento of earlier times, since it was lodged behind a fair-sized

Fallen hemlock at final(?) resting place below Herold

rock. But we were disappointed. The 1996 flood took it out and deposited it against more rocks in the lower Herold bottom below the Fisher Camp, where it remains.

Overall, the 1990s saw three large floods in Birch: 1991, 1994, and 1996. Although data directly related to Birch are not available, the flow measurements at Glendon on Elk River give some indication of the severity of these floods.

The Glendon gaging station is located on the north bank of Elk about thirty yards above the mouth of Birch. Birch would have modest, if any, impact on the data obtained there at low flows, but there is a backup effect when Birch is at flood stage.

The following measurements were obtained:

Flood	Flow	Stage
1991	22,100 cfs	16.02'
1994	21,000 cfs	15.53'
1996	30,300 cfs	18.00' (approx).

The river stage is the height of the water above a zero reference point, which in this case is the Elk River streambed in front of the gage. At normal flows, the stage is around 2.9 feet.

All are impressive figures, especially since Sutton Dam has been taming the flows on main Elk since 1961. The Glendon gaging station has operated continuously since 1959. The 1996 flow of 30,300 cfs is the record for that period.

- - -

Fred Fisher and his wife, Ann, bought a camp on Birch River at Herold in 1952. Ann Fisher wrote poems. "They were scattered throughout the house and written on various kinds of paper," said a daughter, Phyllis Fisher Myers of Ronceverte. One of her poems was about Birch River at flood stage, and it was read on August 30, 1975, at a program dedicating the "Scenic River" sign at the Herold Bridge:

> Beautiful Birch, how angry are your waters;
> Deep yellow is your stream,
> Your dress of green is stained with lustful waves.
>
> The trees that hover over you, as in a dream,
> Bow to your wake;
> Be still, let your bosom lie in peace
> That the children love so well when you sleep.
>
> They race on dancing feet to plunge into the deep;
> Be still, oh Birch, that they may remember thee."
>
> -- Ann Fisher

Birch at flood stage in May 2001;
the high water surrounds a birch tree at Herold (top),
and rages over the falls below Herold (bottom).
Falls photo courtesy of Neal Gentry

Sixteen

The Big Timber Era

And the Final Raft Down Birch

Warder P. Dean was born on February 10, 1899, during a heavy snowstorm in a one-room log cabin on Birch River above Herold. His mother, Melissa Wood Dean, always said it was one of the worst snowstorms ever to hit the Birch Valley. His great aunt, Mary Jane Stephenson, braved the storm to come and serve as midwife at his birth.

The log cabin stood on the farm of his grandfather, Simeon Dean. George Hoylman, a doctor at Gassaway, many years later acquired the property and built a stone cabin and five-hole golf course in the Simeon Dean bottom, which is located on Birch about a half mile above the mouth of Long Run. The Simeon Dean chimney, made of hand cut stone, remains as the lone reminder of the long ago residents.

John Morgan and Melissa Dean and their four sons, Emory, Stanley, French, and Warder, lived in three different locations on the property before they moved to Elk River at Strange Creek in 1912. They made the ten mile journey in a horse-drawn wagon over rutted roads.

When the family moved to Strange Creek, the Birch River property was bought by the Strange Creek Coal and Coke Company, although there is no record of this company having used the land in any way for business purposes.

Warder Dean was named for his uncle, Warder S. Dean, who lived at the Lower Keener Eddy (see "Big Run Meets Lower Keener"). He attended the one room Cleveland School in the Herold area, and graduated from Glenville Normal School (now Glenville State College) in 1921, taught school, and held many other jobs.

In his 1919-20 term at Glenville, he played basketball and tennis and participated in such school organizations as the YMCA, Cosmian Literary Society, Nature Club, Bird Club, and the school band as a trombonist. His studies included second year Latin, English literature, manual training, algebra, practice teaching, and sociology.

- - -

Among his many jobs: B & O trackman, loading coal at Widen; working for a timber contractor at Swandale, an oil refinery on Cabin Creek, an Appalachian Power plant on the Kanawha River, the Goodyear Rubber Company in Akron; as a cook's helper in a mining and lumber camp and weekends at his brother Stanley's Broad Street Cafe in Charleston; installing high-tension electric lines, as a carpenter at Widen, a salesman for a drug company, running a sawmill in partnership with Arthur Gillespie where Elk Valley Dodge of Sutton is now located, timbering in Wyoming County, and helping build a railroad at Cowen. He also was a partner in Little Birch and Little Otter coal mines, a timber buyer for Cotton-Hanlon Lumber Company, a State Road Commission employee, and a teacher.

He taught from 1917 to 1937. Many of his jobs were summertime employment between school terms.

Warder P. Dean

- - -

He was a prolific writer in later years, putting his experiences on paper for the benefit of his sons and grandchildren. His following account of the timbering and rafting era on Birch, written in 1978, is a treasured link to a past that would otherwise have faded into obscurity:

> The first timbering on Birch River of note began in the 1800s by the land owners of the area along the Birch from its mouth at Glendon to a short distance above the village of Birch River.
>
> This stretch of the river was well timbered with virgin stands of Appalachian hardwoods of such valuable species as poplar, black walnut, numerous species of oak, white oak being the best of that family. Then there were many other species of

less value due to the fact that they were not buoyant enough to drift out of the river, which was then the only way to the market.

Another species, the conifer, of which the hemlock is a member, grew profusely along the river from head to mouth. The logs from this tree when drifted to Charleston were used mostly for framing material. The log floated well and was a big help when mixed with other logs of less floatability.

Building was booming in Charleston in those days, and framing lumber was being used extensively, mostly hemlock.

My father, John Morgan Dean, owned 150 acres near Herold on Birch which he had purchased from my grandfather, Simeon Dean. There was virgin timber on this land which my father cut much of and rafted it to Charleston during 1880 and 1900. With the proceeds from this timber he was able to pay for the land.

My father and my older brother helped in cutting and drifting the logs, which were assembled into rafts at the mouth of Birch River.

The drifting of a raft the some seventy miles [to Charleston] was an exciting experience for the young men, but to father it was a way of life. A trip of seventy miles down took about two days depending on the tide in the river. The river had to be up considerably in order to carry over the shallow places and the rocks in the river.

After delivering the raft to the sawmills at the mouth of Elk River and collecting about $50.00 for the 50,000 board feet of logs, father was ready to take off the next morning at daybreak to walk the sixty miles back home in Braxton County. The difference in the miles down and the miles back was that coming back they took the crow's flight route, but in going down the crooks and bends made the difference.

On the way back they spent one night at a farm home who welcomed them as a visitor. They arrived home the evening of the second day, ready to start making another raft.

Next in the timbering line was the cutting and manufacturing of the white oak timber into barrel staves. This was where the whole family took part. First the trees were felled and then the trunks were blocked into sections of forty-four and fifty-four inches with a crosscut saw. Next the bark was removed from the blocks. This process was known as rossing, which was done with a double bitted ax. After the bark was removed, the blocks were split into quarters or smaller according to the diameter of the blocks.

Iron wedges were used to split the blocks, and a tool known as a fro was used to reduce the quarters to pieces two inches thick by six inches wide. This was the finished product, a stave.

The white oak usually grew against the hillside, which was an advantage to the workers since the blocks could be cut and rolled down the hill to the road or river where a wagon or sled could be used to move the staves to the main road. In the case of the river, the staves were split on the river bank and stacked in ricks until dry enough to float down to the road crossing where the staves could be carried out of the river where they were loaded on a wagon and hauled to Sutton where a representative of a cooperage company bought them and shipped them by rail to the company [a cooper is one who makes or repairs wooden barrels or tubs; a cooperage is his place of business].

Later, stave mills moved in and sawed the staves and trucked them to the railroads. If it wasn't for white oak staves there would be no genuine bourbon whiskey. [In a January 1996 article in *Wonderful West Virginia* magazine, Kenneth Carvell wrote that white oak was the only oak that met the needs for tight cooperage, since the vessels in its wood are blocked so that minute amounts of liquid and vapor cannot trickle through].

The next step toward timbering on Birch was the coming of the small circular sawmill powered by a steam engine. This could be moved from place to place near the timber. The lumber from these mills still must be transported to the railroad in Sutton with wagons, which was a huge risk considering the 12 miles of very rough dirt roads.

Timbering really increased with the arrival of the [Coal and Coke] railroad to the mouth of Birch [between 1900 and 1905], and the construction there of a large stationary lumber mill and a log boom at the mill to catch the logs that were drifted from upstream.

Timberland owners began to cut logs and skid them to the river bank where the mill owners, known as the Birch River Boom and Lumber Company, purchased them, and when the river tide was high enough the logs were rolled into the river and a crew of rivermen followed them and broke up log jams that formed, thus keeping them moving down to the log boom at the mill.

Sometimes after a good tide there would be several thousands of feet of logs in the boom. In order to get the logs into the mill, a slide was built from the water up and a drag chain pulled the logs up to the log deck and rolled them onto the log carriage ready to be sawed.

The lumber was loaded onto a small lumber truck and pushed out to the lumber yard to be piled until air dried, ready for shipment in box cars to market.

One of the main obstacles of this method of timbering was the uncertainty of the river flow and the weather, especially in winter, and ice. It seemed that the water was too low most of the time and too high occasionally. One time there was a flood that filled the boom to the breaking point, and hundreds of logs were swept away. Some were retrieved as far away as Charleston in a log boom there.

In order to step up the flow of water, the lumber company built a splash dam far up in Nicholas County [below the mouth of Slabcamp Run] in order to sweep the logs downstream. This was done by building a wall of logs several feet high across the river, with a sluice and a gate that could be raised and lowered after a pool of water accumulated back of the dam. This too was a failure due to the fact that when the gate was opened the water rushed out so fast that the logs were left behind, lodged up on rocks, or washed out on the river banks. This required a lot of extra work to get the logs back in the stream to wait for more water.

Finally the timber was pretty well depleted along the river, and the large mill at the mouth of Birch was dismantled and shipped away. The drifting of logs became a memory. The lumber market declined and all that was left were the little portable mills that still cut mostly crossties. This was the end of the era of timbering in the old days.

- - -

The splash dam at Slabcamp Run existed at least by 1912, according to George Beam, an upper Keener's Ridge resident who recalls hearing

stories about it. The structure was twelve feet to fourteen feet high, and its remains are still visible during periods of low water. Blair Dixon, who was born on upper Keener's Ridge in 1897, fished through the boards at the splash dam when he was a young boy.

Warder Dean retired in 1967 and was living at Gassaway when he passed away in 1985 at age eighty six. His wife,

Remnants of splash dam at Slabcamp Run

Janet Leo Canfield Dean, whom he met at a Teachers Institute at Sutton and married in 1927, is also deceased.

They had two sons. Lowell Dean is semi-retired and manages a block of apartments in Parkersburg; Byron Dean is retired after a 34-year army career, and lives in Fairfax Station, Virginia. He retired as a full colonel, one of the highest ranks ever obtained in the military by a Braxton County native.

- - -

A fitting postscript to Warder P. Dean's account of the big-timber era on Birch is a remembrance by his cousin, Doyle Dean, writing in *The Braxton Citizens' News* in 1986, of the final raft trip down Birch.

In 1931, the year Doyle graduated from Otter District (later Gassaway) High School, he was part of a raft crew that included his father, Warder S. Dean, and Bernard Given, Willis Butcher, and Loring Dean.

Loring Dean, a carpenter and builder of log homes, was living with a daughter, Dixie Simpson, in Charleston. He bought one hundred poplar logs which were cut on the farms of Warder S. Dean, Bernard Given, and Camden McMorrow. These logs were made into two rafts on Birch River in the vicinity of the Lower Keener Eddy, and floated to Charleston.

"I was elated," wrote Doyle Dean, "for it was the first time I had ever been on a log raft, and even if the logs were small, it was a thrill I have never forgotten.

"Neither will I forget the ease with which those two gentlemen [Bernard Given and Willis Butcher] handled the [lead] raft, nor the awe and wonder I felt when they talked about piloting rafts made of huge logs down the Elk to Charleston."

These large rafts were as much as 300 feet long and 60 feet wide, compared to the ones Doyle and his fellow rafters were riding, which were each about 80 feet long and 30 feet wide.

The lead raft in Doyle's procession was made of freshly cut logs, and therefore was more buoyant and faster. The three Deans piloted the slower raft, which was assembled from logs that had been cut several weeks before and had absorbed a considerable amount of water.

Doyle concluded: "I am proud to have had ancestors of pioneer lineage who had a part in the making of a nation. Certain families who lived along the Elk River used their homes for 'hotels' during the boom days of the log rafting. The rafters used their knowledge of the river, and the amount of water flow, so they would arrive at these 'hotels' just before dark."

In summertime, the rafters often camped overnight on the shore. Evening meals frequently included fish they caught while floating through the eddies.

Just as arduous as rafting down Elk was the walk back home. Doyle wrote that the men would leave Charleston early in the morning, and would follow trails across the hills to cut down on the distance. "They would walk all day and night," he said, "with a few short stops for rest, and would arrive back home at Herold, Glendon, or vicinity, by noon the following day."

In 1954, Cass native Warren Blackhurst put a romantic face on the log rafting era with his book, *Riders of the Flood*, about the rafts that were floated down the Greenbrier River. Perhaps a logical sequel would be "Walking Back."

One of the most impressive feats performed among those who walked back up Elk was that of Curtis Mollohan, who lived on upper Keener's Ridge. He was part of a crew that took a raft to Charleston, where, with his share of the proceeds, he bought a saddle for his horse and walked back carrying the saddle. Curtis Mollohan, the grandfather of George Beam, died in 1939.

The Curtis Mollohan raft was made of virgin poplar cut on Birch. One log, George Beam recalls his grandfather telling, measured seven feet in diameter. A hole was bored in it to provide buoyancy. *Forest Trees of West Virginia*, published by the State Forestry Division, says that "the common yellow poplar, or tulip tree, has a height of 80 to 150 feet, and a diameter of 3 to 10 feet."

In addition to riding the last raft down Birch, Doyle also played a role in the last raft that went down Elk: the 1963 centennial raft that was floated from Braxton County to Charleston as part of West Virginia's 100th birthday celebration. The logs were cut on the Elk River Wildlife Management Area, where Doyle was employed.

The centennial raft was plagued by the same problem that faced rafters of an earlier time: low water. It grounded on a shoal near Clay, and didn't reach Charleston until several months later, when the river had raised sufficiently to float it.

Doyle Dean died in 1995 at age eighty five at Stephens City, Virginia. His widow, Evelyn Dean, still lives there.

- - -

Medford Teets saw the final two log rafts go down Birch. He

was eight years old, and in bed with the measles, that common childhood affliction marked by red circular spots, itching, and, one is tempted to think at the time, imminent death. His family lived on the river near the mouth of Leatherwood Run. "My parents saw the rafts coming down," Medford recalled, "and they let me get out of bed and go to the window and watch."

He realized in later years that he had witnessed the end of an era.

~ Seventeen ~

Creatures Large and Small

The Flora and Fauna of Birch River

I once attended a meeting that began with one of the participants saying, "First, let us define our terms." I instinctively knew it was going to be a long day, although in retrospect it wasn't such a bad idea, so allow me to define our terms:

Flora: Plant life.

Fauna: Animal life.

The terms appear relatively simple and straightforward, but as always the devil is in the details. For example, a smallmouth bass, although part of the fauna group, little resembles a whitetail deer, and I've never laid eyes on a hellbender that could hold a candle to a squirrel for cuteness.

Flora is fairly simple; if it grows in the ground, it's flora. But the devil in the details told me to clarify our terms as to birds, fish, frogs, turtles, insects, crayfish, snakes, lizards, and hellbenders, all fauna, when their turn arrives, and for once the devil gave good advice.

First, the flora of the Birch River community. What follows is not intended to be a complete listing, but rather what you would commonly see and perhaps identify on a field trip. A more complete listing with Latin (scientific) names is included at the end of this chapter for the benefit of those who speak Latin, the Italic language of ancient Rome.

The compilation resulted from field trips made in fall 2000 and spring 2001 by Bill Gillespie and Jim Brown (see "The Rocks") and myself. We walked along the river and drove the local byways, and wrote down everything we saw. The list is impressive in its length and also in the diversity of plant life it contains.

Bill explained why Latin is used for scientific names: "It is a 'dead' language, not much used, and therefore not subject to great change over the years. The overall consequence is that people anywhere in the world can recognize the plant from the Latin name, although they may be much confused if the vernacular or common name is used. A scientific name can be used or applied only once, that is, to only one plant" [thus, for example, the common Christmas fern becomes Polystichum acrostichoides].

For purposes of this book, flora is divided into six categories: trees, shrubs, flowers, vines, ferns, and primitives, as follows:

Trees

River birch: Everything else is listed in alphabetical order; river birch deserves to lead off because without it Birch River might have been named Sassafras River; river birch is easily identified by its reddish-brown to cinnamon-red bark that is papery and peels off in layers; it grows up and down the river, and gave its name to the river about two hundred and seven years ago; I've threatened many times to cut the birches that grow in my yard because they are prolific shedders of their limbs, but common sense and decency have always prevailed.

American beech: Its smooth gray bark and cigar-shaped buds are dead giveaways, but if further identification is needed, look for a tree with initials carved on it; ancient hollow beeches are valuable as den sites for squirrels, chipmunks, owls, and pileated woodpeckers, and besides that they are a natural part of the forest progression; old beech trees are "family."

American elm: Found in rich river bottom soil, this magnificent vase-shaped tree with alternating brown and white layers in the deeply fissured bark was once used hereabouts in wagon hubs, so tough is the wood.

American holly: Its evergreen foliage and bright red berries brighten our winter days, and decorate our homes at Christmas, but don't overdo the collecting of it; holly is best enjoyed in a natural outdoor setting, preferably with a light dusting of snow on its leaves.

Basswood: Early settlers braided rope from the tough fiber (called bast) in its bark; its fragrant yellowish-white bloom makes good honey.

Bigtooth aspen: This species isn't common locally, but a few do exist; its larger and coarse-toothed leaves distinguish it from the trembling, or quaking, aspen.

Black birch: The dark horizontal peelings, as is typical only for birchs and cherries, is this tree's fingerprint; the heavy, hard wood is valued by carpenters, and who hasn't enjoyed the wintergreen taste of scraped inner bark in early spring?

Black cherry: A good specimen is worth its weight in gold at the lumberyard because there is furniture... and then there is furniture made from cherry; its durability, grain, and rich dark color spell class; its fruit is beloved by bears, and there aren't many wild cherry trees around whose limbs haven't been broken by bears.

Black gum: Its wood is of little commercial value, and its dark blue berries are sour, hence the colloquial name, sour gum; this tree is virtually impossible to split, although one way is to drive hollow wedges filled with black powder into the tree, light the fuse, and stand back.

Black locust: Who hasn't flinched upon grabbing one of this tree's thorny twigs? The heavy, hard, yellowish wood is decay resistant and makes fine fenceposts; poor soils benefit from the nitrogen it adds.

Black oak: Valued as a timber species, as are most of the oaks, although red oak and white oak usually command higher prices; squirrels and deer cherish the smallish, good-tasting (I suppose) acorns of black oak, and this tree seems to bear more reliably year after year; the bark of black oak is rough and black, even on its large limbs; the inner bark is yellow-orange.

Black walnut: Worth more than all the gold at Fort Knox; its heavy, hard wood makes fine furniture, and landowners who cut their walnut trees for a relative pittance years ago now wish they had them back, or perhaps the landowners' heirs wish that; Maurice Brooks once wrote a small book on plants that die under or near walnuts: apples, potatoes, and tomatoes are three of many; Kentucky bluegrass thrives under a walnut, however.

Buckeye: Widely distributed along the Ohio River and is the Ohio state tree, hence the name of the Ohio State University athletic teams. Also found along moist Birch River banks; an old wives' tale is that half of the buckeye nut is poisonous, and that squirrels know the difference, but actually the nut contains tannin, a non-poisonous but very astringent substance used in tanning, dyeing, ink, and medicine, and squirrels simply know when they've had enough.

Butternut: Also known as white walnut; it is not as common as it once was because of a fungus disease, and butternuts are not long-lived trees in the first place; but some remain.

Cedar: Technically known as Eastern red cedar, it thrives on rough, dry hillsides, and lent its name to one such hillside on lower Birch River, the Cedar Cliffs of "Big Run Meets Lower Keener"; birds relish its pale blue berries.

Chestnut oak: Find a dry, rocky ridge, and you'll find this species with its deeply furrowed bark; its leaves resemble the leaves of the native American chestnut, but without the needle-like tips; chestnut oak is prized for bridge timbers and other rough construction; its lumber sometimes passes for white oak.

Cucumber: Its dark red fruit cone resembles a small garden cucumber; it grows tall, and its close-grained durable wood is a cabinet maker's delight.

Flowering dogwood: According to legend, it was the wood of Jesus' cross; its white to pinkish flowers unfold before the leaves appear, and are a spectacular sight along highways; when the leaves are the size of a squirrel's ear, it's time to reach for the fishing pole.

Hemlock: No cool Birch River hillside is complete without this tall, towering water-loving tree that grows to heights of over one hundred feet; its ascending branches and dark green needles make it a desired ornamental tree as well; deer enjoy its shelter when the snow piles up.

Ironwood: Even a sharp chainsaw has problems cutting this smallish tree that is common along Birch River; it also goes by the names of blue beech, water beech, musclewood (its ripply swirls resemble a well-muscled arm), and hornbeam.

Osage orange: This unique tree was imported from Texas and Oklahoma as an ornamental, and was named for the Osage Indian tribe; its uniqueness is its fruit, which is a large green ball about the size of a softball; osage is not plentiful in the Birch River community, but a few trees do exist; one, for example, stands just below the defunct Adams School.

Pawpaw: Chiefly noted for its greenish-yellow fruit, which resembles a stubby banana in shape, and tastes like, well, like a pawpaw.

Persimmon: Animals, especially opossums, raccoons, and deer, like its fruit, and so, occasionally, do people, although persimmons don't become sweet until after the first frost; sour persimmons may have invented the phrase "puckered lips."

Pignut hickory: A very common tree on well-drained slopes and ridgetops; nearly as common as shagbark hickory; the thick husk has one pointed end that lends a pear-shaped appearance; the bark usually remains tight.

Redbud: Its bright purplish-red flowers announce that spring has arrived; redbud and dogwood blooming in combination are a delight to the senses, and tell us that crappie and bluegills are biting in the lakes.

Red maple: This "common weed of West Virginia forests," also known as soft maple, has gained in popularity as a hard maple substitute, particularly for finishing and interior work, and cabinets.

Red oak: Its inner bark is reddish, its acorns are large and cup-shaped, and the acorn caps have furnished many a "pipe bowl" for youngsters; it is a tall, hardy tree that is cherished for furniture and interior work, and in winter 2000-2001 commanded higher prices than any other oak in the flourishing West Virginia timber industry; the wood, when first split, which it does easily, resembles the color of a slab of salmon at the supermarket.

Sassafras: A small tree that prefers dry soil and abandoned fields; its roots yield a substance called oil of sassafras which is the ingredient of old root beer and sassafras tea, a popular spring potion that is good for whatever ails you, if you are a true believer.

Scarlet oak: Looks similar to red oak, with a lot of dead branches up the trunk; grows on dry sites, like chestnut oak; little value as a timber tree.

Serviceberry: The common "sarvas" or "sarvice" whose white bloom is an early spring delight; its sweet tasting, juicy, dark red berries arrive in July and can be seen scattered along the smooth rock ledges of Birch River; "sarvas" is normally thought to be a corruption of service, but Earl Core, in his book *The Wondrous Year: West Virginia Through the Seasons*, suggests it's the other way around, that "service" is a corruption of sarvas, so perhaps we hillbillies have been pronouncing it correctly all along and didn't know it.

Shagbark hickory: The most common West Virginia hickory; prefers streams and moist hillsides; its thin-shelled nuts are a taste treat in candy, cake, and cookies, and squirrels find them irresistible; its shaggy bark curls are distinctive.

Shellbark hickory: A slightly taller tree than its cousin; some grow to heights of ninety feet; shellbark nuts are enclosed in a thick husk that misleads: when peeled and cracked, the nut is very small.

Slippery elm: The inside of the bark is indeed slippery, and fibrous, and bears will strip the bark and eat the fiber; the inner bark is used for medicinal purposes, hence it is also collected by people.

Sugar maple: The West Virginia state tree; a large, slow growing tree with a beautiful symmetrical crown, it reaches heights of over one hundred feet; also called hard maple or rock maple, it is extremely valuable for flooring, furniture, and other uses; because of its value, many sugar maples have been cut, and are not as plentiful as they once were; tapping sugar maples for sap is still done in West Virginia forests, especially in the higher elevations of the state where sugar maple grows best; the rule of thumb is that about thirty gallons of sap will reduce to a gallon of syrup and up to a pound of sugar.

Sycamore: Along with river birch and hemlock, it perfectly symbolizes the trees of the Birch River corridor; it is a very large tree (maybe the largest in the world); the smooth white surface underneath its scaly bark stands out like an albino deer in the bleak November woods.

White ash: Prefers the rich, moist soils of river bottoms; the toughness and elasticity of its wood makes it prized for baseball bats and tool handles.

White oak: The most stately of West Virginia's and the world's hardwoods and a valuable timber tree, it grows slowly but lives a long time; white oaks of over one hundred and fifty years in age are not uncommon; the oldest was the Mingo Oak, which was five hundred and eighty two years old when it died in the late 1930s; the tree was cut by lumberjacks Paul Criss and Ed Meeks of Webster Springs, using an eight and one-half foot long crosscut saw. Eddy Grey, one of the architects of the map that accompanies this book, had a white oak in his yard in Braxton County that died of lightning, and was two hundred and seventy six years old, and measured sixty and one-quarter inches in diameter; squirrels and deer prefer white oak acorns above all others because they have less tannin and therefore are sweeter.

White pine: The tallest of our pines; the wind moans through it with a melancholy sound that speaks of long ago; its trademark is its six to eight-inch white-tipped cones that curve slightly and are nice for decorative use.

Yellow poplar: Also called tulip tree because of its greenish-yellow tulip-shaped blossoms; honey made from the nectar is highly prized; poplars grow rapidly, reach heights of eighty to one hundred feet or more, and are a valuable timber species of our second growth forests; Poplar Creek of Birch River was named for its abundance of large poplars.

Shrubs

American hazelnut: Its light brown nuts come in clumps of four, and are sweet tasting; it is not an uncommon plant, but usually grows in thickets where it is less likely to be seen (we're dealing here with something very cunning).

Brookside alder: Common in the wet soil along streams in the lower elevations of the state; a member of the birch family and therefore right at home on Birch River; in summer 2000 I sheltered under brookside alder during a light rain while fishing at the Lee Jack Plout of Birch (see "If We Were Counting").

Flame azalea: Maurice Brooks, the late, great naturalist at West Virginia University, said that if he was limited to only one flowering shrub, it would be this one; blooms in late May and early June, and its reddish, orange and yellow flowers can be seen from great distances through the open woods that azaleas prefer, hence they resemble a flame; they also like dry soil, and are therefore generally found on southern exposures; azaleas, mountain laurel, and rhododendron are closely related, botanically speaking, all being members of the heath family.

Leatherwood: Because of its flexible branches and toughness of bark, the Indians used its twigs for twine, and a long-ago farmer or logger on Leatherwood Run of Birch River (see "Leatherwood Country") used it to repair broken oxen harness, thus giving the tributary its name.

Mountain laurel: One of the two shrubs that personify the rugged Birch River streamside, the other being rhododendron; the pinkish-white fragrant bloom of mountain laurel announces the official start of the summer season; it likes everything that Birch has to offer: rocky, gravelly soil along the stream, and the acidic soil of the nearby woods.

Rhododendron: Simply put, Birch is rhododendron country; long stretches of moist, shady river hillsides are covered with this shrub that produces the West Virginia state flower; its limbs are tough and intertwined, thus creating a thicket that is almost impenetrable; but life doesn't get any better than fishing on Birch when the rhododendron is in bloom from late June to mid-July; a colloquial name for rhododendron is "laurel," or "great laurel," but by any name it and mountain laurel epitomize Birch River.

Spicebush: Break off a twig (they are brittle and break easily) and smell the wood, and the name spicebush becomes obvious; the twigs and bark make an aromatic tea; bears feed on the bright red berries.

Staghorn sumac: A very common shrub, and easily identified by its orange-colored wood, densely hairy twigs that resemble a stag's horn in winter, and clumps of oblong-shaped reddish berries.

Squaw honeysuckle: A common sight growing on top of the large rocks of Birch (see "The Rocks"); its berries are so bitter that even birds decline to eat them, but any plant that can cling to life on a rock deserves our respect.

Wild honeysuckle (pink azalea): A common sight growing along country roads in the Birch River community, although its numbers have been reduced by people attempting to transplant it to their yards (usually unsuccessfully); in the glorious era prior to plastic flowers, wild honeysuckle was commonly used to decorate graves on Memorial Day.

Winterberry: This shrub is also known as deciduous holly because it sheds its leaves in winter; another name is black alder; its abundant bright red berries are a delight in late summer and fall along Birch River streambanks.

Witch hazel: If you've nothing else to do, bring some of its seed pods in the house; when brought into a warmer setting, the seeds will pop with a loud noise and propel themselves across the room, and you can amuse yourself by searching for them under the furniture. The city of Louisville often smelled of the delicious odors of their distillation.

Flowers

Ageratum: Its appealing blue flower closely resembles the domestic ageratums of greenhouses; it is also called mist flower and blue boneset; its beauty adds much to fall roadsides.

Black-eyed susan: Also called yellow daisy; ten to twenty yellow petals surround the brown coneshaped center; the flower is from one and one-half to three inches wide; very showy and much beloved.

Bull thistle: Also called common thistle because its purple bloom is a common sight in the fall; its leaves are spiny and prickly and not to be taken lightly; this aggressive weed was introduced from Scotland for reasons that transcend logical thought.

Cardinal flower: Loves moist river situations; its brilliant red flowers are a delight along Birch from July to September; this flower was named for the brightly attired cardinals of the Roman Catholic Church.

Cattail: Euell Gibbons, the wild foods guru, called cattails "the supermarket of the swamp" because they provide many different foods; this tall plant is characterized by its sausage-like head; birds, muskrats, and beaver all feed on cattails; its dark side is that its appearance in farm ponds is a clear indicator that the pond is silting up and becoming "wetland."

Coltsfoot: This dandelion lookalike is a very early spring flower and a fall weed, its half-grown leaves resemble the foot of a colt; early settlers made a tea or syrup from the leaves to treat coughs and colds, and smoked the dried leaves to relieve asthmatic suffering (Joseph Harned, *Wild Flowers of the Alleghanies*).

Dandelion: Named for its bright green leaves, which are cut into very obvious segments, and for the French description of the leaf, which is "tooth of the lion," or "dent de lion"; its bright yellow flowerheads were put on this earth so somebody could be the first each spring to proudly proclaim, "dandelions are blooming already!" Dent de lion greens, anyone?

Goldenrod: Its yellow flowers brighten the fall landscape; some fields appear to have a golden cloth spread over them when this flower is in bloom; there are one hundred and twenty five species in North America, but who's counting? West Virginia has twenty nine of these species; goldenrod is often accused of causing hayfever, but it's a bum rap; most hayfever is caused by ragweed; you'd have to stick your face in goldenrod to get an allergic reaction.

Ironweed: It towers over most autumn flowers, growing to heights of up to nine feet (joe-pye weed, wild lettuce, Jerusalem flower, and ragweed probably grow as tall); ironweed's deep purple flowers are gorgeous, particular in combination with joe-pye, and they do frequently grow together.

Jack in the pulpit: Also called Indian turnip, it's one of the most recognizable and unique plants in the Birch River community; a broad tapering flap unfolds over the floral spike, hence we have Jack in his pulpit; its roots have calcium oxalate crystals that, when stuck in mucous membranes (as when some prankster offers you a bite), cause a hot, excruciating pain on which water has no effect; the pain is worse than that of a toothache.

Jerusalem flower: Tall and showy, it is our largest sunflower; Indians cultivated it because its tubers were a potato substitute, and these tubers are still eaten by wild food gourmets; look for it along roadbanks; its golden flowers are from two to three and one-half inches wide.

Jewelweed: Its orange flowers are a common sight along roads; daub its sap on a bee sting or poison ivy blisters for a soothing effect; its flower pods explode when touched, therefore its more common name, touch-me-not.

Joe-pye weed: Its lavender blooms are an autumn staple; tall and stately, it is also called queen of the meadow; joe-pye's scientific name (Eupatorium fistulosum) honors Mithridates Eupator, 132-63 B.C., who is said to have used it in medicine; joe-pye and ironweed are often confused; a simple way to tell the difference is that joe-pye has a lavender bloom, while ironweed's is deep purple.

Lady's slipper: This beautiful moccasin-shaped orchid loves the sandy soil of secluded Birch River bottoms; the flowers come in both pink and yellow, with the former being by far the most prevalent; unfortunately, deer eat them, and they are becoming quite scarce.

Nettle: Its alternate and dreaded name is stinging nettle; its "fangs" are the bristly hairs on the leaves; when the tip is broken off, it scratches and injects chemicals into the wound, and localized pain follows rapidly, accompanied by redness and prolonged itching; snakebite might be preferable to a nettle sting, depending on the kind of snake. Is often eaten as spinach in Europe, and is used in homeopathic remedies for rheumatism and arthritis.

New England aster: Its aristocratic name doesn't confine it to the bluebloods of New England; it's found elsewhere, including in the Birch River community; it grows tall, and proudly boasts numerous flower heads; its violet-purple petals surrounding an orange-yellow center constitute a strikingly pretty flower.

Ox-eye daisy: An escapee from medicinal herb gardens, this is the common daisy of yards, fields, and roadbanks; it is among the showiest of all our wildflowers because it grows enmasse; unlike most spring flowers, daisies last long into the summer, and without them and their petals to pluck we wouldn't have a clue whether "she loves me, she loves me not."

Pokeweed: Like dandelions, this flower, a.k.a. weed, gives us something to talk about in the spring when it comes time to cook up a "mess" of poke greens from the young leaves; the Indians were said to have used pokeweed berries to make a bright red dye, and perhaps paint their faces before going on the warpath against people who keep saying, "The Indians did this or that."

Queen Anne's lace: Its white flowers cup upward to resemble a bird's nest, with usually one black flower in the center; despite its lacy flower and monarchial name, this Oriental immigrant is a weed, pure and simple, and has taken over many a farmer's fields.

Ragweed: Kerchoo! The bane of existence of ragweed sufferers, this pain in the allergies grows to heights of six or seven feet, thus is difficult to avoid unless you stay inside; the book, *Wild Flowers of the Alleghanies*, says even goats won't eat ragweed.

Red clover: Honeybees and bumblebees love its sweetly-scented nectar, and its crimson red blossom is appealing.

Sheep's sorrel: This low-growing plant with a red top is the one that gardeners love to hate; it invades gardens in late summer and defies all efforts to eradicate it; as was once said whimsically of an Atlanta Braves baseball player who'd had an uncharacteristically good day at the plate, "You can't stop him, you just hope to contain him."

Spanish needles: Also called beggar's sticks or pitchforks, its two barbed spines were undoubtedly put on this earth to torment man and dog; they attach themselves to clothing, fur, and anything else that comes along.

Sunflowers: There are about eighty species of this stately flower, with at least a dozen found in West Virginia; the thinleaved sunflower is the most common in the Birch River community; it has ten petals surrounding its yellowish-brown center, and was a staple in American Indian food pouches.

Tick trefoil: Its small purplish flowers give rise to sticky triangular seeds that stick to clothing like ticks, hence they are also called sticktights.

White snakeroot: Produces a white cluster of flowers; cows eat it, it gets in their milk, and causes "milk sickness" to those who drink it; whole villages once moved because the residents were dying without knowing why, but it was later discovered that it was due to milk sickness.

Wild geranium: Common in open woods and along roadsides, its pink to purple flowers are among the showiest of all wildflowers; seeing wild geranium in bloom is worth a walk in the woods on a spring day.

Wild lettuce: Grows to heights of six feet or more, hence is also called tall lettuce; common along country roadsides; its flowers are yellowish.

Yellow ironweed: Also called wing stem for the flaps of tissue along the stem; it is often mistaken for a sunflower.

Many of the above-listed flowers occur in the fall, and are members of the Composite family, which is the largest of all plant families. Although spring wildflowers get more "press," fall wildflowers are just as showy and longer-lasting.

Vines

Blackberry: My thoughts, prayers, and concerns go out to the hardy breed of people who actually like to pick blackberries; sure, blackberry cobbler and blackberry jam are tasty, but are they worth the scratches, stings, snakes, heat, chiggers, ticks, and assorted other aggravations? Of course not.

Dutchman's pipe: Also called camphor vine; its flower is akin to a curved pipe smoked by the Dutch, and its leaves large and heart shaped; it prefers woods and streambanks.

Fox grapevine: Smaller and thicker than the summer grapevine, it produces a grape that is tart and tasty after the first frost; squirrels and wild turkeys like fox grapes.

Grapevine (summer): This most common grapevine in West Virginia is a high-climbing vine with loose, shreddy bark, and hairy twigs; it has choked many a good hardwood tree into submission, which is why foresters cut grapevines in the process of doing timber stand improvement. It is a wonderful source of water when you're thirsty, and makes attractive wreaths.

Greenbrier:　One of the approximately twenty two shrubs or vines that deer will readily eat; evidence of greenbriers having been browsed by deer can be seen virtually everywhere in the woods surrounding Birch River; also, if you spend even a little time in the woods and have never been tripped and sent sprawling by a greenbrier, raise your hand.

Multiflora rose:　A nuisance if there ever was one; originally introduced as a living fence for livestock and cover for wildlife, it has spread like wildfire and has taken over many fields; versatile if nothing else, it will even climb trees.

Poison ivy:　Those who are allergic to its poisonous ways must remember the saying, "Leaflets three let it be, leaflets five keep it alive," the point being that poison ivy has three leaves and should be avoided, while five-leafed Virginia creeper is completely innocent of any poisonous designs and should be spared.

Ferns

Christmas fern:　West Virginia's most common fern; each leaflet has a telltale "ear" at the base; often used for Christmas decorations because it is green at Christmastime, hence its name; its presence indicates good growing conditions for trees, as do the presence of wood ferns and spicebush.

Cliffbrake fern:　A small fern (ours is the purple variety) that grows on rocks and logs; Thoreau wrote, "It is very pleasant and cheerful nowadays, when the brown and withered leaves strew the ground and almost every plant is fallen withered, to come upon a patch of [cliffbreak fern] on some rocky hillside in the woods, where, in the midst of dry and rustling leaves, defying frost, it stands so freshly green and full of life."

Grape fern:　Also called rattlesnake fern for its long-stalked fertile portion with "rattles" at the end.

Lady fern: More common in the Birch area than the Christmas fern; its fronds are light green and delicate-looking, and are broadest near the base; its stem is deeply grooved and bright pinkish to reddish when growing in heavy shade; often called "the queen of ferns," it is mentioned in several poems; Scott wrote: "Where the morning dew lies longest, there the lady fern grows strongest."

Royal fern: Common in the (now named) Royal Gorge of Birch in the Herold vicinity, it may be the most beautiful member of the fern tribe, and certainly is the tallest; it is easily cultivated in rich soil, but will grow happily in any wet place.

Primitives

(Reproduce from spores instead of seeds)

Algae: Grows on rocks in Birch River, and will put you down quicker than black ice; when my nephew, Rob Johnson, was fifteen, he set a Birch River record of three falls in ten seconds: down, up, down, up, down (after the third fall he stayed down out of respect for an unrelenting and implacable foe).

Bracket fungus: Also known as a conk, it grows, shelf-like, on the sides of trees; artists decorate and sell this tree-hugger.

Ground pine: A relic of the coal swamps of past millenia, it once grew to heights of one hundred feet; now it hugs the ground, probably no more than two to four inches in height; large sections of woodland are covered by ground pine, giving the woods the appearance of Astroturf.

Morel: One of several hundred fungi (parasitic lower plants that lack chlorophyll) found in West Virginia; this one is the tasty mushroom of the spring woods that sprouts about the time of spring gobbler season; fungi decompose or rot bio-logical materials and thus prevent the earth from being buried with foot after foot of leaves.

Moss: A non-flowering plant better known as the soft green carpet of West Virginia woodlands; patches of moss are pleasant in appearance and a spongy delight to walk on; in time, moss covers rocks and logs, thus spawning the term "old mossback" that is commonly applied to whitetail bucks and crafty fish that have lived into their retirement years, and to people of archaic, unbending beliefs who react strongly to ideologies that differ from their own.

Orange moss: Millions of years ago it chose to be orange instead of green; an outstanding example of orange moss can be seen growing on a rock ledge on the south side of W.Va. 82 east of Birch Village and below the mouth of Anthony Creek.

Snakeskin liverwort: Grows on rocks along Birch River; it very much resembles the skin of a snake, which is why my nephew finds this innocent little primitive so repulsive (see the upset canoe episode in "If We Were Counting"); can also be identified by its odor.

Fauna

Fauna includes all manner of creeping, crawling, and flying things, many of them bearing absolutely no resemblance in appearance or in any other way to each other; their one commonality is that they all must eat to survive, so if they tend to eat each other, please forgive them.

Because of the wide diversity of fauna, I promised at the start of this chapter to further define our terms:

Birds: Warm-blooded vertebrates (having a spinal column); also look for something with its body covered by feathers.

Crayfish: A crustacean, or aquatic arthropod (no spinal column) with jointed body and limbs; worldwide, there are twenty six thousand species of crustaceans.

Frogs: Largely aquatic amphibians (can live outside the water);

look for webbed feet.

Insects: Invertebrates; bodies more or less segmented; includes house flies, yellowjackets, butterflies, hornets, moths, mosquitos, tent caterpillars, mayflies, cluster flies, June bugs, fireflies, and other worthy citizens.

Hellbender: A large aquatic salamander.

Lizards: A sub-order of reptile with legs and a tapering tail.

Snakes: Limbless, scaled reptiles; they beguile.

Turtles: Amphibians (except for the Eastern box turtle); watch for creatures that withdraw their heads into a shell.

Fauna is divided into the following five categories:

Mammals

Beaver: They are not abundant on Birch, but signs of fresh beaver cutting appear somewhere along the river every year; the nature of this chisel-toothed, flat-tailed animal is that it eats everything available in a particular area, and moves on.

Black bear: The state animal; bears disappeared from this area in the early 1900s, and didn't resurface again until around 1980 when new hunting regulations adopted by the Division of Natural Resources resulted in their spread from the traditional bear counties in the mountains to all parts of West Virginia; upper Birch has the largest bear population of anywhere along the river, and it always has (see "Skyles and Boggs").

Bobcat: This secretive, nocturnal cat with the stubby tail is at home on the rocky crags and ledges of Birch, although it is by no means plentiful.

Chipmunk: A captivating, striped little creature with pouchy cheeks; chatters and scampers its way through the dry leaves of autumn, making more noise than a squirrel or deer; wisely hibernates in winter.

Coyote: This traditional western animal began to appear in the eastern United States in the 1980s, and has taken up residence; most counties of central West Virginia have a coyote population.

Fairydiddle: This true red squirrel, halfway between a chipmunk and gray squirrel in size, is normally found at elevations of over 3,000 feet, but in recent years has migrated into the Birch area; its traditional habitat is spruce forests, but it has found a home among our hemlocks.

Fox squirrel: Large and red, it is commonly but mistakenly called a "red squirrel"; the true red squirrel is the fairydiddle; the fox squirrel is considerably bigger than a gray squirrel, and prefers a mix of woodland and field habitat.

Gray fox: Smaller than its cousin the red fox, this furtive creature prefers woods and brush; its hair is coarse and therefore its pelt was less valuable than that of red fox when trapping was still in vogue; grays average about twenty eight inches in length, compared to about thirty six inches for reds, and the reds weigh more on average.

Gray squirrel: Its population is cyclic; some people say "there aren't as many squirrels as there once was," and this is undoubtedly true if compared to the days of the American chestnut early in the twentieth century when chestnuts were abundant every year, and squirrels had plenty to eat; but now there are good years and bad years for acorns and such, and the squirrel population bounces back and forth.

Groundhog: A roly-poly weather forecaster that stays in its den during the worst part of winter; some forecaster! but it's the only animal to have a day (February 2) in its honor; you know the drill: if fat boy sees his shadow, it means six more weeks of bad weather.

Little brown bat: A flying mammal that causes hysteria when it gets inside the house, but is relatively harmless; it dips and soars through the air on spring and fall evenings, and eats insects, including mosquitoes, in large quantities.

Mink: Its soft, thick dark-brown coat was once prized by the fur industry, but fur coats have fallen out of favor, and therefore so have fur prices; the mink population on Birch has never been high, and probably never will be; a characteristic of mink is that when angered they spit and squeal. Haven't we all felt like doing that?

Opossum: Our beloved marsupial with beady eyes, scaly tail, naked ears, and a propensity for "playing possum" when threatened; the young take refuge in mother marsupial's pouch.

Rabbit: Habitat in the Birch community no longer favors the cottontail, because farms have grown into woods; but the rabbit is a survivor, and a remnant population exists.

Raccoon: Birch is good raccoon habitat, and this animal's tracks, which resemble a small human foot, are the most common of any animal along the river; its ringed tail, masked bandit face, and flexible fingers make it very appealing, especially as it washes its food, but it's a well-known raider of corn patches; efforts are often made by well-meaning people to tame coons, but as the animal grows older, it reverts to type, and claws and bites.

Red fox: Basically nocturnal, but occasionlly seen in the daytime since it is more likely than the gray fox to frequent open fields and meadows; both reds and grays are superb hunters that catch small mammals, birds, and just about anything else that moves.

Skunk: A cute animal, but cute is as cute smells; capable of spraying its foul-smelling musk at distances of up to ten feet.

Weasel: A small, cantankerous, and rarely seen carniverous animal; back when rural dwellers kept chickens, a dreaded moment was when a weasel got in the chickenhouse.

Whitetail deer: Disappeared from central West Virginia in the early 1900s, but look who's back! Its resurgence began in the 1930s with restocking programs, and deer are now plentiful, although their numbers rise and fall with the annual hunting season kill; the fawning season in May and June has managed so far to replenish the supply; a biological wonder is that bucks shed their antlers in winter, and grow them again the next spring and summer; a sociological wonder is that we had anything to talk about before deer began raiding our gardens; in any event, public fascination with deer continues unabated.

Birds

Barred owl: One of our two "hoot owls," it is slightly smaller than the great horned, the other so-called hoot owl; its numbers remain fairly constant, but it isn't plentiful; it is characterized by its large brown eyes and by the streaks, or bars, on its breast and belly.

Bluejay: Noisy, aggressive; no bird book needed to identify it; look for its bright flashy blue feathers, and arrogance at the feeder.

Canada geese: Not many frequent the smallish waters of Birch, but a few pairs nest on the river, and are seen each spring in the Herold area.

Cardinal: The state bird was well chosen; beautiful red plumage, especially the males, and a year-round resident; a brightly colored cardinal perched in the dark green foliage of rhododendron is an appealing sight.

Chickadee: Smallish bird with black cap and throat, and white cheeks; hangs upside down while feeding; you may want to try this sometime.

Crow: The ultimate survivor, and one of our largest land birds; it has mastered the art of eluding whizzing traffic while feasting on interstate road kills; crows flock together in the spring and fall to migrate, although there is also a resident winter population; in January 2001 I saw a flock of more than one hundred crows near Herold; crows gang up and harass hawks and ravens unmercifully; perhaps it's a turf thing.

Downy woodpecker: Our smallest black and white woodpecker, and the most common; if its tail has black spots on a white outer edge, it's a downy.

Eastern phoebe: Its arrival is a classic sign of spring; builds its nest under roof overhangs; its trademark is the up and down flitting of its tail; catches insects in the air, thus is also called a flycatcher.

Goldfinch: One of our most colorful birds; its gold and black markings stand out; often called a wild canary because it resembles the canaries of pet shops.

Gray catbird: Mimics the mewing of cats perfectly.

Great blue heron: The most stately of Birch River birds; its long legs and fish-spearing beak distinguish it; great blue herons rarely nest in West Virginia, but are spring, summer, and fall visitors; I saw three on Birch in summer 2000.

Great horned owl: Our largest owl, its tufted ears and a call ending in "you-all" distinguish it from barred owls; the great horned attains a wingspan of up to five feet, and is a masterful hunter of small mammals.

House wren: Also called "Jenny wren"; a perky and welcome bird with a spirited song.

Indigo bunting: Often mistakenly called a bluebird because of its deep blue color.

Junco: Also called a snowbird, this gray and white winter visitor loves rhododendron thickets, which makes it right at home on Birch; when it heads north in March or April, it's a sure sign that winter is ending.

Kingfisher: A river bird that dives head-first on its prey, usually minnows; it is blue and white, and has a trademark shaggy head crest.

Mourning dove: Slim bird with a long tail; tends to dominate feeders, but its melancholy call is appealing; flocks together, as in birds of a feather.

Pileated woodpecker: The largest woodpecker, its raucous cry is one of the great sounds of nature; pileateds prefer mature woodlands because of the availability of older trees for nesting cavities; it became scarce when the forests were cut over, but has come back and is now fairly common; fishing quietly along Birch, it's almost a certainty you will hear pileateds.

Raven: Larger than a crow, with a hoarse call that has been described as "a crow with a sore throat"; likes to nest on the ledges of rock cliffs; a nesting pair has taken up residence on the face of a large cliff at Herold.

Red-tailed hawk: Our most common hawk, its piercing cry as it circles looking for prey is unmistakable; its favorite habitats are interstate and Appalachian corridor highway cuts, which offer a high perch from which to pounce on mice and other unfortunates.

Robin: Lord of the yard; it cocks its head, listens, and pounces on unsuspecting earthworms or other cuisine; the traditional "first robin of spring" story is misleading, because robins hang out in the neighborhood year-round, but they do become scarce in yards in winter because of weather conditions and food supply.

Ruffed grouse: The welcome drumming of male grouse in the spring is a sure sign that winter is over, but this great sound of nature is becoming less common; the decline in grouse populations is a mystery; theories abound, but nobody really knows why.

Screech owl: The tremulous call of this little owl is a familiar sound, especially in late summer and early fall; it's purely a creature of the night; its home is usually a tree cavity, although it will also occupy a nest box.

Song sparrow: A common species, but common is as common

does, and song sparrows sing a melodic and cheerful song; look for its streaked breast as an identifying mark.

Turkey vulture: Likes to roost, and probably nest, on the high ridges above Birch River; its return from its winter range in late winter and early spring is a welcome sight; vultures may repel us when feasting on a road kill, but they soar gracefully in flight.

Wild turkey: It has returned after a long absence; its comeback began in 1953 with a trapping and transplanting project begun by the Division of Natural Resources; it has longer legs and neck, smaller head, and a more streamlined body than its domestic counterpart, but anyone seeing a wild turkey gobbler for the first time is usually surprised at its size: gobblers often weigh twenty pounds or more; the resounding call of a gobbler at daybreak on a spring morning is sure to be a wake-up call.

Wood duck: Its head crest always appears to be in need of combing in the back; this smallish duck is frequently seen on the longer eddies of Birch.

Fish

Muskellunge: Once common in the lower eddies of Birch, and as far upriver as Herold, its numbers have become greatly diminished as a result of over-fishing; a fifty inch muskie was caught at the Big Eddy below Herold around 1914 (see "If We Were Counting"); a fifty two and one-half inch muskie caught at the mouth of Birch in 1955 is still the state record for length.

Rock bass: This panfish is fairly abundant in Birch, and goes by many names, including goggle-eye and red-eye; ounce for ounce and inch for inch, it rivals any other fish for tenacity, and will attack a lure larger than it is; my nephew caught a twelve inch rock bass in Birch in summer 2000; the state record is 13.8 inches.

Smallmouth bass: The creme de la creme of game fish in Birch and most other West Virginia rivers; its numbers rise and fall with spawning conditions from year to year; a flood at the height of spawning will virtually wipe out a year's class; the average size of smallmouth caught in West Virginia is from eight to fourteen inches, and in that respect Birch measures up well, but a Birch smallmouth of over seventeen inches is a rarity.

Walleye: Once plentiful in Birch, its numbers have declined in recent years; Birch is the major spawning stream for walleyes in Elk River below Sutton Dam, and one theory is that the walleye population has declined in Elk, thus affecting Birch.

White sucker: The "poor man's trout" of Birch; a bottom feeder and a tasty fish when caught in the cold water of late winter and early spring, but quite bony.

Amphibians

Bullfrog: Its deep, resounding call was once a familiar sound on summer nights on Birch, but it is not as plentiful as before, and has virtually disappeared on parts of the river; the reasons aren't clear, but overharvest has had an impact, and there may be environmental reasons as well; bullfrogs survive in local farm ponds, and on lower Birch, and other rivers as well, including lower Elk, Kanawha, Poca, and, to a lesser extent, New River.

Eastern American toad: This squatty, wart-covered fellow with the big eyes and webbed feet lays its eggs in water, but spends most of its time on land; an old wives' tale is that toads cause warts if handled, but this has no basis in fact. Power mowers and weed eaters are the bane of a toad's existence.

Green treefrog: Its high trill tells us that our midsummer night's dreams are over, forget it, autumn is just around the bend; it mates and lays its eggs in water, but as we may have suspected from its name, it also spends some time in trees.

Hellbender: A reptilian looking aquatic salamander, but totally harmless; it has a flat head, beady, lidless eyes, wrinkled skin, and stubby legs; stays under flat rocks and feeds at night, mostly on crayfish; locally it is called waterdog, but biologically that's another genus; however it may look to us, the presence of hellbenders is an indicator of good water quality.

Hellgrammite: An insect larva that eventually takes wing and becomes the dobsonfly; the larva, or aquatic, stage is excellent bass bait.

Snapping turtle: Give it respect; it has a grouchy disposition and a mean bite; if nothing else, its size sets it apart, but so do the vertical projections on its tail and the edge of its bony shell; feeds on both plant and animal matter, including fingers and toes.

Spring salamander: This "spring lizard" of creeks and hollows is aquatic in the larval stage, but then becomes semi-aquatic; like crayfish and hellgrammites, it is considered an excellent bait for catching bass.

Reptiles

Black rat snake: The common blacksnake and our largest serpent, it grows to lengths of seven feet or more, depending on the vividness of the imagination of those seeing one; five and six-footers are much more likely; feeds on rodents, birds, and bird eggs.

Box turtle: A totally terrestrial tortoise, its high-domed shell is colorfully marked in brown, orange, and yellow; its mortal enemies are weed-eaters, lawnmowers, and vehicles; nothing has a shorter life span than a box turtle crossing the interstate.

Copperhead: One of our two poisonous snakes. Depending on the nature of the bite and size of the snake, its bite can make you very sick; this snake loves to lurk in old lumber piles and sawmill sites; some people say that copperheads have a smell of cucumbers; the hourglass markings on its back, and its narrow neck and diamond shaped head, are distinguishing features; a three foot copperhead is a very large one, although the record is fifty one inches; Glenn Brown of Herold Road once killed a forty two incher in his Locust Stump orchard; he is also the only person I know of who was bitten by a copperhead on Birch River; he was bitten on the left heel as he stepped off a rock ledge just above the Falls near Herold; he never did see the snake whose bite caused him to miss four days' work.

Garter snake: Harmless but persecuted, simply because it's a snake; its color varies from greenish to brownish to grayish; aggressive if picked up, but so are a lot of people.

Milk snake: Unfortunately for the milk snake, it closely resembles a copperhead, therefore is usually killed on sight; this harmless snake grows quite large, even exceeding forty inches.

Ringneck snake: A cute little guy with a yellow ring around its neck on an otherwise shiny black body.

Timber rattlesnake: Our other poisonous snake; virtually non-existent on lower Birch River, but common on Powell's Mountain only ten air miles away; lower Birch's rocky terrain and isolation would seem to appeal to a rattler, but historically that has not been the case; its rattle is its warning, and its bite is very venomous; rattlers scatter hither and yon during summer, but in winter they congregate in dens to hibernate, often with copperheads and other snakes.

Watersnake: This most common of snakes on Birch River is called, appropriately, the common watersnake (formerly known as the northern watersnake). The young are cute and cuddly, if such adjectives can be applied to a snake, but in their  adult years they become belligerent. A case in point was the one whose reaction to having its picture taken at the Martha Butcher Hole led to the capsizing of the canoe in the "If We Were Counting" chapter. Watersnakes become heavy-bodied, grow to lengths of 40 inches or more, feed day and night, and are fond of basking on rocks or logs.

- - -

The flora and fauna described above are some of the more common ones that inhabit the Birch River community. A more complete listing, with Latin names, is found among the appendices

Sketch by Clinton Curtis

~ Eighteen ~

William Strange

And the Legend of Strange Creek

The Preacher in *Ecclesiastes*, probably Solomon, said it first slightly over three thousand years ago: "There is no new thing under the sun." But writers ever since have blissfully ignored the counsel of this wise man and have written about things of which there is obviously nothing new, nor ever will be.

Take the story of Strange Creek, for example. Bill Byrne, who wrote twenty nine hundred and seventy three years after Solomon, conceded that "no one is ever allowed to write anything of or concerning Strange Creek without answering the inevitable and natural question - How did that creek get its name?"

It's almost like those yellow and black "No Trespassing" signs that people seem determined to paste on every tree in West Virginia, warning grimly that "trespassers will be prosecuted [at the very least shot] under full penalty of the law." Conversely, you must write about Strange Creek and the legend of William Strange or face the full penalty of the law.

So, okay.

Solomon may forgive me if I approach this well-traveled subject slightly differently. I propose to reconstruct William Strange's ill-fated footsteps as he wandered toward his eventual doomsday on the head of Turkey Creek, or the mouth of Turkey Creek, or wherever he lay down to die and carved those immortal, doleful words on a tree, if he did.

I may as well even throw in his faithful-to-the-end dog, whose skeletal remains, some say, were found beside those of his master. That twist to the story, if he heard it, may have persuaded Solomon to recon-sider and concede that, yes, maybe there is a new thing under the sun after all.

How much of the Strange Creek legend is fact and how much is fiction that was invented around a campfire or hearth isn't known, except there is a high probability that it was based on an actual historical occurrence. I will introduce genealogical records which show that a man named William Strange did indeed die around 1795, which was when, according to most accounts, William Strange of legend became lost in the Elk Valley wilderness and perished.

Certainly the William Strange story has become the premier legend of central West Virginia. A well-known movie director could have been talking about Strange Creek when he said: "If the legend is more interesting than the facts, forget the facts and print the legend." He would have done just that with the William Strange story.

It is tempting to conclude that the story of his remains being found near a tree on which he had carved his epitaph is no more than a fanciful story, although a good one. But the nagging question remains: Would such a tale be concocted out of thin air? No, it's unlikely that even the best movie script writers could have come up with that one, although the tree carving part requires a considerable leap of imagination.

To set the stage, two forks trickle off the western side of Powell's Mountain, and join at the foot of the mountain near the Big Union Baptist Church of Dille to begin main Strange Creek. The creek turns left at the home of Hettie Browning Bowers of Dille, and flows through an isolated area to enter Elk River at the village of Strange Creek, which was once called Savagetown (another obligatory reference) in honor of brothers Jesse and William Savage, who built an iron furnace on a hillside above the village in 1874.

But William Strange knew none of this. He didn't even know anything about Turkey Creek, much less that he was about to change its name to Strange Creek. In one account he was said to have been "a young greenhorn surveyor's cook" (Peter Silitch in the new *West Virginia Encyclopedia*) for a party that was traversing the wilderness near the mouth of Holly River in Braxton County.

The year is uncertain, but a time period between 1794 and 1795 seems acceptable. That was when surveys of large land grants were being made in what is now West Virginia. According to most accounts, Strange was a member of one of those parties. Also, his fifth and final child was born on July 11, 1794, according to one account. But from that point on, even Solomon in all his wisdom would have become confused at the widely varying stories passed on over the years of the young (if indeed he was young) surveyor's trek into legend. But most of these accounts were written from one hundred to two hundred years after the fact, so it isn't surprising that they vary in content. The four gospels of the New Testament, written only twenty five to sixty years after the death of Jesus, do not agree in all details. And of course there is the familiar rule of thumb that if ten people see a car wreck, they will tell ten different versions of it.

One account has Strange guiding his party, which probably wasn't a role that would have been entrusted to a greenhorn. Two more accounts say he was the party's hunter. Four more accounts say he was the cook, or in charge of the pack horse or horses, or both. On the day he became lost, so most stories go, he was instructed to take the pack horse or horses to a certain location for a rendezvous with the surveyors...an appointment that he eternally never kept.

All of the above discrepancies, except that he was a guide, can be explained by accepting that he was cook, and hunter, and in charge of the pack horses. That he may have been assigned all three duties would not be too unusual, but in all probability he was not the camp hunter. According to the Silitch account, the survey party had set out from Beverly, Randolph County, where Strange was recruited, so he wouldn't have been familiar enough with the daunting wilderness in the Elk and Holly River country to serve as guide or hunter.

Charles T. Dodrill in *Heritage of a Pioneer* writes that the party's guide was Jerry Carpenter, who lived on Elk River above the mouth of Holly. The Carpenters were the first permanent white settlers in what is now Braxton County. They came to the mouth of Holly around 1789 or 1790. Benjamin Carpenter and his wife were killed by Indians in 1792 just below the mouth of Holly. Jerry, a brother of Benjamin, settled in what is now known as the Skidmore bottom across Sutton Lake from the Bakers Run Campground. He was a resourceful woodsman who once built a crude boat out of buffalo skin (*Moccasin Tracks and Other Imprints* by William C. Dodrill). Jerry's oldest son, Solomon, was born under a rock on Laurel Creek where the family had sought refuge from Indians; to this day, the rock is called "Solly's Rock."

All of the accounts that I have pieced together, with one exception, agree that William Strange died on Strange Creek, and the universal assumption over the years has been that every teller and reteller of the story was talking about the Strange Creek we know in Nicholas, Clay, and Braxton Counties, otherwise Strange Creek and its legend would be located somewhere else.

Two of the seven accounts quoted below give the place of his death as the head of Strange Creek, three simply list the site as Turkey Creek or Strange Creek (one and the same), the sixth said his remains

were found at the mouth of Strange Creek, and the seventh lists three possibilities: The head of Strange Creek, the mouth of Strange Creek, or a
startlingly different possibility, Sugar Creek, which is located on the north
side of Elk River near Frametown. The oral tradition among present Dille
residents is that his remains were found at the mouth of Big Run, which
enters Strange Creek about two miles below Dille.

The written accounts:

"Upper reaches of Turkey Creek near the present location of
Dille" (Peter Silitch in the new *West Virginia Encyclopedia*, 2001).

"In a bottom below the forks of the creek" (J.M. Hutchinson in "A
Brief History of Nicholas County's Early Settlement," Nicholas Chronicle,
1910). (Author's note: Strange Creek forks on Powell's Mountain near
Dille).

"A tributary of Elk known as Turkey Creek" (Charles T. Dodrill
in *Heritage of a Pioneer*, 1967).

"On Turkey Run several miles below the Carpenter settlement"
(Virginia Hall in *The Clarksburg Exponent-Telegram*, date of her writing
unknown).

"Wandered to Strange Creek" (John D. Sutton in *History of Braxton County and Central West Virginia*, 1919).

"Along Elk River...on the high river bank at the mouth of the
creek in question [Strange Creek]" (Bill Byrne in *Tale of the Elk,* 1927).

"Mouth of Strange Creek," or "near Dille post office" [head of
Strange Creek], or "Sugar Creek" (Phil Conley in his West Virginia
Review, circa 1930s).

The employer of William Strange is firmly given, rightly or
wrongly, only by Sutton, who said that Strange was a member of a party
that was surveying for Samuel Young, who had received a large land
grant (100,000 acres) along the Holly and Elk Rivers, and that the surveying was being done in 1795. Hutchinson said equivocally that "some connect Strange [to the Hudson Martin surveys of 1794]." The latter survey
was made adjacent to the southern part of the Samuel Young survey.
Hall identifies Strange as a member of a "govenment surveying party
under the command of Henry Jackson" in 1795. Dodrill said that "he
[Strange] came to the Elk Valley with a party of surveyors about the year
1790." Conley writes also that Strange was a member of a surveying
party. Byrne, however, does not say that Strange was a surveyor. Instead,
he wrote that his "bleached but well preserved skeleton" was found by a
party of surveyors who were locating some large land grants made by the
State of Virginia along Elk River.

The Henry Jackson mentioned above also led a survey (no date given) on what is now Granny's Creek in Braxton County, according to Alexander Scott Withers' 1831 *Chronicles of Border Warfare*. One of his hunters, a man named Loudin, "killed a buffalo cow which was so old and tough that the men declared her to be the grandmother of all buffaloes," hence the name Granny's Creek. A hunter named Loudin is also mentioned in at least one account of William Strange's disappearance.

The key to reconstructing William Strange's odyssey into legend is to determine beyond reasonable doubt where he was when he became lost. Silitch, Hall, Sutton, Dodrill, and Conley all place the surveying party on Holly and Elk Rivers near the mouth of Holly (Dodrill is quite specific as to trails and other natural features). Byrne locates the surveyors only as "along Elk River," although he has them at the mouth of Strange Creek where the "bleached skeleton" was found. Hutchinson, writing from a Nicholas County perspective, said this: "An admitted theory is that its [Strange Creek's] name came from a Frenchman by the name of Strange who, while piloting a surveying party, was lost. Some connect him with the party that camped on Mumblethepeg [the aforementioned Hudson Martin survey]."

Of the seven accounts, only Conley names all the members of the party: "Henry Jackson, who was a surveyor, one Hall, one Reger, and William Strange." He thus makes a very convincing case that Strange was indeed in a surveying party. An eighth account, which is given at the conclusion of this chapter to tie loose ends together, indicates that Hall was Joseph Hall, and Reger was Philip Reger.

Dodrill, who in *Heritage of a Pioneer* builds a plausible scenario for Henry Young of Powell's Mountain renown having approached the mountain from Wilson Ridge in Clay County, does the same for the proposition that William Strange came to a forks in a path on Holly River about a mile above the mouth, and took the wrong path, thus, as it turned out, sealing his fate.

Dodrill wrote:

> The next morning [after the previous night's rendezvous] he [Strange] was directed to go down Holly to its junction with Elk River, and then follow the Elk to the Carpenter settlement where he would be met the second night. About a mile above the mouth of Holly, the path he was following forked. One fork crossed the river [Holly] and went up Elk, the other went down Holly a short distance. It then turned to the right, crossed the mountain through a long chestnut flat and came back on the Elk some miles below. Strange did not observe the ford crossing the Holly, and took the right-hand path, thus failing to discover the junction of the Holly and Elk.

There was evidence that he came back to the Elk, a
short distance below the mouth of Holly, where he abandoned
the path and followed the river shore. When he came to impas-
sible narrows, characteristic of the Elk, he became confused,
retraced his steps to the chestnut flat, and tied his horse to a
bush.

Reaching the Carpenter settlement in the late afternoon the members of the surveying party became uneasy when
Strange failed to show up. Early next morning they set out to
search for him. They followed the tracks of his horse until they
found it tied to a bush, but there was no sign of Strange. They
continued their search for quite some time and eventually came
upon a place where he had been lying in the brush. One of the
members of the party fired a gun, and it was thought this might
have frightened Strange, he thinking it might be Indians. After
following his trail for some five or six miles, it was lost in the
wilderness.

There is a high degree of probability that Strange and the other
surveyors knew about the Indian attack of two or three years before, especially if their guide was Jerry Carpenter.

Dodrill then completed his account with the familiar story of the
bones of a man being found some years later on a tributary of Elk known
then as Turkey Creek and now as Strange Creek.

Dodrill's reference to a confused (and probably frightened) William Strange tying his horse to a bush doesn't necessarily conflict with
accounts that he was in charge of a pack train, which might have included
three or four horses. When he became uncertain of the trail, a very natural thing for him to do would be to leave all of the animals there except
the one he was riding, as he searched for the correct trail. Then he would
return and retrieve the other horses, but as we know he never returned.

But according to the Conley account, there was no pack train; just
one horse. "While making the survey," Conley writes, "William Strange
was to do the cooking and have charge of the food and utensils. These
necessities were carried on a horse."

Hall and Conley write that Strange was a member of a surveying
party that departed from what is now Upshur County. The Silitch account
says that the party departed from Beverly, Randolph County (which borders Upshur, therefore both accounts could be right). From one of those
counties, or both, the party came to what is now Braxton County. Hall
gives Strange's duties as cook and in charge of taking the pack horses
from one campsite to another, which is a logical combination. All went
well the first day, she writes, but on the second day when the party was to

meet at the Carpenter settlement, Strange became lost. Hall says simply that he became confused as to which was Elk River and which was Holly River, also logical. Anyone who has deer hunted in modern day West Virginia can probably recall being confused by streams in terrain with which they were not familiar. Strange may have thought he was on Holly River, which he was supposed to descend, but was actually on Elk, and therefore went downstream instead of upstream toward the Carpenter settlement. Hall adds that searching parties went out, but failed to find the lost man.

The accounts by Silitch, Dodrill, Hall, and Conley have just enough differences to indicate they were obtained at least partially from separate sources, but enough similarities to make a persuasive case that William Strange was, indeed, a cook and in charge of a pack horse or horses in a surveying party on the Holly and Elk Rivers around 1794 or 1795, and that he wandered into history on the first or second day of the survey while attempting, alone and in unforgiving, unfamiliar wilderness, to go from one campsite to another.

From that point on, like the final hour in the lives of George Armstrong Custer and his men at the Little Bighorn, there emerged no eyewitnesses to tell us what happened, except at the Little Bighorn there were eyewitness accounts from the Sioux and Northern Cheyenne.

Why William Strange didn't wait until help arrived before he became hopelessly lost is not a logical question, even if it must be asked. People who become lost become frightened, and panic sets in. The almost irresistible tendency is to forge ahead in the belief that something familiar will be found just over the next rise. This is probably what he did.

The legend is that his skeletal remains were found years later on Strange Creek, which at that time was called Turkey Run. Exactly where the remains were found is, like the other elements of the story, elusive, and without such knowledge a reconstruction of his footsteps into history is only speculative. First of all, we must accept on faith and in the interest of a good story that his remains were found on Strange Creek.

The supposed carving on the tree is the heart and soul of the Strange Creek legend, and although the wordings differ in every telling, they all add up to the same thing: A man named Strange was lost and knew he was dying, and carved his own epitaph on a tree. Without this ending, Strange Creek would still be called Turkey Run, and nobody alive today would have ever heard of a man named William Strange.

Would a dying man spend his last hours carving a message on a tree? The probable answer is yes, assuming he had enough strength left. It is human nature to want to leave a legacy, in whatever form. West Virginians, for example, have elevated the practice of carving dates or initials on beech trees to an art form; perhaps the custom originated with the William Strange story.

Byrne said he once talked to a man who claimed to have seen the carving on the tree. If the man gave a location, Byrne didn't pass it along, but presumably it was at the mouth of Strange Creek, where, according to the Byrne version, the skeleton of a man was found at the base of a beech tree, and on the tree was carved:

> Strange is my name,
> And strange the ground,
> And strange that I
> Cannot be found.

Byrne began his law practice at Sutton in 1885 at age twenty three, and, forty two years later, in 1927, began writing his book. It was at some point during this time period that he talked with the man who claimed to have seen the carving.

The Silitch version of the carving in the new West Virginia Encyclopedia, which he says was found on a sycamore tree, is this:

> Strange is my name and strange is the place I
> meet my maker.

Hall says in her story in *The Clarksburg Exponent-Telegram* that the carving was found on a beech tree near the remains. She acknowledged that the words have been quoted differently over the years, and she offered two versions.

The first:

> Strange is my name.
> I am a stranger in a strange land.
> Strange, indeed, I cannot be found.

The second:

> William Strange is my name,
> And in these strange woods I must remain.

Hall says that William Strange's remains were found several years later "on Turkey Run several miles below the Carpenter settlement." She attributed the discovery to "a Mr. Fitzwater, the first settler on Big Buffalo, a tributary of Elk River." Buffalo Creek heads on the western side of Powell's Mountain, as does Strange Creek, so the Fitzwater of Hall's account could have lived near the headwaters of both streams. The "several miles below the Carpenter settlement" could be interpreted as meaning anything from a few miles to thirty or more.

An introduction to her story said that Virginia Hall was the great-great granddaughter of Joseph Hall, who married Ann Hitt Martin Strange, the former wife of William Strange. As we will see later in this chapter, Joseph Hall may have been a member of the surveying party.

Dodrill wrote that the William Strange story "was one that was garnished with a little fancy to make the yarn more interesting and exciting." He was no doubt referring to the conclusion, but like Byrne's reference to an obligatory explanation of how Strange Creek got its name, he obligingly gave his version. He said that several years after Strange's disappearance, "hunters came upon the bones of a man forty miles down Elk from where Strange had left the party." Dodrill says the hunters reported that the tree with the carving was on Turkey Run, a tributary of Elk, but he didn't attempt a specific location. He gave the verse on the tree as follows (which is the version I grew up hearing):

> Strange is my name and I am on strange ground
> And strange it is that I cannot be found.

The same verse is given in a 1925 book, *Know Your Own State*, published by Standard Oil Company of New Jersey. This account adds: "It was supposed that he [Strange] was carried off by the Indians."

Hutchinson's version of the carving in his 1910 series in the Nicholas Chronicle, and the only one to give a date, went this way:

> July 20, 1794. Strange ground I am on; Wm. Strange is
> my name. Lost! Lost! Never to be found again.

Sutton did not say that William Strange's remains were found; only his gun with his initials cut on the stock. But he did mention a carving on a beech tree, which he gave as follows:

> Strange is my name,
> And strange is the woods,
> And strange it is I can not be found.

Conley gives two versions, including this one from L.V. McWhorter's 1915 *Border Settlers of North-Western Virginia*:

William Strange is my name,
And in these strange woods I must remain.

Conley was told another version by someone in the Dille area many years ago:

My name is Strange,
And I'm on strange ground,
I'm lost in the woods and I
Know I'll not be found.

Conley agrees with others that Jerry Carpenter was the party's guide. He says that the party stayed at Carpenter's home the night of Strange's disappearance, and searched for him the next day. From there he says that Strange's trail was followed, that a place was found where he appeared to have slept, and that a shot was fired in hopes of attracting his attention. Conley adds that Carpenter scolded the man who fired his gun, fearing that roaming Indians would hear the shot and ambush them. This differs from other accounts that say Strange heard the shot and feared it was an Indian attack, although both versions could be true.

Conley believes the first printed record of the William Strange story appeared in 1876 in George Atkinson's *History of Kanawha County* (in the 1790s, Kanawha County embraced the area where Strange supposedly disappeared). George Atkinson became the tenth governor of West Virginia in 1897. Writing about him in *West Virginia Governors*, John G. Morgan says that Atkinson was "a scholar, lecturer, and writer." He says that Atkinson's writings "covered subjects ranging from the ridiculous [Strange Creek?] to the sublime."

Atkinson's account of the William Strange legend was reprinted in the aforementioned *Border Settlers*. McWhorter, the author of "Border Settlers," is the one who gives Sugar Creek in Braxton County as the place where Strange's bones were found, although he was only passing along someone else's version. Conley writes that "there is no Sugar Creek in Braxton County," so he searched on Sugar Camp Run (the one on Elk River) for anyone who had heard of a tradition that Strange's bones were found there. He was unsuccessful, and met the same frustration while interviewing oldtime residents of the mouth and head of Strange Creek area. (Author's note: Actually there is a Sugar Creek in Braxton County. It enters Elk River from the north near Frametown).

Conley writes that "although beyond doubt, the interesting legend...is founded on an incident that actually occurred, the embellished story itself is a folk tale pure and simple." Which raises the question: What, then, did happen to William Strange? Conley had a possible answer: "At more than one place in the mountains," he writes, "bones have been discovered that were thought to be those of Strange. Likewise, two or three old rusty guns have been found that were supposed to be the one in his possession when he was lost."

If we accept that the story of the disappearance of William Strange is based on an actual happening, then by most accounts we have him lost in the wilderness on Elk River below the mouth of Holly. But his fate is a blank page until the supposed discovery of the skeleton and the carving many years later on Strange Creek. There are many ways he could have gone, probably none of which would make sense to us unless we accept that he was confused, frightened, and hopelessly lost.

The first possibility is the Direct Route. If he went across country in more or less a straight line, he would have crossed Elk River, then crossed Little Birch River just south of the present community of Little Birch, then crossed Big Birch River a short distance downstream from present Birch Village, crossed over the Brown's Ridge portion of Powell's Mountain, and from there reached the head of Strange Creek near Dille. This is a southwesterly journey of approximately seventeen miles. If he went that route, he wouldn't have followed a straight line exactly. He would have wandered, doubled back, crossed and recrossed streams and ridges, to finally reach the head of Strange Creek where he could go no farther, exhausted and emaciated and accepting of his fate.

The second possibility is the Elk River Route downstream to the mouth of Strange Creek, where the Byrne account said his remains were found. That would be a journey of about thirty five miles. Following a wilderness river that far would be difficult, although it could have been done. We know from the story of Mary Ingles Draper in the book *Follow the River* that she and a companion, identified as the "Old Dutch Woman," escaped from Indian captivity in Ohio and returned to Virginia by following the Kanawha and New Rivers, although frequently climbing the ridges when staying on the river became impossible. Byrne never said that William Strange followed Elk anywhere, but that would be a logical assumption if we accept that he became lost in the vicinity of the mouth of Holly River and that his remains were found at the mouth of Strange Creek.

The third possibility is the Middle Ground Route down Elk to the mouth of Birch River, which he may have mistakenly identified as either Elk or Holly, and followed it upstream to the present vicinity of Birch Village. From there he may have gone up Powell's Creek and crossed over Powell's Mountain into the headwaters of Strange Creek, following the buffalo trails, near Henry Young's even later fateful confrontation with Federal troops. He may have become the first man of European descent, if

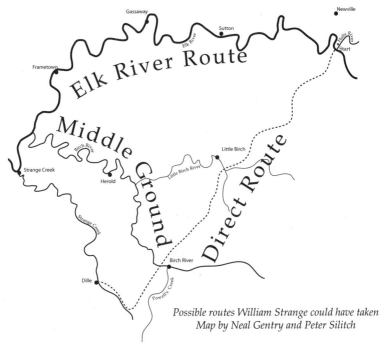

Possible routes William Strange could have taken
Map by Neal Gentry and Peter Silitch

Powell wasn't the first, to follow a buffalo trail that later became the route of the Weston-Gauley Bridge Turnpike, which crossed Powell's Mountain about fifty five years later. In his confusion and naivete he could have mistaken a buffalo trail for a human footpath that gave him hope of finding a settlement or a settler's home. The salt spring that is located about a half mile above present Birch Village was no doubt used by buffalo who followed Anthony Creek or Powell's Creek down off Powell's Mountain, leaving a well-worn trail that enticed William Strange to abandon the river and follow it. Upon reaching the headwaters of Strange Creek, he either died on the headwaters or followed the creek down to the mouth and died there.

The Direct Route poses the question: Why would he cross Elk River and strike out through a forbidding wilderness? One answer is that he became frightened after hearing gunfire, and feared an Indian attack. If that was the case, he sealed his fate by heading into a wilderness that posed far more danger for him than Indian ambush. Another possibility is that he believed the gunfire to be members of his party searching for him, but misread the direction of the gunfire, which deer hunters know is a common occurrence, and went away from the sound rather than toward it.

The Elk River Route had the advantage of being a known quantity, or at least he assumed it did, since he had been instructed to follow Elk upstream to the Carpenter settlement. But he went downstream instead, confusing Elk for Holly. How much wandering over hills and ridges he did on his way down Elk is another question, but it was probably enough to exhaust him.

The Middle Ground Route is enticing in any attempt to account for his wanderings because Birch River is a large enough stream to have led him to believe it was indeed Elk, the river he had been told to follow upstream. This would have been especially so if Birch was swollen by rain.

The mention of Sugar Creek is interesting, because it would keep him on the north side of Elk River, where he started. But in that case, Sugar Creek, and not Turkey Run, would have been renamed.

We will never know, of course, which way he went, or if indeed he did reach Strange Creek and die there, or if in fact his remains were found many years later, or if he did carve his own epitaph on a tree.

But it's a great story, as even Solomon would concede.

Historical authenticity is given the William Strange story, or at least to the existence in the 1790s of a man by that name, in the Hall genealogical records obtained from the Internet (rootsweb.com.). These records list the descendants of Joseph Hall, who was born in England in 1745 and died in Lewis County, Virginia (now West Virginia), in 1825, and served the Colonies in the American Revolution.

About 1795, Joseph Hall married Mary Ann (Hitt) [Martin] Strange, who was born in Fauquier County, Virginia, about 1755 and died in Harrison County, Virginia (now West Virginia) in 1810. And the intriguing clincher: "She was the widow of William George Strange."

An account of the William Strange story that appeared in McWhorter's *Border Settlers* is also helpful in tying most of the loose ends together, or, conversely, creating more of them. McWhorter first gives the Atkinson (former governor of West Virginia) account, and then strikes out on his own with information that appears nowhere else that I could find.

The Atkinson account says that the year was 1790, that the survey party came from Upshur County for the Budd Survey, that Jerry Carpenter was the guide, and that William Strange became lost while attempting to go down Holly River and then up Elk to the Carpenter settlement. Atkinson describes Strange as "a very indifferent woodsman," which presumably led to his demise. As to the conclusion, Atkinson says that the lost man's remains were found many years later on Strange Creek "with his shot-pouch hanging on its ramrod...leaning against the tree at the root of which his bones were lying."

McWhorter disagrees with Atkinson's year of Strange's disappearance. He gives it as the autumn of 1795, which, he says, coincides with family tradition and with the year of a survey made by Henry Jackson "for whom Strange was cook and packer."

McWhorter joins those who give the place of the beech tree carving of legend as near the head of Strange Creek. He says the carving was discovered by "some hunters, who being familiar with the story of Strange, gave it his name." He quotes John Strange Hall, a grandson of William Strange's widow, to the effect that the Mr. Fitzwater of another account "found a gun under a shelving rock, with the stock so badly damaged that it fell to pieces when handled." The grandson did not say that Fitzwater found a carving or remains. "Nothing was ever known touching the history of this gun," the grandson is quoted, "but it was supposed by many to have belonged to the unfortunate Strange, who placed it there before succumbing to death."

McWhorter says that William Strange was born in Fauquier County, Virginia, but he doesn't give a date. He says that William and Mary Ann had five children: Elizabeth, born in 1784, James, born in 1787, John, born in 1789, Sarah, born in 1792, and Margaret, born on July 11, 1794.

Mary Ann Hitt's first husband, Joel Martin, was said to have been a patriot militiaman killed at the Revolutionary War battle of Yorktown in 1781. Therefore, she and William Strange were probably married sometime between 1781 and 1784, when their first child was born.

If she was born about 1755, as previously stated, and he was about the same age, he could have been in his late 20s before he was married, and therefore in his late 30s when he disappeared during the survey. But without a date of his birth, this is only speculation.

McWhorter says that Joseph Hall and the twice-widowed Mary Ann were married in January 1796.

From all this we can conclude that William Strange was indeed an historical figure, that he became lost while with a surveying party on the Elk and Holly Rivers in 1795, and that either his remains, or a carving, or a gun were discovered years later on Strange Creek. The first two conclusions are reasonably documented; the last one is legend, but why doubt it and spoil a good story?

~ Nineteen ~

The Doctor and the Preacher

Two Men Who Defined the Community

Norman Rockwell, who captured rural America of an earlier time in his cover drawings for the *Saturday Evening Post*, should have known Norman Goad and Willie Lewis.

He would have excitedly grabbed pencil and paper and started drawing.

Willie Lewis was a preacher from Keener's Ridge. He never drove or owned a car. He walked or rode a horse. He knew every cow path around, and so, probably, did his favorite horse, Roxy. His trademarks were his cane and Bible.

Norman Goad was a doctor from Strange Creek. He made house calls to every hollow in three or four counties. He rode horseback or drove a Model A Ford. Early on he delivered babies for two dollars. He practiced for forty seven years. And he lavished affection on his foxhounds.

The two men brought a gentleness and humility of spirit to their callings that influenced the lives of many people.

Preacher Willie Lewis (he would never use "Reverend" in front of his name, and would address other preachers only as "Brother" or "Pastor") was born on Upper Keener's Ridge in Nicholas County. He pastored numerous churches in Braxton, Nicholas, and Clay Counties, and preached hundreds of revival sermons in a calling that lasted forty-two years. Perhaps he considered "Reverend," a title commonly used to denote a member of the clergy, as being too exalting of one's self. He wore a watch chain on his vest, but no other jewelry, not even a ring. Like the title "Reverend," he may have considered jewelry too ostentatious. Pictures almost invariably show him wearing a fedora-style hat, and he had an impressive, bushy mustache.

There are stories, probably true, of him walking many miles to preach at a remote country church, receiving a few coins in the collection plate, and then walking home late at night.

Romans 10:15 comes to mind: "How beautiful are the feet of them that preach the gospel of peace."

His daughter, Rosie Lewis Stokes, who lives in Valley Glen, California, in the Los Angeles area, recalls her dad tell about riding horseback over the Powell's Mountain wilderness to hold a revival service and being followed by a panther (possibly a mountain lion or bobcat) when he returned home late at night.

"He did not normally travel [over Powell's Mountain] at night," Rosie Stokes related, but for some reason he got a late start and decided to try to ride home even though it would be dark long before he reached home. He was riding on the narrow dirt road with only the moon to light his way. He soon became aware that he was being followed by a panther [that was his name for the animal] because he could hear its almost human sounding cry. His horse was very much aware of the following panther, because it showed sights of nervousness, almost to the point of panic. I think it speaks volumes of my dad's superb horsemanship that he was able to calm and control the horse so that it didn't panic. He soon came out of the thick trees and the panther did not follow into the area of clearings and small farms. That was a close call!"

"I wish I could say I remember many of my dad's sermons," she continued, "but unfortunately that is not the case [she was a teenager when her father died]. However, there was one I vividly remember and it made a lasting impact on my life. He was preaching about the evils of the Ku Klux Klan, and racism in general. He left no doubt that he believed all men (and women) are created equal in the eyes of God. It is said that God has no 'step children.' I don't think the Klan ever really got a foothold in West Virginia as they did in the deep South, and I like to think it was because West Virginians in general are independent thinkers, not having a herd mentality. I believe I remember this sermon because he spoke so passionately. He really held my attention."

William M. Lewis was born on January 31, 1877. His surviving children aren't sure exactly where, but it was probably in the Morris area. He was baptized by the New Hope Baptist Church of Morris at age fourteen. He was the only son of Charles W. and Margaret Wright Lewis. His mother died in 1899 at age fifty five, and his father, who remarried and had nine children to his second wife, Lucy Walker, died in 1935 at age eighty. His father was a teamster and farmer, served eight years on the Nicholas County School Board, and was a Justice of the Peace.

It was said of Charles W. Lewis at his death: "Few men have done more for humanity according to their means. He was always ready to extend a helping hand to those in sorrow, suffering, and distress."

Charles W. Lewis and his son were both converted and baptized into the fellowship of the New Hope Church in 1891 by Theodore Given. There is no record of where they were baptized, but the nearest place would have been Birch River at the Cora Brown bridge.

Thirteen years later, on July 30, 1904, Willie Lewis was ordained into the ministry by the New Hope Church, and later served as its pastor. His first pastorate, which came prior to his ordination, was at the Big Union Baptist Church at Dille in 1902, when he was twenty-five years old. He was pastor at New Hope in 1905, 1909, 1910, 1919, and 1921.

Other churches he pastored included Big Run, Salem, New Antioch, Little Laurel, Strange Creek, Mount Olive, Birch River, Middle Run, Polemic Run, Flat Fork, Powell's Mountain, and Long Run. On at least three occasions he delivered the principal sermon at annual meetings of the Elk Valley Baptist Association, probably for the final time at Elk River Baptist Church in 1938.

Willie Lewis

Canfield native Gerald Dunn remembered him in his 1987 book, *An Appalachian Boyhood*. "One of our preachers [at Long Run Baptist Church]," Gerald wrote, "was Willie Lewis, who lived on Middle Ridge above Herold. He was a big man with a deep voice, who was considered very well read, largely by self-education. When he got going on religious doctrine or concerns, he was hard to stop."

In a history of the New Hope Church compiled by Mildred Morris Butcher long after the preacher's death, special note was made of Willie Lewis' remarkable photographic memory for dates. If he ever heard a date, he rarely forgot it. He tended to be forgetful in some ways, but not with dates. He had an encyclopedic knowledge of the birthdays of friends, acquaintances, and historic figures, and of the dates of historic events.

Once he pointed out to my grandfather, when they were cutting briers on a hillside above Herold, that Napoleon, the emperor of France from 1804 to 1815, was exactly one hundred years and one day older than Tom Carte. Tom Carte was a traveling man who moved around the community.

His phenomenal memory included Bible scripture. He could cite chapter and verse with the best of them, but never in an argumentative way. The closest he would come would be to say, in response to a doctrinal point or scriptural interpretation: "But what are you going to do about [such and such a verse or passage]"?

He took a test to become a school teacher in his early adult life, and one of the requirements on the test paper was to write a sentence or paragraph containing all the major parts of speech. For his answer, he wrote down *Matthew* 26:39 from Jesus' agony in the Garden of Gethsemane: "And he went a little farther, and fell on his face, and prayed, saying, 'O my father, if it be possible, let this cup pass from me: nevertheless not as I will, but as thou wilt.'"

This passage contains nouns, pronouns, adjectives, indefinite articles, participles, verbs, adverbs, conjunctions, interjections, prepositions, and probably other parts of speech that would require a college English teacher to sort out.

He never wrote in his Bible, nor did he underline or highlight passages.

One of his favorite illustrations about the frailty of human life was to compare a lifespan to that of a tree standing in the field: The tree withstands the storms and tempests of life for decades, but one calm day its time arrives and it simply falls. My mother used that illustration many times, always crediting Willie Lewis.

He married many people. He didn't keep a record, so the number of marriages isn't known. Sometimes the circumstances were unusual. He married at least two couples who rode up to the house on horseback and elected to remain on their horses during the ceremony. Another time, when the Lewis family was living at the Waitman Fast place on the Frametown road, the bride and groom were married, conventionally, inside the house. But when it came to the point in the ceremony where Willie Lewis asked the groom if he took this woman to be his lawful wedded wife, he replied, in an unconventional way, "I reckon."

Alma DeMoss, who lives on upper Keener's Ridge, has the original copy of her parents' marriage certificate, handwritten in pencil by Willie Lewis. It states:

> Teddie Shaver and Walsie Craft were married at my residence near Herold October 25th 1932. They were married by me in the presence of 3 witnesses."
>
> W.M. Lewis

Willie Lewis attended Alderson-Broaddus College at Philippi, but not long enough to get a degree. He decided that college life and being away from home was affecting his health. However, his stay at A-B produced one facet of his life that was little known: he went out for the football team. After seeing three players carried off with injuries, he decided that football could affect his health, too, so he terminated his brief career on the gridiron.

He was married on October 9, 1907, to Fannie Myrtle Acree of Muddlety, Nicholas County. They had seven children. Clyde, Norman, Bessie, and Edith are deceased. Grace and Jim live at the home place near Adams School, and Rosie Lewis Stokes lives in California.

His teaching days came after college and before marriage. He taught at Byfid School, which was located on Keener's Ridge near the Baughman Methodist Church. He may have taught other places as well, including at the Bail School, which was located near the New Hope Church, but there is no record.

He liked to read, especially daily newspapers and books on history, and he enjoyed Zane Gray westerns. When someone expressed surprise at seeing him immersed in a Zane Gray novel, he responded that "Of course there's language I don't approve of, but each one I've read has a good moral to it [good triumphing over bad]." He listened to the news on radio, but preferred newspapers, pointing out that if he saw or heard a word he didn't catch or didn't understand, he had the opportunity with the printed word to go back and review it.

Despite being a voracious reader, Willie Lewis owned only one pair of glasses in his entire life. One day a traveling salesman stopped by and unfolded his wares. The preacher went through them, trying one pair after another until he found a pair that fit his eyes. Those were the only glasses he ever had.

He was not a hunter, and never owned a gun, but sons Clyde and Norman were avid hunters and crack shots. Once they were shooting at a Prince Albert tobacco can with a .22 rifle when their dad surprised everybody by asking, "Wonder if I might try that?" He hit the can with his first shot, and declined the offer of a second shot. "I just wanted to see if I could use one [a gun] if need be," he explained.

He played checkers and dominoes with his kids, and another board game called fox and goose. He never saw a dog or cat he didn't like. He made pets out of everything. He liked to garden, especially when it came to trying new varieties of vegetables. While working in the garden or splitting wood he would hum favorite hymns, usually *Unclouded Day* and *Ninety and Nine*.

The biblical precept of humbleness ("God resisteth the proud, and giveth grace to the humble" of I *Peter* 5:5) meant something to him, because he rarely talked about himself, and then very little. He must not have agreed with the admonition in *Proverbs* 13:24 that "he that spareth his rod hateth his son," because he never spanked his kids.

"My dad had overly strict parents who were often harsh in their discipline, out of proportion to the deed committed," Rosie Lewis Stokes recalls him saying. "As a small boy he was whipped for some minor offense, then whipped again if he cried from the pain inflicted. He said he thought that was unfair of them, and he still believed it was unfair when he became a parent. He said a child should never be whipped for crying, and of course he never did that to us. I expect my grandparents were well meaning and simply trying to follow the admonition, 'Spare the rod, spoil the child.' But they obviously were not as fair-minded as my dad."

He liked to chop wood. "We never lacked for firewood when he was around," daughter Grace remembers. Although his health had begun to deteriorate, he was out in the field cutting locust fence posts during the spring prior to his death on the morning of July 16, 1946. He died of complications from diabetes, an illness that he had for several years, but which made him bedfast only about three weeks prior to his death at age sixty-nine.

He may have preached his final sermon on Powell's Mountain at the Fairview School building, which was the predecessor of the present Powell's Mountain Baptist Church where Linn Schiefer of Tesla has pastored since 1983. Dana Carte now lives in the former school building.

Willie Lewis' funeral was held at his home on a hot summer day. The minister in charge of the service was J.H. McLaughlin, a well-known Baptist preacher himself, who lived on Upper Mill Creek near Frametown. "Preacher Jim" died twenty four years later at age ninety.

After Willie Lewis' death, *The Widen News* carried an item about him, author unknown, entitled "A Wayside Traveler Passes On," which was fitting, given his penchant for walking or riding horseback over the countryside. Said the item: "He walked the highways and hillside paths to bring his gospel message of hope and cheer and salvation to hundreds of God's children."

It would have been appropriate had the item mentioned his cane, which he was virtually never without. He would hang it over the fence at home, or wherever he was visiting, there to await his next journey.

Fannie Lewis died in 1969. She had outlived her husband by twenty three years. Both are buried in the Riffel-Lewis Cemetery on the farm where they were living at the time of their deaths.

Willie Lewis' father is buried at the Walker Cemetery. His grandfather, John Lewis, is buried on a knoll above the Keener's Ridge Community Church.

- - -

Norman Goad was born at Strange Creek on December 1, 1887, in the same house in which he lived virtually all his life. Today, one hundred and fourteen years later, and forty five years after his death, his name recognition still ranks high in the community. Everybody of a certain age has a story to tell about Doctor Goad.

His parents were George and Sarah Frame Goad. George Goad was a native of Carroll County, Virginia. He came to Braxton County in 1875, dealt in horses, was a lumberer (including running log rafts to Charleston), and established a general store at Strange Creek. He served three terms in the House of Delegates from Braxton County in 1899, 1901, and 1903, and served a term as sheriff of Braxton County. He died in 1917; Sarah Frame Goad died in 1937.

John Calhoun, who married Norman Goad's daughter, Mary, found a stamping hammer at Strange Creek with the initial "G" on the head that had been used to stamp George Goad's initial on the end of logs so they would be credited to the proper person upon arrival at Charleston.

George and Sarah Goad had three children: Norman, Nimmie, and Nettie. Nimmie was a schoolteacher, and married Doctor George A. McQueen, who founded Kanawha Valley Hospital in Charleston. Nettie ran the family store at Strange Creek for many years, and later had a store across Elk River on West Virginia Route 4. She married Jack Duvall, who, it was said, came to West Virginia from Missouri in a covered wagon.

Norman Goad married Alice Houghton, a native of the Strange Creek community, on Independence Day, 1929. He was forty two years old.

They had six children. Bessie Mae Goad Magoun, Anna Belle

Goad Duffield, and Opal Ruth Goad Smith are deceased. Norman Robert Goad is retired from Western Electric and lives in Columbus, Ohio, Irma Jean Goad Vaughn lives in St. Albans, and Mary Lou Goad Calhoun lives in Frametown.

Doctor Goad delivered all six of his children at home.

He was a graduate of Valparaiso University in northwest Indiana, and of the Chicago College of Medicine and Surgery, where he not only learned medicine but also learned to tap dance, which he would do occasionally at home. He received his medical degree in 1909, and practiced for a short time at Kanawha Valley Hospital with his brother-in-law. He returned to Strange Creek in 1910 and remained there the rest of his life.

Like all doctors of that era, he performed emergency surgery as the need arose. The stories of rural doctors performing appendectomies are legion, and Doctor Goad was no exception. One night, Mariah Dean, who was eighty years old and lived across Elk River from Strange Creek, suffered an attack of acute appendicitis. Doctor Goad knew she would not live to reach a hospital. He operated on her on the dining room table, under the light of kerosene lamps. She not only came through the operation, but lived another fourteen years.

A similar situation occurred on a remote section of lower Birch River. Ally Long, wife of Willis Long, had severe blood poisoning from a hand wound, and Doctor Goad, convinced she would not live to be taken by train to the hospital the following day, removed her hand. She likewise survived.

One of Doctor Goad's memorable surgeries was performed on his sister, Nettie. He sat her in a chair in the yard at their home and removed her tonsils, perhaps a first and only in the annals of tonsil surgery.

Conditions weren't always ideal for delivering babies. One rainy day he delivered a baby, and soon afterwards the roof began to leak. He and Leota Teets, who was serving as midwife, took shelter under the kitchen table, and waited out the storm.

In the 1930s, Doctor Goad was called to the home of Cecil and Merl McCoy on Tate Creek. Merl McCoy was having difficulty giving birth because of a kidney infection. Doctor Goad and another doctor delivered the baby, but it was dead at birth. Merl McCoy was unconscious and her life in peril because of the infection. Doctor Goad suggested placing sacks of shelled, boiled corn around her body, hopefully to pull out the poison (corn does not cool quickly). Neighbors went to work boiling corn in a big iron kettle. The men kept the fire going and the women kept Mrs. McCoy packed in warm bags of corn. Eventually, she began to perspire profusely, and she recovered and lived many more years.

The day of two-dollar deliveries had passed when my brothers and I were born at home at Herold. Doctor Goad charged twenty dollars for delivering my older brother, ten dollars for me, and five dollars for our younger brother. He told our parents he would deliver the fourth one free, but there was no fourth one.

The first dead person I ever saw was at Doctor Goad's office. I was there with my dad for reasons I've forgotten. A boy had drowned while swimming in nearby Elk River. He was brought to the doctor's office in the back of a truck. The body was placed on a cot in the downstairs hallway of the doctor's home, and kept there overnight. In the process of writing about Doctor Goad, I discovered the drowning victim's name and that he was buried at the Walnut Grove Methodist Church Cemetery on Wilson Ridge in Clay County. I went there one bright spring day in 2000 with a friend, and we searched through the cemetery, which is a very large one with some three hundred graves, and were about to give up when we saw the tombstone: Leonard Anderson, 1918-1935. He was seventeen when he died.

Virgil Houghton, who lives on Hickman Ridge in Clay County, remembers Leonard Anderson. The Houghtons and Andersons were neighbors. Virgil Houghton had just bought a new 12 gauge Western Field shotgun, and Leonard Anderson asked if he could shoot it. That was the evening before he drowned. The day of the drowning was hot, and the youth and a cousin had gone to Elk to swim. The water was muddy, but Leonard Anderson swam across the river, and went under on the return trip. Searchers used poles in the muddy water to locate his body.

Norman Goad

The visit to his grave was a nostalgic moment. I wondered how his life might have turned out had he lived.

Doctor Goad had a remarkable talent for diagnosing illnesses. The late Gassaway physician, Earl Fisher, was said to have remarked that Doctor Goad could hear more with a stethoscope than anyone he knew. That was probably the way Norman Rockwell would have drawn him, listening with his stethoscope placed on the chest of a wide-eyed little country boy with tousled hair and bib overalls.

He maintained an avid interest in medical advances, as all good doctors do. It was an exultant day for him when penicillin, the wonder drug to treat infections, came along.

The doctor pulled teeth, too, although that was not unusual in rural areas many years ago, when a trip to town to the dentist's office was considered either not practical or unnecessary. Every community had its "dentists," and they weren't always medical doctors. In any event, Doctor Goad built up quite a collection of teeth in a jar over the years.

He had a wry sense of humor, including with patients, if they weren't too sick. One day a man brought his slightly ailing son to the doctor's office at Strange Creek. As the man prepared to leave, he asked what foods his son might safely eat. "Anything but bear meat," the doctor is said to have replied. The puzzled father mentioned this to his wife when he got home. "Don't worry," his wife replied, "there aren't any bears around here."

One time he requested that a patient bring in a urine specimen, and they brought it in a perfume bottle. The doctor was puzzled. He said to nobody in particular: "How in the hell did they get it in there? I can't even get it out."

Doctor Goad never weighed more than one hundred and thirty two pounds, soaking wet, which he frequently was. He loved to swim. A favorite place was the Barn Rocks hole, a scenic little spot with a nice sandbar in front of the Strange Creek United Methodist Church. He would often swim across the hole with one of his children on his back. The Barn Rocks were named for a large opening under the rocks that, in local lore, was called a barn. Doctor Goad believed in the healthful benefits of swimming, but more to the point he simply liked to swim.

The Barn Rocks probably also appealed to him because he had a lifelong interest in rocks and rock formations. He would discuss the properties of rocks with his children, or anyone else who would listen.

Another rock formation of legend at Strange Creek is the Buzzard Roost Rocks, which are located on the hillside across the creek from the Goad home. The 1918 book by Albert B. Cunningham, *Manse of the Barren Rocks*, a fictional story set in Strange Creek, drew its title from these rocks. The author lived on Elk River above Strange Creek.

Doctor Goad also swam in Elk, but usually alone. He would swim from Strange Creek upriver toward Glendon, and back. He also fished in Elk occasionally. Fred Nottingham, who accompanied the doctor several times on house calls and fox chases, remembers being invited on a fishing trip. "I dug a can of worms," Nottingham said. "Doctor Goad put on a large pair of bib overalls over his regular clothing. The legs were too long, so he turned them up two or three times, and then he dumped the can of worms into the folds. I suppose he thought they were easier to get to that way." On this particular trip, the doctor caught a nice-sized smallmouth at the mouth of Birch River, took it off the hook, and it flopped out of the boat.

Swimming and fishing were fine, but the doctor's abiding passions were hounds and fox chasing.

He would take them with him on house calls, particularly when he was traveling a ridgetop road. The hounds would trail along as he rode horseback. When he bought a Model A Ford (later a Chevrolet), he would put some of the dogs in the car and release them on the return trip. The baying of the hounds as they pursued the sly fox was music to the doctor's ears. Eventually, the hounds found their own way back home.

In his Model A days, he would carry rocks on the floorboard to throw at the hounds if they congregated in front of the car and impeded his progress.

It is said that he would have fox chases between delivering a baby. He had an uncanny ability to know when the time was near for delivery, and when it wasn't, and if the time wasn't near, he would turn the hounds loose, and return to the house later.

Exactly when he "traded in" his horse for a car is uncertain, but Jennings Fast of Charleston recalls that the doctor was still riding a horse on house calls in 1925. Jennings, who became a Methodist minister, spent two summers as a teenager staying with my grandfather and grandmother, Hampton and Launa Fast Riffel, and he was there when my grandmother died. He remembers that Doctor Goad came to the house on horseback. Fred Nottingham believes the switch occurred around 1936.

The number of hounds Doctor Goad owned at any one time is open to honest debate. His daughter, Mary, suggested a high-water mark of nineteen. Doyle Dean, writing in the Braxton Citizens' News, came up with a figure of twenty-seven.

The doctor's father, George Goad, put it slightly differently in a story passed along by John Calhoun, the doctor's son-in-law: George Goad was at the barber shop in Gassaway and someone asked him how things were going. "Terrible," he replied in his slow Virginia drawl. "The doghouse fell down last night and all but fifteen of the dogs were killed."

Doctor Goad entered his beloved Walker hounds in competition. A cup sat on the piano at home for many years with this inscription:

"All age champion cup. West Virginia Fox Hunters Association, 1921 field trials. Won by Blanche. Bred and owned by Doctor Norman Goad, Strange Creek, West Virginia."

The cup was intended to be passed along from year to year, but Doctor Goad and his dogs won it so many times that the association just gave it to him.

One time one of his hounds, Paul by name, entered into the hen-house of Becky Johnson Davis, my great aunt who lived near Strange Creek, and ate several eggs. When Becky accosted the doctor, he responded, "But Becky, Paul likes eggs."

Fred Nottingham recalls that the doctor's favorite dogs were ones named Drive, Drum, Old Three Toe, and Shine, the latter a female dog that was more attuned to chasing coons than foxes, although she would run foxes, too. She was allowed to sit in the car seat beside the doctor, a rare honor for a member of his canine menagerie, As previously mentioned, Doctor Goad liked to tap dance, and probably he was a jazz fan, too, as evidenced by the fact that he named one of his hounds "Shine," which was also the name of a popular jazz tune immortalized by Louie Armstrong in the early 1930s.

Fred remembers one hunt in particular. They built a fire on Turner Hill near Strange Creek, and released the hounds. They struck a fox and ran it all the way to Runion Ridge in Clay County. At daylight, most of the hounds began to straggle in. Doctor Goad left his coat at the campfire, and the late arrivers curled up beside it to await his return.

Doctor Goad chewed Arbuckle coffee beans while listening to the hounds in joyful pursuit of a fox. "Well, it's just the same as boiled coffee," he would point out.

Doctor Goad was chairman of the board of directors of the Bank of Gassaway at the time of his death, and was a member of the Braxton County Democratic Executive Committee.

He was one of the early stock investors in the community, and followed the market through the *The Wall Street Journal*. My brother, Bob, worked at the Charleston Post Office for a time before starting his career with Columbia Gas, and he recalls placing Doctor Goad's Journal in the mail bag bound for "up Elk." Among the doctor's prized books was one on the art of investing. He also raised Hereford cattle. The Goad store and cattle were joint ventures with his sister, Nettie.

Doctor Goad had surgery for ulcers in his sixty ninth year. Prior to that he was rarely sick. But he never completely regained his health, and died at Gassaway Hospital on March 8, 1956. He and his wife, Alice, are buried on a hillside near the upper Strange Creek bridge. His gravestone says simply: Norman Goad, M.D.

Nettie Goad Duvall and her husband, Jack, are also buried there. Nettie Duvall was ninety eight when she died in 1981. Nimmie Goad McQueen and George McQueen are buried at the Spring Hill Mausoleum in Charleston, as are their two children. Nimmie Goad McQueen died in 1914 at age thirty four.

- - -

Willie Lewis and Norman Goad were born ten years apart, and died ten years apart, both at age sixty nine. Both of their wives died at age seventy eight.

~ Twenty ~

The Indians

Ghosts of Our Past

One September morning, there was a crispness in the air and a tinge of color to the woods as Netowetok pushed aside the deerskin curtains that gave him and his family some sleeping privacy; he stepped outside, stretched, and breathed deeply. He had slept well, and his wife and two children were still sleeping warmly and snugly in their fur robes, but it was a relief to escape the assorted smells of food, bear grease, smoke, and tobacco that permeated the longhouse that was their home, and the home of others of their clan.

Netowetok was a young man, with the dark skin color, broad face, and high cheekbones that were characteristic of his people; he was not a clan chief, but he did aspire to leadership: he hoped that he would soon become a member of the tribal council, which would give him the privilege of sitting with the elders in their decidedly "smoke-filled room" and discussing matters of grave importance.

The year was five hundred A.D., but Netowetok did not know this; he only knew instinctively that it was time to go hunting for winter meat in the wilderness that surrounded his modest little village. The tiny stream that flowed through this wilderness would become known thirteen hundred years later as Diatter Run, but he didn't know that, and never would.

He glanced with a feeling of paternal pride at the spear that was leaning against the longhouse; he had fashioned its sharp, pointed tip from the black rock that was common on another nearby small stream.

*Sketches by
Ben Gibson*

That stream would become known as Leatherwood Run, but he didn't know that either, and never would.

Both of these streams flowed into a larger stream where he had caught fish many times with the tiny hooks that his wife had made from the bones of deer. He had been proud of himself on the occasions he returned from the larger stream with smallmouth bass for dinner, and which his wife had cooked over an open fire.

He did not know the larger stream as Birch; the white men who helped the northern tribes push Netowetok's descendants from their ancestral lands would give it that name twelve hundred years later. Neither did he know that the fish he caught were smallmouth bass; that, too, was a white man's name that would have meant absolutely nothing to him.

But he did know something about the larger stream; his father had told him stories about "the people," which was what they called their ancestors, migrating up this stream from mighty rivers that lay "somewhere out there" (his father had pointed to the west). Netowetok never knew these mysterious rivers as Elk and Kanawha, although, for once, they were not white man's names, but names given them by people who came after Netowetok who were lumped together by the white man as "The Indians," or "savages."

His father, who had been a clan chief, was buried nearby in a grave that was appropriate for a chief: it measured seven feet in height and twenty feet in diameter; Netowetok didn't know these dimensions; he just knew the grave was appropriate for a man of his father's importance in the clan. His father had died of a disease that, much later, the white man's medicine men would call colon cancer, probably the same disease that took the life of another Indian who became much more famous than Netowetok ever thought of being: his name was Cochise.

Not that Netowetok thought of fame or immortality, except in an abstract way; his mind was more occupied with killing deer, bear, and woodland buffalo for food and clothing. Yet without thinking about it, he and others of his clan had become part of what archaeologists of the white man would call "a culture of mound builders," or "the burial mound era." His father's grave was proof of that.

But enough reflection: it was time to hunt. He picked up the spear, put a spare point in the deerskin pouch where he also carried some tobacco and ground corn, and thought briefly about his sleeping wife, who, like other women of the clan, did most of the farm work such as growing and grinding the corn that he would have for lunch; women also cured the meat, and tanned the hides.

Netowetok was a hunter; he killed the deer that his wife sewed into clothing, including the moccasins he was wearing that were insulated with deer hair; they were careful to use hairs from the deer's winter coat, which were hollow and thus provided better insulation. Netowetok respected the deer, and he killed no more than his family needed.

But he wasn't just a hunter; he also fished, and he made the weapons and tools that were necessary for his family's survival.

He paused to eat a piece of bear meat from the turtle shell dish around which his family had gathered for the previous evening's meal; he had speared the turtle in the river he never knew as Birch. He barely glanced at two objects that were lying nearby: a polished stone that his wife used to grind corn, and an axe that he used to chop firewood.

Then he stepped into the wilderness.

- - -

Fourteen hundred years later, a white man, plowing his cornfield, picked up a polished stone, turned it over and over in his calloused hands with great curiosity, and took it home to show his wife. He didn't know, and would never know, that it had belonged to Netowetok.

One week later, hoeing his garden, the white man turned up another object that was shaped like a crude axe; it was the implement that Netowetok had used for chopping firewood, and had casually looked at on the morning of his hunt; the white man never knew that.

The white man found other objects over the years, among them the spear points that Netowetok had carefully chipped from the black rock he found on the stream he never knew as Leatherwood. The white man knew none of this either.

- - -

But he had a curious mind, and he knew from the books on the shelf of his comfortable living room that the Indians of Netowetok's time lived in the archaeological period known as Middle Woodland, which ranged from 100 B.C. to 500 A.D. This was the period during which Indians began to live in villages, as we think of them, and to grow crops.

Most of the artifacts that people find today were products of this period and the ones that followed it called Late Woodland and Late Prehistoric, which lasted until around 1675. The finding of numerous artifacts in a particular area means that there was at least a seasonal camp there; the old myth that West Virginia was only a hunting ground through which nomadic Indians roamed is just that, a myth, although it became more or less true later when village life ended.

This disruption of native cultures is known as the Removal period, a chilling term that describes the time when Indians of the Woodland and Late Prehistoric eras were being pushed from their ancestral lands. We tend to associate this removal with the arrival of the white settlers, but that's not entirely true. By the time the Europeans arrived, many major Indian settlements were already deserted, either as a result of disease, or incursions by tribes from the north.

One or both scenarios probably spelled the death knell for Netowetok's little village; the prehistoric Indians of which Netowetok was a part were gone from West Virginia by 1700, if not earlier.

The beginning of the end for all of the Indians of the eastern United States can be traced to 1607, when the first permanent European settlement occurred at Jamestown, Virginia. The final slide was well under way by 1750 when contact with white men had been firmly established. The eastern woodland Indians were mostly gone by 1800, either killed, decimated by white man's diseases, or pushed westward where they assimilated with other tribes.

If we were to assign a date to the official disappearance of the Indian in central West Virginia, it would be 1792. That was when the last documented killings of white settlers by Indians occurred in what are now Braxton and Nicholas Counties: Benjamin Carpenter and his wife at their log cabin home on Elk River just below the mouth of Holly (see "William Strange"), and Elizabeth and Margaret Morris on Peter's Creek near present day Lockwood. The Morris girls were driving their cows home when the Indians killed and scalped them.

There were several known Indian trails in West Virginia, among them the Pocahontas Trail that bisected Nicholas County east to west; unfortunately for the Morris girls, Lockwood lay almost precisely on this path.

The tribal identity of the Indians involved in the Carpenter and Morris killings is unknown, but they were probably Shawnees from across the Ohio River.

In his 1915 book, *Moccasin Tracks and Other Imprints*, William C. Dodrill places the end of the line for the Indian in West Virginia as 1795. Certainly there is no mention in any of the literature I have come across that tells of the early settlers on Birch River, beginning with English Bill Dodrill in 1799, as having encountered Indians.

The book, *Heritage of Webster County*, records only one incident in which white settlers were killed by Indians in Webster County: the killing of Peter Stroud and his wife and children on Stroud's Creek in 1772 or 1773. The Shawnee were blamed, but ironically this incident led to the revenge killing of several members of a peaceful village of Delaware Indians at Bulltown in Braxton County.

The presence of the Delaware at Bulltown was an anomaly; this tribe was more commonly associated with the states of Delaware, Pennsylvania, New Jersey, and New York. Supposedly, Captain Bull, a Delaware chief, had moved south with five families of Delaware after his village was burned in New York state, settling at Bulltown in what is still the only recorded Indian settlement in central West Virginia. In retribution for the killing of the Stroud family, so the story goes, a party of renegade whites went to Bulltown in 1773 and massacred all the inhabitants of that peaceful little village.

As with many historical events that occurred in the twilight zone before the existence of CNN and *The New York Times*, there is more than one version of the carnage at Bulltown: one version is that Captain Bull and some of his braves were on a hunting trip and therefore survived; another version is that he and all the rest of his clan were killed; we will never know which is the correct version, and had CNN and the *Times* been around then, they probably couldn't have sorted it all out either.

- - -

The Indian archaeological record is more complete for Nicholas County than for Webster and Braxton, partly as the result of the late Edward McMichael's 1965 *Archaeological Survey of Nicholas County*. The original impetus for this study was the construction of the Summersville Reservoir.

Most of the Nicholas sites documented by McMichael were in the southern end of the county, which isn't surprising, because the early Indians tended to follow the large waterways, even one as rough as Gauley River; rivers were threads that ran through their lives, providing food and transportation arteries; the broad bottoms of the Kanawha and Ohio Rivers were particularly favored.

Only two of the Nicholas sites listed by McMichael were on the Birch drainage, which lies in the northern end of the county: one was a stone mound near Dryhouse Run of Anthony Creek that measured about twenty five feet in diameter, and three to four feet in height. Like the earthen mound on Diatter Run (see "The Blue Hole"), it showed signs of having been excavated, although perhaps not extensively. Curiously, many rock mounds have been found along Nicholas County ridgetops, and they are a classic archaeological mystery: nobody knows exactly who made them, or why. But Mike Anslinger of Cultural Resource Analysts of

Hurricane said such stone mounds are fairly common, date primarily to the Late Woodland period (500 to 1000 A.D.), and in most cases are probably burial mounds.

The second site on the Birch drainage was on the north slope of Powell's Mountain just off U.S. 19 near Powell's Creek and Shanty Branch. It was believed to be a campsite at a rock shelter, and, based on scanty finds, its affiliation was believed to be the Archaic (7000 B.C. to 4000 B.C.) period.

McMichael also mentioned a rock shelter (not a mound) near the top of Powell's Mountain on the north fork of Brushy Fork of the Muddlety Creek drainage that showed signs of Indian occupation during three archaeological periods covering at least 1,500 years: Early, Middle, and Late Woodland. This is most likely the rock formation known as Flanders Camp (see "Powell's Mountain").

Painter Rocks, an impressive collection of rocks on the western side of the mountain near the head of Strange Creek, has also been a treasure trove for Indian artifacts over the years, although it was not mentioned.

But artifacts have been found in large numbers in all three counties. Point Mountain in Webster County near Webster Springs has yielded many artifacts, for example, and Roger Hollandsworth, who lives near Boggs on upper Birch River, told me that artifacts and even skeletons have been found at a large overhanging rock on the head of Two Lick Run, a Birch tributary. Similar finds of artifacts have been made in probably every community in the three counties.

Henry Given, who lives on lower Birch and attended Fairview Grade School on Keener's Ridge, said that the students found a surprisingly large number of artifacts of all sizes; the largest, which appeared to be a hatchet-type implement, was found by a teacher, Newman Baughman.

Randall Butcher, who lives on Coon Creek, an Elk tributary, has found hundreds of artifacts while plowing his corn field and garden. In April 2001, I took eight of these artifacts to the State Historic Preservation Office at the Cultural Center in Charleston, where they were identified by senior archaeologist Joanna Wilson as being from the Late Woodland (500 A.D. to 1000 A.D.) and Late Prehistoric (1000 A.D. to 1675 A.D.) periods.

The five largest projectiles most likely came from the Late Woodland period, while three small ones, called "bird points," most likely came from the Late Prehistoric period. Five of the eight were notched, which, archaeologically speaking, assigns them to the Late Woodland period; the remaining three were not notched, and were quite small, which assigns them to the Late Prehistoric period when the Indians had developed bow and arrow technology. For this, they wanted very light and very sharp points.

Three of the projectiles in the Butcher collection were made of a light-colored flint-like quartz called chert. This indicated to Wilson that they were "imports" from quarries in other states, probably Ohio, Kentucky, or Pennsylvania, although there were also two such quarries located in eastern West Virginia.

The Indians were great traders, Wilson pointed out, and probably obtained the quartz through trade. "By the time the Late Prehistoric villages were in full swing," she said, "Indians were obtaining such items as conch shells from the Gulf of Mexico, and obsidian [volcanic glass] from the Pacific Northwest. Later, after the Europeans arrived, they traded for beads and iron-related items."

Because of the large number of artifacts found at the Coon Creek site, she suspects it was occupied over different periods of time, and perhaps the same group of Indians would return there periodically.

The south ridgetop above Herold was a well-known place for finding "arrowheads" when it was being cultivated about eighty years ago, and Pershing and Bobby Keener, who live on Long Run near Herold, have found many artifacts when plowing their garden.

Apparently I had Indians for "neighbors," although I never knew them. Ben Gibson of Herold, who drew the mythical Netowetok for this chapter, told me that he and his brother, Jeremiah, once found an arrowhead or spear point in a small cave across the river from my home.

John Hymes Jr., former Glenville State College history professor, said in a 1982 article: "One can conclude that the Birch River and surrounding areas were probably utilized by Archaic peoples but most likely not to the extent that such cultures existed along the arteries of the Ohio and Greater Kanawha River valley areas."

- - -

Very few Indian artifacts found in West Virginia are associated with the period following the arrival of the white man, because Indians quickly found that guns were better than spears and bows, as were other implements of the white man such as steel hatchets. The desire on the part of the Indians for all these things spawned the fur trading era; the Shawnee, for example, began trading with the French in the late 1600s, and the British in the 1700s.

But anyone with a desire to do so can collect a surprising number of Indian artifacts that predate the Shawnee and other named tribes. "The whole state of West Virginia is one big artifact," says state archaeologist Wilson. "The Indians pitched a lot of stuff, although not as much as our litterbugs do today."

Ray Reip, who lived on Keener's Fork, a tributary of Diatter Run, found many artifacts over the years prior to his death in 1987. He found most of these in a relatively small area, leading him to believe that a village was located on Keener's Fork.

The artifacts pictured in this chapter were part of Ray's collection. I took them to the Historic Preservation Office in March 2001, where Wilson and Andrea Keller and Lora Lamarre of her staff identified them as being from the Woodland period. That takes in a lot of territory, beginning in 1000 B.C. and ending in 500 to 1000 A.D., but most likely, I was told, they are from the Late Woodland (500 A.D. to 1000 A.D.) period, the tipoff being the triangular-shaped spear points.

Artifacts from the Ray Reip collection
Photo by Ferrell Friend

Wilson said the polished stone from the collection is called a celt, which is a prehistoric stone shaped like an axe head. It is not flint, but a basaltic (dense, hard-grained) rock that lends itself to polishing. Its use cannot be pinned down to any definitive degree; the Indians most likely had as many different uses for the same tool as we do. It would be as if someone a thousand years from now would dig up a Black and Decker hammer and exclaim, "I wonder what they used this for? Cracking walnuts?"

The notched implement from the Reip collection is flint, and was probably used as an axe, or maybe a hoe. The "arrowheads" were most likely spear points. "The wider one is an excellent example of a Middle Woodland projectile point, and was probably attached to a spear handle," said Wilson, and "the narrower point probably had the same use." She said the points were made from Kanawha Black, a very common flint, which, when heated, can be chipped into a desired shape.

William C. Dodrill wrote in *Moccasin Tracks*: "Masses of flint weighing as much as eight or ten tons have been found on the Elk, the Gauley and the Birch Rivers."

The Indians of Netowetok's time did not have bows and arrows; that technology was developed in the Late Prehistoric period from 1000 to 1675. Of course the "ultimate" weapon, the gun, came with the white man. Greg Carroll, historian in the archives and history section of the Division of Culture and History, points out that among eastern Indians, the Mohawks and other Iroquois people from north of here became dominant first because they were the first to obtain guns from the early Dutch traders.

- - -

Nor did the Indians of Netowetok's time have a tribal identification. Any attempt to determine what tribes of Indians lived in central West Virginia, or indeed anywhere in West Virginia, in Netowetok's time is doomed to failure because there weren't any tribal names then. Just as Netowetok would never have known a name for the stream called Birch, neither would he have heard of an Indian tribe called the Shawnee. That was a name the Shawnee gave themselves long after Netowetok's time. In the absence of written records for many Indian cultures, white anthropologists gave them scientific names for classification and cultural diffusion.

Netowetok would have been further bewildered, just as students of Indians are today, had he known that in the history of the Indians of the United States there were from one thousand to two thousand languages and cultures.

"It's complex, and covers a huge time period," said historian Carroll. "The Shawnee, Mingo, Delaware, and Seneca [four tribes that moved through West Virginia] were all mobile tribes that belonged to different language groups. The Shawnee and Delaware belonged to the Algonquian language family, for example, while the Senecas and Mingo belonged to the Iroquoian. Whites tend to 'tribe' a particular Indian group, but that doesn't necessarily work either, because, for example, there were five different factions of Shawnee."

Further complications arise from the fact that Indians didn't leave written records of their existence until the 1700s and 1800s. But after that there is a rich history of beautiful and poignant use of the written and spoken word. One of the best known is Chief Logan's famous lament: "Who is there to mourn for Logan? Not one." Logan was a Mingo chief whose family had been massacred by white renegades. Invited to peace negotiations in what is now the state of Ohio, the wary chief wrote down his thoughts instead, and sent them by messenger. Today those final nine words are a haunting reminder of the period when the Indians were making their last stand in the eastern United States.

In the west, Chief Joseph of the Nez Perce spoke words which were just as illustrative of the Indians' plight, and which have resonated across the years: "From where the sun now stands I will fight no more forever." Joseph and his little band had been chased across two thousand miles of the western landscape, and were within a day's ride of sanctuary in Canada when they were cut off and forced to surrender to the U.S. Army in October 1877 in the Battle of Bear Paw Mountain in Montana.

The last stand of the Western Plains Indian is well documented, particularly in army records. The Apache warrior, Geronimo, was interviewed many times by whites, as was Sitting Bull, the spiritual leader of the Sioux at the Battle of the Little Bighorn. The book, *Black Elk Speaks*, gives a keen insight into the Sioux mind in the late 1800s when their lands and lifestyle were slipping away; Black Elk was an Oglala Sioux priest whose words were recorded by a white author, John Neihardt, and which are a classic chronicle of Black Elk's prophetic visions of the future; in essence, it is an Indian version of the Bible's *Book of the Revelation*. Crazy Horse, the famous Oglala warrior, was, like his second cousin Black Elk, a mystic. Black Elk said of Crazy Horse: "He [seemed] always part way into that world of his vision."

- - -

Neil Boggs, Clay County native and former NBC newsman, taught at the University of New Mexico after his television career. In the interest of political correctness, he once asked an Indian student what designation he preferred: Native American, Indian, or Zuni, which was his ethnic affiliation. The student grinned and said, "What's with you people? Nobody cares except you. I'm an Indian, and calling me anything else doesn't change that. Not that I want to change it."

Another time the faculty was asked to come up with programs aimed at snagging foundation money and new government grants. Neil suggested that the university create a George Armstrong Custer Chair of Native American Studies! After a few gasps, the meeting moved on.

- - -

I grew up thinking that all Indians were either Shawnee or Seneca, and I was chagrined when, at 4-H Camp, I was placed in some "inferior" tribe, the name of which I've forgotten. Just as the Sioux and Apache were the major antagonists of the cavalry in the American West, so were the Shawnee "our" Indians of the 1700s and early 1800s because they had the greater presence in West Virginia.

The Shawnee were warlike and nomadic, and fiercely resisted

the white movement into the Ohio Valley (the *Gale Encyclopedia of Native American Tribes* calls them "mysterious wanderers of the eastern woodlands"). This lifestyle put them on an inevitable collision course with white settlers coming across the Allegheny Mountains. Neither did they endear themselves to the settlers when they sided with the French in the French and Indian War of 1754-1755, nor when they later cast their lot with the British in the War of 1812.

The Indians were diplomats, both with whites and each other, and were usually adept at it, although their diplomacy sometimes backfired, as when the Shawnee cast their lot with the losing sides in two wars. When the Iroquois tried to control the Ohio Valley, they attempted to placate the Shawnee by referring to them as "Little Brothers," a ploy that the Shawnee resented mightily.

"The Shawnee were good at playing off the British against the French, and then the British against the Americans," said state historian Carroll. "That way, they got gunpowder from both sides" [and delayed the settlement of their hunting grounds by Europeans].

- - -

Standard reading for West Virginia schoolchildren of an earlier generation was the story of Lewis Wetzel, the frontiersman who settled near Wheeling in the 1700s, and whose life's work was fighting the Shawnee. It is said that he and his brother, Jacob, were captured by Shawnee when they were young, but managed to escape; another brother, however, was killed, and Lewis went to his grave bearing an unyielding hatred of Shawnee.

He died of pneumonia at Rosetta, Mississippi, in 1808, at forty four years of age, after he had moved to New Orleans; his remains were returned to West Virginia's Northern Panhandle in 1942, where he is buried at the McCreary Cemetery at Limestone, Marshall County, near Moundsville. A new stone was erected in 1992 by the McCreary Cemetery Preservation Foundation that includes an etching of him and the words: "Legendary frontier scout Lewis Wetzel," and underneath that the sobriquet: "Deathwind."

Daniel Boone, born near Reading, Pennsylvania, in 1734, was the most famous of the frontiersmen who matched wits with the Shawnee, although he is better known as a hunter, trapper, explorer, surveyor, and politician. He was captured by the Shawnee in 1778, and spent five months in captivity before escaping. He came to Point Pleasant in 1788, and lived in West Virginia for about ten years, including near Charleston, where he was elected a delegate to the Virginia Legislature from Kanawha

County in 1791. But his eternal wanderlust directed his path west to Missouri, and he died there in 1820 at age eighty six. The remains of Daniel and his wife, Rebecca, who died in 1813, were moved to Frankfort, Kentucky, in 1845.

The best known Shawnee were Cornstalk and Tecumseh. Cornstalk is believed to have been born on the Greenbrier River in 1709; he directed the Indians in the October 10, 1774, Battle of Point Pleasant that is often referred to incorrectly as "the first battle of the American Revolution," when in actuality the war didn't begin until a year and a half later at Lexington and Concord in Massachusetts. But the Battle of Point Pleasant did create a three-year period of peace between the Americans and the Indians which helped the American cause.

In 1777, Cornstalk went to a fort near Point Pleasant to warn that the Shawnee were going to take up arms against the Americans; while he was there, a soldier was shot (not by Cornstalk), but vengeful settlers killed him in retaliation.

Tecumseh, the last great war chief of the Shawnee, was an implacable foe of whites, and his death at the Battle of the Thames in Ontario, Canada, in 1813 basically ended Shawnee resistance to the westward movement of the settlers. Characteristically, he died fighting Americans, which the settlers were by then called. They had chased him into Canada from Detroit.

We are indebted to the Shawnee for naming both the Elk and Kanawha Rivers: Tiskelwah, or river of fat elk, for the Elk, and Keninsheka, or river of evil spirits, for the Kanawha. They may even be given credit for inventing soccer, because they played a soccer-like game with a soccer-like ball.

The Delaware gave another of our local streams its name: Gauley, a French derivation of Tokobelloke, or the falling creek. Today we applaud their acumen, because the Gauley's rapids have spawned a multi-million dollar whitewater rafting industry.

- - -

The Seneca were historically located in New York state, one of five tribes that comprised the Iroquois Confederation. "They were fantastic capitalists," said Ruth Brinker, retired archaeologist on the Monongahela National Forest at Elkins. "The tribes divvied up their economic spheres of influence, and the Seneca got this area [eastern West Virginia and Pennsylvania], and they ruled it with a heavy hand."

They were here long enough to have a trail, a rock formation, a creek, and a post office named for them: the Seneca Trail that began at the mouth of the South Branch of the Potomac River and ran westerly to Elkins; Seneca Rocks, located on the North Fork of the South Branch in Pendleton County; Seneca Creek, which enters the North Fork at the rocks; and Seneca Rocks Post Office (zip code 26884).

Seneca Creek is one of twelve streams in the state that have fishable populations of naturally spawning rainbow trout. Two of the best known of the others are Little Black Fork of Shaver's Fork in Randolph County, and Turkey Creek in Monroe County.

The Seneca Trail was an avenue of commerce that led the Indians to new fishing grounds, new flyways for hunting waterfowl, and such. "They were always moving to new resources," Brinker said, "plus there was undoubtedly a desire to see what was on the other side of the mountain."

In 1994-95, the U.S. Forest Service contracted for the excavation of two ancient Indian villages at Seneca Rocks whose residents lived during the Late Prehistoric period (six hundred to eight hundred years ago), long before the nomadic Seneca. "These were permanent villages where whole families lived," said Brinker.

A discovery that fascinated archaeologists was that these long ago villagers had a consistent unit of measurement, just as we do today. This measurement showed up time after time in their construction work, and was approximately from the end of the middle finger to the elbow in an adult (the same unit used by the ancient Hebrews and their neighbors - the cubit). The villages were named "Yokum" and "Harper," for the Mouth of Seneca motels and stores owned by Shirley Yokum and Joe Harper.

The entertaining legend of Seneca Rocks, as told by Julie Fosbender, director of the Seneca Rocks Discovery Center, is that Snow Bird, a princess of the Seneca Indians, informed her seven suitors that she would give "my hand, my heart and my life" to the one who could follow her to the top of the rocks; one by one, her suitors fell by the wayside, until there was only one remaining; he slipped on a ledge near the top, but she took his hand and saved him.

Between 125,000 and 140,000 people a year visit the Discovery Center, which is located at the junction of W.Va. 28 and U.S. 33 east of Elkins.

The Seneca, although a powerful tribe in their day, made a grievous error: they sided with the British during the American Revolution, and after that they had negligible bargaining power with the American government, and lost their holdings in the Ohio Valley.

The Seneca had a limited presence in central West Virginia, as did the Mingo. The latter were most prevalent in Ohio and the Northern Panhandle of West Virginia, but a small band is believed to have lived at what is now Mingo Flats in Randolph County. Likewise, the Cherokee claimed a portion of southeastern West Virginia, but did not have a presence in the center of the state except for later refugee families trying to escape their removal to Oklahoma in the 1820s and 1830s over the celebrated "Trail of Tears."

But exactly what Indians lived where in West Virginia, and who controlled this or that portion of the state, remains an unanswered question two hundred years after their departure.

- - -

We can conclude from the historical record that the "modern" Indians of the 1700s were not fulltime dwellers in West Virginia, but that the state was a favorite hunting ground in the fall; then the larger tribes would disperse to "winter camps" in the hills of West Virginia, and in the spring and summer reform into larger groups and travel to the flatlands of the Ohio Valley and elsewhere to plant crops.

After the harvest, war parties were often sent out; the "Indian summer" period of late fall was a time for raiding, not necessarily for enjoying the last warm rays of sunshine.

- - -

ARCHAEOLOGICAL PERIODS AND CULTURES

Paleo-Indians (15,000 B.C. to 8000 B.C.): They hunted the woolly mammoth, a type of now extinct elephant with body hair; there was no strong presence of the Paleo-Indians in West Virginia, but a few artifacts have been found, including at the St. Albans "digs," which date from 10,000 to 9000 B.C.

Archaic (7000 B.C. to 4000 B.C.): They hunted present-day game species, and gathered nuts and berries; their presence in central West Virginia has been documented sparingly.

Early Woodland (1000 B.C. to 100 B.C.): Few Indians of this period lived in central West Virginia, preferring instead the broad river valleys; this period gave rise to the burial mound culture, which in turn gave rise to some far-out theories, including one that the mound builders were one of the biblical Lost Tribes of Israel (it turns out they were simply Native Americans).

Middle Woodland (100 B.C. to 500 A.D.): Scattered hamlets of these hunters and crop-growers appeared in central West Virginia, and many artifacts have been found; our mythical Netowetok lived late in this period. The Indians of this period grew squash, sunflowers, and local grasses and herbs; corn didn't appear until late in the period.

Late Woodland (500 A.D. to 1000 A.D.): Decline of earthen mound building, and the ascent of stone mounds, such as the one recorded by Edward McMichael on Dryhouse Run of Anthony Creek on the Birch River drainage, even though he makes no cultural attribution.

Late Prehistoric (1000 A.D. to 1675 A.D.): A quantum leap in warfare among clans or tribes; many artifacts remain, including a few found in central West Virginia, although most have been found south of Charleston, and on New River.

Historic (1675 A.D. to 1750 A.D.): Contact made with the European white settlers; trade with the whites drastically altered the tribal balance; this period was the beginning of the end for the eastern woodland Indians; few artifacts remain; the Indians were mostly gone when a young George Washington surveyed for the Virginia Commonwealth in the late 1740s, although winter hunting in our area was still very important to tribes such as the Shawnee, Cherokee, Iroquois, etc.

Removal (1750 A.D. to 1800 A.D.): The period of disruption and removal of native cultures; very few artifacts have been found, because by this time the Indians were using the white man's implements; West Virginia had become an occasional hunting ground; native cultures were trapped between rival colonial powers and then crushed by American lust for land.

~ Twenty One ~

The Poem

Thomas Dixon Immortalizes Birch River

Around 1875, Thomas Dixon, a Virginian, moved to upper Keener's Ridge in Nicholas County. His farm was on a ridge above Birch River, about three-quarters of a mile off the Keener's Ridge Road. The river at high flow could clearly be heard from his home. If you were to walk downhill to the river, you would come to Birch below Slabcamp Run.

Some years after his arrival on Keener's Ridge, Thomas Dixon wrote a poem, or more precisely a letter in poetic form, about his community. That piece of literary work has endured over the generations. Although known only locally, it deserves wider recognition because it is humorous, philosophical and imaginative, and is history because it tells of a rural West Virginia community in the late 1800s.

Pictures of the author show him as a tall man with Burnside whiskers. That style was fairly common around the Civil War and afterwards. In fact, because of his beard, height, and facial features, he very much resembled General James Longstreet, the senior lieutenant in Robert E. Lee's Army of Northern Virginia, who was also tall, and, at an old age, wore Burnsides. It is said that Thomas Dixon kept a chest of Confederate money in his barn.

Thomas Dixon and his wife, Elvira McCutchan Dixon, were married in 1858 in Augusta County, Virginia, and had three sons and three daughters. One son ran away and returned to Virginia soon after they moved to Keener's Ridge, but they went back and retrieved him.

One can envision Thomas Dixon sitting by an oil lamp, or perhaps on the porch of his home on a Sunday afternoon, composing *The Hills of Birch River*, although another scenario is that he wrote it while plowing

with his mule. According to this version, he would
write while he was resting.

He was a voracious reader and a prolific
writer of letters. He supposedly titled this particular composition "News From Birch River," or simply
"Birch River News." "The Hills of Birch River" title
gradually evolved over the years from the poem's
opening words.

In more recent years, common usage of the
latter title was solidified when a community news
column began to appear in *The Nicholas Chronicle*
called "The Hills of Birch River." The column heading came at the suggestion of Beulah Brown, who
started the column after she retired from teaching in
1975.

The year in which the poem was written
isn't known. A time frame between 1875 and 1885
appears most likely. Writing about the poem in the
January 17, 1991, edition of the Chronicle, Beulah
Brown states that the composition was mailed to the
James H. Callahan family in Middlebrook, Virginia,
Thomas Dixon indicates as much in the next to last

Thomas Dixon
Photo courtesy
of Dixon family

paragraph of his poem: "I send my best wishes to one and all that live on
the farms of James H. Callahan."

The Callahans were friends of Thomas Dixon when he lived in
Virginia. One could assume that an early date would be plausible for the
penning of the poem, since he would have been eager to share his impressions of his new surroundings on Keener's Ridge.

The town of Middlebrook, organized in 1799, is located a few
miles south of Staunton in Augusta County in the Shenandoah Valley,
and was a stop on the stage coach line from Staunton to Lexington. Today
it is a charming little community of well-kept homes, many of them dating
back to the Civil War era, that have been restored by people who have
migrated into the picturesque valley.

Beulah Brown's 1991 story says that the Callahans "thought it
[the poem] worth publishing in their Virginia newspaper." She further
writes that "James Gibson from Herold, W.Va. [a few miles down Keener's Ridge]" was a subscriber to this newspaper so he clipped it out and
kept it." That scenario would explain how the poem began circulating in
the Keener's Ridge area.

But another version is that Thomas Dixon wrote the poem and

then decided not to mail it to his Virginia friends for fear it would offend some of his Keener's Ridge neighbors who were mentioned. This version has it that he hid the poem in a bed, where it was found by family members, who subsequently placed it into circulation.

Either way, it eventually saw the light of day, and most likely the present-day descendants of families mentioned in the 102-line poem are pleased to be included in what has become a part of local lore.

- - -

The contents of the poem are, like the date of its writing, open to speculation and interpretation as to what Thomas Dixon was describing.

For example, the part about a dance that was held in the woods in the moonlight, which constitutes a large middle section of the poem, is clearly fictional, but nonetheless delightfully-written fiction. The author makes it clear that it is fictional : "I will speak of a dance and that very soon that never took place by the light of the moon." Then he goes on to say that "They went to the woods, cleared off the ground, and all night long they footed it down."

Thirteen family surnames are mentioned as participants in the fictional dance, and most of those names are familiar ones in the area to this day. Probably most have ancestors dating back to that time period.

The only individual mentioned is Jimmy Gibson, of whom it is written: "The greatest wonder that happened of all, Old Jimmy Gibson danced down the last one at the ball." Probably that is the same James Gibson mentioned above as having lived at Herold. Whether he actually lived at Herold could not be confirmed, but a reference to a James Gibson in a 1984-85 publication of the Webster County Historical Society is enlightening. An article on the Baughman family history in West Virginia states that John Baughman, a son of Samuel Baughman, the first Baughman settler on upper Keener's Ridge, married Margaret Gibson, daughter of James and Matilda Cox Gibson, in 1870. If James Gibson was still living a few years after this marriage, he would most certainly be the "Old Jimmy Gibson" of Thomas Dixon's literary work.

Beulah Brown recalled reading in *The Richwood News-Leader* that the original copy of *Hills of Birch River* was in the possession of P.A. Gibson of Sutton, a grandson of Jimmy Gibson. P. A. Gibson died many years ago, and his children are deceased also. The last one, Staley Gibson of Sutton, died in February of 2000. But when I talked with him a few weeks before his death, he had no knowledge of a poem manuscript in the family.

- - -

Although Thomas Dixon obviously was writing of a dance that never took place, he may have based it on something real that happened in the community. Different scenarios have been suggested. One is that he was writing about a church revival. He was a Presbyterian, and Presbyterians are not traditionally known for their fervent revival meetings, so he may have been intrigued by the passion of local revivals of a different cloth. Another version is that the fervent ones didn't believe in dancing, and that he whimsically invented a dance for them.

Maybe. But writers can take poetic license with almost anything to create interesting copy. I think it's plausible that Thomas Dixon did just that. He wanted to work the community families into his writing, and an imaginary dance became his vehicle, and a very effective one.

Beulah Brown seemed to think so, too. In her *Nicholas Chronicle* article, she wrote: "It was just a newsy humorous letter written in rhyme from one friend to another in which he penned some of the activities in and around his new home and farmland."

Thomas Dixon's writing was a local homespun example of a style that was popular around the time in which he lived. Among the American poets who exemplified this style were Washington Irving (*Legend of Sleepy Hollow*), Nathaniel Hawthorne (*The Scarlet Letter*), and John Greenleaf Whittier (*The Barefoot Boy*).

- - -

Although Birch River is mentioned only peripherally, the poem immortalizes the river with its opening lines: "On the hills of Birch River, the place we call home, where the rattlesnakes crawl, and the catamounts roam." I submit it would be difficult to write a better opening for Thomas Dixon's purposes. First, the author identifies the Birch River hills as the place where he not only hangs his hat, but also where his heart is ("the place we call home"). Then he proceeds to give those hills the lurking menace of rattlesnakes and catamounts. Thus the seed of adventure is planted in the minds of his readers. Rattlesnakes have always been around, and mountain lions indeed existed in the area until the latter part of the 1800s.

Birch River is further alluded to in a line that goes this way: "The neighbors are kind and seem honest and true, and everyone paddles his own gum tree canoe." Where else but nearby Birch River to paddle? However, this reference could also be allegorical. The expression about paddling your own canoe, or, putting it another way, being independent, has been around a long time.

There is a miniature sermon tucked away in the poem:

Food for the ravens He hath always supplied (Book of Job).
He watches the sparrows high up in the air (The fowls of the air
from the Sermon on the Mount).
He holds out the rainbow (Noah and the flood).
He clothes the lilies in colors so rare (Consider the lilies of the
field from the Sermon on the Mount).

Birch River Post Office gets its fifteen minutes of fame in the concluding lines, which are classic: "My name is a secret, you never shall know, but direct your letters to Birch River P.O." The Birch River P.O., founded in 1840, is located a few miles from upper Keener's Ridge.

- - -

Perhaps Thomas Dixon really didn't want his poem to "get out." But if it hadn't, future generations would have been deprived of a fine piece of writing that has stood the test of time.

Beulah Brown, now Beulah Brown Neil, lives in Daytona Beach, Florida. "The poem always meant so much to me," she recalled. "Aunt Ella Johnson Frame [her great aunt] said that poem to me many times when I was growing up. I just couldn't believe anyone could repeat all that from memory. It sounded like she was reading it."

Ella Johnson Frame memorized the poem for a last day of school program when she was age twelve or thirteen, and never forgot it, even though she lived into her nineties. She last recited it publicly at a 4-H talent show at Birch River Elementary in the 1960s.

Illene Cutlip, one of Beulah Brown's students at Birch River Elementary School, learned the poem for a PTA program as a sixth grader, and, according to the teacher, "could do it as well as Aunt Ella." Illene Cutlip, now Illene Cutlip Lewis, lives on Keener's Ridge in Braxton County and is a teacher at Frametown Elementary School.

"It took me a while," Illene remembered. "My mom and dad [Mary and Herman Cutlip of Bays] listened for hours as I recited it. I would take it a stanza at a time, and kept adding stanzas until I learned them all." The poem has mostly faded from her memory over the years, but she also learned in elementary school to name all fifty-five West Virginia counties in alphabetical order, and she hasn't forgotten that because she requires her second-graders at Frametown to memorize the counties.

- - -

Thomas Dixon died at age eighty eight on January 8, 1917, during the flu epidemic. He is buried with his wife, Elvira McCutchan Dixon, in the Dixon Cemetery about one hundred yards from his homesite. His wife died in 1883 at only forty seven years of age.

At the time of his death, Thomas Dixon was visiting a daughter in Gassaway. For those who believe in omens, or tokens, or signs, there was one that night. A grandson, Blair Dixon, a brother-in-law, Addison Wilson, and a daughter-in-law, Salina Riffel Dixon, were at Thomas Dixon's home and all three of them heard the distinct sound of a wagon clanging and creaking its way around the hill in the dark. The next day they received word that he had died.

The line from a song, "Time has made a change in the old home place," came to my mind one day in June 2000 when I visited the Thomas Dixon gravesite in the company of Denzil Baughman and Bill Dixon, the latter a great grandson of the poem writer. The only remaining evidence of the house was a neat row of foundation stones, a well, and stones from outbuildings. The house faced the steep river hillside, but the ground around the site ranges from level to gently rolling. The entire area is now completely wooded. Bill Dixon showed us a picture of a 1938 family reunion at the house, which was then still standing, and the only tree visible was a large, stately maple. That tree, and another like it, are still there.

The cemetery is on a nicely rounded knoll, as cemeteries frequently tend to be. The cemetery, like the house site, is now surrounded by woods. There are perhaps fifteen graves there, among them, of course, that of the writer of *The Hills of Birch River*.

Thirteen direct descendants of Thomas Dixon are still living. They are granddaughter Ruth Dixon Brown of upper Keener's Ridge; great granddaughters Evelyn Dixon Powell of Fayetteville, Juanita Dixon Pellot of Oak Hill, Bernadine Dixon Wilson of Montgomery, Avalene Dixon Brown of Grand Prairie, Texas, and Sue Dixon Casey of Morrison, Tennessee; and great grandsons Bob Dixon of Charleston, Bill Dixon of Warren, Ohio, Gene Dixon of Keener's Ridge, Gene Baughman of Florida and Tennessee, Bernell Baughman of Ravenswood, Herald Baughman of Charleston, Darrel Cox of Charleston, and many great great grandchildren.

THE HILLS OF BIRCH RIVER

On the hills of Birch River, the place we call home,
Where the rattlesnakes crawl, and the catamounts roam;
Living in poverty, living in peace,
Is better than working poor land on a lease.

No longer a renter, not exactly a slave,
For we live in the land of the free and the brave;
No grasping landowner is here to complain
If the Lord should send down a shower of rain.

No hardened old sinner to howl like a hound
If the rain washes off a spoonful of ground;
No miserly wretch to bray like an ass
If the horse when he's grazing should trample the grass.

Nor walk o'er the land and carry a spade
To fill up the tracks the kildees have made.
But with something to eat, and something to wear,
We feel just as free as the birds of the air.

The children are healthy and well they may be,
For they live in the land of the brave and the free.
Then why should we grumble; why should we complain,
The Lord sends us sunshine as well as the rain.

Food for the ravens He hath always supplied,
And bread for the children will surely provide.
He watches the sparrows high up in the air,
And extends to the children his bountiful care.

He holds out the rainbow and rides on the storm,
And tempers the wind to the lamb that is shorn;
He clothes the lilies in colors so rare,
That kings in their glory can never compare.

Then why should we grumble; why should we repine,
Today may be cloudy, tomorrow sunshine.
The neighbors are kind and seem honest and true,
And everyone paddles his own gum tree canoe.

You meet them abroad and find them at home,
They mind their own business and let yours alone.
I have spoken of facts - I will now speak of fiction,

And don't be surprised if you find contradiction.

I will speak of a dance and that very soon,
That never took place by the light of the moon;
When natives all met in very high glee,
All being determined in having a spree.

And when they consented and wanted more room,
Said they would dance by the light of the moon.
They went to the woods, cleared off the ground,
And all night long they footed it down.

Backward and forward - the left and the right,
They footed it down by the pale moonlight.
Gibsons, Mathenys and Stephensons there,
Walkers and Deans turned out by the pair.

Givens and Baughmans belonged to the band,
Browns and Johnsons are always on hand.
Barnes and Bowers to the front likewise,
Grimmetts and Dixons to my surprise.

The greatest wonder that happened of all,
Old Jimmy Gibson danced down the last one at the ball.
Soon the next morning in passing around,
I went to the place - took a view of the ground.

And such a sight, eye seldom hath seen,
As the wreck that was scattered around on the green.
If I only would lie, I might say the bright sun
Ne'er saw such a sight since the fight at Bull Run.

Of things that are useful and things that are gay,
And things that are worn by the folks every day.
Things for the hands, the feet and the face,
And things for which "Old Nick" could never find place.

Now speaking of "Nick" I want you to know,
I mean the old fellow who lives down below.
Jews-harps and tooth picks scattered around,
Corsets and ribbons covered the ground.

Overcoats, shawls, bracelets and rings,
Hickory bark garters and wire shoe strings.
Calico, cotton, whale bone and sheeps wool.
And toenails - I picked up a double hand full.

Some large, some small, but all very neat,

Which came off the lads and lassies bare feet.
Some sharp like a pen knife, some like a spoon,
Which the natives danced off by the light of the moon.

To this part of the story I'll never make oath,
I want you to take it for what it is worth.
But don't tell the folks I spoke of the dance,
They would kick me across the ocean into France.

If one single word they ever should hear,
They would give me a coat of feathers to wear.
Then they would try to make it look neat,
With a gallon of tar they would make it complete.

But I guess you will think I have been lieing enough,
You are tired of reading such horrible stuff.
So now for the present I'll bid you goodbye,
And out on the hills of Birch River I hie.

And follow the plan that other folks do,
And paddle around in my gum tree canoe.
When weary of rowing, I'll rest in the shade,
No one to molest or make me afraid.

And on with my wife and my children I'll roam,
In the corn patch around our little cabin home.
Then write me a letter and write very soon,
I'll read it aloud by the light of the moon.

And when you are writing, please tell me the news.
Say, are you able to paddle your own canoes?
I send my best wishes to one and all,
That live on the farms of James H. Callahan.

My name is a secret, you never shall know,
But direct your letters to Birch River P.O.

Twenty Two

A Much-Studied River

But Not So Well Known

For a small stream, 36.6 miles in length, tucked away in the middle of Nowhere, W.Va., a large body of information exists on Birch River. It has been documented in depth by the Army Corps of Engineers, the National Park Service, the U.S. Fish and Wildlife Service, and the state Division of Natural Resources.

Birch should be flattered by all this attention.

The Corps of Engineers had its eyes on Birch in the 1960s and 1970s for a dam, and the feasibility study done by this federal agency provided the first large body of information to be compiled on the physiography and geology of the river, and of the soils at the dam site. This report was called the "Feasibility Study of Authorized Birch Reservoir Project," and was issued in June 1966 by the Corps' Huntington District.

The project would have changed the face of the community in dramatic ways: A dam that might have been larger than Sutton Dam; a lake that would have inundated ten or more miles of natural stream; an 1,196-foot tunnel through the mountain at the Lower Turn Hole; and a bridge over Elk River at Glendon.

Authorization for the Birch study was the Flood Control Act of June 28, 1938, otherwise known as Public Law Number 761, which was passed by the 75th Congress. This was the law that spawned the building of numerous dams around the nation, among them Sutton, Summersville, and Burnsville in West Virginia. The fuel that fanned the flames out of which Public Law Number 761 emerged was a series of disastrous floods in the 1930s. To localize this picture, raging floods on Elk River in 1932,

1936, 1937, and 1939 were among the largest of the century, although all were exceeded by the 1861 flood of record on Elk, and one in 1918 that sent waters running down the main street of Sutton.

One must wonder if those who lived through the 1930s, and were old enough to think about such things, might have imagined that the Apocalypse had arrived, given the floods, the Great Depression, the dust-bowl droughts, and the retirement of Babe Ruth that occurred in that decade.

The floods of the 1930s were preceded by the most severe drought ever to hit the area. In 1930 it didn't rain enough to wet the ground from spring to fall. Crops and wells dried up, and so almost did Birch River. One of the legends of the 1930 drought is that Warder S. Dean, who lived at the Lower Keener Eddy, stopped the entire flow of Birch River by sticking his hand in a crevice where the stream trickled over a ledge.

The 1930 drought was the most severe in recorded history in West Virginia, and indeed in most of the United States ("West Virginia Floods and Droughts," U.S. Geological Survey). Although 1930 was the peak of drought, it was only part of an extended drought that started in 1929 and ended, more or less, in 1932. In spring and early summer of 1930, daily temperatures averaged about ninety-five degrees.

Thirty six years later, the spectre facing Birch River residents was not too little water, but too much. The Birch Reservoir proposal was front-page news in *The Charleston Gazette*. A story by staff writer John Morgan, now retired and still living in Charleston, said the reservoir would provide remarkable relief for water quality needs in the Kanawha Valley. Although water quality (low-flow augmentation for Kanawha Valley industry and water users generally) was the primary thrust of the proposed dam, that alone would not have justified it. Additional flood control benefits for lower Elk figured in the equation, too, since Birch and its 143-square mile watershed is the largest uncontrolled tributary of Elk. Also, the recreational attractions of a reservoir in such a scenic rural setting were not overlooked. Ironically, it was the recreational appeal of a free-flowing river that helped tip the scales against the Birch project.

The Fish and Wildlife Service and state Division of Natural Resources (DNR) did a cooperative study of the fish and wildlife resources in relation to the proposed reservoir, under authority of the Fish and Wildlife Coordination Act, and issued their joint report on May 17, l966. The report took aim at the recreational benefits of a reservoir versus those of a free-flowing stream, ultimately contending that irreversible fish and wildlife losses would occur with the building of a reservoir. The lack of support from these two federal and state wildlife agencies probably had more to do with the demise of the Birch project than anything else.

The third and final study of Birch to date was conducted in the early 1980s by the National Park Service at the official request of the late Congressman John M. Slack Jr. It qualified Birch for possible inclusion in the National Wild and Scenic Rivers System, a possibility which, like the reservoir, didn't materialize.

But as a result of all of the above studies, the following basic information on Birch, as well as a lot more, can be chiseled in stone:

> Length: 36.6 miles.
> Total drainage area: 143 square miles.
> Elevation at source: 2,300 feet.
> Elevation at mouth: 775 feet.
> Total fall: 1,525 feet (an average of 42 feet per mile).

Birch is the second largest tributary of Elk River. Following are the major tributaries, ranked by drainage area:

> Holly River, 148 square miles.
> Birch River, 143 square miles.
> Big Sandy Creek, 133 square miles.
> Buffalo Creek, 113 square miles.
> Blue Creek, 80 square miles.
> Back Fork of Elk, 70 square miles.
> Laurel Creek, 67 square miles.
> Little Sandy Creek, 51 square miles.

Birch is the largest tributary of Elk in mileage, if the two forks of Holly River are counted separately:

> Birch River, 36.6 miles.
> Blue Creek, 25.31 miles.
> Left Fork of Holly, 25.12 miles.
> Back Fork of Elk, 24.78 miles.
> Right Fork of Holly, 23.91 miles.
> Buffalo Creek, 23.81 miles.
> Laurel Creek, 19.83 miles.

Little Birch River, a tributary of Big Birch, is 19.84 miles long, giving the two a combined length of 56.44 miles. The two forks of Holly plus an additional 3.85 miles of Holly below the forks total 52.88 miles.

The meanders of Birch, an apt word for a river that has more twists and turns than a jigsaw puzzle, take it on a northwesterly course from near Cowen, Webster County, to Glendon, Braxton County, at Elk River Milepost 80.7. Turn left and Charleston would be that far away.

Turn right and Sutton Dam would be 20.4 miles upstream at Elk River Milepost 101.1.

Although Birch in total is not well known, the mouth of Birch is a walleye and muskie fishing landmark on Elk River Road (W.Va. 4), a road that has known life in the slow lane since Interstate 79 was completed to through traffic in 1981 (the official dedication came in 1982). The interstate has siphoned off all but local traffic, leaving W.Va. 4 as a scenic and leisurely drive.

The Birch River Basin is roughly diamond-shaped as it contours its way through Webster, Nicholas, and Braxton Counties, and, as befits its setting on the western slopes of the Allegheny Plateau, is quite hilly, even mountainous, with many elevations in its upper reaches over two-thousand feet. Although the total drainage area is usually rounded off at 143 square miles, the U.S. Geological Survey lists it as 142.3 square miles. The USGS measures areas with an instrument called a planimeter that gives fairly precise readings.

Physiographers (those who study the evolution of land forms) tell us that the hills and ridge summits of Birch represent the remains of an ancient peneplain, which by definition is a land surface of considerable area shaped by erosion. This peneplain was formed in the Tertiary period approximately 65 million years ago, when dinosaurs began to disappear.

But everything is relative in the context of the earth's evolvement. The Tertiary period is just a youngster compared to, say, the Jurassic period of the Steven Spielberg movie, *Jurassic Park*, which depicted the dinosaur era of approximately 205 million years ago.

The steep hills of Birch are prevalent throughout its course. For example, although the valley floor elevation at Herold, 9.7 miles above the mouth, is only 927 feet, the surrounding ridgetops rise to 1,300 feet on the north side of the river (Fast Knob), and 1,453 feet on the south side (head of Bob Given Hollow).

The isolation of Birch from the Cora Brown Bridge downstream becomes evident by looking at a West Virginia Highway Map. Herold is the only settlement, tiny though it is, on the final seventeen miles of river. The Fish and Wildlife Service expressed it well: "The [dam project] area is largely rural and generally inaccessible."

Birch would, of course, have become better known had it eventually evolved into Birch Reservoir, or Birch Lake.

The proposed dam location was 1.3 miles above the mouth, or immediately above the Lower Turn Hole, the last named place on Birch before the river straightens out into the Mouth of Birch Eddy and makes its final approach to Elk. Six possible damsites were looked at on the last six miles of Birch, with the above site the preferred choice. The Turn Hole is appropriately named, because the river makes a sweeping 4,500-foot turn there, one of several such loops below Herold.

The physical proportions of the proposed Birch Dam, and the size of the lake that would have been created, were drawn up in two different proposals. The first set of figures came with the 1966 feasibility study. In 1971, the Corps of Engineers published a one and one-half inch thick volume called the "Kanawha River Comprehensive Basin Study." This was a plan for water and related resource development and management in the basin, as recommended by an interagency task force.

This latter study would have dramatically increased the size of the Birch Dam, and therefore would have created a larger impoundment. A map shows backwater going all the way to the mouth of Little Birch River. In the 1966 feasibility study, the backwater would have ended near the mouth of Long Run, about two miles below the mouth of Little Birch.

All of this must include, however, the caveat that plans for such projects as dams are often modified up until the last few months prior to start of construction. That could have been the case with the Birch project, had it been built. Additionally, whether the 1971 proposal would have superceded the earlier one is a matter of conjecture.

The following chart compares the two plans:

	1966	1971
Dam site	Lower Turh Hole	Lower Turn Hole
Composition	Earth and rock	Earth and rock
Height	190 feet	234 feet
Top length of dam	670 feet	1,080 feet
Length of backwater	9.6 miles	11.8 miles
Summer pool	1,050 acres	1,710 acres
Winter pool	940 acres	1,420 acres
Max. summer depth	152 feet	200 feet
Avg. summer depth	43 feet	50 feet
Land purchase	6,600 acres	* See below
Cost	$13.1 million	$26.7 million

* Land purchase for the 1971 project was given as fol-
lows: "Acquisition will include about 1,710 acres within the maximum flood control pool and a continuous strip a minimum of 300 feet in width landward from the flood control pool line. Selected additional land along the shore line and downstream from the dam will be acquired for public access and use."

Birch dam would have been built at this site above the Lower Turn Hole

The average summer depth of 50 feet for Birch Lake in the 1971 plan illustrates what a deep lake it would have been. Neighboring Burnsville Lake, by contrast, has an average depth of only 14 feet. Given the relative infertility of the Birch water in the first place, a deep lake with insufficient shallow spawning areas for fish raised the eyebrows of federal and state wildlife agencies.

Access to the Birch Dam, whichever plan might have been adopted, would still have been via a 460-foot bridge spanning Elk River and connecting to W.Va. 4, and an access road to the dam of six-tenths of a mile.

Water releases from either proposal would have been fed into an 1,196-foot tunnel that would have completely bypassed the Lower Turn Hole loop. This bypass tunnel would have been unique for a dam in West Virginia with the exception of the one at Hawks Nest on New River.

Recreational development would have been part of both proposals. The 1966 proposal showed two developed campsites with adjacent boat launching ramps. One was called Leatherwood Run Camping Area, and would have been located on the north side of the lake on the ridge above a prominent geological feature of lower Birch called Devil's Backbone. The boat launching ramp was designated for nearby Leatherwood Run, which would have been an arm of the reservoir. The other developed campsite was called Herold Camping Area, and would have been located on the south side of the reservoir in the vicinity of the Herold Bridge. A boat launching ramp was designated for the large bottom below the Herold Bridge. Primitive camping sites were planned in the Herold/Wolfpen Run vicinity, and on the extreme lower end of the reservoir. The 1971 proposal presumably would have retained all of the above, and would have added a recreational development on Long Run, although the exact location and type of development for the latter was not given.

The terrain of Birch helped sway the Fish and Wildlife Service and DNR in their decision not to support the reservoir project. Because of the narrow river valley and steep hillsides rising close by, the reservoir would have been deep and sterile. The river valley at the proposed dam site is only 100 feet wide, yet is approximately 1,000 feet wide a short way up the hillside; in other words, a classic "V."

The Fish and Wildlife Service and DNR response to the Birch Reservoir concentrated on Birch as an important, and maybe the only, walleye spawning ground in the lower Elk River watershed. This would have been lost had the natural stream been inundated by a reservoir, although the two agencies suggested an alternative: the building of a walleye hatchery downstream from the dam to mitigate losses to the Elk River walleye fishery.

The Corps of Engineers deferred the project for restudy in the early 1980s, and then deactivated it in November 1986. As much as anything, the environmental and social climate for building more dams had run its course somewhere along the way between 1966 and 1986. Deactivation of a Corps of Engineers project means that the planning stops. Projects that are deactivated could be reactivated if some momentous event or events occur in the future, but the odds are against it.

- - -

The most compelling case for Birch as a local and regional natural treasure was the Wild and Scenic River Study conducted by the Mid-Atlantic Regional Office of the National Park Service at Philadelphia in 1981-83, and made public in August, 1983.

The Birch study was authorized on March 5, 1980, under the authority of the Wild and Scenic Rivers Act of October, 1968 (Public Law 90-542). Field trips were made along the river corridor by NPS personnel in October, 1981, and May, 1982, to see the river under different flow conditions.

The NPS looked at the final seventeen miles of the river for possible inclusion in the system. This is the same stretch from the Cora Brown bridge to the mouth that is covered in the State Natural Streams Preservation Act. It includes four miles in Nicholas County and thirteen miles in Braxton County.

"It has been determined," the NPS concluded, "that the study segment of the Birch River is eligible for inclusion in the National Wild and Scenic Rivers System."

That was the good news for Birch, but then the other shoe dropped. The river, although found eligible, was found not to qualify for a federally administered component of the system.

The NPS suggested various scenarios for local-state management, one of which would have been a River Corridor Commission composed of representatives from Nicholas and Braxton Counties, private landowners, local interest groups, regional planning and development councils, and the state. None of these scenarios got off the ground because of local opposition or disinterest.

Proposed Birch River Reservoir, 1971 version (right)
Graphic by Neal Gentry

Long Run

Herold

Middle Run

Wolfpen Run

Dialter Run

I-79

Leatherwood Run

Exit 52, Frametown

Water Release Tunnel

Rt. 4

Proposed Dam Site

Elk River

Strange Creek

Epilogue

As I grow older, I find, more and more, I drift off searching for a simpler time, a place of comfort, to ease this life's burdens. I don't really know what I am looking for, other than a little peace, as I search my mind to relive some of my favorite memories. The day I finally discovered where this place of comfort was, I was truly amazed.

My family had traveled to Herold, West Virginia, to visit my uncle. My children, Kevin and Kenny, always love visiting "the country," as we call it. As I watched my children fishing with Mama, searching out "good" rocks to throw with Papa, climbing across the rock path to reach "the Big Rock," and just having a fun time at the river, I saw in my children's eyes the wonder and joyful innocence that only a child has for the simple pleasures of life. In that very instant, I had a unique revelation.

I recognized that look of joy on their faces! I remembered seeing that same look of wonder in my brother and sister's eyes as we spent summer days long ago on Birch River! Watching my children play, I can picture myself, Robbie, and Vicki in that same spot, full of that same innocence and wonder and delight as we played exactly as they do now! Wading with my grandmother, watching my family fish, climbing rocks that seemed huge at the time, catching "crawl crabs" for bait (at least finding them under the rocks and yelling for someone, anyone but Daddy, who wouldn't touch them, to come catch them). Never will I forget the happiness of those wonderful summer days.

Who would have thought that Birch River, simple and unassuming, would have such a profound affect on a life? Who would have thought that Birch River in its quiet beauty could teach so many of life's lessons? Patience is learned while fishing, determination is learned while trying to skip a rock, trust is learned with beginning swimming lessons, an appreciation of nature is learned upon seeing your first snake, a belief in God can never be doubted while sitting on a rock watching the river gently flow!

I guess I shouldn't be surprised that it took two small children to show me what I was missing. As I grow older, I tend to get wrapped up in my responsibilities and end up letting life live me, forgetting to revel in the special joys each day brings, however big or small they may be.

What a pleasure it is to close my eyes and for those few minutes allow myself to live my life again as I did as a child, full of awe and excitement at each little turn. What excitement there was at turning over a rock and finding a "crawl crab," but yet somehow understanding if there wasn't one, not to be disappointed but to just move on and turn over the next rock. Who knows what's waiting there to be found?

I understand now, this truly is my place of comfort! Thank you Birch River for all the memories and joy you have given my family, in summers past, in current days, and for all the joy you will continue to bring us in the future. Simple pleasures are truly a gift from God and I am thankful we were given this one to share.

-- Karen Johnson Yurasek

Sunset on the lower Birch River drainage

The Tributaries of Birch River

(Alphabetically)

Tributary	County	Mileage
Anthony Creek	Nicholas	4.75
Back Fork	Webster	2.35
Barnett Run	Webster	2.35
Baughman Draft	Webster	0.8
Bee Run	Webster	0.8
Big Run	Nicholas	1.9
Big Run	Braxton	2.4
Bragg Run (Laurel Fork)*	Webster	3.04
Chuffy Run	Webster	1.3
Coal Hollow	Webster	0.75
Coalbed Run	Nicholas	1.85
Cobb Run	Webster	0.6
Davis Run	Braxton	1.50
Deep Hollow	Webster	0.95
Diatter Run	Braxton	3.35
Fast Hollow	Braxton	0.6
Feedtrough Run	Nicholas	1.52
Jacks Run	Webster	1.31
Johnson Branch	Webster	1.35
Kate Run	Webster	1.1
Leatherwood Run	Braxton	2.27
Little Birch River**	Nicholas, Braxton	19.84
Long Run	Braxton	4.64
Madison Run***	Nicholas	0.9
Meadow Fork	Webster	2.1
Middle Run	Braxton	3.85
Mill Creek (upper)	Nicholas	4.67
Mill Creek (lower)	Nicholas	4.18
Ming Run	Webster	1.35
Otter Hole	Webster	1.25
Poplar Creek	Nicholas	6.27
Powell's Creek	Nicholas	6.08
Rich Fork	Webster	1.55
Road Fork of Skyles Ck.****	Webster	3.05
Rose Run	Nicholas	1.5
Silk Run	Webster	1.0
Skyles Creek*****	Nicholas, Webster	4.18
Slabcamp Run	Nicholas	1.2

Sutton Run	Nicholas	1.33
Two Lick Run	Webster	1.4
Williams Branch	Webster	1.15
Wolfpen Run	Braxton	2.54

* Bragg Run was originally called Laurel Fork.

** The mouth of Little Birch River defines a corner of the Nicholas and Braxton County line.

*** Madison Run enters Birch River from the south at the Cora Brown Bridge.

**** Road Fork of Skyles Creek originates in Webster County, and crosses into Nicholas County before returning to Webster County to join Skyles Creek.

***** The mouth of Skyles Creek defines a corner of the Nicholas and Webster County line.

As They Occur (head to mouth)

Tributary	County
Meadow Fork	Webster
Back Fork	Webster
Jacks Run	Webster
Deep Hollow	Webster
Coal Hollow	Webster
Williams Branch	Webster
Johnson Branch	Webster
Bee Run	Webster
Baughman Draft	Webster
Two Lick Run	Webster
Chuffy Run	Webster
Cobb Run	Webster
Kate Run	Webster
Silk Run	Webster
Otter Hole	Webster
Bragg Run	Webster
Barnett Run	Webster
Ming Run	Webster
Rich Fork	Webster
Skyles Creek and Road Fork	Webster and Nicholas
Rose Run	Nicholas
Poplar Creek	Nicholas
Anthony Creek	Nicholas
Upper Mill Creek	Nicholas
Powell's Creek	Nicholas

Sutton Run	Nicholas
Lower Mill Creek	Nicholas
Madison Run	Nicholas
Slabcamp Run	Nicholas
Big Run	Nicholas
Feedtrough Run	Nicholas
Coalbed Run	Nicholas
Little Birch River	Nicholas and Braxton
Long Run	Braxton
Wolfpen Run	Braxton
Fast Hollow	Braxton
Middle Run	Braxton
Diatter Run	Braxton
Big Run	Braxton
Leatherwood Run	Braxton
Davis Run	Braxton

The Top Ten (in length)

Tributary	*Mileage*
Little Birch River	19.84
Poplar Creek	6.27
Powell's Creek	6.08
Anthony Creek	4.75
Mill Creek (upper)	4.67
Long Run	4.64
Skyles Creek	4.18
Mill Creek (lower)	4.18
Middle Run	3.85
Diatter Run	3.35

(This list of Birch River tributaries and their mileage was obtained from the water resources section of the State Division of Environmental Protection. In instances where tributaries extend into more that one county, the county in which the mouth of the tributary occurs is given).

Flora

Trees

Common name	Latin name
American beech	Fagus grandifolia
American chestnut	Castanea dentata
American elm	Ulmus americana
American holly	Ilex opaca
Basswood	Tilia spp.
Bigtooth aspen	Populus grandidentata
Black birch	Betula lenta
Black cherry	Prunus serotina
Black gum	Nyssa sylvatica
Black locust	Robinia pseudo-acacia
Black oak	Quercus velutina
Black walnut	Juglans nigra
Black willow	Salix nigra
Box elder	Acer negundo
Buckeye	Aesculus octandra
Butternut	Juglans cinerea
Chestnut oak	Quercus prinus
Cucumber tree	Magnolia acuminata
Eastern red cedar	Juniperus virginiana
Flowering dogwood	Cornus florida
Hemlock	Tsuga canadensis
Mockernut hickory	Carya tomentosa
Ironwood	Carpinus caroliniana
Osage orange	Maclura pomifera
Pawpaw	Asimina triloba
Persimmon	Diospyros virginiana
Pignut hickory	Carya glabra
Pitch pine	Pinus rigida
Redbud	Cercis canadensis
Red maple	Acer rubrum
Red oak	Quercus rubra
River birch	Betula nigra
Sassafras	Sassafras albidum
Scarlet oak	Quercus coccanea
Serviceberry	Amelanchier spp.
Shagbark hickory	Carya ovata
Silver maple	Acer saccharinum

Slippery elm	Ulmus rubra
Sourwood	Oxydendrum arboreum
Sugar maple	Acer saccharum
Sycamore	Platanus occidentalis
Umbrella magnolia	Magnolia tripetala
Virginia pine	Pinus virginiana
White ash	Fraxinus americana
White oak	Quercus alba
White pine	Pinus strobus
Yellow birch	Betula alleghaniensis
Yellow poplar	Liriodendron tulipifera

Flowers

Ageratum (mist flower)	Eupatorium coelestrium
Black-eyed susan	Rudbeckia hirta
Bloodroot	Sanguinaria canadensis
Bluebell	Campanula rotundifolia
Blue cohosh	Caulophyllum thalictroides
Bluets	Houstonia caerueli
Broomsedge	Andropogon virginicus
Bull thistle	Cirsium vulgare
Buttercup	Ranunculus acris
Cardinal flower	Lobelia cardinalis
Cattail	Typha latifolia
Chicory	Cichorium intybus
Cinquefoil	Potentilla tridentata
Coltsfoot	Tussilago farfara
Columbine	Aquilegia canadensis
Common blue violet	Viola papilionacea
Crownbeard	Verbesina occidentalis
Dandelion	Taraxacum officinale
Dutchman's breeches	Dicentra cucullaria
Dutchman's pipe	Aristolochia durior
Dwarf ginseng	Panax trifolium
Foam flower	Tiarella cordifolia
Ginseng	Panax quinquefolius
Golden ragwort	Senecio aureus
Goldenrod	Solidago spp.
Great chickweed	Stellaria media
Hercules club	Aralia spinosa
Ironweed (tall)	Veronia altissima
Jack in the pulpit	A. triphyllum
Jerusalem artichoke	Helianthus tuberosus

Jewelweed	Impatiens pallida
Joe-pye weed (common)	Eupatorium fistulosum
Lady's slipper (pink)	Cypripedium acaule
Mayapple	Podophyllum peltatum
Milkweed	Asclepias syriaca
Nettle	Urtica dioica
New England aster	Aster novae-angliae
Ox-eye daisy	Chrysanthemum leucanthemum
Pokeweed	Phytolacca americana
Plantain	Plantago major
Queen Anne's lace	Daucus carota
Ragweed	Ambrosia artemisiifolia
Red clover	Trifolium pratense
Robin's plantain	Erigeron pulchellus
Rue anemone	Anemonella thalictroides
Sheep's sorrel	Rumex acetosella
Skunk cabbage	Symplocarpus foetidus
Small-flowered crowfoot	Ranunculus micranthus
Snakeroot (white)	Eupatorium perfoliatum
Solomon's seal (common)	Polygonatum biflorum
Spanish needles	Bidens bipinnata
Spring beauty	Claytonia virginica
Sunflower (common)	Helianthus annuus
Tick trefoil	Desmodium canescens
Tiger lily	Lilium tigrinum
Toothwort (two-leaved)	Dentaria diphylla
Toothwort (cut-leaved)	Dentaria laciniata
Trillium (white)	Trillium grandiflorum
Trillium (red)	Trillium erectum
Violet (common blue)	Viola papilionacea
Violet (smooth yellow)	Viola pensylvanica
Violet (long-spurred)	Viola rostrata
Violet (sweet white)	Viola blanda
Wild geranium	Geranium maculatum
Wild lettuce	Lactuca canadensis
Wild strawberry	Fragaria virginiana
Winter cress (creasy greens)	Barbarea vulgaris
Wood anemone	Anemone quinquefolia
Yellow fawn lily	Erythronium americanum

Shrubs

American hazelnut	Corylus americana
Black elderberry	Sambucus canadensis

Brookside alder	Alnus serrulata
Flame azalea	Rhododendron calendulaceum
Hercules club	Aralia spinosa
Leatherwood	Dirca palustris
Mountain laurel	Kalmia latifolia
Rhododendron	Rhododendron maximum
Spicebush	Lindera benzoin
Squaw huckleberry	Vaccinium caesium
Staghorn sumac	Rhus typhana
Wild honeysuckle	Rhododendron nudiflorum
Witch hazel	Hamamelis virginiana
Yellowroot	Hydrastis canadensis

Vines

Blackberry	Rubus spp.
Fox grape	Vitus labrusca
Greenbrier	Smilax rotundifolia
Ground pine	Lycopodium complanatum
Kudzu	Pueraria lobata
Multiflora rose	Rosa multiflora
Poison ivy	Rhus radicans
Summer grape	Vitis aestivalis
Virginia creeper	Psedera quinquefolia

Ferns

Christmas fern	Polystichum acrostichoides
Cliffbrake fern (purple)	Pellaea atropurpurea
Interrupted fern	Osmunda claytoniana
Lady fern (glade)	Athyrium pycnocarpon
Maidenhair fern	Adiantum pedatum
New York fern	Dryopteris nuveboracensis
Royal fern	Osmunda regalis
Sensitive fern	Onoclea sensibilis

Primitives

Algae (green)	Spyrogyra
Apple moss	Bartramia pomiformis
Bracket fungus	Fomes spp.
Matchstick lichen	Cladonia cristalella
Moss (cushion)	Leucobryum glaucum
Reindeer moss (lichen)	Cladonia rangiferina
Snake liverwort	Conocephalum conicum

Fauna

Mammals

Common name	*Latin name*
Beaver	Castor canadensis
Black bear	Ursus americanus
Bobcat	Felis rufa
Chipmunk	Tamias striatus
Cottontail rabbit	Sylvilagus floridanus
Coyote	Canis latrans
Fairydiddle (red squirrel)	Tamiasciurus hudsonicus
Field mouse	Mus musculus
Flying squirrel	Glaucomys volans
Fox squirrel	Sciurus niger
Gray fox	Urocyon cinereoargenteus
Gray squirrel	Sciurus carolinensis
Groundhog (whistlepig)	Marmota momax
Little brown bat	Myotis lucifugus
Mink	Mustela vison
Mountain lion	Felix concolor
Muskrat	Ondatra zibethica
Norway rat (river)	Rattus norvegieus
Opossum	Didelphis virginiana
Raccoon	Procyon lotor
Red fox	Vulpes vulpes
Skunk (striped)	Mephitis mephitis
Weasel	Mustela frenata
White-footed mouse	Peromyscus leucopus
Whitetail deer	Odocoileus virginianus

Birds

Barred owl	Strix varia
Bluejay	Cyanocitta cristata
Canada goose	Branta canadensis
Cardinal	Cardinalis cardinalis
Chickadee	Parus atricapillus
Crow	Corvus brachyrhynchos
Downy woodpecker	Picoides pubescens
Eastern bluebird	Sialia sialis
Eastern phoebe	Sayornis phoebe

Goldfinch	Carduelis tristis
Gray catbird	Dumetella carolinensis
Great blue heron	Ardea herodias
Great horned owl	Bubo virginianus
House wren	Troglodytes aedon
Indigo bunting	Passerina cyanea
Junco	Junco hymelis
Killdeer	Charadrius vociferus
Kingfisher	Ceryle aleyon
Mourning dove	Zenaidura macroura
Pileated woodpecker	Dryocopus pileatus
Raven	Corvus corax
Red-tailed hawk	Buteo jamaicensis
Redwing blackbird	Agelaisus phoeniceus
Robin	Turdus migratorius
Ruby throated hummingbird	Archilochus colubris
Ruffed grouse	Bonasa umbellus
Scarlet tanager	Piranga olivacea
Screech owl	Otus asio
Song sparrow	Melospiza melodia
Starling	Sturnus vulgaris
Tufted titmouse	Parus bicolor
Turkey vulture	Cathartes aura
Whip-poor-will	Caprimulgus vociferus
Wild turkey	Meleagris gallopavo
Wood duck	Aix sponsa
Wood thrush	Hylocichla mustelina

Fish

Carp	Cyprinus carpio
Flathead catfish	Pylodictis olivaris
Gar	Lepisosteus osseus
Largemouth bass	Micropterus salmoides
Muskellunge	Esox masquinongy
Rock bass	Ambloplites rupestris
Smallmouth bass	Micropterus dolomieu
Spotted bass (Kentucky)	Micropterus punctulatus
Sunfish (longear)	Lepomis megalotis
Walleye	Stizostedion vitreum
White sucker	Catostomus commersoni

Amphibians

Bullfrog	Rana catesbeiana
Crayfish	19 species found in W.Va.
Eastern American toad	Bufo a. americanus
Gray treefrog	Hyla chrysoscelis
Hellbender	Cryptobranchus alleganiensis
Hellgrammite (dobsonfly)	Corydalus cornutus
Northern spring peeper	Hyla c. crucifer
Red-spotted newt	Noto phthalmus viridescens
Snapping turtle	Chelydra serpentina serpentina
Spring salamander	Desmognathus fuscus

Reptiles

Black racer	Coluber c. constrictor
Black rat snake	Elaphe o. obsoleta
Box turtle	Terrapene carolina carolina
Copperhead	Agkistrodoncontortrix mokasen
Garter snake	Thamnophis s. sirtalis
Hognose snake	Heterodon platyrhinos
Milk snake	Lampropeltis t. triangulum
Ringneck snake	Diadophis punctatus edwardsii
Timber rattlesnake	Crotalus horridus
Watersnake (common)	Nerodia s. sipedon

Populations in the Birch River Counties: 1860-2000

These charts tell the story: The Webster County population peaked in 1940 and has since declined almost fifty percent; the Nicholas County population peaked in 1950, but today is not far below that benchmark; and the Braxton County population peaked in 1920, but has shown an upward trend since 1990.

Webster, where Birch River begins, is relatively isolated. There is no interstate or Appalachian highway running through Webster, unlike Nicholas (U.S. 19) and Braxton (I-79).

Nicholas has benefitted greatly from four-lane U.S. 19 and a large amount of gently rolling land along the highway corridor that has led to development.

Braxton, likewise, has benefitted from I-79, which bisects the county, and to development along that highway, particularly at Flatwoods.

The population trends in all three counties reflect a changing lifestyle: largely rural and agricultural in the first half of the twentieth century, and then, beginning in World War II, a population shift away from the farms and to the cities.

In the cases of Nicholas and Braxton, this trend is showing a reversal, as superhighways have made it easier to live in the country and work in the city.

Census Year	Webster County	Nicholas County	Braxton County
1860	1,555	4,627	4,992
1870	1,730	4,458	6,480
1880	3,207	7,223	9,787
1890	4,783	9,307	13,928
1900	8,862	11,403	18,904
1910	9,680	17,699	23,023
1920	11,562	20,717	23,973
1930	14,216	20,686	22,579
1940	18,080	24,070	21,658
1950	17,888	27,696	18,082
1960	13,719	25,414	15,152
1970	9,809	22,552	12,666
1980	12,245	26,126	13,894
1990	10,729	26,775	12,998
2000	9,719	26,562	14,702

373

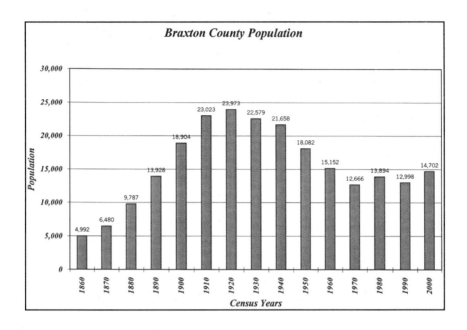

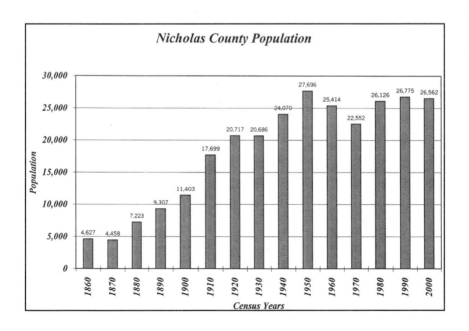

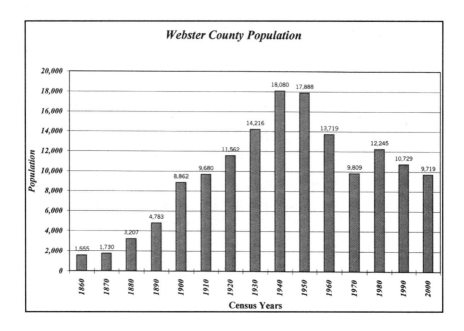

Population Graphs by Lyle Stokes

Bibliography

Army Corps of Engineers, *Feasibility Study of Authorized Birch Reservoir Project.*

Army Corps of Engineers, *Kanawha River Comprehensive Basin Study.*

Batty, Ken, *Significant Floods and Flash Floods in West Virginia Since 1900*, National Weather Service.

Byrne, W.E.R., *Tale of the Elk*, Mountain State Press.

Callahan, James, *Semi-Centennial History of West Virginia.*

Cohen, Stan, with Richard Andre, *Kanawha County Images*, Pictorial Histories Publishing Company and Kanawha Bicentennial Inc.

Colton, J.H., *1865 Map of the State of West Virginia.*

Conley, Phil, *West Virginia Review.*

Core, Earl L., *The Wondrous Years: West Virginia Through the Seasons*, Seneca Books.

Core, Earl L., and Guthrie, Roland L., *Forest Trees of West Virginia*, West Virginia Department of Agriculture, revised edition.

Cunningham, Albert B., *Manse of the Barren Rocks.*

Dodrill, Charles T., *Heritage of a Pioneer.*

Dodrill, William Christian, *Moccasin Tracks and Other Imprints*, third printing by McClain Printing Company.

Dunn, Gerald, *An Appalachian Boyhood.*

Gale's Encyclopedia of Native American Tribes.

Green, N. Bayard, and Pauley, Thomas, *Amphibians and Reptiles in West Virginia*, University of Pittsburgh Press in cooperation with the West Virginia Division of Natural Resources nongame wildlife program.

Hall, George A., *West Virginia Birds*, Carnegie Museum of Natural History.

Hammon, Neal, Ed., *My Father, Daniel Boone*, the Draper interviews with Nathan Boone, The University Press of Kentucky.

Hansroth, Andy, and Morgado, Alex, *Nothing But Mountain State Fishing*, the Charleston Gazette.

Hardesty's Braxton County.

Hardway, Ronald, *Heritage of Webster County*, Webster County Historical Society.

Hardwoods of West Virginia, West Virginia Department of Agriculture.

Harned, Joseph, *Wild Flowers of the Alleghanies*, Press of the Sincell Printing Company.

Kessler, Thelma and Kent, *Doctor Dan.*

Lee, David D., *Sergeant York: An American Hero*, The University Press of Kentucky.

Lowry, Terry, *September Blood: The Battle of Carnifex Ferry*, Pictorial Histories Publishing Company.

McGuffey, W.H., *McGuffey's Third Reader.*

McMichael, Edward, *Archaeological Survey of Nicholas County.*

McWhorter, L.V., *Border Settlers of North-Western Virginia.*

Nicholas County Heritage, the Nicholas County Historical and Genealogical Society.

Pauley, Thomas, *Toads and Frogs of West Virginia*, for the DNR nongame wildlife and Natural Heritage programs.

Pauley, Thomas, and Seidel, Michael, *Turtles and Lizards of West Virginia*, for the DNR nongame wildlife and Natural Heritage programs.

Peterson, Roger Tory, and McKenny, Margaret, *Northeastern Wildflowers*, the Easton Press.

Reip, Donna, *Journal of the Braxton County Historical Society*.

Shalaway, Scott, *The Wild Side* (two volumes) and *Birds, Bats, Butterflies...and Other Backyard Beasts*, Saddle Ridge Press.

Simon, Hilda, *Easy Identification Guide to North American Snakes*.

Skidmore, Warren, *History of Skidmore Family*.

Strausbaugh, P.D., and Core, Earl L., *Flora of West Virginia*.

Sutton, John D., *History of Braxton County and Central West Virginia*, reprint by McClain Printing Company.

The Wild Turkey in West Virginia, West Virginia DNR.

Venable, Norma Jean, *Introduction to Ferns of West Virginia*, cooperative extension service, West Virginia University.

Warden, William E., *West Virginia Logging Railroads*, TLC Publishing..

Water Resources Data, West Virginia Water Year 1998, U.S. Geological Survey in cooperation with the state of West Virginia and with other agencies.

West Virginia: A Guide to the Mountain State, Works Progress Administration, 1941 booklet.

West Virginia Common Snakes, DNR nongame wildlife program.

West Virginia Floods and Droughts, U.S. Geological Survey.

White, I.C., *1917 West Virginia Geological Survey report.*

Withers, Alexander Scott, *Chronicles of Border Warfare.*

Index

A. T. Massey, 3, 195
Abbott, Larry, 213
Abner, 150, 158, 184, 193-194, 202, 212
Acuff, Roy, 169
Adams Ridge, xii, 129, 161, 164, 170, 177, 206, 215, 219, 231
Adams School, 79, 170, 217, 224, 236, 273, 315
Allen, Margaret, 223
Allen, Peck, 222-224
Allen, Savina Samples, 244
Ambrose, Stephen, ix
American Electric Power Company, 187
Anderson, L. T., 6
Anderson, Leonard, 319
Anderson, W. C., 17
Anderson Davis Knob, 206, 212, 236
Anthony Creek, 49, 58, 62-64, 68, 132, 285, 308, 330, 340, 362-364
Appalachian Power, 262
Archaeological periods and cultures, 339
Arcuri, Mike, xi
Armentrout, Bill, ix, 11, 60
Armstrong, Louie, 322
Army Corps of Engineers, xi, 162, 169, 229, 241, 252, 254, 351, 375
Artifacts, 223, 328, 331-333, 339-340
Ashton, Ken, 11, 211
Ashton Place, 11-12
Atkinson, George, 306
Augusta Heritage Center, xii, 33
Ayers Rock, 144
B&O Railroad, 4, 29, 115
B&O Museum, 45
Baby Overland, 26
Back Fork of Elk, 36, 251, 256, 353
Bacon, Edward R., 37
Bail, David, 218-219
Bail, Bryan, 218
Bail, Faye Cowger, 212
Bail, Virgil, 212
Bail School, 315
Bailes, Junior, 242
Bakers Run Campground, 299
Ballengee, Chris, 139
Ballengee, Ray, 139
Baltimore, Md, 4, 45, 89, 92, 211, 224
Bank of Gassaway, 322
Bark Peelers Convention, 43
Barkley, Artie, xi
Barn Rocks, 320
Barnett, Charlotte Rose, 22

Barnett, Levi, 22
Barnett, Levi J., 22
Barnett, William C., 21
Barnett Cemetery, 21-22
Barnett Run, 15, 18-20, 27, 29, 32, 255, 362-363
Barnette, Doy, 97
Barnette, Perl, 44
Barnette, Wilkie, 28
Barnette, Dicey Burroughs, 97
Barnettsville, 22
Barnhart, Henry, 46
Barnhart Log Loader, 42, 46
Barren Rocks, 320
Bath County, Va, 24
Batterson, Phil, 213
Battle of Bear Paw Mountain, 335
Battle of Bulltown, 120
Battle of Carnifex Ferry, 52-53, 74-75, 82, 106, 376
Battle of Guadalcanal, 244
Battle of Point Pleasant, 20, 337
Batty, Ken, 253, 375
Baughman, Audrey, 209
Baughman, B. F., 122
Baughman, Bernell, 346
Baughman, Christopher, 22-23, 32, 59, 128
Baughman, Clora, 88
Baughman, Cornelius, 97, 115
Baughman, Denzil, 43, 132, 147, 191, 203, 208, 214, 346
Baughman, Ed, 191
Baughman, Gene, 346
Baughman, Gerry, xii
Baughman, Heinrich, 24
Baughman, Henry, 23, 128, 133, 136
Baughman, Herald, 346
Baughman, J. E., 138
Baughman, John, 343
Baughman, Newman, 331
Baughman, Rachel Glasburn, 23
Baughman, Samuel, 23, 343
Baughman Cemetery, 170
Baughman Draft, 362-363
Baughman Methodist Church, 315
Bays, 56, 104, 345
Beall, Ernest, 236
Beall, Willis & Ward, 118
Beall Cemetery, 236
Beam, Doris, xii

Beam, George, xii, 98, 265, 267
Beam, John, 97
Bear Run, 107, 115, 117-118, 120
Bear Run Road, 115, 117
Bearhunter Billy Barnett, 20-21, 23, 27-28, 35
Becker, Henry, 235
Bee Run, 362-363
Belva, 52, 82, 254
Bennett, Joseph H., 16
Bennett, Randy, 65
Bennett, W. G., 17
Benson, Dick, 133
Benton Given Cemetery, 230, 237
Bergoo, 39, 214
Big Bend Tunnel, 167
Big Buffalo Creek, 36, 115, 118
Big Coon Den, 104
Big Ditch Lake, 2-4
Big Eddy, 126, 148-149, 151-152, 154, 180,
    189-190, 261, 292
Big Eddy Rock, 148, 151-152, 154, 180
Big Otter, 133
Big Run, Braxton, 161-162, 224, 362, 364
Big Run, Nicholas, 142, 362, 364
Big Run School, 93
Big Union Baptist Church, 298, 313
Bill Johnson Campground, 109
Birch Boom and Lumber Company, 97, 243,
    246, 264
Birch District, 222, 250
Birch Hill, 3
Birch Mountain, 2-3, 52, 56, 83, 101, 106
Birch Reservoir, 162, 169, 200, 229, 241,
    351-352, 354, 357-358, 375
Birch River, vi-x, xii, 1, 3, 8-9, 11-12, 19, 22-25,
    28-38, 40-43, 45, 48-49, 51, 53-65, 68-69, 71,
    76, 79, 82-83, 85-88, 91-94, 96-97, 99, 101, 103,
    106, 108-109, 111-112, 115-116, 120, 124,
    132, 134-137, 141, 144-145, 148, 153, 161,
    166-167, 176, 185, 189, 192, 195-196, 199,
    201-205, 208-209, 211-213, 219-220, 223, 226,
    229-232, 235, 237, 239, 250, 252-254, 256-257,
    259, 261-264, 266, 269-270, 272-277, 279-281,
    283-285, 290, 292, 294-295, 307, 309, 313, 318,
    321, 329, 331-332, 340-347, 349, 351-355, 358,
    360-365, 372
Birch River Baptist Church, 56-58, 120
Birch River Bigfoot, 232
Birch River Elementary School, 57-58, 256, 345
Birch River Junction, 115-116, 235
Birch River Little League, 65
Birch River Post Office, 60-61, 345
Birch River Ruritan Club, 250
Birch River Volunteer Fire Department, 58
Birch Valley Lumber Company, 6, 45, 48-49,
    63, 91
Birch Village, 13, 20, 25, 41, 48, 51-66, 69, 76,
    78, 87, 91-92, 98, 102, 107, 120, 195, 249-250,
    253, 255-256, 262, 285, 307-308
Bird River, 55

Bison, WV, 115
Black, Samuel, 79
Black Betsy Coal, 38
Black Elk Speaks, 335
Black Jack Line, 244
Blair-Berthy, 49
Blake, John, 207
Blake, Wilbur, 207
Blankenship, Alva, 58
Blankenship, Don, 34-35
Blankenship, Mike, 34
Blarney Castle, 144
Blattenberger, Donald, 9
Blattenberger, Joyce, 9
Bliss, 125
Blue Creek, 36, 353
Blue Hole, 20, 79, 108, 158, 163, 169, 177, 195,
    197-198, 205-210, 213, 215, 219, 228, 237, 241,
    330
Bluegrass Connection, 52, 58
Board Fork of Beaver Creek, 19
Bob Given Hollow, 108, 354
Bobbitt, Chilton, 10
Boggs, Bill, 95
Boggs, Billy, 15, 19
Boggs, David, 19
Boggs, Leo, 220, 224
Boggs, Neil, 144, 335
Boggs Cemetery, 18, 21, 29, 32
Boggs Store, 13-15, 19, 32
Boone, Daniel, 25, 30, 59, 336, 376
Boone, James, 59
Boone, Nathan, 59, 376
Bossie, Vicki Johnson, viii
Bottlenose Rock, 160
Bowers, Hettie Browning, 298
Bowers, Robert, 29, 255
Bowles, M. V., 81
Bowman, Lec, xii
Boy Scout Troop, 173
Bradley, Mabel Warren, 142
Bradley, Omar, 63
Brady, Larry, 226
Brady Hollow, 157
Brady Rock, 157, 203
Bragg, Abb, 29
Bragg, Clint, 29
Bragg, Ellen Greene, 29
Bragg, Goldie, 219
Bragg, Guy, 195
Bragg, Jim, 29
Bragg, Lewis, 29
Bragg, Luther, 41
Bragg, Tom, 29
Bragg Run, 27, 29, 31, 362-363
Branham, George, 15
Braxton County Circuit Clerk, xi, 225
Braxton County Commission, 118, 132
Braxton County Courthouse, 246
Braxton County DOH Maintenance Head-

quarters, 226
Braxton County High School, 65, 237
Braxton County Population, 372
Brenner, Margaret, xii
Brinker, Ruth, 337
Brooks, Judy Bragg, 195
Brooks, Maurice, 272, 276
Brooks Run Coal Company, 3, 5, 37, 89, 104
Brooks Run School, 104
Brown, Ancel, 96-97
Brown, Avalene Dixon, 346
Brown, Bert, 26, 44
Brown, Bobby, 235
Brown, Cora A., 85-86, 88
Brown, Emil, 62, 88, 91, 98
Brown, Emza, 190
Brown, Glenn, 137, 225, 294
Brown, I. Pat, 87
Brown, Israel, 138
Brown, James F., 54, 120
Brown, Jim, xi, 146, 155, 159, 270
Brown, John, 54
Brown, Juanita, 88-91, 253
Brown, Kitty Young, 73
Brown, Lela, 97
Brown, Ozzie, 88
Brown, Pat, 98
Brown, Ruth Dixon, 346
Brown, Sarah Frame, 96
Brown, Willa Coulter, 233
Brown Forestry, 159
Browning, Joy, 256
Browning, Okey, 97-98
Browning, Rachel, 97
Broyles, Betty, 223
Brushy Fork, 69, 71, 331
Bubbie Hole, 58, 64, 255-256
Buck Fork, 121-122, 125
Buckhannon, 29, 35, 48
Buckhannon River, 35
Bucks Garden, 69
Bucktail High, 43
Bug Ridge, 104
Bull Run, 348
Bullfrogs, 137, 207, 293
Bunyan, Paul, 143, 152
Burge, Mae Sartin, 105
Burke, Billy, 132-133
Burns, Mildred Fisher, 47
Burns, Robert, 47
Burnsville, 33, 39, 41, 93, 351, 356
Butcher, Carl, 244
Butcher, Delila Keener, 163, 169, 210
Butcher, Elliott, 231, 240, 244
Butcher, James, 170
Butcher, Martha, 158, 169-171, 186-188, 192, 210, 254, 295
Butcher, Mildred Morris, 313
Butcher, Randall, 118-119, 210, 331
Butcher, Rose, 244

Butcher, Tyburtis, 137
Butcher, Warning, 244
Butcher, Willis, 266
Butler, Jack, 139, 177
Buzzard Roost Rocks, 320
Byfid School, 315
Byrne, Bill, 7-8, 14, 20, 24-25, 226, 297, 300
Byrnes, Eleanor Carte xii
Byrne, Rufus, 223
C. W. Wright Construction Company, 65
Cabin Creek, 262
Cacapon River, 257
Cal Fleming Tombstone, 18
Calhoun, John, 317, 321
Calhoun, Mary Goad, xii, 318, 321
Callahan, James, 39
Callahan, James H., 342, 349
Called Shot, 198
Camden, Johnson N., 7-8
Camp Claiborne, 63
Camp Gordon, 63
Camp Porcupine, 139
Camp Restawhile, 133, 135
Camp Wesley, 139
Canaan Valley, 106, 133
Canfield, Benjamin T., 115
Canfield, George, 115
Canfield, Harry, 115
Canfield, Kenny, 189
Canfield, Veda Garee, 114
Canfield Cemetery, 115-116
Captain Bull, 330
Captain Henry M. Beckley, 75
Captain John S. Sprigg, 251
Carl Morris Construction Company, 87
Carnifex Ferry, Battle of, 106
Carpenter, Benjamin, 299, 329
Carpenter, Harold, 4-5, 10
Carpenter, Howard, 219
Carpenter, Jerry, 299, 302, 306
Carpenter, Solomon, 10
Carpenter Fork, 101, 103-104, 106
Carr, Bill, 109
Carroll, Greg, xi, 334
Cart, Cynthia, 161
Cart, Levi, 79
Carte, Belle, 129, 217
Carte, Dana, 70, 316
Carte, Glenn, 173
Carte, Jink, 52
Carte, Judy, xii
Carte, Orlan, 133
Carte, Tom, 314
Carte, Wesley, 139, 191
Carvell, Kenneth, 264
Case, Howard, 26
Casey, Sue Dixon, 346
Cash, Cecil, 232
Cass Scenic Railroad, xi, 34, 38, 45-46
Cat Heaven, 101-102

Cedar Cliffs, 171, 237, 272
Cedar Creek, 47
Centennial Muskie, 239
Central Hotel, 7
Centralia, 6, 36, 97, 101, 251
Century Inn Restaurant, 166
Chaffee Branch, 45
Chamberlain, George, 120
Chamberlain, Kate, 129
Chandler, Wm. J., 17
Chapel Cemetery, 78-79
Charleston Gazette, xii, 6, 171, 238, 352, 376
Charleston Lumber Company, 165
Charleston Post Office, 322
Charleston Town Center, 141
Cheat Mountain, 34, 36
Cherry River Boom and Lumber Company, 5, 50
Chicago College of Medicine, 318
Chicago Connection, 33
Chicago Cubs, 198
Chicago World's Fair, 130
Chief Joseph, 175, 335
Chief Logan, 334
Chris Hollow, 2-3
Chuffy Run, 362-363
Civil War Atlas, 33, 76
Clarksburg, 4, 38, 55, 74, 82, 98, 300, 304
Clay, xi, 34, 58-59, 66-67, 73, 77-80, 85, 144, 167, 174, 190, 192, 213, 226, 235, 251, 255, 267, 299, 301, 311, 319, 322, 335
Clay County, 34, 58-59, 66, 73, 77, 79-80, 144, 167, 174, 190, 192, 213, 235, 255, 301, 319, 322, 335
Clay County Board of Education, 79
Clay County Courthouse, 192
Clay County High School, 255
Cleveland, Grover, 138
Cleveland School, 108, 138-139, 261
Cliffs, 68, 71, 93, 143, 149, 153-158, 171-172, 193, 237, 272, 291
Clifton, Carlin, 105
Clifton, Joe, 134, 219
Clifton, Oma Baughman, 93
Clifton, Oscar, 212
Clifton, Virgie Brown, 88
Climax Engine, 45
Coal and Coke Railroad, 244, 264
Coal Hollow, 362-363
Coalbed Run, 23, 97-98, 362, 364
Cobb Run, 362-363
Cochise, 327
Cochran, Steve, 213
Coffman, Gaylord, 58
Coffman, Guy, 57
Coffman, Jack, 57-59, 61-62, 107
Coffman, Ophie, 58
Coffman Motel, 60-62
Cogar, Clara Rose, 114
Cold Knob, 37

Cole, Tom, 208
Cole, Ed, 208
Cole, James B., 208
Cole, Walter, 208
College League, 65
Collins, Jasper, 41
Collins, Ronnie, 20
Columbia Gas, 322
Comeback Hole, 200
Comstock, Jim, 125
Concrete Steel Bridge Company, 55
Connelley, William, 67
Conrad, Roger, xi
Continental Navy, 121
Cook, Nell, 56
Coon Creek, 21, 111, 210-211, 226, 331-332
Coon Knob Interstate Maintenance Garage, 225
Cora Brown Bridge, 85-87, 91-92, 100, 108, 132, 207, 313, 354, 357, 363
Cora Frame Post Office, 61
Corley, Dana, 246
Corley, Dolsie Ramsey, 246
Cornstalk, 337
Costner, Kevin, 208
Cottle, 18-19, 137
Cotton-Hanlon Lumber Company, 262
Coulter, Ches, 59, 78, 87
Coulter, Glenn, 218, 232-233
Coulter Lumber Company, 218
Country Apple, 118
Cowen, John K., 7
Cowen Grade School, 9-10
Cowen High School, 9-10
Cowen Post Office, 9
Cowger, Junior, 211
Cowger, Mariah Duffield, 211
Cowger, Nancy Davis, 211
Cowger, Sam, 211-212
Cox, Darrel, 346
Cox, James, 45
Craft, George, 222
Craft, Walsie, 130, 315
Craigsville, xi, 5-6, 10, 16
Cranberry River, 132
Crayfish, 197-198, 269, 285, 293-294, 371
Crazy Horse, 335
Creasey, William D., 52, 120
Criss, Claude, 60
Criss, Jean, 60
Criss, Jim, 56
Criss, Paul, 275
Crites, Dencil, 36
Crites, Georgia, 9
Crites, Irene, xii
Crites, John, 104-105
Crites, Margaret Skidmore, 104-105
Crites, Naham, 105
Crites, Riley, 105
Crites Mountain, 41, 101-106

Crites Mountain Cemetery, 105-106
Crites Mountain School, 106
Crosby Rock, 145-146
Crosscut Saw, 97
Crossties, 35, 165, 265
CSX, 3-4, 6, 36
Cultural Center, 331
Cummings, James, 107
Cunningham, Dale, 95
Cunningham, Norman, 234
Curry, Scott, 57
Curt Rock, 231
Curtis, Clinton, 139, 296
Curtis, Mick, 139, 145
Curtis, Sarah Crosby, 145
Custer, George Armstrong, 303, 335
Cutlip, Esker, 103
Cutlip, Henry, 23
Cutlip, Herman, 345
Cutlip Cabin, 78
Cutright, Boyd, 35
Daugherty, Rebecca Lewis, 30
Dave Long Hill, 112
Davis, Becky Johnson, 322
Davis, Carl, 21
Davis, Henry Gassaway, 245
Davis, Squire George, 212
Davis, Steve, 6
Davis, Vaughn, 69, 102, 104
Davis, Wesley, 116
Davis, William Anderson, 212
Davis Knob, 206, 212, 236
Davis Memorial Presbyterian, 241
Davis Run, 241, 362, 364
Davis-Eakin Lumber Company, 38
Dean, Bracky, 26, 48
Dean, Byron, 266
Dean, Doyle, 165, 243, 246, 266-267, 321
Dean, E. B., 48
Dean, Ebb, 40
Dean, Elizabeth Teeter, 128
Dean, Evelyn, 267
Dean, Gene, 26
Dean, J. Clark, 128, 243, 246
Dean, Janet Leo Canfield, 266
Dean, John, sawmill, 95
Dean, John Morgan, 261, 263
Dean, Johnny, 190
Dean, Loring, 266
Dean, Lowell, 266
Dean, Mariah, 163, 318
Dean, Melissa Wood, 261
Dean, S. Clark, 108, 126, 128, 133
Dean, Sarah McMorrow, 178
Dean, Simeon, 108, 163, 261, 263
Dean, Warder P., 97, 185, 187, 189-190, 193-194, 196-197, 199-200, 261-263, 265-266
Dean, Warder S., 129, 162-165, 178, 246, 261, 266, 352
Deathwind, 336

Deep Hollow, 362-363
Delaware Indians, 330
Delung, Earl, 26
DeMoss, Jeff, 34
DeMoss, Luther, 35
DeMoss, Randy, 34
DeMoss, Rick, 34
DeMoss, Rose, xii
Depression, 42, 49, 56, 87, 93, 132, 237, 352
DeSoto, 113
Deveraux Lumber Company, 39
Diada Falls, 189
Diadda, Frank, 221-222
Diadda Run, 189, 221-222, 226
Diadda Spring Run, 189
Diado Falls, 189
Diatta Falls, 189
Diatter Run, 108, 154, 162, 189, 196, 205, 210, 213, 217, 219-220, 222-224, 226, 228, 234, 325, 330, 333, 362, 364
Dilley, Gary, 28, 35, 255
Dilley, Michael, 24, 53
Dixie, 18, 266
Dixon, Thomas, xii, 210, 341-346
Dixon, Bill, xii, 210, 346
Dixon, Blair, 243, 265, 346
Dixon, Bob, 346
Dixon, Elvira McCutchan, 341, 346
Dixon, Emma, 130
Dixon, Salina Riffel, 346
Dixon Cemetery, 346
Doddridge Run, 31
Dodrill, Big John, 26, 41, 63-64
Dodrill, Carl, 255
Dodrill, Charles T., 10, 29-30, 49, 62, 76, 299-300, 375
Dodrill, Sherman & Dale, 103
Dodrill, Elmer, 62-64, 255
Dodrill, Fannie, 137-138
Dodrill, Frank, 49
Dodrill, George, 44
Dodrill, John, 26, 41, 63-64
Dodrill, Rebecca, 30
Dodrill, Wendell, 57
Dodrill, William C., 20, 22-23, 299, 329, 333
Dodrill Cemetery, 32
Dodson, Elmer, 232
Dominion-Hope Gas Company, 196, 219
Downey, Cherie, xii
Draper, Mary Ingles, 307
Droop Mountain, 120
Dry Fork School, 224
Dudley Nottingham Plout, 167
Duffey, Connie, 127
Duffield, Anna Belle Goad, 317
Duffield, Florence, 240
Duffield, Frank, 221, 224
Duffield, Lillie, 244
Duffield, Rhoda, 240
Duffield, Rose, 239-240

Duffield, Samuel, 244
Duffield, Scott, 242
Duffield Cemetery, 240-241, 244
Duffield Eddy, 230, 238-239
Duffy, John, 165
Dundon, 68
Dunn, Bernice Dent, 118
Dunn, Bill, ix, 117-118, 129
Dunn, Byrne, 112, 116
Dunn, Gerald, 64, 114, 118, 146, 313, 376
Dunn, Hugh, 41
Dunn, Ida, 129
Dunn, J. Martin, 116, 120
Dunn, Jim, 107
Dunn, Paul, 116-117
Dunn, Ralph, 41
Dunn Brothers Grocery, 116
Dunn Cemetery, 117, 119
Duvall, Jack, 317
Duvall, Nettie Goad, 323
Eakin, Elizabeth Woods, 42
Eakin, Pete, 34, 36, 40, 42
Earp, Wyatt, 13
Eighty-second Division, 63
Elk River Baptist Church, 218, 313
Elk River Coal and Lumber Company, 34, 92-93, 162, 169, 210
Elk River Road, 354
Elk River Wildlife Management Area, 166, 242, 267
Elk Tunnel, 6
Elk Valley, 77, 250, 252, 262, 298, 300, 313
Elk Valley Baptist Association, 313
Elk Valley Soil District, 250
Elkins, xii, 22, 33, 45, 70, 133, 159, 337-338
Elliott, John, 80
Ely, Ralph, 42
Ely-Thomas Lumber Company, 42
English, Harry, 92
English Bill Dodrill, 25, 29-31, 329
Erbacon Road, 9, 101, 104
Eureka Church Cemetery, 174
Eureka Methodist Church, 212, 229, 236
Evans, Ann Rowan, x
Evans, Caroline, x
Evans, Dave, 237
Evans, Jack, 28
Evans, William, x
Evergreen Mining Company, 1, 5, 12, 29, 37
Exline, Goldie, 9
Facemire, Charley, 102
Facemire, Juanita Sartin, 105
Fairview Grade School, 331
Fajardo River, 208
Falls at Boggs, 27-28, 180, 255
Falls below Herold, 136, 143, 189, 191, 201, 260
Falls Mill, 52
Falls Rock, 143-145, 147, 152, 179, 199
Fast, Delia, 147

Fast, Jennings, 131, 321
Fast, Waitman, 47, 210, 214, 314
Fast Hollow, 147-149, 151-152, 177, 179, 183, 198, 205, 212, 362, 364
Fast Hollow Rock, 147-148, 152, 179, 198
Fast Knob, 147, 354
Fayette County, 167, 208
Fayetteville, 82, 94, 346
Federal Power Commission, 169
Feedtrough Run, 85, 94, 362, 364
Ferguson, Ewell, xii
Final Raft Down Birch, 261, 266
Fingerstone Rock, 171, 231
First National Bank of Webster Springs, 125
Fisher, Ann, 259
Fisher, Earl, 319
Fisher, Fred, 135, 259
Fisher Camp, 135, 201, 258
Fishing, 3, 20, 96, 135-136, 142, 148, 151, 157, 159, 163-164, 170, 174-178, 185-187, 189-190, 193-195, 197-204, 209, 219, 230, 237-239, 241, 243, 245, 247, 272, 276-277, 291, 321, 338, 354, 360, 376
Fitch, R. P., 82
Fitzwater, Omer, 45
Flanders Camp, 71, 331
Flash Floods, 253, 375
Flat Fork, 313
Flatfish, 209
Flatwoods, 36, 47, 109, 372
Fleming, Cal, 18
Fleming, Catherine Vanover, 18
Fleming, Henon, 8, 14-19
Fleming Cemetery, 18
Fletcher, Anna Mae Woods, 3-4
Floods of Birch, 97, 144, 151, 232, 246, 249-250
Floyd, John B., 73
Fockler School, 83-84
Fort Duquesne, 221
Fosbender, Julie, 338
Frame, Antonia, 210
Frame, Bailey, 52
Frame, Bernard Roy Jr., 62
Frame, Curtis, 231
Frame, Ella Johnson, 345
Frame, Ellis, 40
Frame, James, 62
Frame, John, 75
Frame, L. M., 75
Frame, Martha Davis, 174
Frame, Molly, 62
Frame, Nimmie Tanner, 231
Frame, Paul, 52, 56-57
Frame, Pearl, 174, 230-231
Frame, Penn, 61
Frame, Sarah Friend, 54
Frame, Thurman, 60, 62
Frame, Wade, 61
Frametown Elementary School, 345
Frametown Road, 147, 210, 213-214, 217,

221-222, 224-225, 314
Frank Given Hole, 93-94
Freda Wood Eddy, 190
Freda Wood Rock, 151-152
Freeman, Robert, 225
Friend, Ferrell, xii, 248, 333
Fulton, Ella, 72
Furbee, Connie, 115, 235-236
Gainer, Carl, 132-133
Galeton, Pa, 42-43
Gandee, Harold, 224
Gann, Ernest, 133
Gardner, Emma, 9
Garee, Dale, 114
Garee, John, 111-115
Garee, Naomi Cogar, 114
Garee, Zela Baughman, 115
Garee Low Gap, 112-113, 115, 122-123, 225
Garland, Jim, 65
Garrett County, 45
Garvin, Lewis, 17
Gassaway Hospital, 322
Gassaway Public Library, xii
Gauley Bridge, 52, 54, 82, 106, 208
Gauley Bridge Turnpike, 52, 106
Gauley Mills, 41
Gauley Mountain, 208
Gauley River, 2, 4, 6, 49, 68-69, 71, 133,
253-254, 330
Gauley Sanitarium, 9
Gawthrop, Frank, 26, 40-41
Gawthrop, John, 109
Gentry, Neal, xi, 138-140, 260, 308, 358
Geothermals, 211
Geronimo, 166, 335
Gettysburg, 43, 62, 120
Ghost Wagon, 29
Gibbons, Euell, 278
Gibson, Ben, 326, 332
Gibson, Betty, Birch Village, 56-57
Gibson, Betty, Canfield, 118
Gibson, Butch, 127
Gibson, Chad, 156
Gibson, James, 342-343
Gibson, Jimmy, 343, 348
Gibson, Jeremiah, 332
Gibson, John, 118
Gibson, Mabel, 127, 134
Gibson, Margaret, 343
Gibson, Matilda Cox, 343
Gibson, Matt, 118
Gibson, Mike, 135
Gibson, P. A., 343
Gibson, Phillip, 108
Gibson, Raymond, 225-226
Gibson, Richard, 109
Gibson, Sam, Birch Village, 56
Gibson, Sam (Unk), Herold, 148, 156
Gibson, Sandra, 156
Gibson, Staley, 343

Gibson, Steve, 162-163
Gillespie, Bill, xi, 141, 144, 146, 149-150, 155,
157-158, 172, 270
Gillespie, William H., 158
Gillespie Forestry Services, 158-159
Given, Arthur, 244
Given, Belle, 93
Given, Benton, 229-230, 237
Given, Bernard, 165, 266
Given, Clara Mae, 58
Given, Doug, 109, 241-242, 248
Given, Ed, 109
Given, Frank, 93-94
Given, Henry, 174, 226, 244, 331
Given, Isabel Pierson, 87
Given, Ivy, 169
Given, J. Arthur, 244
Given, Jasper, 79-80
Given, Lola, xii
Given, Mary Agnes Young, 79
Given, Phala Dean, 178
Given, Reynolds, 167-168, 237
Given, Robert, 108, 164, 235-237
Given, Theodore, 169, 313
Given Cemetery, 164, 218, 230, 233, 235-237
Glade Elementary School, 10
Glenville, 24, 76, 89, 128, 159, 166, 223, 262, 332
Glenville Normal School, 262
Glenville State College, 24, 76, 89, 128, 159,
223, 262, 332
Goad, George, 317, 321
Goad, Norman, 129, 311, 317-319, 322-323
Goad, Norman Robert, 318
Goad, Sarah, 317
Goad, Sarah Frame, 317
Graff, Jacob, 17
Graham, Kenny, 93
Graham, Wade, 93
Grand Old Opry, 97
Grannies Creek, 223
Grass Run, 81
Gray, Zane, 315
Great Depression, 352
Green Valley Coal Company, 65
Greenbrier River, 24, 80, 132-133, 154, 208, 252,
267, 337
Greene, Carroll, 4
Greenville, 65
Gregory, Oley, 107
Grey, Eddy, x, 164, 217, 275
Grist Mill, 27, 29, 59-60, 62, 108, 117, 128, 136,
238
Groves, Charles, 121
Grumman, 189, 202
GTR, xii
Guadalcanal, 114, 244
Gulf of Mexico, 332
Hall, Cap, 13, 15
Hall, John Strange, 310
Hall, Joseph, 301, 305, 309-310

Hammon, Neal O., 59
Hammons, Sampson, 16
Hamric, Curg, 245
Hamric, Don, 148, 238, 245, 247
Hamrick, Carsel, 115-116
Hamrick, Dale, 119
Hamrick, Hale, 137
Handschumacher, Dorothy, 6
Hardway, Ronald, 22, 376
Harold, Mayme, 9
Harper, Joe, 338
Harris, Frank, 26, 38
Harris, John Q., 119
Harris, Rosie, 233
Harrison, George, 45
Harrison County, 192, 309
Harrison Trail, 104
Harrouff, Bob, 59
Harrouff, Lola George, 59
Hart, Sharon, xi
Harvey, L. T., 58
Hatfield, Devil Anse, 18
Hawkins , T. H., 81
Hawkins, Lorraine, 255
Hawks Nest, 356
Hawthorne, Nathaniel, 344
Hayes, Lester Jr., 242, 245, 248
Hayes, Rutherford B., 52
Heisler engine, 45
Hellgrammite, 197, 294
Hemingway, Ernest, 143
Hemingway, Patrick, 143
Henderson, Lanky, 4, 8, 16
Henry, John, 167, 234
Henry Long Hollow, 103
Henry Young Monument, 81
Henshelwood, J. V., 92
Henshelwood Eddy, 92, 100
Herold, George A., 9, 15, 125-127
Herold, Viola Hill, 126
Herold Bridge, 131-132, 250, 255, 259, 357
Herold Homemakers Club, 133
Herold Quadrangle, 212
Herold-Frametown Road, 79, 211
Hickman, Brenda, xii, 78-79
Hickman, Delma Justus, 60
Hickman, Dolly, 11
Hickman, Hamilton Burton, 77, 79-80
Hickman, Henry Preston, 78-79
Hickman, Rodney, 109
Hickman, Sarah Jane Young, 79-80
Hickman, Virginia Tinnel, 60
Hickman Ridge, 319
Hickory Flats, 36, 101-104
Hickory Flats School, 104
Hill, Rebecca L., 76
Hines, S. S., 17
Hines, Will, 116
Hinkle, Beecher, 10
Hinkle, Ed, 47

Hinkle, Eleanor, 47
Hinkle, Jacob, 17
Historic Preservation Office, 331, 333
Hitt, Mary Ann, 309-310
Hivick, Madalene, 18, 20
Hoard, Junior, 116
Holbrook, Guy, 255
Holbrook, Harry, 35
Holbrook Fork, 35
Holcomb, Rex, 104
Holister, Eva, 9
Hollandsworth, Ella, 255
Hollandsworth, Roger, 331
Holly Fork of Long Run, 119
Holly River, 36, 96, 298-299, 301, 303, 307, 309, 353
Home Hotel, 4
Homewood sandstone, 153-154
Hookersville, 83, 125
Hoover, Byrne, 34
Hoover, Leht, 41
Hoover Post Office, 225
Hope Natural Gas Company, 196, 218
Horan, A. J., 14
Horan, Emily Scott, 54, 61
Horry Georgetown Technical College, 223
Hosey, Conley, 34
Houghton, Virgil, 319
Hoylman, George, 108-109, 163-164, 261
Huckleberry Rock, 145, 199
Huff, Doug, xii
Huffman, A. E., 39
Huffman, J. R., 39
Huffman, Jacob, 107
Huffman, L. J., 120
Huffman, Levi J., 57
Huffman, Roy, xii
Humphreys, Clinton, 104
Hungry Spring Run of Bear Run, 120
Huntington, xi, 10, 200, 213, 351
Hupmobile, 26
Hurley, Elizabeth, 64
Hurricane Hazel, 255-256
Hutchinson, J. M., 53, 68, 80, 300
Hyde, Arnout Jr., 256
Hymes, John Jr., 24, 76, 128, 223, 241, 332
Iroquois, 334, 336-337, 340
Isenhart, E. J., 17
Island Creek Coal Company, 11
Jack Johnston Rock, vii
Jacks Run, 362-363
Jackson, Amos, 106-107
Jackson, Angie, 106
Jackson, Bertha, 213
Jackson, Byrd, 256
Jackson, David, 106
Jackson, Dick, 213-214
Jackson, Dottie Snyder, 107
Jackson, Ira, 119
Jackson, Okey, 118

Jackson, Oleta, 106
Jackson County, 105
Jackson, Henry, 300-301, 310
Jackson School, 107, 117
James, Bill, 165
James, Ellott, 165
James, Fred, 109
James, Jesse, 221
James, Jill, 237
James, Lowell, 156
James, Patty Cowger, 211-212
James, Roy, 235-236
James, Scott, 212
James Knob, 212
Jamestown, 329
Jarvis, Fred, 116
Jean, Norma, 377
Jennings Post Office, 257
Jerryville, 2, 5
Jewish Wailing Wall, 240
Jews-harps, 348
Jitterbug, 178
Johnboats, 208
Johnson, Barrett, 233
Johnson, Bob, author's brother, 136-137, 197
Johnson, Bob, logger, 138-139, 241
Johnson, Carmel, 131
Johnson, Carmine, 31, 202
Johnson, Carolyn Gibson, 127
Johnson, Floyd, 129
Johnson, George S., 127
Johnson, Isabel Young, 91, 126
Johnson, Jane Given, 164
Johnson, Justin, 136
Johnson, Louis, 126-127, 130, 134, 164
Johnson, Mabel, 133
Johnson, Rebekah, 135
Johnson, Rob, x, xii, 132, 174-177, 185-187,
    189-190, 192-194, 197-198, 201, 241, 284
Johnson, Travis, 136, 174-176
Johnson, Walt, 136, 173-174
Johnson, William, 164, 235
Johnson Branch, 362-363
Johnson Campground, 109, 204
Johnson Cemetery, 164, 235
Johnston, Earl, 94
Johnston, Frank, xii, 106, 118
Johnston, Jack, 94, 100, 153
Johnston, Lee, 95, 117
Johnston, Orva, 95, 118, 129
Joins, Robert, 213
Jones, Randall, 93
Jucovich, Sarah Frame Walker, 174
Justice, Matthew, 62
Justus, Don, 116
Justus, Howard, 58
Kanawha Black flint, 333
Kanawha County, 16, 21, 30, 78, 135, 244, 306,
    336, 375
Kanawha River, 30, 223, 251, 262, 332, 355, 375

Kanawha Valley Hospital, 317-318
Karickhoff, David, xi
Kate Run, 362-363
Keaton, Arnold, 213
Keeley Construction, 83-84
Keener, Andrew, 163, 214, 220
Keener, Berkley, 207
Keener, Bobby, 214, 332
Keener, Charles D., 75
Keener, Charley, 129, 190
Keener, John, 75
Keener, Nettie, 214
Keener, Pershing, 190, 210, 214
Keener, Samuel, 163
Keener, Tilden, 243
Keener, Willis, 129
Keener Eddies, 177, 196, 202, 220, 230
Keener's Ridge, xi-xii, 23, 76, 85, 87-88, 90,
    92-93, 96-97, 126, 128, 130, 132, 161, 164, 170,
    178, 210, 217, 229, 235, 265, 267, 311, 314-315,
    317, 331, 341-343, 345-346
Keener's Ridge Community Church, 317
Keener's Ridge Road, 76, 217, 229, 341
Kelford, Teri, 244
Keller, Andrea, 333
Kelly, Charles, 95
Kent, Chris, 151
Kerns, Chester, 19
Kessler, Doctor Dan, 8, 10, 41
Key, Jimmy, 65
Kiger, Sally, 119
Kimberling, Arlene Jackson, 213
King, Clara, 214
King, Ruth, 14, 16-19
King Tut, 146-147
Kinslow, Dee, 35
Kirkham, R. F., 83-84
Knapps Creek, 132
Kniceley, Loran, 109
Knight, George, 216
Knight, Lowell, xii
Knight, Mabelle, 216
Knight, Nancy, xii
Knottingham, Jack, 75
Korean War, 114
Kreutz, Phillip, 105
Kruk, John, 65
Ku Klux Klan, 312
Kuhl, Erma James, 217
Kuhl, Suzanne, 244
Kuhl, Virgil, 217
Lamarre, Lora, 333
Lanes Bottom, 78
Laurel Creek of Elk River, 3, 101
Laurel Run School, 107
Lazy Ike, 245
Lazy Ned, 233-234
Leaning Beech Coon, 206
Leaning Hemlock Rock, 151-152
Leatherwood Eddy, 195, 230-232, 239-240

Leatherwood Ford, 226, 229, 231, 237, 244
Leatherwood Road, 210, 226, 229, 237
Leatherwood Run, 167, 174, 189, 195, 205, 210, 216, 219, 221, 226, 228-230, 233-237, 240, 254, 268, 276, 327, 356, 362, 364
Leatherwood School, 233, 237
Leatherwood Shoal, 203
Lee, Robert E., 62, 341
Lee Jack Bass, 193-194
Lee Jack Plout, 157-158, 182, 191, 193, 213, 276
Left Fork of Holly, 256, 353
Legend of Strange Creek, 96, 297, 320
Leslie, Clyde Sr., 10
Leslie, John, 11
Leslie, Larry, 11
Leslie Bros, 10-11
Levi Cart Cemetery, 79
Lewis, Andrew Jr., 30
Lewis, Anna Lee, xii
Lewis, Betty, 37
Lewis, Charles W., 313
Lewis, Dale, 161, 177, 206
Lewis, Fannie, 214, 317
Lewis, George, 30
Lewis, Illene Cutlip, 51, 345
Lewis, Jim, xii, 231
Lewis, John, 317
Lewis, Margaret Wright, 312
Lewis, Ruth, xii, 161
Lewis, Thomas, 30
Lewis, Willie, 97, 121, 311-317, 323
Lewis, William, 30
Lewis County, 7, 42, 309
Lewisburg, 86
Libbey-Owens-Ford, 212
Lick Fork, 35
Lima Locomotive Works, 37, 44
Little Bighorn, 303, 335
Little Birch Mountain, 101, 106
Little Birch School, 106, 117
Little Black Fork of Shaver, 338
Little Buffalo Creek, 111, 225
Little Laurel Creek, 42, 313
Little Otter, 262
Lockwood, 52, 329
Locust Stump, 118, 225, 294
Locust Stump School, 225
Logan County Wildcats, 75
Logan High School, 76
Lombard, Louis, 140
Lone Grave, 78, 81
Long, Austin, 240
Long, Dave, 112
Long, Harold, 106, 132-133
Long, Harry, 232
Long, James, 111-112, 197
Long, Patty, 113, 138
Long Cemetery, 112-113
Long Hole, 95-96, 196
Long Run, 106, 111-113, 115-116, 118-122, 124,

129, 160, 197, 210, 212, 225, 250, 261, 313, 332, 355, 357, 362, 364
Long Run Baptist Church, 112, 120-122, 313
Long Shoal, 166, 175-178
Long,Willis, 166-167, 187-188, 232, 318
Longacre, Glenn Jr., xii, 18, 39
Longstreet, James, 341
Lost Tribes of Israel, 339
Louis, Joe, 97
Louisa, Melcina, 54
Lower Birch, ix, 9, 27, 51, 95, 125, 155, 157-158, 162, 166, 169-170, 172, 187, 193, 196-197, 200, 203, 205-207, 212, 215, 217, 230-231, 236-237, 239, 242, 254, 256, 272, 293, 295, 318, 331, 356, 361
Lower Freeport sandstone, 118
Lower Keener Eddies, 196, 230
Lower Mill Creek, 217, 362, 364
Lower Turn Hole, 139, 169, 196, 203, 205, 240-242, 248, 351, 354-356
Lucas, Tim & Dawn, 232
Lyd Wilson Ridge, 102
Lyda Wilson Ridge, 101-102
Lynch, Dana, xi
Macal River, 208
Madison Run, 91, 362-364
Magoun, Bessie Mae Goad, 317
Manchin, A. James, 70
Margaret Johnson Rock, 151-152, 250
Marion Powel Shovel Company, 46
Marsh, Anna, 242
Marshall, Bert, 26
Marshall, Erie King, 214
Marshall, George, 213-214, 217
Marshall, Jim, 213
Marshall, Russ, 26
Marshall County, 336
Marshall University, xi, 207
Martin, Hudson, 300-301
Martin, Joel, 310
Martin, Louie, 65-66, 102
Martin, Ola Johnson, 164
Martin, Tony, 65
Matheny, Pierce, 78
Matterhorn, 186
May Fork, 35
McClung, Fielding, 81
McCoplin, May, 9
McCormick, Jim, xi
McCourt, Hans, 4
McCoy, Buck, 28
McCoy, Dave, 65-66
McCoy, Kathryn, 17, 19
McCoy, Maggie, 29
McCoy, Merl, 318
McCoy, Moody, 45
McCoy, Richard Scott, 73
McCoy, W. L., 28
McCoy, William, 73
McCreary Cemetery, 336

McCreary Cemetery Preservation Foundation, 336
McElwain, Charles, 3
McGraw, John T., 5
McGuffey, W. H., 234, 376
McGuffey Readers, 234
McGuire, P. J., 17
McKinley, William, 52
McLaughlin, Dennis, 64
McLaughlin, J. H., 316
McLaughlin, James H., 120-121
McLaughlin, Marco, 57
McMillion, James, 80
McMorrow, Camden, 165, 266
McMorrow Buck, 243
McPherson, Joe, 2
McQueen, George A., 317
McQueen, Nimmie Goad, 323
Mead-Speer Lumber Company, 39, 47, 257
Meadow Bridge, 10
Meadow Fork, 1-3, 11-12, 59, 362-363
Meadow Fork Road, 11
Meadville, 79, 257
Meeks, Ed, 275
Middle Ground Route, 307, 309
Middle Ridge Passway, 213
Middle Run, 79, 91, 119, 163, 174, 196-198, 205, 207, 209-220, 225, 233-234, 236, 238, 313, 362, 364
Middle Run Baptist Church, 163, 196, 214, 217
Middle Run Cemetery, 79, 119, 209-211, 213, 218, 236
Middle Run School, 211-212, 233
Middlebrook, Va., 342
Middletown, Ct., 127
Milky Way candy, 140
Mill Creek-Erbacon Road, 69
Miller, Chris, 2
Miller, Ernest, 9
Miller, Paul, 49
Miller, Ralph, 2
Miller, Sampson N., 32
Milnes,Gerry, xii, 20, 22-23, 26, 33-35, 70
Ming Run, 362-363
Mingo Flats, 339
Mingo Oak, 275
Mississippi Delta, 149
Mississippi River, 7
Missouri Run, 33, 36-37, 104
Moccasin Rangers of Cowen, 7
Model A Ford, 26-27, 93, 112, 123, 129, 311, 321
Model T Ford, 26-27, 112, 123, 129
Mohawks, 334
Mohicans, 128, 253
Mollahan, Eck, 26
Mollahan, Herb, 44
Mollahan, Okey, 34, 41
Mollahan, Curtis, 267
Mollohan, George, 24, 32
Mollohan, Ira, 98

Mollohan, Jack, 56-57
Mollohan, Roy, 56-57, 60
Mollohan, Vina, 98
Mollohan Drive, 60, 256
Monongahela National Forest, 337
Monterville, 16
Montgomery, 24, 71, 107, 235, 346
Morgan, John G., 306
Morgantown, 43, 82, 139
Morley, 244
Morris, xi, 23, 52, 87-88, 195, 218, 312-313, 329
Morris, Doug, 195
Morris, Karen, xi
Morris, Margaret, 329
Morris, Phillip, 52
Morton, Amanda Young, 78
Morton, E. H., 16
Morton, Francis, 78, 80, 236
Morton, Joe, 195
Morton, Shirley, 29
Moundsville, 336
Mount Eagle, 43
Mount Everest, 11
Mount Nebo, 146, 159
Mount Olive Church Cemetery, 178
Mouth of Birch, ix, 13, 38, 107-108, 125, 128, 157, 167, 174, 185, 189, 195-196, 201, 221, 229-230, 239, 241-246, 258, 263-265, 292, 307, 321, 354-355, 363
Mouth of Birch Eddy, 196, 241, 243, 354
Mouth of Middle Run, 197-198, 205, 207, 209, 213, 215-217, 238
Mouth of Seneca, 338
Mouth of Strange Creek, 300-301, 304, 306-307
Mower Lumber Company, 46
Muddlety Creek, 5-6, 69, 71, 80, 125, 331
Muddy Creek, 24, 69, 80
Mullins, Butch, 72
Mullins, Mike, 72
Mumble-the-Peg Township, 79-80
Mumblethepeg, 79-80, 301
Mummelpeck Creek, 80
Murphy, Annie, xii
Murphy, Bill, 87
Murphy, Edmund, 137
Murphy, Kathy, 89
Murphy, Leonard, 137
Murphy, Margaret Shaver, 210
Murphy, Mark, 58, 65, 89, 93-94, 96-98
Murphy, Mike, 98
Murphy, Nora King, 216
Murphy, Vernon Jr., 52, 58, 65-66, 87, 89, 91, 98
Myers, Phyllis Fisher, 135, 259
Nance, Kenny, 213
Nantucket Island, 121
Napier, Bob, 222, 224
Napier, Rita Tyo, 222
National Park Service, 51, 86, 92, 96, 207, 223, 351, 353, 357

National Register of Historic Places, 107
National Weather Service, 253, 375
Natural Resources Committee, 133
Nauman, Gene & Jane, 138
Naylor, Tim, 163
Neal, Jake, 26, 47
Neal, Sarah, 133
Neihardt, John, 335
Neil, Beulah Brown, 88, 92, 345
Nettles, Brad, 162
Nettles, Harry, 206
New Hope Baptist Church, 88, 312
New River, 132, 208, 293, 340, 356
New York Yankees, 65, 130
Newman, Paul, 208
Newton, Sir Isaac, 187
Nez Perce, 335
Nicholas, Steve, xii
Nicholas County Commission, 54, 250
Nicholas County Courthouse, 80
Nicholas County High School, 65
Nicholas County Population, 372
Nicholas County School Board, 313
Nichols, Benjie, 156, 167, 171, 195, 231, 239
Nichols, Jean, 167
Nichols, Woody, 239
Nidiffer, Mike & Judy, 244
North Pole Ice Company, 155
Northcraft, Granville, 91
Northern Cheyenne, 303
Northern Panhandle of West Virginia, 339
Nottingham, Bennie, 216, 232
Nottingham, Charley, 168
Nottingham, Dudley, 167-168, 173, 231
Nottingham, Fred, 168, 320-322
O. K. Corral, 13
O Brien, Adam, 20, 32
O Dell, Irving, 129
Odell, Granville, 55
Oglala Sioux, 335
Ohio Infantry, 53, 75
Ohio River, 221, 253, 256, 272, 329
Ohio State University, 272
Ohio Valley, 336, 338-339
Old Moon, 137
Ontario, 7, 69, 337
Otter Hole, 362-363
Outline Map of Braxton County, 225
Packard, 26
Paddy Ridge, 192
Paddy Run, 83
Painter Fork, 101, 104, 234
Painter Rocks, 71, 331
Paintiff, Jim, 232
Panther Lick Branch, 25
Pardee-Curtin Lumber Company, 39, 49, 214
Pardue, Eleanor, 232
Parkersburg, 7, 266
Pauley, Tom, xi, 207
Pearl Harbor, 37, 48

Pellot, Juanita Dixon, 346
Pembroke, R. H., 243
Pendleton County, 128, 338
Pennsylvania Lumber Museum, 42, 46
Perrine, Delbert, 104
Perrine, Larry, 2-3
Perrine, Lewis, 165
Perrine Ford, 164-165, 169, 235
Peters Creek, 31, 68-69
Pettit, Joe, 116
Pfister, Phillip, 187
Phillips, David L., 76
Phillips, Jack, 109
Pierce Arrow, 123
Pierson, Burton, 207, 226, 242
Pierson, George R., 126-127
Pierson, Grover, 224
Pierson, Hampton, 91
Pierson, Jim, 118
Pierson, Jonathan, 221
Pierson, Kitty Cowger, 91
Pierson, Ocie Given, 224
Pierson, Waitman, 94, 212
Pierson, Walter, 177, 203
Pierson, William R., 220, 224
Pierson,John, 222
Pig Shoal, 170-171, 173, 187
Pig Shoal Plout, 170
Pilegge, Betty Clifton, 131
Pillar Rock, 158, 215
Pilot Knob, 101, 104
Pilot Knob Road, 104
Pilots Quartet, 57
Piney Island, 194-195
Pinnacle Rock, 158
Pinnell, Brenda, 170
Pinney, Eddie, 66, 248
Pittsburgh Pirates, 130
Plantation Fork, 121
Pletcher, John, 172
Pletcher, Skeeter, 172, 196, 230
Pletcher Pontiac Company, 172
Plymouth Rock, 144
Pocahontas County, 34, 111
Pocahontas Trail, 329
Point Mountain, 12, 142, 331
Point Pleasant, 20, 25, 30, 336-337
Polemic Run, 57, 93, 102, 107-108, 212, 313
Poplar Creek, 20, 22, 25, 32, 49, 62, 276, 362-364
Popovich, Paul, 10
Posey, Andrea Smith, 233, 237
Posey, Mart, 44
Potomac River, 45, 338
Potter County, Pa., 42
Pound Gap, Va., 14, 17
Powell, Evelyn Dixon, 346
Powell, William, 68-69, 93
Powell Creek, 34, 49, 54-56, 58, 62, 67-71, 73,
    75-76, 84, 250, 307-308, 331, 362-364
Powell Mountain, xii, 6, 34, 45, 49, 52-54, 56,

59, 66-84, 87, 93, 102, 154, 192, 212, 236, 295, 298, 300-301, 305, 307-308, 312-313, 316, 331
Product Distributors of Little Birch, 106
Pudding Stones, 142-143
Putnam County, 170
Queen Shoals, 251, 254
Quinwood, 41
Rainelle, 17, 65
Ramp Run, 101
Randolph, Roger, 170-171
Randolph County, 54, 159, 299, 302, 338-339
Rapala, 186-187
Ratcliff, Trace, 27
Raven Eddy, 142, 158, 181, 185, 190, 206-208, 213, 215, 228
Ravenswood, 95, 346
Reger, Blanche Tinnel, 48
Reger, Emery, 48
Reger, Philip, 301
Reger, Roscoe, 48, 50
Reger, Tom, 26, 48, 50
Reip, Betty Dent, 233
Reip, Bland, 234
Reip, Donna, 224, 230, 377
Reip, Newton, 224
Reip, Ray, 221-222, 333
Remage, J. C., 243
Revolutionary War, 20, 30, 32, 209, 309-310, 337-338
Reynolds Rock, 167-168, 237
Ricci, Lon, 213
Rich, Domineck, 38
Rich Fork, 221, 362-363
Richardson, Tom, 213
Riddle, Bill, 19
Riddle, Elmore, 216
Riddle, Gaylord, 216
Riddle, Myrtle Roberts, 27
Riddle, Sharon, 19
Riddles,Nida, 216
Riffel, Hampton, 131, 219, 321
Riffel, Launa Fast, 147, 321
Riffel, Perry, 164
Riffel Eddy, 230-232
Riffel-Lewis Cemetery, 231, 317
Riffle, John, 230
Riffle, Larry, 2
Riffle, Randy, 172
Right Fork of Holly, 256, 353
Ritchie County, 217
River Runt, 209
Road Fork of Skyles Creek, 20, 33, 363
Road Run, 102, 107, 115, 117, 210, 212
Roane County, 79
Robert Given Cemetery, 164, 235-237
Roberts, Dick, 29
Roberts, Fred, 22, 70
Roberts, Glen, 29
Roberts, Maston, 70
Roberts, Neal, 22

Roberts, Ruby Boggs, 29, 255
Roberts, Skip, 29
Roberts, William, 19
Roche, Paul, x, 191, 208
Rockwell, Norman, 311, 320
Rollyson, Martin, 241
Rose, Cleat, 57
Rose, Fielding, 20
Rose, Goldie Carpenter, 102, 104
Rose, Isaac, 20, 32, 220
Rose, Jack, 56-57, 59
Rose, Julianna, 163, 220
Rose, Margaret Forsythe, 20
Rose, Martha Persinger, 220
Rose, Sarah Jane, 220
Rose, Strosie, 106
Rose, William, 20, 163, 220
Rose Hill Methodist Church, 103
Rose Hill School, 88
Rose Run, 53, 220, 362-363
Rosecrans, William, 73, 77
Rowan, Eddie, x
Rowh, Benson, 22
Rowh, Rose Barnett, 22
Royal Fern Rock, 183
Royal Gorge, 149, 151-152, 284
Royal Gorge Rock, 151-152
Runion Ridge, 77, 80, 322
Ruppert, Jacob, 130
Ruth, Babe, 130, 198, 352
Salt Works, 63
Samples, Corbett, 244
Samples, Elliott, 242
Sampson, Laura, 169
Sanders, Elizabeth Wiggins, 220
Sanson, Lise, 24, 32
Sartin, Asenath Nesselrotte, 105
Sartin, George, 105-106
Sartin, Marion, 106
Sartin, Myrtle Wines, 106
Sartin, Robert, 106
Sassafras River, 270
Savage, Jesse & William, 87, 298
Savagetown, 298
Scenic Birch River Sign, 124
Scenic River Study, 357
Scenic Rivers System, 51, 86, 92, 207, 223, 353, 358
Schiefer, Linn, 316
Schuemacher, Phillip, 16
Sciles River, 33
Scootin Falls, 27
Scott, Richard, 54, 73
Searfoss, James, 97
Selbyville, 48
Seneca Creek, 338
Seneca Indians, 338
Seneca Rocks, 338
Seneca Rocks Discovery Center, 338
Seneca Rocks Post Office, 338

Seneca Trail, 337-338
Seng Run, 102
Sergeant York, 63, 376
Sexton, John, 213
Shaffer, David, 210
Shakespeare, 118
Shanty Branch, 56, 73, 75-76, 78, 331
Shaver, Henry, 197, 209-210
Shaver, James, 209
Shaver, Keith, 225
Shaver, Margaret Butcher, 197, 209
Shaver, Teddie, 315
Shaver Eddy, 197
Shavers Mountain, 16
Shawnee Hills Center, 232
Shawnee Indians, 24, 329-330, 334-337
Shawver, Beldon, 235-236
Shawver, Jerald, 174, 235-236
Shay, Ephraim, 37
Shenandoah Valley, 342
Sigman, May, 36
Silitch, Elizabeth, x, 123, 141, 210
Silitch, Peter, x, 123, 141, 210, 298, 300, 308
Silk Run, 362-363
Simmons, Harold, xi
Simon, Hilda, 186, 377
Singleton, Page, 109
Sitting Bull, 335
Sizemore, D. H., 17
Skidmore, Hilliard, 120
Skidmore Addition, 252
Skidmore Cemetery, 122
Skyles, Jacob, 13
Skyles Creek, 13, 20, 23, 32-35, 70, 103, 255-256, 362-364
Slabcamp Run, 85, 97, 243, 265, 341, 362, 364
Slack, John M. Jr., 353
Slaughter, Dolly Butcher, 244
Slaven Cabin Road, 16
Smallmouth, 148, 164, 175-178, 193-194, 196-198, 200, 269, 292-293, 321, 327, 370
Smiley Face, 103
Smith, Arimetha, 217
Smith, Clyde, 4
Smith, Dolly, 218
Smith, Erman, 217, 219, 226
Smith, John, 9
Smith, Lon, 196, 217-219
Smith, Mickey, 10
Smith, Opal Ruth Goad, 318
Smith, S. Austin, 244
Smith, Spurgeon, 218, 232
Snodgrass, Ralph, 213
Snow, Ron, 29
Sommerville, Boonie, xi
South Branch, 338
South Charleston, 115, 240, 340
Spencer, Ruby Reger, 48
Spielberg, Steven, 354
Sprague, John W., 53

Spring Hill Mausoleum, 323
Spring Ridge, 104
Spring Ridge Road, 104
Squaw Honeysuckle, 277
St. Albans, 139, 318, 339
St. Louis Cardinals, 130
St. Thomas Catholic Church, 241
Starbuck, David, 122
Starbuck, Edward, 121
Starbuck, Martha Barnett, 122
Starbuck, Mathew, 121
Starbuck, Paul, 121
State Archives, 106
State Historic Preservation Office, 331
State Magazine Section, 6
State Natural Streams Preservation Act, 86, 92, 106, 109, 132, 358
State Road Bureau, 55
State Road Commission, 82, 225, 262
State Soil Conservation Committee, 4
Statue of Liberty, 136
Stavis, J. H., 126
Stearns-Knight, 26
Steer Creek, 222
Stephens City, Va., 267
Stephenson,Mary Jane, 261
Stokes, Lyle, xi, 374
Stokes, Rosie Lewis, 312, 315-316
Stolzman, Pat Clifton, 134
Stonecoal Lake, 242
Stonewall Jackson Grill, 72
Stonewall Jackson Highway, 56, 72
Stonewall Jackson Hospital, 210
Strait of Gibraltar, 144
Strange, Ann Hitt Martin, 305, 309
Strange, William, 68, 87, 96, 297-310, 329
Strange Creek Coal and Coke, 261
Strange Creek United Methodist Church, 320
Strickland, Dean, 166
Strickland, Valeria Dean, 164-165, 171, 210
Strickland Low Gap, 97
Stroud, Adam, 6
Stroud, Peter, 329
Strouds Creek, 5-6
Studebaker, 26
Sturdivant, B. B., 41
Stutler, Boyd, 28
Stutler, Bud, 10
Stutz, 26, 123
Sugar Camp Run, 79, 161, 306
Sugar Creek, 218, 300, 306, 309
Sugar Creek Cemetery, 218
Sullivan, Charlie, 213
Summersville Little League, 65-66
Summersville Reservoir, 330
Sunset Memorial Park, 240
Sutton, John D., 74, 77, 122, 252, 300, 377
Sutton Bridge, 6, 251
Sutton Dam, 10, 253, 258, 293, 351, 354
Sutton High School, 113

Sutton Hospital, 88
Sutton Lake, xi, 6, 299
Sutton Public Library, 113
Sutton Run, 113, 363-364
Svet, Don, 10
Swandale, 262
Swindall, Dock, 15
Talbert, Clyde, 9
Tanner, Christina, 115
Tanner, Tim, 114
Tate Creek, 245, 318
Tate Creek Road, 245
Tecumseh, 337
Teets, Cleo, 168, 232
Teets, Kevin, xi
Teets, Leota, 318
Teets, Medford, ix, 170, 216, 233, 254, 267
Teets, Ray, 206
Teets, Royce, 177
Teets, Thelma Butcher, 169, 254
Tennessee, 10, 346
Tenney, James, 197-198, 201
Tenney, Peggy, 122, 197, 209
Tenney, Roger, 93, 122, 197
Tesla, 41, 102, 107, 225, 316
Tesla, Nikola, 102
Tesla Post Office, 102
Tesla Road, 102, 107
Tetrick, Enoch, 243
Thayer, Del, xii
Thomas, John, 95
Thomas, Randall, 37
Thomas, Wellington, 42
Thomas Walsh of Grafton, 243
Tidewater Grill, 141
Tilden Buck, 243
Tinnel, Daisy, 60
Tinnel, Ernest, 60, 98
Tinnel, Frank, 71
Tinnel, Joe, 59
Tinnel, Morgan, 59
Tinney, Burl, 255
Tioga Coal Corporation, 45
Tioga County, Pa., 48-49
Tioga Lumber Company, 45, 49
Titanic, 148, 208
Tokobelloke, 337
Tollgate Rocks, 3
Trail of Tears, 339
Tributaries of Birch River, 35, 94, 361-362, 364
Trinity Baptist Church, 58, 250
Truman, Harry, 134
Truman, Merle, 135
Tucker, Mel, 118, 224
Tucker County, 7, 89
Tug Fork, 71, 84
Turkey Creek, 297-300, 302, 338
Turkey Run, 300, 303-305, 309
Turner, A. S., 86
Turner Hill, 322

Twistville P. O., 225
Twistville Road, 224-226
Two Lick Run, 49, 331, 363
Tyo, Leonard, 222
Tyree, Retta Faye Murphy, 210
Tyree, Winifrede Ballengee, 139
U. S. Army, 63, 335
U. S. Forest Service, 338
U. S. Postal Service, 7, 102, 244
U. S. Senate, 7
U. S. Soil Conservation Service, 3, 233
U. S. Treasury, 201
Uldrich, Tom, 108
Underwood, Harry, 109
University of New Hampshire, 146
University of New Mexico, 335
University of Virginia, 117, 234, 376
Upshur County, 23, 36, 48, 104, 302, 309
USGS, 251-253, 257, 354
Valley Head, 16
Valparaiso University, 318
Vance, Tom, xii
Vaughn, Irma Jean Goad, 318
Virginia, State of, 300
Virginia General Assembly, 30
Wadepuhl, Berniece Brown, 88
Waggy, Henry, 103
Waggy, William, 103
Waggy Coal Company, 38
Waggy Post Office, 103
Wainville, 8, 10, 36
Walker, Bailey, 91, 93, 97
Walker, Curt, 129, 137
Walker, Lucy, 313
Walker Cemetery, 87, 92, 97, 317
Walkersville, 52
Walleye, 95, 109, 163, 167, 178, 200, 209, 245, 293, 354, 357, 370
Walnut Grove Methodist Church Cemetery, 79, 319
Walnut Grove United Methodist Church, 19, 255
Walsh, James, 130
Walsh, Jim, 129
Walsh, Thomas, 129-130
Ward, Thomas, 89, 91
Washington, George, 340
Washington Monument, 136
Wattsville, 77
Wayne County, 154
Webster, Daniel, 7
Webster County, xi, 1, 4, 7-10, 14-19, 21, 23-24, 27, 29, 32, 35, 37, 39-40, 48-49, 71, 78, 101, 125, 142, 158, 214, 329, 331, 343, 353, 363, 372, 376
Webster County Board of Education, 8
Webster County Circuit Court, 14, 16
Webster County Courthouse, 16
Webster County Development Commission, 29
Webster County High School, 10, 71

Webster County Population, 372
Webster Glades, 7
Welsh Glades, 3-4
West Virginia & Pittsburgh Railroad Company, 4
West Virginia, State of, 76, 333, 375, 377
West Virginia Bar Association, 117
West Virginia Department of Agriculture, 117
West Virginia Department of Highways, xi, 29, 51, 67
West Virginia Division of Culture & History, xi, 334
West Virginia Division of Environmental Protection, xi, 154, 364
West Virginia Division of Forestry, 159, 267
West Virginia Division of Natural Resources, 3, 95, 166, 286, 292, 351-352, 376
West Virginia Encyclopedia, 125, 298, 300, 304
West Virginia Floods, 253, 352, 375, 377
West Virginia Fox Hunters Association, 322
West Virginia Geological Survey, xi, 3, 11, 16, 50, 71, 98, 118, 131, 154-155, 211, 221, 240, 378
West Virginia Legislature, 9, 106, 132
West Virginia University, 39, 43, 114, 117, 159, 276, 376-377
West Virginia University College of Law, 117
Western Field Shotgun, 319
Western Maryland Railroad, 45
Westfall, Burl, 108
Weston, 9, 38, 42, 46-47, 52, 82, 106, 210
Weston-Gauley Bridge Turnpike, 52, 55, 74, 84, 308
Wetzel, Lewis, 336
Wheeler, Lois, 54
Wheeling Area Historical Society, xii
White, Herb & Ann, xii
White, I. C., 155, 378
White Cemetery, 192
White Oak Fork Road, 59
Whittaker Station, 45
Whittier, John Greenleaf, 344
Wickline, Monty, 148
Widen High School, 58
Williams Branch, 363
Williams River, 9
Williamson,W. T., 244
Willis Long Plout, 166-167, 187-188
Willys Jeep of World War II, 26
Willys Knight, 26
Wilson, Addison, 346
Wilson, Bernadine Dixon, 346
Wilson, Carl Sr., 78, 192
Wilson, Joanna, xi, 331
Wilson, Lyda Greene, 102
Wilson Ridge, 77, 79, 101-102, 301, 319
Windom, Lee, 26
Windy Run, 107
Windy Run Historical Association, 107
Wineman, S., 243
Wines, Homer, 104
Wines, Sebert, 104
Wirt County, 78, 80
Wise County, Va., 14
Wolf Creek, 104
Wolfpen Digital, xi, 139
Wolfpen Run, xi, 108, 125, 137-139, 189-190, 357, 363-364
Wonderful West Virginia, 29, 255-256, 264
Wood, Freda, 134, 151-152, 190, 217, 257
Wood, Hugh, 137, 190
Wood, Lee Jack, 192
Wood, Lee Roy, 192
Wood, Ray, 109
Wood, Tim, 98
Wood, Tom, 109
Wood Eddy, 109, 190
Woods, Bill, 2-3
Woods, Cindy, 257
Woods, Frank, 3
Woods, Jane McElwain, 3
Woods, Lee Jack, 191-192
Woods, Rebecca, 9
Woods, Sally Pardue, 192
World Series, 65, 130, 198
World War I, 63, 91, 113, 129
World War II, 26, 37, 48, 57, 63, 106, 114, 133, 214, 222-223, 244, 372
Wyoming County, 262
Yankee Stadium, 130
Yellowstone National Park, 211
Yoho, O. J., 83
Yokum, Shirley, 338
York, Alvin, 63
Yorktown, Va., 30
Young, Henry, xii, 53, 66, 72-82, 301, 307
Young, Bazel, 78, 80
Young, David, 80
Young, Dreama Nichols, 216
Young, Hie, 75-76
Young, Johnny, 161
Young, Lucinda James, 72, 78, 81
Young, Mandy, 79
Young, Marjorie Teets, ix, 174, 216
Young, Mortimer, 80
Young, Raban, 209
Young, Ross, 174
Young, Samuel, 300
Youngs Monument Road, 72
Yucca, 18, 209
Yurasek, Karen Johnson, 361
Zengerle, Jim, 213